ILLINOIS

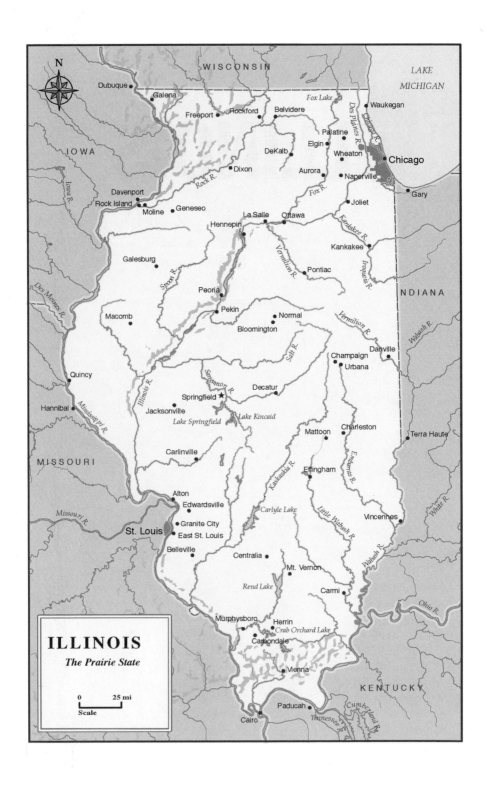

N

WISCONSIN

LAKE MICHIGAN

IOWA

INDIANA

MISSOURI

KENTUCKY

Dubuque
Galena
Freeport
Rockford
Belvidere
Fox Lake
Waukegan
Palatine
Elgin
DeKalb
Wheaton
Chicago
Dixon
Aurora
Naperville
Gary
Davenport
Joliet
Rock Island
Moline
Geneseo
La Salle
Ottawa
Hennepin
Galesburg
Kankakee
Peoria
Pontiac
Pekin
Normal
Macomb
Bloomington
Quincy
Danville
Champaign
Urbana
Hannibal
Decatur
Springfield ★
Jacksonville
Lake Springfield
Lake Kincaid
Mattoon
Charleston
Terra Haute
Carlinville
Effingham
Alton
Edwardsville
Carlyle Lake
Vincennes
Granite City
St. Louis
East St. Louis
Belleville
Centralia
Mt. Vernon
Rend Lake
Carmi
Murphysboro
Herrin
Crab Orchard Lake
Carbondale
Vienna
Paducah
Cairo

Des Plaines R.
Chicago R.
Fox R.
Rock R.
Iowa R.
Kankakee R.
Iroquois R.
Vermilion R.
Spoon R.
Des Moines R.
Vermilion R.
Illinois R.
Salt R.
Sangamon R.
Wabash R.
Mississippi R.
Kaskaskia R.
Embarras R.
Little Wabash R.
Wabash R.
White R.
Missouri R.
Ohio R.
Cumberland R.
Tennessee R.

ILLINOIS

The Prairie State

0   25 mi
Scale

ILLINOIS

A History of the Land and Its People

Roger Biles

NORTHERN

ILLINOIS

UNIVERSITY

PRESS

DeKalb

Published by the Northern Illinois University Press, DeKalb, Illinois   60115

Manufactured in the United States using acid-free paper

Design by Julia Fauci

Library of Congress Cataloging-in-Publication Data

Biles, Roger, 1950–

Illinois : a history of the land and its people / Roger Biles.

   p.   cm.

Includes bibliographical references and index.

ISBN-13: 978-0-87580-349-4 (acid-free paper)

ISBN-10: 0-87580-349-0 (acid-free paper)

ISBN-13: 978-0-87580-604-4 (pbk.: acid-free paper)

ISBN-10: 0-87580-604-X (pbk.: acid-free paper)

1. Illinois—History. I. Title.

F541.3.B55 2006

977.3—dc22

2005007279

JACKET / COVER CREDITS: Chicago skyline photo by Steve Smedley; Abraham
Lincoln and Wa-Kawn, the Library of Congress; Harold Washington photo by Antonio
B. Dickey, Special Collections and Preservation Division, Chicago Public Library; Jane
Addams, Jane Addams Memorial Collection (JAMC 1003), The University Library,
University of Illinois at Chicago; John Deere, the Deere & Company Archives;
pastoral scene photo by Cathy McKinty, Acclaim Stock Photography.

CONTENTS

LIST OF MAPS

PREFACE

This book explores the changing populations in Illinois over time and discusses the major events of the centuries as seen through the lens of demographic shifts. While providing a chronological framework to help understand the state's development and devoting attention to the touchstones of its history, this is not simply a straightforward political chronicle recounting the procession of gubernatorial administrations. Just as surely as politicians, captains of industry, military heroes, and other famous men receive considerable attention here, so too do the "ordinary people"— including women, African Americans, and other minorities—whose lives have contributed in many ways to the development of the state. A brief biographical essay in each chapter highlights the significance of a key individual in that era. As the author of many books and articles on Chicago, I am fully aware of the leading role played by that city in the state's development. No thorough history could ignore the giant shadow cast across the Illinois prairie by the metropolis on Lake Michigan. At the same time, I am sensitive to the need for balance and also relate the crucial experiences of people inhabiting the state's farms, small towns, and medium-size cities. A brief essay in each chapter examines the story of a key community at each stage of the state's development and underscores the significance of places other than the Windy City. The result is a book that presents a broad overview, rather than a comprehensive history, of the state's development.

I am pleased to thank the people who helped in the preparation of this book. Robert McColley and Roger Bridges gave the manuscript a thorough reading, saving me from countless errors and questionable interpretations. Any shortcomings that remain are due to my own obstinacy and not to any dearth of useful suggestions on their part. Harvey Smith made the necessary arrangements for me to spend a year teaching at Northern Illinois University, which allowed me to work closely with the staff at Northern Illinois University Press in finishing the book and to teach Illinois history to an able, enthusiastic, and inquisitive class of undergraduates. Dave Dallstream was a superb teaching assistant for that class. Thanks to Mary Lincoln, Julia Fauci, Susan Bean, and the other fine folks at Northern Illinois University Press for their hard work to make this a better book. David Kyvig, Christine Worobec, and Kenton and Marlee Clymer made the year in DeKalb enjoyable as well as productive. Russell Lewis at the Chicago Historical Society and Mary Michals at the Abraham Lincoln Presidential Library were very helpful in procuring illustrations for the book. Finally, my greatest thanks go to my wife, Mary Claire, and my children, Brian, Jeanne, and Grant, for their love and unwavering support.

ILLINOIS

The Indians and the French

The first European explorers to navigate Illinois rivers found that, when they left their canoes and walked beyond the clumps of trees alongside the water, vast prairies extended as far as the eye could see. Accustomed to the dense forests of Europe and the timberlands of eastern Canada, they marveled at the miles of treeless land interrupted only occasionally by isolated strips of forest. In an 1842 visit to the Illinois prairie, Charles Dickens called the landscape "oppressive in its barren monotony"; a later unimpressed observer termed the flatlands "Illinoleum."[1] The volatile weather, both unpredictable and often extreme, annoyed many newcomers. Hot humid summers, violent thunderstorms, and the seasonal threat of tornadoes alternated with bitterly cold winters, biting winds, and heavy snowfalls. Some newcomers adapted to the climate and found beauty in the prairie grass that grew taller than a man on horseback and rippled in the stiff summer breezes. Adorned with a rich variety of wildflowers, the colorful grasslands changed their hues seasonally. Most encouraging to European newcomers, the fertile soils capable of supporting such vegetation gave promise for a variety of crops that could sustain large populations of frontiersmen—and without their having to labor for years to cut down trees and clear land. Indeed, Illinois became one of the most fertile agricultural areas in the world.

The topography discovered by the Europeans, a product of gradual change over centuries, owed its character largely to the impact of glaciers. The Illinois countryside looked altogether different before the earth's ice ages, containing more hills and lacking extensive stretches of prairie. The transformation of the terrain resulted from prolonged periods of frigid weather that kept winter snows from melting and led to the formation of giant glaciers. These massive sheets of ice leveled hills and valleys and deposited layers of rocks and dirt that had been slowly pushed southward from Canada. When the ice ages ended and the glaciers receded, lakes,

rivers, and streams remained in the newly created crevices. An estimated fifteen thousand years ago, in the wake of the last retreating glacier, strong dry
winds scattered a thick layer of topsoil known as loess across the state. Following the period of glacial activity, centuries of rainfall, climate changes,
and erosion then shaped the glacial drift into the rich Illinois soils.

Geologists have identified four separate glaciers that, over the centuries,
covered all or parts of Illinois. The soil deposits of the first two ice sheets,
which arrived during the so-called Kansan and Nebraskan geologic periods, later gave way almost entirely to the third glacier of the Illinoian era.
(A small portion of the Kansan drift can still be found on the surface of the
land around Quincy.) The Illinoian glacier arrived an estimated 100–150
thousand years ago and extended as far south as Carbondale. Approximately 15–50 thousand years ago, the Wisconsinan glacier covered
roughly the northeastern half of the state extending as far south as Peoria
and Mattoon. The Illinoian and Wisconsinan glaciers principally accounted for the contours of the land and the richness of the soil.

Although much of Illinois became flat, the distances advanced by the
glaciers explain geographical deviations in various areas of the state. Dis-
crete prairies varied from a few acres to several miles in width and were frequently separated by groves of trees. Treeless prairies predominated
throughout northern and central Illinois so that a man could travel three
hundred miles south from Wisconsin and not discover more than five
miles of woodland at a time; timber proved more plentiful in the southern
reaches of the state. The glaciers mostly bypassed the northwestern corner
of the state, which accounts for the gently rolling hills there and around
Galena. Extensive erosion over thousands of years has removed the glacial
drift from the area around the confluence of the Mississippi and Illinois
rivers. Because the ice sheets extended only as far as Jackson, Williamson,
Saline, and Gallatin counties, a hilly extension of the Ozark Highland covers the southernmost area of the state. Throughout the rest of the state,
scattered moraines and modest valleys interrupt the level terrain.

Beneath the surface, layers of sedimentary rock contained a host of
valuable minerals. Bituminous coal in beds sometimes fifteen feet thick
rested below ground throughout two-thirds of the state. The presence of
lead ore in the northwestern part of Illinois made Galena an important
town early in the state's history, and settlers later found modest deposits of
oil and gas as well. Glacial deposits included sand, gravel, stone, cement,
and clay, which proved useful in the making of bricks and concrete for
buildings, pavement, and drainage tile. Prospectors found traces of silver
and iron ore but not in sufficient quantities to have an economic impact
on the state's development.

The glaciers also played a role in the original settlement of the Illinois
area. When large portions of the earth's water froze into gigantic ice sheets
and ocean levels fell, Stone Age immigrants from Asia traveled across a

land bridge connecting Siberia with Alaska. As glaciers receded, opening avenues into North America, these Paleo-Indians drifted southward. They hunted on foot and followed herds of wild animals, probably mastodons, bison, tapirs, ground sloths, and camels. Moving frequently from place to place, these hunters and their families dwelled in caves and makeshift shelters. For generations, hunting parties periodically returned to a campsite under a rock overhang now known as the Modoc Rock Shelter near the village of Prairie du Roche in southern Illinois. Archaeologists have discovered spear points and other artifacts that suggest these first arrivals came to Illinois as early as ten thousand years ago.

Changes in vegetation, when the climate of North America became warmer and drier, and the hunting of some species to the point of extinction eliminated many large animals from the region. The Paleo-Indians accordingly looked to smaller animals and plants for their food supply. By about 2000 BC, they began establishing villages near waterways, cultivating plants, and weaving baskets for storing food. The villagers erected small huts, using tree branches for frames and filling in the tops and sides with thatch, mud, and animal hides. They still dispatched hunting parties but began to rely on crops such as corn and squash for food. Archaeologists have discovered cooking utensils, tools, and weapons in small burial mounds built by the Paleo-Indians. The accumulation of ceramic pottery, stone implements, weapons, and tools reflects their adoption of a more sedentary existence. The unearthing of more exotic artifacts not indigenous to Illinois, such as marine shells from the Gulf of Mexico and copper from the Northeast, indicates that the Indians participated in far-ranging trade networks. As in later centuries, the Indians apparently made the area a crossroads for commerce and a juncture for cultural exchange.

Sometime around AD 1000, the members of a culture that archaeologists have named Middle Mississippian constructed a massive community covering six square miles near present-day Cahokia, southeast of St. Louis. The estimated twenty thousand inhabitants living in that early community, the ancestors of latter-day Indian tribes, raised crops, engaged in extensive trade networks, and exhibited signs of a highly developed civilization. They left lasting monuments in the form of earthen mounds, some of which assumed massive proportions. Monks' Mound, which has been judged the largest prehistoric earthwork in North America, sprawls over seventeen acres and stands 100 feet high, 700 feet wide, and 1,080 feet long. Nearly a hundred other mounds existed within the vicinity, which indicates that great numbers of people resided there permanently. These earthworks seem to have held great religious significance for the residents, with temples and arenas built atop the mounds where priests and other community leaders staged sacred rituals and athletic contests. A scattering of towns smaller than the early Cahokia dotted the Illinois River valley to the north, and archaeologists believe that mounds indicating additional settlements may have been leveled by farmers or land developers in the nineteenth and twentieth centuries.

By the early decades of the sixteenth century, the Middle Mississippian culture had vanished and the once-vibrant cities of that area lay vacant. The reasons for the decline of these people remain obscure, although there are some possible explanations. Perhaps the depletion of food and game left such large numbers of people unable to sustain themselves. Warfare with other tribes may have been influential, or the beginnings of trade with Europeans may have introduced lethal diseases to which the people had no immunities. Whatever the reasons, when the first European traders and trappers reached Illinois, a different tribe of Indians had replaced the Middle Mississippian people.

Early in the sixteenth century, a group of Algonquian-speaking Indians who called themselves the Illini or the Illiniwek left southern Michigan, migrated west along the southern edge of Lake Michigan, and arrived in northern Illinois and southern Wisconsin. By the middle of the century, they predominated in most of Illinois as well as parts of Wisconsin, Iowa, Missouri, and Arkansas. A loose confederation of a dozen bands, the most notable of which were the Cahokia, Kaskaskia, Michigamea, Moingwena, Peoria, and Tamaroa, the Illini numbered about eight thousand in the early 1500s. Although a grand chief nominally ruled all members of the Illini tribe, the bands lived separately and exercised a great deal of autonomy.

Combining agriculture with hunting, the Illini adopted a cyclical routine tied closely to the changing of the seasons. In the spring, the women planted corn, beans, pumpkins, melons, squash, and other staple crops in the fields adjoining their villages. In the summer, using spears and bows and arrows, all members of the village participated in a buffalo hunt that

Cahokia as it would have looked around AD 1100 from the top of Twin Mounds across the plaza with Monks' Mound in the distance. Covering more than seventeen acres, Monks' Mound may have been the largest prehistoric earthwork in North America.
Illinois State Historical Library

lasted from three to six weeks. In late summer and early autumn, they returned to the village to harvest crops, cure the meat, and tan the animal hides. As winter approached, they retired to scattered camps where individuals and small groups hunted periodically as needed. In the early spring, the winter encampments dissolved as the Illini made their way back to the larger villages, and the cycle began again. As one observer noted, such a life "consisted of alternating periods of strenuous effort and of almost complete inactivity."[2]

Males received special recognition for prowess in hunting, athletic contests, and gambling, and particularly for success on the battlefield. Braves attained status within the tribe through their valor in warfare as they defended their villages or launched attacks against neighboring tribes. The Illini recognized successful warriors in elaborate ceremonies, after which the heroes wore distinctive tattoos to signify their elevated station. Typically, the most heralded warriors assumed positions of wealth, prestige, and leadership in the community. Village leaders buried war chiefs slain in battle with special honors. Virtually every spring, war parties attacked rival villages or hunting parties to avenge earlier wartime deaths, to acquire slaves, or to add new tribal members to replace those who had died. Raiding parties usually consisted of six or seven braves, although occasionally as many as twenty men would act together. In the 1660s, Illini warriors began to use firearms obtained in trade from eastern tribes and thereby enjoyed a great advantage against many of their enemies. In 1673 a Frenchman noted the psychological edge that guns gave the Illini, who "use [these weapons] especially to inspire, through their noise and smoke, terror in their Enemies." He added: "The latter do not use guns and have never seen any, since they live too Far toward the West."[3]

If the Illini fared well in their struggles with tribes located to the west, the same could not be said of their efforts against increasingly dangerous rivals to the east. Like many other Algonquin tribes along the Atlantic coastline, the Illini suffered at the hands of the powerful Iroquois confederation (the Cayuga, Mohawk, Oneida, Onondaga, and Seneca tribes) based in New York. Notorious for their ferocity and skill as warriors, the Iroquois became even more formidable when they became the first Native Americans to acquire firearms. Appreciative of their renowned martial skill, one French observer wrote, "The Iroquois approach like foxes, fight like lions, and fly away like birds."[4] Trading furs to the Dutch and the English in exchange for guns, rum, and other valued goods, the Iroquois controlled the area from New York and Pennsylvania to the Great Lakes. When the rapacious Iroquois moved farther west and dislodged the Huron, Sauk, Fox, Potawatomi, Kickapoo, Shawnee, and Miami, these tribes in turn fled into the territory previously controlled by the Illini and struggles for living space inevitably resulted. By the middle of the seventeenth century, the Iroquois themselves arrived in Illinois in search of new hunting and trapping grounds. Outnumbered, disorganized, and armed with fewer guns, the Illini stood little chance against the Iroquois, and in the 1660s they relocated across the Mississippi River in southeastern Iowa, eastern Missouri, and northeastern Arkansas. By the early 1670s, a reduced Iroquois presence and the arrival of growing numbers of French settlers persuaded the Illini to return to the Illinois country.

By the time the French arrived in Illinois, the Illini were clearly in decline. The tribe lost more than 40 percent of its people in the last quarter of the seventeenth century, and precipitous population losses continued in the eighteenth century. From a high of thirteen thousand in the 1650s, the tribal population had dwindled to around seven hundred a century later. Indeed, even though the beleaguered Illini welcomed the French and promptly forged a close alliance with the European newcomers, their fortunes continued to ebb. The French eliminated the Iroquois from the area south of Lake Michigan, but the Illini still warred against several other tribes such as the Fox and the Chickasaw in northern Illinois. In addition, close contact with Europeans resulted in high incidents of disease, alcoholism, and factionalism among the tribal branches. The French acknowledged their intention of subjugating the Indians—"to bring them into total dependence by these means, by gentle treatment, a few presents, and embassies," according to one Frenchman—and proved remarkably successful with the Illini.[5] By 1800, only eighty members of the tribe continued to reside in their former lands east of the Mississippi River.

The French who came to the Illinois country in the seventeenth century sought to extend their nation's control of the lucrative fur trade into the interior of the North American continent. Having established a series of forts and trading posts from the maritime provinces of Canada to the Great Lakes, the *coureurs de bois* (fur traders) next turned southward in search of new sources of beaver pelts. They listened intently to the Indians' descriptions of a great river in the interior that might serve as a pathway to the Pacific Ocean. Such a waterway, which the Indians called "Misi Sipi" (big river), would be critical to the French maintenance of their fur-trade monopoly. Thus, at a time when English settlements remained tightly restricted to the land east of the Appalachian Mountains, the French looked to expand their New World empire into uncharted wilderness.

In 1663 King Louis XIV made New France a royal colony and dispatched additional soldiers to protect French interests there. According to the dictates of the king's finance minister Jean-Baptiste Colbert, French forces concentrated around the St. Lawrence settlements and discouraged forays into the interior. Nonetheless, fur traders and Roman Catholic missionaries drifted westward individually and in small groups. The first official expedition into Illinois came after representatives of the French government laid claim to the interior of the continent at an elaborate ceremony staged at a Chippewa village near Sault Ste. Marie in 1671. As bewildered Indians from fourteen different tribes watched in silence, a high-ranking French official unfurled the fleur-de-lis, proclaimed the king's ownership of Illinois and adjacent lands, and sternly recited the punishment for trespassing. The French in fact had scant notion of what lands they had claimed and soon began to prepare an expedition into the interior to survey the area and search for the great river described by the Indians.

To lead the expedition westward in 1673, the governor of New France, Louis de Buade, Comte de Frontenac et Palluau, named a twenty-seven-year-old Canadian, Louis Jolliet. A fur trader who had traveled extensively through the Great Lakes, Jolliet also possessed considerable skills as a mapmaker. Frontenac selected a thirty-five-year-old Jesuit priest, Father Jacques Marquette, to carry Catholicism into the North American interior. Having emigrated from France in 1666, Father Marquette had organized a mission on Lake Superior and then moved to St. Ignace on the Straits of Mackinac. He learned several dialects of the Algonquian language and looked forward to establishing a mission among the Illini tribe, whose members he had met at St. Ignace. On May 17, 1673, Jolliet, Marquette, and the other five members of their crew left St. Ignace in two canoes to explore the Mississippi Valley.

In all likelihood, other white men had earlier traversed the same rivers, but they had not left any record of their journey, whereas Jolliet and Marquette took great care to document their exact whereabouts at all times. After paddling across Lake Michigan to Green Bay, Wisconsin, they followed Miami Indians down the Fox River and carried their canoes the short distance to the Wisconsin River. Ignoring the Indians' warnings not to proceed any farther, they entered the Mississippi River on June 17. Floating down the wide waterway for hundreds of miles, they noted the changes in scenery as the surrounding hills gave way to flatter terrain. Below the mouth of the Illinois River, the explorers saw a colorful painting on a rocky bluff. Father Marquette described the creature drawn on the rock as a composite of a man's face, a tiger's beard, a deer's horns, and a serpent's tail. The gigantic pictograph, later called the Piasa Bird, seems to have been the depiction of a storm spirit or other religious figure of the Illini tribe.

Some distance below the mouth of the Ohio River, the expedition encountered Indians who informed them that they still needed to travel for ten days before the Mississippi River emptied into the Gulf of Mexico. Realizing that they would not find a waterway to the Pacific Ocean and concerned that they might encounter hostile Indians or Spanish farther downriver, Jolliet and his party decided to head back to Canada with their information. Following the advice of friendly Indians, they left the Mississippi and paddled up the Illinois and DesPlaines rivers to reach Lake Michigan. Along the way, they encountered a band of Kaskaskia Indians who seemed particularly receptive to Father Marquette's evangelism. He promised to return and establish a mission among them, and the Frenchmen continued northward. Father Marquette had become ill on the

An artist's representation of Native Americans gazing at the Piasa Rock located on the Mississippi River below the mouth of the Illinois River, a pictograph that was probably a religious figure of the Illini tribe. *Illinois State Historical Library*

journey, and he remained at Green Bay to recuperate while the others headed eastward. As Jolliet approached the outskirts of Montreal, his canoe capsized in rapids and the two men riding with him perished. He lost his maps and records and could only attempt to reconstruct the details of their journey from memory. As a result, Father Marquette's journal, which French officials later transferred from St. Ignace to Montreal, remained the only official record of the expedition.

Completing his convalescence at Green Bay, Father Marquette headed back to the Kaskaskia village but suffered a relapse at the Chicago portage and remained there for several months. Partially recovered, he finally established the Mission of the Immaculate Conception of the Blessed Virgin among the Kaskaskia and lived long enough to preach to a gathering of fifteen hundred Indians on Easter Sunday 1675. Again seriously ill, he left for St. Ignace but died on May 18, 1675, before reaching his destination. Jolliet fell out of favor with the governor and other top officials in Montreal, and they denied his request to lead another expedition to Illinois and establish a French colony there. Although he conducted several expeditions throughout eastern Canada, Jolliet never returned to the Illinois country.

Having denied Jolliet the opportunity to develop the Illinois country, Governor Frontenac selected instead his friend and secret business partner, René-Robert Cavelier, sieur de la Salle. The governor sent La Salle to the Mississippi River valley in search of precious minerals and the elusive waterway to the Pacific Ocean, in return for which he granted the explorer an exclusive monopoly to the fur trade south of the Great Lakes. Born into a noble family in France, La Salle came to Canada in 1666 and, after a brief stint as a farmer, became a highly successful explorer. Arrogant, domineering, and cocksure, he dreamed of establishing a great French empire in the New World and of personally acquiring fame and fortune. Before heading westward, he made two trips to France to enlist financial support for his explorations. In addition to a substantial amount of capital, he returned to Canada with a worthy lieutenant for his expeditions, Henri de Tonti. An Italian soldier of fortune, Tonti wore an iron hook in place of the right hand he had lost in battle; Indians marveled at this metal hand, thinking it invested Tonti with mystical powers.

In subsequent years, La Salle and Tonti initiated the French settlement of Illinois, but only after a series of adventures and misadventures. They built the first sailing vessel on the Great Lakes, the forty-five-ton *Griffon*, which transported them and their crew to Green Bay. Loaded with furs and heading back to Fort Frontenac, the *Griffon* mysteriously disappeared; the loss of the fur cargo exacerbated La Salle's already tenuous financial situation. On his first trip into the area, La Salle traveled down the Kankakee River to the Illinois River and built Fort Crèvecoeur on the future site of Peoria. Pressed hard by creditors, he returned to Canada to search for the *Griffon*, and in his absence, the men stationed at Fort Crèvecoeur mutinied, plundered, and obliterated the three-month-old structure. When La Salle returned to Illinois with a new cohort of men, he not only found Fort Crèvecoeur in ruins but also discovered that the Iroquois, urged on by the British, had destroyed the Kaskaskia town founded earlier by Father Marquette. He likewise learned that Tonti had been severely wounded while fighting the Iroquois but had survived.

In the spring of 1682, accompanied by twenty-five Frenchmen and eighteen Indians, La Salle and Tonti traveled down the Mississippi River to the Gulf of Mexico. At the mouth of the river, the French explorer laid claim on behalf of the king to all of the lands touched by all the rivers that flowed into the Mississippi River—an area extending from the Appalachian to the Rocky mountains—and called the tract Louisiana after Louis XIV. As part of his grandiose scheme, La Salle hoped to be named governor of a new French colony in the lower Mississippi Valley and to drive the Spanish out of northern Mexico.

Returning north, La Salle and Tonti built Fort St. Louis on a promontory known as Starved Rock, high above the Illinois River. (According to Indian legend, a heroic band of Illini starved to death there while under siege by Potawatomi warriors.) The Frenchmen gathered nearly four thousand warriors from several Indian tribes around the fort for protection against the Iroquois. Obstacles to La Salle's dreams of empire arose, however, when Governor Frontenac returned to France and his replacement, Antoine le Febvre de la Barre, initiated new policies that restricted activity in the Mississippi Valley. Tonti remained at the fort and successfully defended the site against a massive Iroquois attack, while La Salle returned to France to plead his case to King Louis XIV. The flamboyant adventurer proposed to assemble an army of thousands of Indians for an invasion of Spanish territory west of the Mississippi River and asked for two ships; on July 24, 1684, he left France with four ships and an army of 250 men. The armada met a series of misfortunes, however, and his grand plan unraveled. The Spanish captured one of the ships, the others lost their way in the Gulf of Mexico, and La Salle's boat ran aground in Texas. During a desperate attempt to reach the Mississippi delta by land in 1687, the disgruntled men in La Salle's party turned on their leader and killed him. They left him unburied where he fell.

Tonti resumed La Salle's work and during the following fifteen years increased the French presence in Illinois. He and his Indian allies vacated the fort at Starved Rock and built a larger one called Fort Pimitoui on the banks of the Illinois River above Lake Peoria, and this became a thriving French village and mission. As relations with the Fox Indians deteriorated in northern Illinois, the French increasingly sought to build supply depots and communities in the southern portion of the state. In 1698 François-Xavier de Montmorency Laval, the bishop of Quebec, inquired about a location in southern Illinois for a new Catholic mission. As Tonti recommended, the French built the Church of the Holy Family among the Tamaroa and Cahokia Indians and called the adjacent village Cahokia. In his last years, Tonti explored in the lower Mississippi Valley and represented the French in negotiations with the indigenous Indian tribes. In 1704 he died of yellow fever in Mobile.

As the seventeenth century ended, the Fox Indians became increasingly hostile and the French withdrew from the northern reaches of Illinois. In 1700 the Jesuits abandoned the Mission of the Guardian Angel, which they had established four years earlier at the site of present-day Chicago, as well as the village at Fort Pimitoui. In the following years, the French built a series of villages and missions in the rich bottomlands east of the Mississippi River, below the mouth of the Missouri River, that they called the *Paradis Terreste* and that later became known as the American Bottom. In 1703 they founded Kaskaskia, which became the third site of Marquette's Mission of the Immaculate Conception, about fifty miles south of Cahokia. Kaskaskia became, for the next century, the leading French settlement in Illinois and the commercial and cultural capital of the area. Approximately fifteen miles north of Kaskaskia, French colonists established the village of Prairie du Roche and, five miles farther west, Fort de Chartres, which became the administrative center for the region. Using the Illinois and Wabash rivers to the north and east, the inhabitants of southern Illinois maintained contact with French Canada. The *coureurs de bois* sent their pelts to Detroit, which had been founded in 1701 by Antoine Laumet de la Mothe, sieur de Cadillac, and then down the Mississippi River to New Orleans.

Although the fur trade continued to thrive in Illinois, the French sought economic diversification as well. As remote trading posts gave way to frontier settlements, France developed a variety of plans to increase the profitability of the colonies in the New World. In 1717 Louisiana annexed the Illinois country, which had previously been part of Canada. The following year, the government turned the administration of Louisiana over to John Law of Lauriston, an entrepreneurial Scotsman who had devised a scheme for the economic development of the French colonies. In return for a trade monopoly and ownership of all mines in Louisiana, Law and his partners aimed to found new communities, recruit settlers, import slaves, improve colonial administration, and bolster defense. Law's scheme foundered in 1720, and his ruined company was reorganized as the Company of the West, which in turn went bankrupt and forfeited its charter. In 1732 Louisiana, including the province of Illinois, became a royal colony and remained under the direct control of the crown for the remainder of the French presence in the New World.

During the years of the Law regime, the French first imported African slaves into the Illinois country to supplement the number of Indian bondsmen already at work. Philippe Renault, the French director of mines, originally hoped to discover gold, but soon he initiated lead-mining operations instead. Renault arrived in Illinois in 1720, bringing along an estimated five hundred African slaves he had purchased in Santo Domingo for work in the mines. When Law's financial scheme unraveled, Renault left to prospect for precious metals elsewhere in North America and sold his slaves to French families living in the area. In subsequent decades, French villagers and priests throughout southern Illinois owned chattel. A few free blacks resided in the *Paradis Terreste*, and manumission over the years added to their numbers.

The French population of Illinois never exceeded a few thousand, most of whom resided in Kaskaskia, Prairie du Roche, Fort de Chartres, Cahokia, and a handful of other small villages in the *Paradis Terreste*. The government mandated that annual censuses be taken but few of them have survived, and questions about their accuracy persist. A 1723 census in Kaskaskia, for example, counted 193 inhabitants, excluding slaves: 61

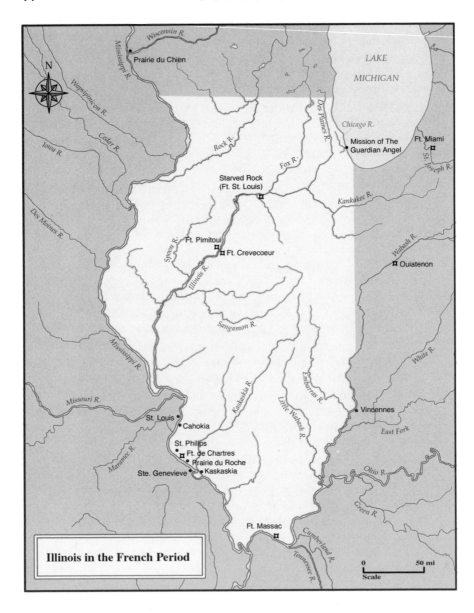

Illinois in the French Period

farmers, 41 laborers, 37 women, and 54 children. In all likelihood, the censuses undercounted the number of village residents and altogether missed the rural and migrant populations. A 1752 sampling of the entire population in the *Paradis Terreste* listed 767 men, women, and children, as well as 250 slaves, in the French towns. In fact, historian Natalia Belting notes, a better estimate would be one thousand men, women, and children, along with four hundred slaves. Owing to the shortage of women, many Frenchmen married Indian women, and census takers noted a sizable métis population.

French Canadians always comprised the majority of the white population of the Illinois country during the years of French dominance, but heterogeneity increased during the eighteenth century. With the establishment of regular traffic on the Mississippi River connecting Illinois with New Orleans, an increasing number of settlers came from Europe rather than from Canada. French investors recruited Catholics from France, the Lowlands, and the Swiss cantons. The French also employed men of various nationalities in the military, including Swedes, Germans, Spaniards, Irish, Scots, Italians, and even a few English. After their tours of duty, many of these mercenaries remained on the frontier; a good number adopted the Gallic spelling of their names and became fully acculturated in French communities.

Although the villages remained compact, the small number of farmers made the *Paradis Terreste* the granary for the entire French population of Louisiana. Lower Louisiana failed at cereal grain production, and by the 1730s the Illinois Country became the principal supplier of wheat to New Orleans and its surroundings. The patterns of settlement and the operation of agriculture in Illinois, at first comparable to practices in French Canada, actually owed more to traditional patterns in northern France. The *habitants* of the St. Lawrence Valley cultivated their own narrow strips of land (known as longlots), and although these longlots appeared in other regions of French influence throughout North America, the system of agriculture that developed in Illinois proved unique in the New World. (In New France, the word *habitant* referred to a sedentary agricultural settler, whereas the term *voyageur* described a transient.) The longlots in the *Paradis Terreste* extended outward from the Mississippi River but, as in Europe, operated as open fields rather than as individually owned plots. The longlot or ribbon farms, sometimes from just thirty to forty feet wide, extended as much as a quarter of a mile from the rivers. The *habitants* resided in nuclear villages, jointly cultivated open fields, and pastured their livestock in common areas. By the late eighteenth century, this system began to disintegrate as some gentry in the communities laid out large estates that were separate from the traditional villages. Even so, open-field agriculture persisted well into the nineteenth century in the *Paradis Terreste* before the dispersed farmsteads common throughout much of Illinois predominated there as well.

Even though many Frenchmen in Illinois had relocated from Canada, the common-field agriculture that developed in the Mississippi River valley more closely resembled the patterns employed in the plains of northern Europe than in the St. Lawrence River valley. Reinforcing the cultural baggage brought from France, the circumstances in Illinois led the *habitants* to opt for open-field farming. French colonists in the *Paradis Terreste* huddled together in compact villages for reasons of security, most notably as protection against hostile Indians, and quickly found common-field agriculture the best means of cultivating the rich soil of the adjacent bottomlands. They designated lands that proved too rocky, marshy, or otherwise unsuitable for cultivation to be used as commons for pasturage. Open-field farming required a sense of altruism, a commitment to the ideal of community, and a rejection of freehold landownership. To adjudicate any disputes that arose over the communal farmlands, the residents elected *assemblées des habitants* (village assemblies) that dealt with all issues involving pastureland, livestock, fences, roads, and so forth. In short, all issues related to the management of communal agriculture fell to the village assemblies.

In the Illinois villages, *habitants,* Indians, slaves, merchants, government officials, and *engagés* (indentured servants) lived together in densely populated communities. The *habitants* lived in modest one-story wooden homes separated by narrow streets. Wealthy merchants, government officials, and nobles resided in greater luxury in their larger homes adorned with furniture and china that they had managed to import from France. Slave residences dotted the townscapes, as slaveholders usually established living quarters for their bondsmen near their own homes. Groups of Indians nestled on the fringes of the communities. Peripatetic *coureurs de bois* and *voyageurs* came and went at irregular intervals. In all, these communities bustled with an energy deriving from the heterogeneous population, as whites, Africans, Indians, and people of mixed heritage toiled together in the fields and lived alongside each other.

The French communities of the Illinois country thrived for decades in relative isolation from other European groups, as colonists from Great Britain remained in settlements east of the Appalachian Mountains, but by the middle of the eighteenth century, the struggle for the Ohio Valley was under way. During King George's War from 1744 to 1748, the French suspected British frontiersmen of inciting the Indians to wage war against whites in the Illinois country. In 1749 King George II of England presented a group of investors with a land grant of several hundred thousand acres in the Ohio Valley. To the French protest that La Salle had claimed the interior of the continent for France long before the first British settlers even arrived in the New World, the British responded that their own John Cabot had staked the British claim to all of North America in the fifteenth century, two centuries before any French explorers sighted the land in question. During 1753 and 1754, the French closed portages from the Great Lakes to the Ohio River in an attempt to stanch the flow of British settlers westward.

In 1756 the Seven Years' War between England and France commenced in Europe, and the struggle over the Ohio region became an important issue in the international conflict. The French living in the Illinois country played

A drawing of a typical French house in the *Paradis Terreste,* a modest one-story structure made of wood with a wraparound porch. Unlike British settlers, the French
stacked logs vertically to form the sides of their dwellings. *Illinois State Historical Library*

a minor role in the French and Indian War, as it came to be known in North
America. They sent wheat grown in the *Paradis Terreste* to French garrisons
and a modest number of soldiers to distant battlefields in the East where the
military outcome was decided. In 1763 the Treaty of Paris ending the war
compelled France to cede all of its territory east of the Mississippi River (except New Orleans, which went to Spain) to the victorious British.

In the two years following the Treaty of Paris, the British altogether ignored the Illinois country. They were more involved in quelling the large-
scale uprising led in the trans-Appalachian West by the Ottawa chief Pontiac. Having finally put down the Pontiac Conspiracy, the British began to
establish outposts in the newly acquired frontier and to occupy forts constructed by the French. In 1765 the last vestiges of French rule in Illinois
disappeared as a British regiment marched into Fort de Chartres, and the
remaining twenty-two soldiers in the garrison ferried across the Mississippi
River to St. Louis. Learning that the Illinois country had been transferred
to Protestant England, many Frenchmen expected religious persecution
and feared the loss of their slaves, although in fact the British allowed the
French to retain their chattel. Some of the French fled downriver to New
Orleans, while others relocated across the river in such Missouri communities as St. Louis and Ste. Genevieve. Those who remained in the *Paradis
Terreste* did so with considerable trepidation. The French dreaded the coming of the Anglo-Americans, whom they viewed as uncouth scoundrels—

"whiskey boys," one Frenchman called them. The *habitants* were delighted when no immediate influx of the British ensued.[6]

By the late 1780s, as more Anglo-Americans arrived, the ethnic mix of the Illinois country began to change. The few hundred Frenchmen remaining in the *Paradis Terreste* eventually became insignificant among hundreds of thousands of immigrants from England and other European nations who arrived in subsequent decades. The traditional open-field system of farming gave way to the patterns of individual landownership that had long predominated in the British colonies of North America. A smattering of French place names and oddly configured landholdings remained, but everywhere in the *Paradis Terreste* the Anglo-American culture became ascendant. The French dreams of empire in North America expired, as did French control of that small portion of Illinois settled by Europeans.

Cahokia

The extensive complex of mounds on the east bank of the Mississippi River across from St. Louis constitutes an impressive yet enigmatic remnant of a civilization that flourished in Illinois many centuries ago. A tourist attraction that has long intrigued the viewing public, the mounds have left archaeologists important clues about the character and activities of the people who built the structures. At the same time, however, not all archaeologists agree that the impressive size of the mounds necessarily confirms that a societal complexity existed among the inhabitants. Nor are all archaeologists and historians prepared to call the Cahokia of centuries ago a city, considering the vast array of activities usually associated with urban life. As the first and largest of the Mississippian communities established in North America, Cahokia no doubt affected the many other settlements that developed around it. Nevertheless, the extent of its political and economic influence remains unclear. Students of Cahokia have answered many questions about the site, but several mysteries remain.

Sometime around AD 1050, a group of elites subdued the common people living in the area that would later become known as the American Bottom. The elites—including a chief, religious leaders, and mortuary officials—beheaded the commoners who resisted and then interred them in subordinate positions below the deceased members of the favored classes. The residents of Cahokia lived in a rigidly hierarchical society with clear class distinctions. The common people resided in modest dwellings and provided the agricultural and craft labor essential to the society. By contrast, the wealthy members of Cahokia lived in relative splendor, in large dwellings, and enjoyed their pick of the best game, agricultural produce, and manufactured goods available at the time. Artifacts and engravings painstakingly preserved at archaeological digs provide snapshots of the religious and civil ceremonies conducted by the people of a surprisingly sophisticated civilization.

The powerful elites marshaled a workforce that constructed the massive Cahokia mounds and plazas. A phalanx of hundreds of laborers, over a period of fifty years, built the Grand Plaza, an extraordinarily complex edifice completed around AD 1000. Large enough to accommodate Cahokia's entire population for religious ceremonies, the plaza stood near the largest mound, Monks' Mound, a towering structure one hundred feet tall, seven hundred feet wide, more than one thousand feet long, and covering seventeen acres. In all, the natives constructed dozens of mounds at various times over a period of three hundred years.

Sometime in the eleventh century, the population of Cahokia reached approximately fifteen thousand. By the end of the thirteenth century, the number of inhabitants had fallen to just a few thousand. Although the decline of the community has not been fully explained, students of the period point to the inherent instability of the organizational structure and to deadly rivalries between competing chiefs. Cahokia had been totally abandoned by around AD 1400, and its inhabitants scattered in many directions. The Cahokian diaspora may have produced a number of different Indian groups, including a number of Siouan-speaking tribes, but evidence for establishing this lineage remains fragmentary. Like the particulars of Cahokia's existence, the circumstances surrounding its demise continue to intrigue us.

Marie Rouensa

The Jesuit missionaries who sought to convert the Indians of North America to Roman Catholicism observed that they frequently had the most success with the women of the tribes. The missionaries found that if they could win over a number of women, the men usually followed in time. According to Father Jacques Gravier, his proselytizing efforts among the Illini in the late seventeenth century bore fruit after the successful conversion of Marie Rouensa, daughter of Chief Rouensa of the Kaskaskia tribe. Marie persuaded her father and mother to embrace Christianity, then many Kaskaskians did likewise, and the Indians' assimilation into French culture accelerated.

In 1694 seventeen-year-old Marie Rouensa converted to Christianity while the Kaskaskia Indians were residing near Peoria. She became such a devout Christian that she initially refused to marry Michel Accault, the

French *voyageur* her father had selected to be her husband, so that she might be unencumbered in her service to Jesus Christ. (A French Canadian who had served at Fort Crèvecoeur with La Salle and Tonti, Accault was a trader who probably considered marriage to the daughter of a Kaskaskia chief a way to improve his business prospects in the Illinois frontier.) Enraged by his daughter's defiance, Chief Rouensa expelled her naked from his lodge and threatened worse punishment. Marie eventually agreed to marry the Frenchman only when Father Gravier convinced her that she could continue to devote her life to Jesus as a married woman. She took pride in the hasty conversion of her new husband, whose debaucheries in previous years had made him one of the Illinois country's legendary rakes. The couple insisted that their two sons, born in 1695 and 1702, be baptized and raised as Roman Catholics.

Clashes with the Fox and Iroquois Indians led the Kaskaskia and their French allies to vacate the Peoria region and relocate farther south in the Illinois country. They settled in 1700 on the Mississippi River's west bank at the mouth of the DesPeres River. In 1703 the Indians, Jesuit missionaries, and fur traders established a new community where the Kaskaskia River flows into the Mississippi. Michel Accault died shortly after the birth of his second son, and in 1704 Marie married another French trader, Michael Phillipe, who became a captain of the local militia and one of the fledgling community's leading citizens. During the next fifteen years, Marie gave birth to six more children, who grew up as members of a leading Kaskaskia family. Fully acculturated to the mixed society in Kaskaskia, Marie strongly disapproved when her second son chose to live with his mother's people in total isolation from European civilization. In a codicil to her will, completed shortly before her death in 1725, Marie expressed her intentions to disinherit the prodigal son unless he returned to reside among the French.

In Kaskaskia, Marie remained a devout Roman Catholic and continued to aid the Jesuits in their attempts to win converts among the Indians. She died a very wealthy woman, her estate including considerable landholdings and five slaves. The Jesuits interred her remains beneath the family pew in the parish church—a singular honor afforded no other woman in Kaskaskia's history. Marie's children lived in various French villages in the Illinois country and in other parts of Louisiana and generally married persons of property and high social standing. Her status and the ready assimilation of her children say much about Franco-Indian culture in late seventeenth- and early eighteenth-century Illinois.

British Colonial Rule
and American Independence

Having dispatched the French from North America, the British suddenly possessed an immense tract of land stretching from the Atlantic Ocean to the Mississippi River and from the Hudson Bay to the Gulf of Mexico (except the city of New Orleans). The newly expanded colony in North America represented great potential wealth, but Great Britain was in many ways ill prepared to develop the bonanza it had acquired. Having just waged a series of costly wars against France that spanned much of the eighteenth century, Great Britain was facing an empty treasury and severe economic problems. The French and Indian War alone cost millions of pounds and saddled the nation with an imposing debt. The acquisition of lands west of the Appalachian Mountains certainly created an opportunity for future prosperity, but it also brought increased responsibilities, and the price of developing the frontier and protecting British subjects loomed large. The cost of administering an expanded empire was a troublesome prospect at a time calling for financial retrenchment. Although the French had ostensibly been removed from the Ohio Valley, hostile Indians— most of whom had fought against the British in the French and Indian War—remained to harry any British settlers who sought to push westward. Committed to a policy of economy, the British government balked at the cost of safeguarding its subjects from Indian attacks, and this attitude was reinforced by the difficulties encountered in subjugating Pontiac and his followers. The British saw no economic incentive in expediting the settlement of the West as long as Spain controlled New Orleans, the destination of the furs and crops originating in the Illinois country. The British would be able to reap profits from their possessions in the West only after they acquired New Orleans, or after trade could be diverted to the Great Lakes and the St. Lawrence River, both eventualities that seemed far in the future. Accordingly, in 1763 the British government issued a proclamation prohibiting any settlement west of a line drawn roughly along the headwaters of the rivers flowing from the Appalachian Mountains into the Atlantic Ocean. The Proclamation Line would ensure the safety of British subjects while also allowing colonial authorities to maintain tighter control of the North American population.

From the outset, however, the new policy proved problematic. British settlers had already migrated west of the Appalachians and had no intention of retreating eastward. More important, great numbers of colonists anticipated that the defeat of France would create additional opportunities for westward movement; indeed, they believed that the French and Indian War had been fought specifically for that reason, and they summarily ignored the Proclamation Line. Eager to buy and sell land, speculators and boosters ignored any restrictions on their activities in the West. The French had been unable to retain their colonial possessions in North America precisely because they had not established a strong presence in the trans-Appalachian region, argued Benjamin Franklin and other colonists who traveled to England to lobby against the new policy. Hugely unpopular from the first and extremely difficult to enforce, the Proclamation Line deterred relatively few colonists from moving into the continent's interior. After the trappers and other frontiersmen came land speculators and farmers. Years later, a high-ranking British official acknowledged the policy's failure and conceded, "A very silly proclamation it was."[1]

Population spilled over the Appalachian Mountains into the Ohio Valley, but at first very few settlers reached the Illinois country. The fate of Fort de Chartres illustrated how little influence the British exerted in the years following the Treaty of Paris. The new inhabitants of the garrison planned to emulate the French example and administer the civil and military affairs of the American Bottom from that site. In the following years, however, no trained civil servants arrived at the outpost, and the military personnel established no courts or civilian law enforcement agencies. The military garrison languished from inattention. Soldiers died, and no reinforcements arrived to replace them. The Mississippi River's spring floods eroded the landscape, and soon the fort stood in a sorry state of disrepair. In 1772 the shrunken British military force destroyed Fort de Chartres and took up residence at Fort Gage near Kaskaskia. Four year later, the remains of the British contingent vacated the Illinois country altogether, leaving Kaskaskia in the hands of Phillippe François de Rastel, chevalier de Rocheblave, a somewhat disreputable Frenchman who had pledged his allegiance to the new British regime after the Treaty of Paris.

In 1774, in response to the cry for administrative reform in Canada, the British Parliament adopted the Quebec Act, which was designed principally to mollify the substantial French population continuing to reside in the British dominion. This legislation authorized the open practice of Roman Catholicism, restored the French system of laws, and appointed a new council as the colony's official governing body to replace the elected legislature. In addition, the measure expanded the boundaries of Quebec to include the area east of the Mississippi River and north of the Ohio River and designated lieutenant governors to administer affairs at Detroit, Vincennes, and Kaskaskia. By restoring French law and establishing tighter administrative control in the wilderness, the British government sought to deter land speculators and settlers from penetrating farther into the trans-Appalachian West. A British official candidly admitted at the time that the Quebec Act had "the avowed purpose of excluding all further settlements [in the interior]." Announced in the wake of the Coercive Acts and at the same time as the Boston Tea Party, the Quebec Act generated little reaction in the Illinois country and quickly faded into inconsequence as the widening split between Great Britain and its North American colonies turned into revolution.[2]

Most of the fighting in the American Revolution occurred far away from the Illinois country, as in the French and Indian War a generation earlier. Indeed, because the overwhelming majority of the military engagements took place elsewhere, a number of the inhabitants of the American Bottom initially remained oblivious to developments in the colonies east of the Appalachians. Yet events in the West and strategic considerations intervened to force residents to pay attention to the war for independence. An increase in the number of attacks on isolated colonial settlements perpetrated by Indians allied with the British aroused resentment. Moreover, their control of the Ohio and Mississippi valleys would allow the British to put economic and military pressure on the rebellious colonies along the East Coast. Even if the thirteen original colonies succeeded in securing their freedom, the fate of the British possessions between the Appalachian Mountains and the Mississippi River would remain uncertain. To many of the colonists residing in the densely populated East, continued access to the Western lands would be essential for the future health of an independent nation.

Among the revolutionaries who espoused the critical importance of the Western lands, no one argued more forcefully than George Rogers Clark. A native Virginian who had moved to Kentucky and acquired extensive farmlands near the site of Louisville, Clark argued that "if a country was not worth protecting, it was not worth claiming." He believed that the Americans could neutralize their enemy west of the Appalachians by capturing the strategically vital British fort at Detroit but that their ability to achieve this goal hinged upon first controlling the Illinois country. By seizing Kaskaskia, the Americans could limit Detroit's river communications to the south, curtail the British fort's supply routes, and subdue the troublesome Indian tribes in the Mississippi Valley. For Clark, Detroit remained the ultimate prize in the frontier war, but control of the Illinois country became the linchpin of his design.[3]

The strictures of the Quebec Act notwithstanding, Virginians believed that a seventeenth-century charter granting the London Company suzerainty from sea to sea entitled the colony of Virginia to all lands immediately westward on the continent—including Illinois. Therefore, to seek support for his plan, Clark pleaded his case to the Virginia governor, Patrick Henry. According to spies in the Illinois country, Clark told the governor, very few British soldiers manned their garrisons there and the French population would welcome the military defeat of their longtime enemies. Before the British could strengthen their presence in the area, Clark proposed to conquer, in turn, Kaskaskia, Cahokia, and Vincennes, a small settlement on the Wabash River. Then his force could link up with another contingent from Fort Pitt for the culminating attack on Detroit. With colonial resources already overextended, Governor Henry could provide little assistance, but he approved Clark's daring plan. Armed with a vaguely worded act from the Virginia Assembly approving an expedition "to march against and attack any of our western enemies" and authorized to spend twelve hundred pounds for supplies, Clark left Williamsburg, Virginia, on January 18, 1778.[4]

Although Clark originally indicated to Governor Henry that he would lead an army of 200–300 into the Illinois country, he enlisted only 175 men for the expedition. Leaving Kentucky on June 24, 1778, Clark and his tiny detachment floated down the Ohio River as far as Fort Massac at the mouth of the Tennessee River, and knowing that the British were closely monitoring river traffic at the intersection of the Mississippi and Ohio rivers, they marched the remaining 120 miles to their destination. Arriving in Kaskaskia in the middle of the night, the American detachment took the British soldiers by surprise and seized the fort without firing a shot. On July 4, Rocheblave awoke to find his command in the hands of the enemy, and he formally surrendered. Clark assembled the townspeople and explained to them in detail why the colonists had chosen to make war against the mother country. He promised the Kaskaskians, many of whom were of French Catholic ancestry, that they would enjoy all rights and privileges of citizenship, including freedom of religious worship, if they joined the Americans in the fight. The French had chafed under British rule since 1763, believing they had been alternately ignored and abused, so the prospect of an American regime excited some interest. When Clark related the news that France had allied with the colonies against the British, the townspeople readily agreed to join the alliance. Clark successfully negotiated treaties with more than ten Indian tribes, and his men quickly occupied the neighboring villages of Prairie du Roche, St. Philippe, and Cahokia as well. In just three days, without any fighting at all, the Americans secured control of the entire American Bottom. Equally important, the Indian treaties neutralized the powerful allies upon whom the British had relied so heavily.

Next Clark considered Vincennes, which he believed the Americans must hold in order to protect supply lines between Kentucky and the newly acquired Illinois country. He sent Father Pierre Gibault, the French priest in charge of the Illinois settlements, as an emissary to negotiate with the Vincennes townspeople. Father Gibault found Vincennes virtually defenseless and the inhabitants amenable to the same sort of arrangement as was concluded at Kaskaskia. The small detachment of British soldiers quickly surrendered, and Clark's men immediately assumed control of Fort Sackville as well as the adjacent village. Once again, the Americans secured a key objective without firing a shot.

When word of Clark's bloodless triumphs reached Williamsburg, the jubilant members of the Virginia Assembly declared Illinois a county of the Old Dominion. The news of the creation of Illinois County prompted a much different reaction in Detroit, however, where the alarmed British commander, Lieutenant Henry Hamilton, expressed shock and anger. Known as the "Hair Buyer" because he purportedly paid Britain's Indian allies for American scalps, Hamilton immediately conceived a plan to recapture the outposts. He promptly assembled a force of thirty-five British regulars, seventy-eight French mercenaries, and approximately sixty Indians, and he set out for Vincennes; along the way, he recruited several hundred more Indians. In mid-December, Hamilton's force easily overpowered the token American force Clark had left in Vincennes—the local French population refused to honor their new alliance in fighting against their countrymen from Detroit—and reclaimed the British fort on the Wabash River. Isolated in the Illinois country and certain that no reinforcements would be forthcoming from Virginia, Clark feared Hamilton and his army would merely wait for better weather in the spring before moving against the Americans to reclaim Kaskaskia and its surroundings.

Having learned that Hamilton had allowed his Indian allies to return home for the winter and supposing that the British commander would never expect the Americans to attack before spring, Clark boldly opted for a preemptive strike. With an army of 170 men, he left Kaskaskia on February 5, 1779, and commenced the 140-mile journey to Vincennes. The unusually mild winter of 1778–1779 had produced more rain than snow, leaving much of southern Illinois a quagmire. The terrain became even more impassable as the Americans came closer to the Wabash River and its swollen tributaries, where flooding had left much of the countryside underwater. With no dry ground available for sleeping and unable to light fires for warmth, the miserable soldiers plodded waist-deep through icy waters for the last six days of their journey. On the very last day of their journey, the exhausted men waded across the Wabash River with water up to their shoulders. Having survived extreme hardship, the army promptly gained control of Vincennes and laid siege to the British garrison at Fort Sackville. His position untenable, Hamilton surrendered on February 25, 1779, and Clark dispatched the British commander to a prison in Williamsburg, Virginia.

Clark's daring exploits made him an instant celebrity in the East, and he hoped that his great victories would build additional support in Virginia for his next venture. He immediately sought to attack Detroit as the final step in his grand design to liberate the West from British control. The eager frontiersman wanted to move against Detroit in the summer of 1779, but a force of three hundred Kentuckians, scheduled to participate in the campaign with his Illinois army, inexplicably wandered off to pursue a band of Indians. Clark planned another attack on Detroit in the spring of 1781, but again the lack of sufficient troops forced cancellation. Never able to mount an attack on Detroit, Clark unhappily spent the rest of the war defending Vincennes and other Illinois settlements against British counterattacks.

In 1780 the British launched an expedition from Detroit under Lieutenant Governor Patrick Sinclair to recapture the Illinois country at the same time that another detachment from the south under General Campbell moved northward into the Mississippi Valley. Sinclair's army of 750 men moved down the Mississippi but never received the expected support from General Campbell's forces, which had been engaged by Spanish forces farther south. After losing to the Spanish at St. Louis and to Clark's forces at Cahokia, Sinclair's army and its Indian allies retreated in disarray. Clark sent part of his army under Colonel John Montgomery to pursue the retreating British as far as Lake Michigan and then to burn the village of the principal British allies (the Sauk and Fox Indians) at Rock Island. Later that year, Augustin La Balme, a mysterious French cavalryman who had received the rank of lieutenant colonel from the Continental Congress, assembled an army of Illinois Frenchmen for an assault on Detroit. The attack failed, and La Balme and an estimated thirty of his men perished at the hands of Indians. In 1781 a Spanish militia captain, Eugenio Pierre, led an expedition of thirty Spaniards, twenty men from Cahokia, and two hundred Indians to capture a British trading post at St. Joseph (near Niles, Michigan) and raised the Spanish flag before retreating to the safety of territory held by American forces. Clark's dreams of driving the enemy from Detroit never materialized, but his military victories in 1778–1780 succeeded in undermining any British claims to the Illinois country. Thanks in large measure to Clark's escapades, the rebellious thirteen colonies metamorphosed into a new nation, encompassing lands that extended beyond the Appalachian Mountains and included the Illinois country.

Like the French and British before them, the Virginians found governing the distant Illinois country a daunting challenge. Most of the population of southwestern Illinois—which by then had come to be called the American Bottom, to distinguish it from the Spanish settlements across the Mississippi River—continued to be concentrated in a few communities.

With five hundred white settlers and an equal number of slaves, Kaskaskia remained the metropolis of the region. Cahokia claimed three hundred whites and eighty blacks, while Prairie du Roche's population stood at an estimated one hundred whites and eighty slaves. A handful of families resided in St. Phillipe and Prairie du Pont, and an equally small number congregated outside the ruins of Fort de Chartres. Altogether, the American Bottom contained approximately two thousand whites and one thousand black slaves. A few scattered outposts in remote locations such as Peoria essentially completed the American presence in the Illinois country.

Shortly after Illinois officially became a part of Virginia (as Illinois County), Governor Henry appointed John Todd its first county lieutenant and charged him with the task of administering the county's affairs. In a letter of instructions, the governor advised Todd to "befriend the French and Indians and to teach them the value of democracy." The county lieutenant arrived in Kaskaskia in May 1779 and found the American Bottom in a deplorable state. In particular, economic problems beset the Illinois County, where the depletion of the Virginia treasury had left a mountain of unpaid bills. Local merchants soon realized that the Virginia currency offered for the purchase of supplies was practically worthless. George Rogers Clark had spent his own money and relied on the generous extension of credit by some hopeful French businessmen to keep his army in the field (Gabriel Cerre, the wealthiest resident of Kaskaskia, had been especially magnanimous), but the reservoir of goodwill toward the American government was drying up. The French residents of Illinois villages complained that American soldiers stole their livestock for food; Clark expressed sympathy for the Frenchmen's concerns but saw no alternative ways to feed his men.[5]

Todd discovered that, just as the flow of Easterners into the Illinois country was beginning to increase, relations between the Americans and the longtime French residents were deteriorating. In 1779 the first American settlement appeared in Bellefontaine just south of present-day Waterloo, and the second came quickly after at Grand Ruisseau near Cahokia. Virginians established New Design a few miles south of Bellefontaine, and additional communities followed in subsequent years. The Americans often erected stockades for their protection and simply began farming land on which they held no legal claim. Having hoped for better treatment from the Americans than they had enjoyed under British rule, the French expressed increasing disillusionment when the newcomers disregarded existing property lines, sold liquor to the Indians, and stole cattle, flour, and other commodities from the *habitants*. Contemptuous of the French language, religion, and customs, the Americans evidenced little regard for the sensibilities of the people whose ancestors had occupied the area for generations. To escape the encroachments of the Americans, many of the French accepted the Spanish commandant's offer of free land and relocated across the Mississippi River. Even Father Gibault, who had earlier extolled the virtues of the Americans to the residents of Vincennes, joined the French migration to the west bank of the Mississippi River.

Overwhelmed by the combination of problems facing him, Lieutenant Todd remained at his post for only five months before returning to Kentucky. Ignoring the rejection of his resignation letter, he appointed his deputy Richard Winston to be his successor and simply left the county. What little civil authority had existed under Todd quickly dissolved. John Dodge, an unscrupulous land speculator from Connecticut, arrived on the scene in 1780 and declared himself captain commandant of Illinois County. He accused Winston of conspiring with the Spanish, convinced the military commander to imprison him for treason, and with the approval of the burgeoning American population launched a reign of terror against the French. When Winston secured his release from prison, he dissolved the ineffectual county court at Kaskaskia, appointed Timothe de Monbreun as his successor, and fled to Virginia. De Monbreun enjoyed no greater success at controlling Dodge, who continued his ruthless persecution of the beleaguered French, whose exodus intensified. Virginia experienced nothing but frustration in its attempt to govern its Western lands and therefore allowed the law that created Illinois County to expire on January 5, 1782.

In the years during and immediately following the American Revolution, several of the states vied for control of the land above the Ohio River known as the Northwest Territory. Conflicting land claims threatened to undermine the new nation's unity, so in 1784 Virginia surrendered all of its lands to the national government, after the other states claiming land in the area had agreed to do the same. Thomas Jefferson devised a scheme for dividing the Northwest Territory into seven rectangular states, all with Indian and Greek names—Sylvania, Michigania, Cherronesus, Metropotamia, Assenisipia, Polypotamia, and Illinoia. (According to his configuration, different sections of modern Illinois would have been contained in Assenisipia, Polypotamia, and Illinoia.) Jefferson's proposal generated less support than an assessment by James Monroe, who believed that, because the wilderness seemed unlikely to attract many settlers at all, the number of people who would settle in the Northwest Territory's 265,878 square miles could easily be accommodated by the creation of three, four, or five states. In 1785 Congress established a system for surveying the territory and passed the Land Ordinance Act, which provided for the division of land into 6-mile-square townships, with each township containing 36 sections of 640 acres apiece. Roads adjacent to section lines intersected at right angles, creating checkerboard patterns throughout the countryside. Squabbles over real estate ownership recurred in later years, but the clarity and simplicity of the land surveys precluded endless boundary wrangles. Following Monroe's lead, the Northwest Ordinance mandated the creation of no fewer than three and no more than five states. The five states eventually carved out of the Northwest Territory were Ohio (1803), Indiana (1816), Illinois (1818), Michigan (1837), and Wisconsin (1848).

Residents of Illinois welcomed the creation of the Northwest Territory and eagerly awaited the arrival of the newly appointed governor, Revolutionary War hero Arthur St. Clair, because they hoped the governmental

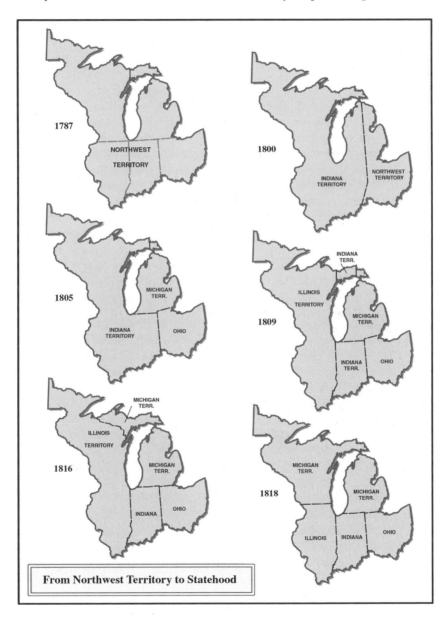

From Northwest Territory to Statehood

reorganization would bring law and order to the frontier. Certainly, chaos had reigned in the preceding years. John Dodge continued to act with impunity, living in palatial splendor and exploiting the French at every turn. The Spanish closed the Mississippi River to American commerce and incited Indian attacks against the relatively defenseless villages in Illinois. The emboldened Indians—principally members of the Miami, Wea, Kickapoo, and Potawatomi tribes—stole livestock and destroyed crops at will. Long after the American Revolution, the British continued to cause problems for the American settlers. The British-owned Michilimackinac Company maintained a trading post in Cahokia for supplying Indians, and scores of British fur companies operated in the American Bottom. The ineffectuality of the Kaskaskia court resulted in rampant lawlessness among the white settlers. In response to a flood of petitions from Illinois settlers, Congress sent the commander of American forces in the West, General Josiah Harmar, on an inspection trip in 1787. Swayed by Dodge's blandishments, however, Harmar dismissed the residents' complaints as exaggerations and urged the French to obey the law and be patient.

The clash of ethnic cultures and the struggle for land produced the potential for hostilities to erupt at any time. The relatively few Americans sought government assistance against the Indians, Spanish, and British while simultaneously trying to maintain control of a depleted French population. The French appealed for government intervention to protect them from the Americans, the British, and the Spanish, even as they saw their traditionally good relations with the Indians deteriorate. The assorted Indian tribes, whose alliances with various European powers had failed to stem the tide of white immigration, fought a desperate holding action trying to retain control of their dwindling hunting grounds. "The situation in Illinois was a complicated one," concluded one historian, "and probably the numerical weakness of the population alone saved the country from disastrous results."[6]

In 1788 Governor St. Clair established territorial headquarters at Marietta, Ohio, and in 1790 he arrived in Kaskaskia for his first look at the American Bottom. He initiated the process of sound government by creating a county, which he named after himself, and appointing his cousin, William St. Clair, court clerk. (St. Clair County sprawled across approximately one-third of the current state of Illinois.) Shortly after his arrival, he confronted a controversy—the issue of slavery—that threatened to divide the population of Illinois. Having feared that the existence of slavery in the Northwest Territory would upset New Englanders and thereby retard population growth in the West, Congress inserted in Article VI of the Northwest Ordinance a sentence prohibiting slavery and involuntary servitude. Many settlers already owned slaves, however, and feared that the new legislation would force a change in the existing arrangement. St. Clair mollified the slaveholders by interpreting Article VI to mean only that no new bondsmen could be brought into the territory.

The persistent threat from hostile Indians presented the governor with another nettlesome problem he could not ignore. In fact, conflicts confronted Americans throughout the Northwest Territory, with the Indians wreaking the most havoc far to the north and east of the American Bottom. In 1790 General Harmar's army fought a disastrous battle against the Indian tribes near the Maumee River in which 180 U.S. soldiers died. The following year, the Miami Indians inflicted a humiliating defeat on a large army led by Governor St. Clair; American casualties numbered 630 dead and 285 wounded. The Indians demanded that whites evacuate the Northwest Territory, and the demoralized Americans assented to peace negotiations. In 1794, however, General "Mad Anthony" Wayne turned the tide in favor of the Americans with his complete rout of the Indians at the Battle of Fallen Timbers in Ohio's Maumee Valley. Wayne's decisive victory— followed by the Treaty of Greenville, which he bullied the Indians into signing the following year—gave the Americans undisputed control of much of the Northwest Territory.

The Treaty of Greenville included several provisions of importance for the development of Illinois. The defeated Indians relinquished their claim to the land at the mouth of the Chicago River, which gave the whites control of the portage there and provided the site for the future construction of Fort Dearborn. Similarly, the Indians ceded strategically situated parcels of land at Peoria, at Fort Massac, and at the mouth of the Illinois River. The treaty forced the Indians to surrender all claims to lands in Illinois that were already settled by whites while acknowledging that the rest of the land in the state belonged to the Native Americans. A number of the Indian tribes, including the Kaskaskia, Potawatomi, and Kickapoo, also received the promise of annual payments in trade goods.

In the American Bottom, the temporary curtailment of hostilities with the Indians resulted in a slight increase in the pace of immigration. Although many Frenchmen continued to leave for Spanish territory across the Mississippi River, a number of French settlers arrived in the Illinois country as well. These French Canadians, unlike the more humble *voyageurs* and *habitants* of earlier times, included several men of considerable means who contributed significantly to the economic development of the area. Pierre Menard, a Kaskaskia merchant, became known as a generous philanthropist and served in the territorial legislature. Nicholas Jarrott, another prosperous French businessman, built an impressive mansion that was probably the first brick house constructed in Illinois. Yet despite the notable achievements of such French newcomers, no Roman Catholic churches remained in the American Bottom by 1800, and French communicants relied upon the priests who infrequently visited from across the Mississippi River. Early in the nineteenth century, a group of Trappist monks established a monastery at Monks' Mound near Cahokia in the hopes of converting the Indians. After several years of crop failures and sickness, the Trappist monks withdrew to the East Coast and then to France.

Protestant churches gradually began to appear. In 1787 James Smith, a Separate Baptist elder, became the first Protestant to preach in Illinois, and in 1790 the Reverend Daniel Badgley established the first Baptist church in the state at New Design. By 1807 Baptists from five churches that collectively claimed a membership of more than one hundred persons formed an association. In 1793 the Reverend Joseph Lillard became the first Methodist minister to preach in Illinois; the Reverend Benjamin Young rode the circuit for the Methodists in the state ten years later. At the end of the eighteenth century, primarily the Baptists and Methodists attended to the spiritual needs of the estimated twenty-five hundred people living in the American Bottom and a handful of other scattered settlements.

By 1798 more than a thousand white males resided throughout the Northwest Territory, so Governor St. Clair began preparations for the next stage of territorial development by holding an election for a new legislature. Two inhabitants of Illinois—Shadrach Bond and John Edgar, both of Kaskaskia—served in the twenty-three-member legislature in Cincinnati. The Northwest Ordinance also granted the people the right to elect a nonvoting delegate to the U.S. Congress, and territorial voters chose William Henry Harrison to fill the post. An aide-de-camp to Mad Anthony Wayne at the Battle of Fallen Timbers, Harrison had achieved fame as a military hero and then resigned from the army in 1798 to become secretary of the Northwest Territory. Bowing to complaints from residents of the future states of Illinois and Indiana that the remote seat of government in Ohio proved insensitive to the needs of Westerners, Harrison used his position as chairman of the House Committee on Public Lands to secure passage of a law in 1800 that divided the Northwest Territory into two: the Territory of Indiana (including the modern states of Illinois, Indiana, and Wisconsin, as well as parts of Michigan and Minnesota) and the Northwest Territory (consisting of the modern state of Ohio and part of Michigan). Harrison assumed the governorship of the Indiana Territory, with Vincennes selected as its first capital.

At the westernmost edge of the new territory, Illinois remained an unimpressive backwater. According to the 1800 census, Illinois could claim only 2,458 residents, about the same population as was counted in the middle of the eighteenth century. Settlements continued to exist alongside navigable waterways because transportation remained of paramount importance in the frontier. Population numbers in the principal villages remained small— 719 in Cahokia, 467 in Kaskaskia, 286 in Bellefontaine, and 212 in Prairie du Roche. Approximately 100 people, mostly French, lived in and around Peoria, and a roughly equal number resided in the vicinity of Fort Massac. The census reported no settlers at all living in the expanse of southern Illinois between Kaskaskia and the Wabash River. The startling lack of population growth resulted from the persistence of harsh frontier conditions, recurring troubles with Indians, lack of effective government, the attendant lawlessness, and delays in the opening of land for sale.

The disposition of public lands, a troublesome problem that had earlier confounded Governor St. Clair, continued to retard population growth in the early nineteenth century as the U.S. government refused to sell any public land in Illinois prior to the settlement of all extant claims. Legislation in 1796, offering land in increments no less than 640 acres at two dollars an acre, set the price too high for the vast majority of potential landowners. Subsequent laws made land available first in 320-acre parcels and later in 160-acre allotments, but the federal government determined to sort out previous land grants before commencing surveys and land sales. The government encountered the greatest difficulty in uncovering what had happened to the 400-acre grants extended by Congress in 1788 to French heads of families. Concerned about the increasingly hostile environment they encountered in the American Bottom, many of the French sold their grants at ridiculously low prices to wealthy land speculators such as John Edgar and William Morrison. An investigatory commission found that these land speculators had not only illegally acquired many land titles from the French but had also manufactured false improvement claims and engaged in other shady land grabs. The attempt to identify fraudulent land claims dragged on for years amid charges and countercharges while impatient settlers and speculators chafed at their inability to acquire land. Potential migrants to Illinois faced a dispiriting choice between either purchasing French claims that had not been fully adjudicated or squatting on government land and making improvements without any assurances of ownership. It was not surprising that they often looked elsewhere.

Edgar, Morrison, and other leading speculators became bitter enemies of Governor Harrison, whom they accused of favoritism and incompetence. Charging that the Indiana Territory consistently ignored the interests of Westerners, in 1803 they called for separation from the Vincennes government and annexation to the new Louisiana Territory; they petitioned for the creation of a separate Illinois territory in 1805, 1806, and 1808. The issue of slavery in the territory widened the rift between the speculators and the governor and his supporters. Both factions argued for the legalization of slavery and based their argument upon the shortage of labor in Illinois, but they disagreed on the best method to circumvent the proscriptions of the Northwest Ordinance. In 1803 Harrison and territorial judges adopted a measure that provided for the indenture of African Americans, an attempt to establish slavery by another name. Calling the governor's initiative inadequate, the speculators advocated moving to the second stage of territorial government so they could have a delegate lobby for slavery in Congress. In 1804 Harrison surprisingly supported this proposal, which his enemies promptly deserted, and it carried in a public referendum. In 1805 and 1807, the legislature passed new indenture laws that consigned African American men and their families to extended periods of servitude.

Not everyone in the large Indiana Territory favored slavery, however, and in some quarters the new laws countenancing indentured servitude raised cries of protest. In Dearborn County in eastern Indiana, for example, antislavery residents petitioned to become part of the free state of Ohio. Other settlers in the eastern sections of the territory urged detaching the Illinois country from the Indiana Territory, to forge an antislavery majority in the area remaining. As a result, the agitation for separation from the west became widespread, and in 1808 politicians on both sides of the issue consented to work together for a common end. Jesse B. Thomas, a resident of Dearborn County and speaker of the territorial House of Representatives, won election to Congress with the overwhelming support of the separatists from the Illinois country. Thomas completed the bargain by working successfully for a law that created Illinois as a separate territory. On March 1, 1809, the Illinois Territory officially came into existence, with Kaskaskia designated as its capital. Bordered by a line running south from Canada to Vincennes, the Wabash, Ohio, and Mississippi rivers, and a line running from the Mississippi River to the Lake of the Woods, the territory included an area roughly two and a half times the size of the modern state.

In large measure, the desires of the settlers residing in the Illinois country to achieve their independence from the Indiana Territory replicated a pattern established earlier on the American frontier. Just as the pioneers in Kentucky had sought their independence from Virginia, and frontiersmen in Tennessee had yearned to be separated from North Carolina, a similar situation developed west of the Wabash River. Frontier minorities on the farthest outposts of civilization thought their needs were being overlooked by distant ruling groups to the east. Discontent and eventual separation resulted. The political deal that created the Illinois Territory left a residue of bitterness in its wake. Harrison and many other officials expressed resentment toward the separatists as they proceeded to reorganize the government of the Indiana Territory. Bitter over Jesse Thomas's role in the creation of the Illinois Territory, some residents of Vincennes burned him in effigy. An unidentified assailant killed a member of the anti-Harrison faction in Kaskaskia, and the governor's foes tried to implicate the land commissioner. As the strife continued, factionalism and intractable issues remained in the new territory. Contested land claims, the controversy over slavery, querulous relations with the Indians, and a host of other challenges lay ahead.

Kaskaskia

In 1703 a number of French traders and trappers, many of whom had married into the Kaskaskia Indian tribe, founded a village where the Kaskaskia River emptied into the Mississippi River. Unlike the settlement of New Orleans

and Mobile, where French officials surveyed the land before carefully laying out streets and lots in an identifiable pattern, Kaskaskia grew in an entirely random fashion. The Frenchmen and a number of Jesuit priests who
sought to convert the Indians to Roman Catholicism built a huge church
complete with three chapels, a baptismal font, and a steeple as the centerpiece of the village, and houses scattered haphazardly around the mission.
Habitants worked alongside Indians in the field growing maize, wheat, vegetables, and melons. An epidemic in 1714 took a terrible toll in Kaskaskia
and its surroundings, killing four or five people a day during the summer
months. Despite that year's carnage, however, the population gradually increased. A census taken in 1723 found 105 white men, 37 married women,
and 54 children in the village. In 1767 the village contained an estimated
600 men, women, and children.

The French in Kaskaskia built houses that were readily distinguishable
from structures built by the British or Spanish. While the British laid
long narrow striplings or pieces of wood on top of each other to form
log cabins, for example, the French stood the wooden strips on end to
form a *maison de poteaux en terre* (a house of posts in the ground). They
filled the gaps between the logs with a mixture of clay and grass or stone
rubble. Sometimes, to avoid the problem of rotting logs, they erected
wooden frames on foundations of limestone that had been quarried
from the nearby river bluffs. Most of the community's residents hailed
from French Canada, but their houses were of a different structure.
Homes in Kaskaskia often included wide porches that wrapped around
the structure on two, three, or even all four sides. Although stone chim-
neys were not uncommon in the 1720s and 1730s, wooden houses predominated in the community until the middle of the eighteenth century. The *habitants* often built stables, slave quarters, chicken coops, and
pigpens near their homes.

From its early origins, Kaskaskia became the heart of French Illinois as
well as the civic and cultural capital of the American Bottom. Between
1787 and 1790, at the height of anarchy in the Illinois country, great numbers of French fled across the Mississippi River, and the community actually lost population. The 1800 census listed only 467 residents. Despite
stagnant population growth, however, Kaskaskia remained the center of
Illinois government. In 1795 the village became the county seat of newly
created Randolph County; in 1809 when Illinois became a territory,
Kaskaskia became its capital. The aging French community, small in population and shabby in appearance, nevertheless remained the capital when
Illinois became a state in 1818. Scarcely a year later, however, land speculators suggested that the state capital should be moved to a more central location, because Kaskaskia was located in the southwestern part of the state.
The capital relocated to Vandalia in 1819, and Kaskaskia's fortunes continued to ebb. Years of flooding drove families to higher ground, and by 1881,

constant erosion left the village stranded on an island. More buildings crumbled as the Mississippi River crept closer, and eventually the village disappeared altogether. The tiny island that remains is the last vestige of what was once the leading metropolis of French Illinois.

George Rogers Clark

George Rogers Clark was born on November 19, 1752, in Albemarle County, Virginia, and grew up on a plantation adjacent to Thomas Jefferson's birthplace. He attended school briefly with another neighbor, James Madison, before becoming a tobacco farmer at an early age. Like George Washington, whom he believed he resembled, Clark became a surveyor and part-time soldier. At the age of twenty-three, he headed west and acquired land in Kentucky. When Indian war parties launched raids across the Ohio River into Kentucky, Clark organized the settlers in defense. Arguing convincingly that

George Rogers Clark and his men cross the swollen Wabash River prior to their attack on Vincennes, Indiana, as illustrated by George I. Parrish, Jr. *Illinois State Historical Library*

the protection of the Virginia frontier depended upon the defense of the Kentucky settlements, he lobbied successfully for the creation of Kentucky County in 1776 and became known as the founder of the Commonwealth. With the onset of the revolution against Great Britain, Clark devoted himself to the advancement of American interests and the removal of the British from the frontier. In his view, these goals could be achieved by the capture of the British stronghold at Detroit and by subsequent American control of the trans-Appalachian region. Clark envisioned the conquest of the Illinois country as the first step in the process.

In 1778–1779 Clark and his small army of Virginians, Frenchmen, and Indians executed a series of military maneuvers that achieved victory over the British with very few casualties and occasionally without one shot being fired. After taking the British outpost at Kaskaskia and then Cahokia and the other villages in the American Bottom in 1778, Clark signed treaties with Indians who had previously been allied with the British, and he captured the British fort at Vincennes. When a British force from Detroit under the command of Lieutenant Henry Hamilton defeated a token force that Clark had left to defend Vincennes, Clark and his men conducted a daring campaign in the middle of winter to reclaim the prize. Crossing the flooded southern Illinois prairie undetected in February 1779, the American force again took the unsuspecting British by surprise and forced immediate capitulation. The recapture of Vincennes marked the high point of Clark's military career, for, although he earnestly desired to follow up this victory with an attack on Detroit, circumstances prevented him from ever launching that northern campaign. Instead, he fought British forces again only in defense of the Illinois country in 1780.

Clark's triumphs negated any British claims to the trans-Appalachian West and thereby played a substantial role in securing for the United States a generous western boundary. A great national hero at the age of thirty, Clark saw his reputation plummet in subsequent years. Beset by creditors and unable to collect money owed him by the Virginia government, he nevertheless monitored the distribution of land grants to the soldiers who had served under his command during the Revolution. His attempt to lead an unauthorized expedition against warring Indians ended ingloriously when his Kentucky troops mutinied. With repeated business failures, he sank deeper and deeper into poverty and alcoholism. Forgotten by the nation he had served so nobly, he entered into several intrigues with the French and Spanish over the disposition of Louisiana. He lost his right leg in an accident and, partially paralyzed by a stroke, lived his last years as an invalid. He died at the age of sixty-six in 1818—ironically the same year that Illinois became a state.

CHAPTER THREE

From Territory to Statehood

A number of politicians in Kaskaskia who had fought to create the Illinois Territory aspired to be its first governor, but President James Madison neatly sidestepped potential problems by naming an outsider to the post. Madison chose Ninian Edwards, a wealthy aristocrat from Kentucky, to be governor of the Illinois Territory. Edwards required some time to put his affairs in Kentucky in order and to transport his livestock and slaves to his new home, so he did not arrive in Kaskaskia until six months after the establishment of territorial government. During that time, the conduct of the governor's business fell to the territorial secretary, Nathaniel Pope, Edwards's cousin and the brother of Kentucky Senator John Pope. A successful attorney who spoke fluent French, the twenty-four-year-old Pope attended to the day-to-day affairs of governor and settled minor disputes between individuals, but the major problems immediately facing the new territory—the question of who would exercise the franchise and the perennially perplexing issue of landownership—awaited the arrival of Governor Edwards.

According to the Northwest Ordinance of 1787, only landowners could vote. Such a restrictive franchise proved extremely unpopular in the Illinois Territory where only about 220 of the estimated 12,000 inhabitants could demonstrate landownership. Under such circumstances, continuing wrangling over land claims deprived some of the territory's leading citizens of the right to vote. Sentiment in the West—including Illinois—was moving toward broader participation in politics and government, and in 1809 the residents of Indiana Territory obtained the right to elect their own delegate to Congress. In response to the rising clamor for greater political participation in the Illinois Territory, Governor Edwards called for a public referendum on the question. When the results of the referendum indicated an overwhelming majority in favor of expanding the franchise, Edwards successfully petitioned Congress for a law granting Illinois second-grade territorial government. Under the new arrangement, all free white males who had resided in the territory for at least one year and paid any territorial or county taxes at all would be eligible to vote. Squatters as well as landowners voted in October 1812 and elected the members of the territory's first legislature as well as its representative to the U.S. Congress, Shadrach Bond.

The other pressing problem confronting the new territorial government concerned land distribution, a conundrum that had plagued the Illinois country for decades. The French had parceled out land according to a feudal system that later arrivals either contested or disregarded altogether. British officials had repeatedly ignored existing French claims, often discarding records that would have established ownership, and cavalierly awarded land to newcomers. Fraud abounded under the British, and the payment of bribes and kickbacks had allowed some speculators to amass massive tracts of land. After the American Revolution, the Confederation government reversed British policies and affirmed French titles. Many of the French who had scuttled their claims and sold their land at ridiculously low prices found their previous holdings to be extremely valuable, especially as talk began to spread of statehood. At the same time, Congress awarded as much as four hundred acres of land to each Revolutionary War veteran who had resided in Illinois prior to 1783.

Sorting out legitimate from illegitimate land claims proved a Herculean task. Most of the land acquired from the French belonged to a small group of wealthy and influential men who had never allowed laws or scruples to stand in the way of constructing real estate empires. John Edgar, an Irish immigrant and former seaman in the British Navy, came to Kaskaskia in the 1780s and acquired title to more than forty-nine thousand acres in an area spanning eight counties. He often collaborated with William Morrison, who had come to Kaskaskia from Philadelphia along with his five brothers and obtained more than fifteen thousand acres of land. Two federal commissioners reported to the secretary of the treasury in 1810 that Edgar, Morrison, and other speculators had been guilty of forgery, perjury, and suborning witnesses to authenticate their claims falsely. In all, the commissioners found almost nine hundred land claims to be fraudulent and proclaimed them illegal.

As government officials struggled to make sense of existing land titles, in 1810 surveyors began to establish township and section lines in preparation for public land sales. In 1814 the government finally offered land in the public domain for sale at the existing land offices in Kaskaskia and Shawneetown; two years later a third land office opened at Edwardsville. The regularization of land sales still left one problem unsolved, however, for those squatters who had earlier established domiciles and improved their holdings had no legal claim on their land and feared that they would have to compete all over again with newly arriving settlers. With the help of Shadrach Bond, they successfully petitioned Congress to pass a preemption law that gave them the first chance to purchase the land on which they were residing. The sale of land in Illinois accelerated after the conclusion of the War of 1812 as settlers and speculators bought most tracts at the attractive price of two dollars an acre. Most buyers relied on credit and took advantage of the generous terms offered by the government. Purchase of land required only a 5 percent down payment, another 20 percent within forty days, and the balance in three annual installments with no interest. The government claimed the right of foreclosure if buyers failed to meet their obligations within five years.

In the early nineteenth century, increasingly liberal policies in the nation's capital meant that land in the Illinois Territory became available in smaller tracts and at lower prices. For example, a law in 1800 allowed individuals to purchase a minimum of 320 acres (a half-section) at $2.00 an acre; an amendment in 1804 authorized the sale of 160 acres (a quarter-section); and another alteration in 1817 permitted the sale of 80-acre holdings. In 1820 Congress reduced the price to $1.25 an acre for an 80-acre plot, which then remained the standard for as long as the government sold land in Illinois. Such favorable terms meant that anyone with $100.00 could obtain title to an 80-acre farm without being saddled with any debt at all.

While tens of millions of acres became available for settlement under this generous policy, Congress reserved 3.5 million acres between the Illinois and Mississippi rivers for War of 1812 veterans. In 1816 Governor Edwards persuaded the Indian tribes to concede white ownership of what became known as the Military Tract, and the disbursement of 160-acre plots commenced the following year. Within four months of the policy's enactment, the general land office in Washington, D.C., distributed eighteen thousand warrants, each of which granted 160 acres to a veteran or his heirs. Because the law failed to require that veterans remain on the land they received and the warrants could be sold immediately, Eastern speculators acquired most of the land in the Military Tract, often paying as little as ten cents an acre. The U.S. government created two regional military tracts, and because the tract in Louisiana Territory attracted mostly veterans from the Southeast, settlers in Illinois came disproportionately from Northern states. As in countless other instances in Illinois and throughout the West, an exceedingly generous national land policy designed to benefit individual homesteaders ended up distributing the lion's share of acreage to speculative interests.

The resolution of the perplexing land question made the Illinois Territory a much more inviting destination for westward-bound migrants, but the frontier remained hazardous because of the continued threat of Indian warfare. Americans in the West blamed British agitators based in Canada for their uneasy relations with many of the Indian tribes. The provocative behavior of British traders and military forces no doubt contributed to the increasingly volatile situation on the frontier, but the Indians would have undoubtedly resisted the Americans' invasion of their land in any event. An inchoate coalition of tribes under the leadership of the Shawnee chief Tecumseh and his brother Tenskwatawa, known as the Prophet, dissolved after William Henry Harrison's decisive victory in November 1811 at the Tippecanoe River in Indiana, but bad feelings remained throughout the West. Harrison's triumph forestalled the creation of a massive tribal alliance, but many of the Indians joined forces with the British at the outset of the War of 1812.

In the Illinois Territory, in which the Indians still outnumbered the white settlers by a ratio of nearly ten to one, roving bands of Potawatomi, Kickapoo, and Winnebago raided isolated settlements and homesteads, stealing horses and killing white settlers. Believing the possibility of war with the Indians imminent, Congress sent four companies of rangers to Illinois and placed the soldiers already stationed in the territory on alert. Governor Edwards paid the expenses for other militia companies out of his own pocket and ordered the construction of Fort Russell near Edwardsville as well as a series of blockhouses to protect scattered white settlements. Rising fear among the settlers led the governor in February 1812 to write the secretary of war: "The alarms and apprehensions of the people are becoming so universal that I really should not be surprised if we should, in three months, lose more than one-half of our present population. In places, in my opinion, entirely out of danger, many are removing. In other places, large settlements are about to be totally deserted."[1]

The violence dreaded by the denizens of the Illinois Territory came not in the heart of white settlement in the more densely populated south but in the relative isolation of Fort Dearborn on the shores of Lake Michigan. Jean Baptiste Point du Sable, part French and part African American with an Indian wife, had established a trading post near the lake as early as 1779, but the future site of Chicago remained for decades nothing more than a tiny village where a few Indians and fur traders commingled in an ethnic and racial middle ground. In 1803, after Du Sable had abandoned his home, the U.S. government erected Fort Dearborn and stationed a small detachment of soldiers there. After the outbreak of war against the British in 1812, General William Hull at Fort Detroit feared an immediate strike by Britain's Indian allies. He sent orders to the commander at Fort Dearborn, Captain Nathan Heald, to dispose of all arms and ammunition, to distribute nonmilitary goods to friendly Indians living in the surrounding area, and then to abandon his post. The Indian who brought the orders from Detroit and John Kinzie, a fur trader who lived nearby, both urged Heald to disregard the orders and remain within the safety of the fort. If Heald felt compelled to abandon his position, Kinzie advised, he should do so promptly before the Indians could marshal their forces for an attack. Heald dithered for five days before coming to the decision to follow orders. In the view of Kinzie and several experienced junior officers, the commander at Fort Dearborn made an unwise decision and then compounded the error by waiting too long to act.[2]

On August 15, 1812, Heald disposed of the goods in the fort as instructed and led his party eastward on a march bound for Fort Wayne, Indiana. He foolishly destroyed virtually all of the garrison's ammunition, leaving the soldiers with just twenty-five rounds apiece for the entire journey. Almost immediately after the column vacated the fort, the Potawatomi guides escorting the marchers and their allies who waited in ambush launched an attack. In the ensuing battle, the Indians killed sixty men, two women, and twelve children and took five women captive; the fate of several children remained unknown. Long after the army officers surrendered, the Indians tomahawked some of the wounded and tortured to death five surviving soldiers. They spared the lives of Heald, who had been wounded during the fight, and his wife. In the tumult Kinzie loaded his family onto a boat and sent them off to safety, and he also survived the ordeal. The day's carnage ended with the victorious Indians burning Fort Dearborn.

In the aftermath of the Fort Dearborn massacre, as it came to be known, land sales virtually ceased and the flow of new arrivals into the Illinois Territory declined to a trickle. As Governor Edwards had predicted to the secretary of war, a great number of settlers fled the territory for purportedly safer locations elsewhere. Seeking retribution, the governor mustered an army of eight hundred men at Fort Russell and personally led a campaign

An artist's rendering of the Fort Dearborn massacre on August 15, 1812, when Indians burned the fort and killed more than seventy men, women, and children. *Illinois State Historical Library*

against the largest gatherings of Indians in the area. The American force destroyed two Kickapoo villages near the future site of Springfield, then moved toward Miami and Kickapoo villages near Lake Peoria. Discipline evaporated, and the militia degenerated into a mob. The marauding whites torched several villages and killed an estimated twenty to thirty Indians as they fled. A second punitive expedition against the Indians, led by Captain Thomas E. Craig rather than by the governor himself, resulted in a similar loss of discipline, and the militia burned and plundered an Indian village near Peoria; later, Edwards used government funds to compensate the peaceful Indians for their losses. Two expeditions by American forces against Sauk and Fox encampments on the Mississippi River near Rock Island, which were strategically important locations reinforced by the British, ended in failure.

The end of the War of 1812, very little of which had been fought within the Illinois Territory, brought to a halt most of the hostilities against the Indians, but considerable enmity remained. In 1814, just ten days after the signing of the peace treaty in Ghent, Belgium, the territorial legislature announced a system of bounties for the killing of hostile Indians. The territory promised to pay civilians one hundred dollars for each warrior killed in Indian country, fifty dollars for each one killed within a white settlement, and comparable amounts for women or children captured. In 1816 the Americans erected a new Fort Dearborn and built Fort Armstrong at Rock Island. Existing treaties left much of the northern part of the territory and a sliver of land in the eastern section in the possession of Indian tribes—areas generally not yet in demand by settlers—but the federal government could claim legal ownership of most of the eventual state of Illinois.

The return of peace to the Illinois Territory led to an increase in immigration. In the years following the end of the War of 1812, most of the new arrivals came from Southern states. Whereas many migrants from the New England region moved into New York and then farther west into Ohio, Michigan, and Indiana, those who arrived in Illinois hailed principally from the mountainous areas of the region known as the Upland South. A sample of one-tenth of the population that entered the territory between 1815 and 1818 showed that 71 percent came from Kentucky, Tennessee, Virginia, Maryland, Georgia, and the Carolinas. Some settlers made the trip overland in wagons or buggies and others walked, but most followed water routes west. From the Kentucky and Cumberland rivers and along numerous other tributaries, they made their way to the Ohio River, the early nineteenth-century highway to the West. Although the first steamboat traveled down the Ohio River in the winter of 1811–1812, navigation in Western waterways proceeded slowly at first, and the first steamboat did not reach St. Louis until 1817. Travel on steamboats proved prohibitively expensive for most immigrants, and instead they usually loaded their livestock and other personal possessions on flatboats and floated down the Ohio River. Easy and inexpensive to construct, flatboats could transport between twenty-five and one hundred tons of cargo in a single trip. Utilized as "a mixture of log cabin, fort, floating barnyard and country grocery," these crude vessels could be dismantled at their destinations and sold for lumber. Immigrants traveling down the Ohio disembarked at Shawneetown, the gateway to the Illinois Territory, and then proceeded westward. In later years, many settlers arrived via the Cumberland Road, the national highway that wound from Wheeling, Virginia, through southern Ohio, Indiana, and Illinois to Vandalia.[3]

When Indiana became a state in 1816, no groundswell of popular opinion for statehood yet existed in the Illinois Territory. Farther west, more remote to immigrants and still struggling to subdue a substantial Indian population, Illinois had been growing at a much slower rate than its neighbor to the east. Indeed, considering the country's sparse population and dearth of economic development, statehood for Illinois may well have been premature at that time. Nevertheless, in 1817 Daniel Pope Cook, the nephew of Congressman Nathaniel Pope and future son-in-law of Governor Edwards, initiated a campaign for statehood. Cook had come to Illinois from Kentucky in 1815 to practice law and, although only twenty years old at the time, quickly made a name for himself as a young man of great energy and ambition. He purchased an interest in the *Illinois Herald,* the territory's first newspaper, and Governor Edwards appointed him the state's auditor of public accounts. He used the *Illinois Herald*—later renamed the *Western Intelligencer* and then the *Illinois Intelligencer*—to advance his arguments for statehood. Enumerating the deficiencies of territorial government, he lamented the extraordinary power delegated to the governor because of his irreversible veto, the powerlessness of the general assembly, and the ineffectuality of representatives to the U.S. Congress who could offer their views but could not cast votes. Cook conceded that the state would be obligated to pay the salaries of public officials, a financial responsibility the federal government bore for the territories, but argued that the increase in the value of land brought by statehood would more than offset that cost.

Having been elected clerk of the territorial House of Representatives, Cook found himself in an even more advantageous position from which to work for statehood. Addressing the legislature at the opening of the session on December 2, 1817, Governor Edwards recommended that a population census be taken in preparation for an application for statehood at the next session. Unwilling to await the results of a census or to postpone their activities in behalf of statehood for a year, members of a house committee followed Cook's urging and immediately drew up a petition for statehood that estimated the territory's population at forty thousand. The governor assented, the entire legislature voted affirmatively on December 10, and the petition went forward to the U.S. Congress.

Advocates for statehood received the encouraging news from Washington that Nathaniel Pope, Illinois's representative to Congress and Cook's uncle, had been appointed chairman of the committee that would consider the petition. Pope thought the estimated population of forty thousand seriously inflated and considered the hastily composed petition in need of several amendments, but he voiced none of his concerns publicly and worked arduously in behalf of statehood. Noting that Indiana, when it became a state, had rejected the northern boundary given it under the Northwest Ordinance and had moved the line northward to acquire an additional forty-five miles of shoreline along Lake Michigan, Pope drafted an amendment for the Illinois petition that pushed its northern border, then situated south of Lake Michigan, forty miles northward. He justified this adjustment to the readers of the *Illinois Intelligencer* by noting the importance of having access to Lake Michigan and control of a proposed canal that would link the Illinois River to commerce on the lake. Establishing this connection to the Great Lakes and northern trade, he speculated, would also increase the likelihood that Illinois would become a free state rather than a slave state. As a result of his prescience, the new state acquired roughly eight thousand square miles (eventually parts of fourteen counties) and the future site of Chicago.

Pope proposed several other amendments to the petition, the most important of which dealt with the money derived from the sale of public land. In recent cases, 5 percent of the proceeds from land sales had been reserved for the new states. In Indiana, for example, this revenue had been designated for the construction of roads and canals. In an unprecedented departure from existing practice, Pope's amendment stipulated that the 5 percent be divided up in the following fashion: 2 percent would be allocated for roads and the remaining 3 percent given to the state legislature "for the encouragement of learning, of which one-sixth part shall be exclusively bestowed on a college or university." Pope reinforced his interest in education by mandating that section 16 of each township in the state be set aside for use by schools. On April 14, 1818, Congress approved the petition with Pope's amendments, and President James Monroe completed the first step toward statehood by signing the enabling act on April 18.[4]

The next step toward statehood involved the drafting of a state constitution, a process that commenced in July 1818 when the people of the territory elected thirty-three delegates for that purpose. At a time when political parties remained largely unformed on the frontier, the residents of the Illinois Territory chose as their representatives to the constitutional convention their friends, neighbors, and others with similar views on the leading issues of the day. The delegates, a disparate lot, included three attorneys, three physicians, two peace officers, a minister, a land office official, and assorted farmers and laborers representing fifteen counties. The constitutional convention convened on the first Monday of August 1818 in Kaskaskia, with Judge Jesse B. Thomas as its chairman.

Even as the convention began its deliberations, the delegates expressed concern that the population of the territory fell far short of the requisite forty thousand. Pope had been able to deflect a proposal in Congress that the census be conducted by a federal commissioner, but an official count administered by the state remained necessary. Governor Edwards had arranged to have a census taken between April 1 and June 1 of that year, but the territorial legislature extended the terminal date to December 1 when it became apparent that the reported population would fall well below the required number. Territorial officials began the creative compiling of numbers. Census takers counted some settlers several times, included in their tallies migrants passing through Illinois on their way to Missouri, and submitted generous estimates for the populations of isolated outposts in remote areas of the territory. The final total also included some communities, such as Prairie du Chien, located inside the existing territory but clearly outside the proposed boundaries for the state. The census takers triumphantly reported a population of 40,258, a figure that fortunately went unchallenged. A federal report issued later concluded that the Illinois Territory had a population of only 34,620 in 1818.

The constitutional convention selected a committee of fifteen men, one representative from each of the territory's counties, to produce a rough draft of the governing document. The committee completed its work in one week, largely because of the indefatigable efforts of a young delegate from Randolph County, Elias Kent Kane. Having carefully scrutinized other states' constitutions and relying most heavily on the New York, Ohio, and Kentucky constitutions, Kane dominated the discussions in the committee, suggested the exact wording to be used, and revised drafts between meetings. The finished product, a compact document including a preamble and eight articles, quickly found approval within the whole convention. Because popular ratification of state constitutions did not become mandatory until 1820, the Illinois constitution then went directly to the U.S. Congress for approval.

The constitutional convention generally performed its work quickly and efficiently, but prolonged and spirited discussions ensued over the article concerning slavery. The Northwest Ordinance had outlawed slavery, but the French had introduced slaves to the region generations earlier, and neither the British nor the Virginians had challenged existing practices. The constitutional convention delegates offered a variety of arguments concerning the propriety and efficacy of the peculiar institution. Some supporters of human bondage contended that slaveholders enjoyed certain property rights and government lacked the authority to deprive a man of his chattel. Others noted the critical shortage of labor on the frontier and argued that slaves would be necessary for the newly admitted states to compete economically with the Eastern states. Opponents questioned the suitability of the Illinois prairie for slavery and posited that bondsmen might prove an economic detriment in the new state. Some saw slavery as a threat to free labor and wondered whether yeoman farmers could compete effectively against slave labor. Some rejected slavery because they did not want blacks living in Illinois. Others thought the institution of slavery morally wrong and embraced abolitionism. The issue prompted acrimonious debate throughout the duration of the convention.

The final version of the constitution contained a series of compromises that both failed to end slavery and stopped short of assuring its perpetuation. The document upheld existing property rights by maintaining the status of slaves and indentured servants at that time. Yet it also forbade the future introduction of slavery, except for a provision that slaves could be used at the salt springs near Shawneetown until 1825. Indentures would be honored but could not be extended; male children of indentured servants would be freed at the age of twenty-one and female children at the age of eighteen. Although the constitution failed to uphold the institution, many proslavery delegates voted for the pertinent articles—no doubt because they suspected Congress would reject any constitution explicitly countenancing slavery in a state north of the Ohio River.

While the convention readied the finished constitution for submission to the U.S. Congress, the territory held elections on September 17–19, 1818, in preparation for the establishment of a new state government. Shadrach Bond ran unopposed for governor, and Pierre Menard, the acknowledged leader of the territory's remaining French population, easily defeated two opponents for lieutenant governor. John McLean of Shawneetown narrowly defeated Kane to become Illinois's first U.S. congressman. When the newly elected general assembly convened on October 5, its members chose Ninian Edwards and Jesse B. Thomas as U.S. senators. Edwards and Thomas drew straws to determine which of them would serve the long term, and Thomas won. Congress had not yet approved statehood, so the state legislature declined to conduct additional business and adjourned.

On November 16, 1818, the U.S. House of Representatives commenced consideration of the Illinois constitution, and although a select committee submitted a favorable report considerable discourse followed. Congressmen from the New England states, New York, New Jersey, and Pennsylvania questioned whether the document contained adequate safeguards against slavery. Supporters provided the necessary assurances, and the House voted 117 to 34 for approval. After much less discussion, the Senate followed suit on December 1. President Monroe signed the resolution on December 3, making Illinois the twenty-first state. On December 16 Governor Edwards announced that the new state legislature would convene on the third Monday of January 1819.

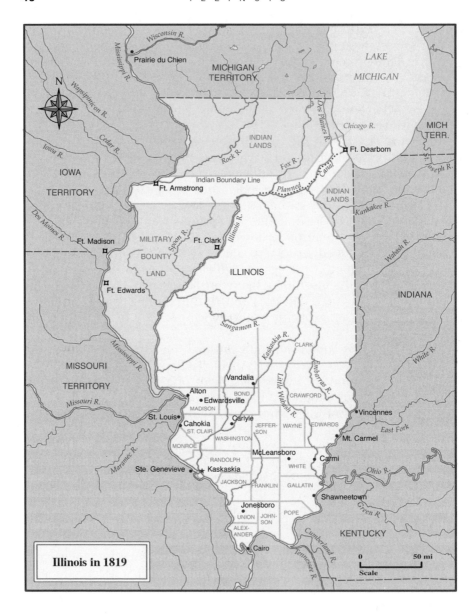

Illinois in 1819

Congress failed, however, to provide land for a seat of government as it had done for several other recently admitted states. Land speculators eager to make a profit by opening up the wilderness for settlement argued that the state capital should be located in a more central location than Kaskaskia, and politicians began urging the adoption of several sites northeast of the existing capital. The first general assembly petitioned Congress for a parcel of land on the Kaskaskia River to serve as the state capital for twenty years. Arguing that such a grant would boost the value of remote public land, Senators Thomas and Edwards prevailed upon their colleagues in Washington to award Illinois four sections in the unpopulated wilderness. Five state legislators chose a location eighty-two miles from the existing capital on the river's west bank, and surveyors began laying out the town of Vandalia even before laborers began clearing the first trees from the dense forest. With construction of the unimposing, two-story statehouse barely completed, the second general assembly convened in Vandalia on December 4, 1820. Not much else existed in the tiny community, and when the legislative session concluded in February 1821, Governor Edwards and a host of elected officials promptly evacuated the capital and headed for what they regarded as the comforts of civilization. A fire on the night of December 9, 1823, destroyed the state capitol, and the residents of Vandalia quickly erected a replacement that proved equally plain and incommodious.

The state's population growth in the early years was very slow, largely because of widely publicized economic setbacks. The Panic of 1819, a nationwide phenomenon, took a particularly heavy toll in Illinois, where inchoate financial institutions struggled to gain a sound footing. Throughout most of the state, a crude system of barter continued to exist because of the absence of currency. Many settlers used the little money they brought with them for the purchase of land, and land offices usually compounded the problem by immediately transferring this currency to Eastern banks. A number of private banks chartered earlier in the Illinois Territory failed to provide relief and went bankrupt in the early statehood years. The demand for relief from the large and growing number of debtors led the general assembly in 1821 to create the State Bank of Illinois, without any capital. Individuals could obtain loans up to one hundred dollars without any security or collateral at all, a policy so generous—and unsound—that borrowers quickly consumed all of the bank's funds. The general assembly in 1825 adjudged the bank notes worth only one-third their face value and initiated liquidation proceedings against the State Bank in 1830. As in other Western states, state-chartered banks struggled unsuccessfully to create credit and maintain the necessary amounts of currency without adequate capital.

In addition to being notorious for financial instability, Illinois suffered from widespread belief that its living conditions were unhealthy. In the frontier era, before widespread acceptance of the germ theory of disease, physicians as well as the uneducated masses believed that miasmas and noxious vapors arising from ponds, swamps, and sloughs caused disease. Such wet places, common in the flat and poorly drained state, existed most often near the waterways where the population initially preferred to settle. Scientists had not yet identified mosquitoes as the carriers of malaria, and the disease wreaked havoc among the population. Known

variously as "the fever," "the ague," and "the ager," malaria killed a relatively small percentage of those afflicted but proved debilitating for a time
and frequently recurred during people's lifetimes. Physicians prescribed
quinine with much success, but the drug's scarcity and expense limited its
effectiveness on the frontier. Weakened by their bouts with malaria, pa-
tients sometimes then succumbed to other ailments. Health did not generally improve until scientific breakthroughs in hygiene and medical knowledge took place later in the century.

Along with these other problems, the new state continued to grapple
with the unresolved issue of slavery. The territory's political leaders in Congress had dealt carefully with this inflammatory issue in order to secure approval for statehood, but events of subsequent years show the degree to
which sentiment in Illinois persisted in favor of slavery. In 1819 the state
listed only 168 slaves as permanent residents, but up to two thousand
bondsmen who were leased from owners in Kentucky and Tennessee
labored in the salt wells west of Shawneetown. Also in 1819, the general assembly passed legislation known as the Black Laws, which remained in effect even after the Civil War, a collection of measures limiting the freedom
of slaves and indentured servants. According to these laws, whites could not
bring slaves into the state for the purpose of manumission. Free blacks had
to provide certificates of freedom for filing at county seats. State statutes
prohibited indentured servants from testifying in court or bringing suit
against citizens. Whites found guilty of harboring runaway slaves, a felony,
faced a fine or thirty-five lashes. In short, the Black Laws differed very little
in severity from the slave codes adopted in the antebellum South.

The fate of slavery in neighboring Missouri, which applied for statehood in 1819 as a slave state, elicited strong sentiment in Illinois. Some
residents of Illinois voiced their concern that respectable Southerners seeking to relocate westward would bypass a free state and settle in the slave
state just across the Mississippi River. Others decried the shortage of cheap
labor in Illinois, which not only left farmers with more work before land
became arable but also handicapped their wives because of the dearth of
domestic help. Congressman John McLean's unpopular vote to deny Missouri admission as a slave state figured prominently in his reelection loss
to Daniel Pope Cook in 1820. Illinois's two senators supported slavery, and
Jesse Thomas introduced the bill providing for the Missouri Compromise,
which admitted Missouri as a slave state but prohibited slavery in the balance of the Louisiana Territory north of latitude 36 degrees 30 minutes.

Slavery emerged as the most important issue in the 1822 Illinois elections. The voters chose Edward Coles as governor, a patrician from Virginia
who had freed his slaves before arriving in Illinois and who ran on an antislavery platform. Coles won with just 33 percent of the vote and owed his
election to the fact that three other candidates, two of whom openly em-

braced slavery, divided the remaining ballots. Proslavery forces could take solace, however, in the election of a sympathetic lieutenant governor and solid proslavery majorities in both houses of the general assembly. Pleased with the Missouri Compromise and emboldened by the outcome of the 1822 elections, proslavery legislators in Illinois proposed an amendment to the state constitution in 1823 that would have formally legalized slavery. Under the provisions of the first state constitution, amendment could occur only at another constitutional convention that required the consent of three-fourths of the members of the general assembly as well as a majority of the state's voters. When the vote in the general assembly fell one vote short of the required three-fourths majority, the proslavery advocates (the "conventionists") engineered the removal of one legislator, replaced him with their own man, and subsequently received the necessary vote totals.

The conventionists proffered a complex economic, social, and political case for slavery. They acknowledged that settlers barely able to buy a quarter-section of land could ill afford to purchase a slave at the going rate of between three and six hundred dollars; but they argued, benefits would accrue from the increased immigration that would inevitably result from the legalization of slavery. At a time of economic torpor, they asserted, the influx of prosperous slaveholding Southerners would bring thousands of desperately needed dollars into the state. The conventionists tied slavery to the state's economic development again when they contended that the cultivation of the state's rich bottomlands awaited massive clearing efforts that could only be achieved by the gang labor afforded by slavery. Finally, they linked slaveholding to republicanism by identifying their goal as the creation of a republic of white yeoman farmers—an idealized vision that appealed to the upwardly mobile white immigrants from the Upland South who had recently arrived in the state. The conventionists portrayed the political battle as a class conflict between virtuous, hardworking, ambitious men and elites like the aristocratic governor who jealously guarded their own economic advantages. For the conventionists, more than anything else, slavery meant a means of advancement at a time of economic stagnation.

In his first inaugural address, Governor Coles called for the repeal of the Black Laws and the abolition of slavery altogether, and he led a coalition of like-minded politicians, clergymen, and abolitionists in an impassioned campaign against the proposal. The governor claimed the high moral ground inherent in abolitionism and contended that, contrary to the conventionists' claims, slavery would retard progress in Illinois by inhibiting immigration. A number of antislavery societies appeared throughout the state. The Baptist "Friends of Humanity" and circuit-riding Methodist ministers excoriated the sinfulness of human bondage, and Quaker immigrants from the East Coast distributed antislavery pamphlets. The famous British radical Morris Birkbeck, who had recently moved to Illinois and become a good friend of the governor, argued forcefully that the tolerance of slavery degraded the dignity of labor. In a series of letters written under the pseudonym of Jonathan Freeman, Birkbeck persuasively reassured the state's farmers that they could develop the land without the help of slave labor.

For eighteen months following the general assembly's adjournment in February 1823, the convention question monopolized Illinois politics. The state's four newspapers were divided on the issue: the *Illinois Intelligencer* and the *Edwardsville Spectator* supported the governor, and the *Kaskaskia Republican* and the *Illinois Gazette* of Shawneetown called for another constitutional convention. Partisans on both sides of the issue assailed each other, as Thomas Ford put it, "with much personal abuse . . . a perfect lava of detraction." Angry grogshop debates degenerated into fisticuffs, a conventionist mob in Vandalia burned Governor Coles in effigy, and contemporaries attributed several murders to passions inflamed by the slavery issue. On August 4, 1824, the public voted 6,640 to 4,972 not to call a second constitutional convention, and Illinois remained officially a free state.[5]

The tumultuous events of 1822–1824 in Illinois punctuated the shift from territorial status to statehood and demonstrated that slavery remained an extremely volatile issue. Hard economic times curtailed the pace of immigration and disappointed the new state's boosters who had envisioned immediate and substantial population gains. Most of the populous settlements still existed along the Mississippi, Ohio, Wabash, and Illinois rivers in the southern reaches of the state. The most notable additions to the Illinois population by the 1820s had come from the Upland South with comparatively few newcomers hailing from the Northern states. The next several decades, however, would bring considerable change.

Shawneetown

Hoping to curtail the movement of British settlers from the East into the Illinois Country, the French first toyed with the idea of erecting a fort on the Ohio River near the mouth of the Wabash River and then decided to persuade some of their Indian allies to settle there instead. At the urging of the French, the Shawnee Indians established a village in 1745 on the north bank of the Ohio River near the mouth of the Tennessee River, but they remained only a few years before dispersing. For decades the site remained uninhabited, but a community reappeared there in the early nineteenth century because of the saltworks twelve miles away, located on a ten-by-thirteen-mile reservation that was leased by the federal government in 1803 and transferred to Illinois in

1818. Slaves labored at the salt wells, drove the wagons to nearby Shawneetown, and loaded the salt onto keelboats bound for markets in Indiana, Tennessee, Kentucky, and Missouri.

The U.S. government platted a village near the saltworks and made lots available at auction in 1814. In the years before the Civil War, residents of Shawneetown took pride in the fact that only their community and Washington, D.C., had been planned by the national government rather than by private interests. In 1818 a visitor described Shawneetown as little more than a few log cabins, yet he also marveled at the constant bustle of activity in the community, which served as the principal gateway to Illinois and Missouri from the Ohio River. A steady stream of horses, wagons, and passengers disembarked from flatboats and keelboats, while prospective settlers purchased provisions at dry goods stores, precious gems at a jewelry store, and alcoholic beverages at local taverns before resuming their journeys. Westbound travelers left Shawneetown on the Goshen Road for Carlyle, Edwardsville, Alton, and Kaskaskia; the Goshen Road connected to a trail linking Vincennes, Indiana, with St. Louis. Many new arrivals purchased land in eastern Illinois at one of the state's two land offices (in 1820 about 35 percent of the state's land sales occurred in Shawneetown) and transacted their financial business at one of the state's two banks. In 1818 a printer arrived on a flatboat from Pittsburgh with a printing press and began publishing the territory's second newspaper, the *Emigrant*. Most of the space in its weekly issues was devoted to the printing of national laws and political affairs, but the *Emigrant* also contained advertisements for goods and services offered by local businessmen. The concentration of mercantile establishments and government offices made Shawneetown the state's foremost metropolis in the early nineteenth century.

Despite its early prominence, however, Shawneetown failed to keep pace with the growth experienced by other communities in Illinois. Annual spring floods often left much of the village submerged, and heavy rains at other times made the streets impassable. Local residents never responded to the perennial flooding problem until 1937, when they moved many buildings to adjacent hills and abandoned Old Shawneetown for higher ground. Plans to construct a railroad linking Shawneetown with the western part of the state never came to fruition. The saltworks continued to operate profitably for several decades but then struggled to compete with a better brine produced near Charleston, West Virginia. In 1847 the state sold the reservation to a private concern, which closed the salines for good in 1873. The opening of the Erie Canal, the increasing importance of the Great Lakes as a route into the Upper Midwest, and population growth in northern Illinois diminished Shawneetown's importance as an entrepot.

Ninian Edwards

Ninian Edwards became the most prominent political figure in the first generation of Illinois history, spanning the territorial and the early statehood years. A wealthy aristocrat who lacked the common touch, he won the respect and admiration of Illinois voters though not perhaps their affection. Although he lived the life of a grandee, he generally espoused positions that found favor with the unlettered masses. In the days before truly national political parties formed in the state, politicians divided into two factions—those who supported Edwards and those who opposed him.

Born in Montgomery County, Maryland, on March 17, 1775, he grew up in a prominent local family. His father, Benjamin Edwards, had been a member of the Maryland convention that ratified the U.S. Constitution. Educated at Dickinson College in Pennsylvania, Ninian moved to Kentucky at the age of nineteen and began managing a farm for his father. Despite a prodigious appetite for drinking and gambling, he became a successful attorney and added to his already considerable fortune. After serving two terms in the Kentucky legislature, he became presiding judge of the general court, circuit judge, and chief justice of the court of appeals. He persuaded Henry Clay to nominate him for the governorship of Illinois Territory, a post he assumed at the age of thirty-four.

In the hardscrabble conditions of frontier Illinois, Edwards ostentatiously displayed his considerable wealth. Accepting a thousand acres of land as a perquisite of office, he established a sprawling farm near Kaskaskia. He purchased thousands of additional acres of land from the federal government, maintained a stable of thoroughbred horses, and owned several stores and mills in the Illinois and Missouri territories. Riding everywhere in a carriage driven by one of his slaves, he dressed flamboyantly in expensive broadcloth coats and ruffled shirts. Widely ridiculed by his enemies as pompous and verbose, Edwards nevertheless impressed many observers as a distinguished and refined gentleman whose wealth and accomplishments seemed all the more impressive in the humble surroundings of the new territory. When Illinois became a state in 1818, the first general assembly overwhelmingly chose him as the U.S. senator for the short term; the following year, he was reelected for a full term. In the Senate, he argued in favor of cheap land for settlers in the Western states and supported the admission of Missouri as a slave state. In 1824 he left the Senate to become minister to Mexico but quickly resigned that office after a highly publicized run-in with secretary of the treasury William H. Crawford. Quite recklessly, he charged Crawford with complicity in the failure of the State Bank of Edwardsville but could not prove his case and left the capital in disgrace.

Ninian Edwards, the most influential politician in the state's early days. *Chicago Historical Society*

Edwards attempted to resurrect his political career in 1826 when he sought election as Illinois's third governor. During and after the election, which he won by a narrow margin, he bitterly attacked a number of prominent men in the state whom he charged with being involved in the Bank of Edwardsville affair. Although he clashed frequently with a general assembly dominated by his political enemies, Edwards won popular approbation with his repeated calls for the removal of the remaining Indian tribes from the state and for government's adoption of a more generous land policy. In 1830 he decided not to seek reelection and two years later lost an election for a seat in the U.S. Congress. On July 20, 1833, he died of cholera, which he contracted while ministering to his stricken St. Clair County neighbors.

CHAPTER FOUR

Settling the Frontier

In 1830 Illinois remained a sparsely populated state with most of its inhabitants living south of the state capital, Vandalia. The U.S. census reported Illinois's population as being 157,445, showing an increase of 117,187 during the twelve years since its admission as a state (an average increase of less than ten thousand per year). Some of the immigrants had come from Pennsylvania, New York, and the New England states, but most had come from the Upland South. According to the testimony of Easterners who visited the state, Southern accents predominated in most settlements. A French influence lingered, especially in the American Bottom, and more slaves resided in Illinois than in any of the other states or territories of the Old Northwest. The nascent settlement that would become Chicago amounted to nothing more than a jumble of cabins and trading posts. Settlers began to appear in the Military Tract and the Sangamon Valley, while scattered farmsteads and an occasional village dotted the countryside north of Peoria. Few settlers ventured into northern Illinois, the last area of the state in which significant numbers of Indians roamed and still constituted a real threat against the advancing white population. Yet for all the state's apparent quietude, a rising spirit of expansionism was already sending ambitious adventurers in search of land and opportunity.

The opening of the Illinois frontier coincided with the Age of Jackson, the era of American history defined by the political rise and administration of Andrew Jackson. Denied the presidency in what he and his supporters called a corrupt bargain in 1824, the nation's greatest War of 1812 hero won the White House in 1828 and 1832 and cemented the Democratic party's national dominance. The Whig party originated in the 1830s in opposition to what dissenters referred to as King Andrew I's tyrannical policies. For nearly a generation, no politician in Illinois could be elected unless he identified himself as a staunch Jackson man, a condition resulting from the extraordinary popularity of the ideals for which the president purportedly stood. "Jacksonian Democracy" meant greater political participation, an expansion of the franchise for adult white males, and decentralization of power on behalf of the states. Both before and during his entry into electoral politics, Jackson stood for enhancing economic opportunities for the common man in the West through the passage of more liberal land laws. A heralded Indian fighter, he readily accepted the necessity of uprooting the remaining Native Americans from the land coveted by his political constituency.

The first clash in the decisive campaign to remove the remaining Indian tribes from Illinois came with the Winnebago War of 1827. Defending the honor of some of their women, Winnebago warriors killed two white men near Fort Crawford in southern Wisconsin Territory. When Illinois Governor Ninian Edwards sent a regiment to investigate and militias assembled from Chicago to Danville, Chief Red Bird prudently extradited the six men responsible for the murders. To the sound of sabers rattling in white settlements, the Winnebagos and other tribes signed three treaties in 1828–1829 that surrendered 4.5 million acres of land in northern Illinois in return for a tract in eastern Iowa, annual cash payments, tobacco, and other gratuities. A number of settlers abandoned their homes, and white regiments marched menacingly around the region, but prompt submission by the Winnebagos averted considerable bloodshed. Chief Red Bird died in prison, one of the few casualties of the minor skirmish that served as a prelude to the more serious Black Hawk War of 1832.

Chief Black Hawk and his Sauk, Fox, and Kickapoo followers farmed in the Rock River valley and refused to abide by an 1804 treaty signed by Sauk and Fox chiefs that surrendered the land to whites in return for an annuity. Questioning the validity of the treaty, Black Hawk and his band stubbornly remained in the valley until marauding whites burned the Indians' lodges and destroyed their cornfields. Still decrying the treaty, the Indians reluctantly fled across the Mississippi River into Iowa but found conditions no more hospitable there. Attacked by Sioux Indians and beset by crop failures, malnutrition, and the threat of starvation, Black Hawk and his men returned to Illinois in 1831, ordered white squatters to leave, and burned cabins in the Rock River valley. Confronted by an army of twenty-five hundred sent by Governor John Reynolds, Black Hawk and his three hundred braves withdrew again to Iowa after signing a treaty promising not to return.

Following the severe winter of 1831–1832, during which disease and inadequate food supplies further decimated the tribe, Black Hawk led the Indians once more back into Illinois. The band of 500 men and 1,000 women and children headed north for Prophetstown, where, according to what is written in Black Hawk's autobiography, they hoped to raise corn with the few Winnebagos remaining in the area and live in peace. Authorities in Illinois, however, viewed the Indians' return as a hostile act in clear violation of the recent treaty. Governor Reynolds assembled an army of 1,000 regulars and 1,935 militiamen (including a young Abraham Lincoln) at Fort Armstrong and headed up the Rock River intent upon removing the Indians from the state. Initially, the outnumbered Indians won a number of minor victories. A war party of 40 braves led by Black Hawk routed a volunteer company of 275 in Ogle County and killed 12 men. A separate group of Potawatomi killed 16 men, women, and children at the so-called Indian Creek massacre in La Salle County. Black Hawk's modest forces never posed a serious threat in northern Illinois, but their enemies sought to avenge the Fort Dearborn massacre and other successful raids on white settlements. The size of the Illinois army grew exponentially as news of the Indian successes spread through a panicked white population. Soon the few hundred tired, hungry warriors, women, and children with Black Hawk found themselves heavily outnumbered. The Indians fled into southern Wisconsin to escape an army of federal and state soldiers numbering more than 4,000.

Their numbers depleted, unable to recruit other Indians as allies, and resigned to defeat, Black Hawk and his followers hoped to elude their pursuers and escape across the Mississippi River into Iowa. They failed. The men fought a successful rearguard action against the whites while some of the women and children crossed the Wisconsin River, but the end came several days later on August 2, 1832, at the Battle of Bad Axe on the Mississippi River. Driven into the river by the soldiers advancing behind them and shelled by an armed steamboat in front of them, the Indians fell victim to a lethal crossfire. Sioux Indians waiting on the west bank attacked those who thought they had swum to safety. More than 300 Indians, including women, children, and the elderly, perished in the water, and approximately 120 surrendered; Black Hawk escaped but was soon captured. In September 1833, the remaining Indians in Illinois, whether they had fought in the Black Hawk War or not, ceded their land and left the state; even the members of the Kaskaskia tribe, who had joined the American forces, forfeited their land. Removal of the tribes proved so thorough that, unlike other neighboring states, Illinois contained no Indian reservations thereafter.

The disposition of the Indian problem removed an impediment to settlement of the Illinois prairie, and the numbers of immigrants increased dramatically in the 1830s. Between 1830 and 1835, despite the Black Hawk War, the population of the state increased by 114,982 to 272,427, and between 1835 and 1840, despite the nationwide economic collapse known as the Panic of 1837, by another 203,756 to 476,183. In fact, some historians have argued, the Panic of 1837 may have compelled the destitute to head westward in search of cheap land. Some migrants to Illinois decided to move there because of positive portrayals of the state in newspaper advertisements or because of encouraging letters from relatives and friends.

Many newcomers chose to come to the state because they had read highly flattering accounts in a series of gazetteers published in the 1830s and 1840s. John Mason Peck, a Baptist minister from Connecticut who moved to St. Louis in 1817 and then to St. Clair County in Illinois in 1822, became the author of the most widely read and influential books in the genre. In *A Gazetteer of Illinois* (1837), a classic example of the booster literature, Peck's vivid imagery depicted his new home state in idyllic terms. He described the Illinois landscape as "beautiful groves of timber, and rich, undulating, and dry prairies; richest quality; an undulating surface, a rich, deep, black, sandy, calcareous soil; a beautiful situated village; the most extensive and fertile-tract; a soil of exhaustless fertility." Such promotional literature, written with more than a touch of hyperbole, helped burnish the image of Illinois at the same time that other factors combined to increase the likelihood of westward migration.[1]

The heightened pace of immigration derived mostly from improved transportation in the older states to the east. The National Road, a wide thoroughfare with a macadamized surface, originated in Cumberland, Maryland, and wound through Wheeling, Virginia, Columbus, Ohio, and Indianapolis, Indiana, to reach Vandalia in 1839. Thousands of migrants' wagons traversed the lavish roadway as an alternative to the steamboats that had by the 1830s become commonplace on the Ohio River and its tributaries. Some pedestrians arrived from Detroit around the southern tip of Lake Michigan via the Chicago Road, which the federal government had constructed after the War of 1812 for defense purposes. Steam vessels had appeared on the Great Lakes as early as 1818, and migrants could soon travel by water from Buffalo, New York, to Detroit, Michigan, and then by regular stagecoach service to Chicago.

The opening of the Erie Canal in 1825 linked Chicago to the eastern seaboard and provided migrants and merchants a remarkably quicker and more comfortable means of reaching Illinois than by land. Forty feet wide and four feet deep, the canal stretched 363 miles from the Hudson River at Albany to the Lake Erie port of Buffalo. Its impact on commerce proved immediate and profound, for Midwestern farmers who might previously have sent their crops to Canada via the Great Lakes and the St. Lawrence River began to ship them instead to New York City. At the same time, the canal provided Illinois farmers with a better alternative than floating their crops down the Mississippi River to New Orleans. Within a generation, the value of canal freight easily exceeded the value of riverine commerce, and residents of Illinois began to look north to the Great Lakes for connections to the Northeast rather than southward toward the Crescent City. Most important for the growth of the state, the Great Lakes opened wide an inviting door to migrants from the Northeast who sought easy access to the Midwest. By 1841 improved steamship technology had cut the Buffalo–Chicago trip down to nine days, and with the coming of the railroad later in the decade, the New York City to Chicago trip could be completed in five days. The fare for the Buffalo–Chicago trip on the Great Lakes cost twenty dollars in 1840 and fell in 1850 to ten dollars (only five dollars for steerage).

By the 1830s and 1840s, thousands of residents of the New England and Mid-Atlantic states were finding compelling reasons to relocate elsewhere. Overcrowding, the prohibitively high cost of land, and the depletion of soils from generations of use left many Northeastern farmers hard pressed to sustain themselves. Relocation in the cities brought them little relief because of the high population densities, unemployment caused by the introduction of new technology, and depressed wages that resulted from the competition for jobs with European immigrants who were willing to work for very little compensation. Some emigrants headed north looking for unclaimed land in New Hampshire and Maine, but a much greater number looked westward for economic opportunity.

Land sales in Illinois boomed. In the years following statehood, the three federal land offices (at Kaskaskia, Edwardsville, and Shawneetown) had sold merely a few thousand acres of public domain land. By 1836, however, the state had been constrained to add an additional seven land offices (at Chicago, Galena, Quincy, Springfield, Danville, Vandalia, and Palestine), and altogether the ten offices had sold more than three million acres. In particular, sales boomed in the northwestern corner of the state, the Military Tract, and the Sangamon Valley. For the first time, settlers acquired tracts of land lying far from navigable rivers. Land sales proved brisk in northern Illinois, and then in the mid-state prairies where conventional wisdom suggested that the sparsity of trees indicated poor soils. Here settlers discovered that, after their teams of oxen broke the tough prairie sod, the rich black soil of central Illinois produced bountiful yields.

The land-buying craze of the 1830s and 1840s in Illinois, replicated in other Midwestern states, led to rampant speculation. Some settlers bought land at government land offices for the price of $1.25 an acre that had been established earlier, but speculators probably purchased more than half of the real estate before reselling it to farmers. Many speculators operated on a decidedly modest scale in areas near their own homes. Small farmers acquired more land than they could cultivate themselves, for example, while merchants, bankers, lawyers, and politicians merely invested on the side in local real estate. Boom and bust conditions alternated, and just as surely as some speculators netted considerable fortunes, economic downturns such as the Panic of 1837 sent land prices plummeting and drove many investors into bankruptcy. High-stakes speculation left small farmers embittered. Local landowners accepted speculative buying by their neighbors but looked askance at the financial manipulations of remote capitalists on the East Coast who purchased thousands of acres in expectation of a rise in market value and a quick resale. The machinations of wealthy New York capitalists proved especially distasteful to the Illinois sodbusters. To many of the state's longtime residents, the speculative mania seemed simply another by-product of the massive ongoing demographic shift in Illinois—the arrival of so many newcomers from the Northeast.

The Yankee invasion of the 1830s and 1840s triggered a series of cultural conflicts. The predominant population in the southern part of the state warily assessed the new arrivals, who were generally better educated and more affluent. The Yankees valued hard work, thrift, and order; they believed in progress and proved aggressive businessmen. Sober and industrious, they worked hard and advocated higher taxes to improve the commonweal. Puritan ideals survived in Congregationalism and Unitarianism, and many New Englanders transplanted to the Midwest brought with them a strong sense of mission and an unyielding commitment to community. They viewed the denizens of southern Illinois as lazy and decadent, attributing the primitive conditions throughout much of the state to the indolence of the earlier inhabitants. Imbued with a sense of altruism and eager to perfect themselves and others, many of these Northerners eagerly embraced a variety of reform causes ranging from abolitionism to temperance.

Accustomed to living at a slower pace, seemingly less determined to succeed economically, and indifferent—if not openly hostile—to formal education, most Southerners possessed values typical of their Scots-Irish or Anglo-Celtic roots. They viewed the Yankees as greedy, grasping peddlers who could not be trusted. Being "Yankeed," Southerners said, meant to be swindled by a fast-talking salesman from the Northeast. Often distrustful of institutions, Southerners felt overwhelmed by the number and influence of the schools, churches, and voluntary associations established in Illinois by transplanted Northerners. Perhaps worst of all, the moralistic Yankees perpetrated a kind of cultural imperialism whereby they sought to remake other people in their own image—an image that Southerners suspected was more imaginary than real. High-minded Yankee rhetoric masked base motives, Southerners believed, as moral crusades often conveniently allowed reformers to advance their own economic interests.[2]

The stark difference between the Southerners and the Yankees showed clearly in their respective attitudes toward education. Whereas Yankees avidly supported education and built numerous schools and colleges in the northern part of the state, the Southerners showed altogether less enthusiasm for book learning. As a result, despite the allocation of one township in every thirty-six for education, private schools predominated in the first half of the nineteenth century. In 1855 Yankees finally forged a working majority in the general assembly and passed laws mandating the establishment of public schools statewide; even so, compliance in southern counties came only with the promise of double the state revenue allotted to the northern counties. Springfield established a public school system in 1856, and communities throughout the state followed suit. In the same decade, the absence of qualified instructors led to the founding of the Illinois State Normal School near Bloomington, followed by other teachers' colleges in Peoria, Carbondale, and Chicago. Although disparities in local funding persisted, the commitment to public education solidified in the second half of the nineteenth century.

Along with the influx of Yankees came significant numbers of immigrants from foreign countries. Some individuals came alone to Illinois from the European nations, but more commonly, foreigners came in groups, to establish whole communities and new lives in completely different environments. Some Europeans fled their home countries to escape oppressive regimes, the threat of conscription, or the kind of political turmoil that ended in revolution in France, Germany, and Italy in 1848. Others emigrated to escape religious intolerance and sought refuge in America where they yearned to worship freely. Crop failures throughout western Europe in the 1840s, most notably the Irish potato famine that drove as much as one-fifth of the population overseas, propelled many destitute farmers toward North America and the promise of cheap land. Many Europeans reacted to rising populations and stagnant economies in their homelands by setting off to seek their fortunes in the American Midwest. In the early years of migration, these foreigners congregated in the more settled areas of southern Illinois such as in St. Clair, Madison, and Edwards counties, but increasingly they established residences in the north alongside the Yankees.

The Germans, the largest group of immigrants in Illinois in the decades before the Civil War, numbered 38,000 by 1850 and 131,000 ten years later. A diverse group of farmers, laborers, merchants, and intellectuals, they settled at first in huge numbers in St. Clair County. Hardworking and frugal, according to popular belief, German farmers built sturdy, spacious barns before they even constructed their own houses. Those without the resources to acquire real estate immediately worked instead as agricultural laborers or found employment in towns and saved their money for the opportunity to purchase their own land. As immigration swelled after the European political upheavals of 1848, substantial German communities developed in Illinois towns such as Quincy, Alton, Peoria, Springfield, Galena, and Peru. In 1854 in Peru, for example, the Germans numbered 1,000 out of a total population of 3,500. After the Civil War, substantial communities of East Frisians (immigrants from the northwestern corner of Germany) migrated from the Peoria-Pekin area into eastern Illinois and played a key role in the draining and cultivating of the flat, swampy terrain there.

The second-largest group of immigrants, the Irish, numbered 27,800 in 1850 and 87,600 in 1860. Devastated by a series of famines in the 1840s in Ireland, which took more than one million lives, the Irish came to America with virtually nothing. In many instances, landlords and local officials in Ireland underwrote the emigration of the rural poor out of a sense of desperation. Lacking the funds to buy land and chary of engaging in farming because of their recent experiences, the Irish labored in the mines of northwestern Illinois, found work in the cities, and toiled on such large-scale construction projects as the Illinois and Michigan Canal and the Illinois Central Railroad. Their reputed aversion to agriculture notwithstanding, many Irish canal workers took the scrip they had been paid and cashed it in for land along the canal site and north of Peoria. Despite the concentration of the Irish in Chicago and other large cities, recent historical studies show that about one-third of immigrants from Ireland were engaged in agriculture by 1850.

Although not as numerous as the Germans or the Irish, other European immigrants came in significant numbers and made an imprint on the developing state. In the late 1840s and early 1850s, several hundred Dutch families arrived in Illinois and settled in Chicago; some bought land south of the city and established farms and communities such as South Holland and Roseland. A visiting Englishman marveled at the prairie state's heterogeneity in 1842, observing in Randolph County a diverse mixture of people that included "Dutch, Germans, Swiss, Yankees, Irish, Scotch, a few English, and a number from the more southern states." By 1850 the number of first-generation immigrants in Illinois totaled 111,860, just over 13 percent of the state's population.[3]

Newcomers to Illinois, European immigrants as well as Yankees, expressed their amazement at the seemingly endless prairies that still covered much of the state. The prairie grasses of central Illinois appeared to a British journalist to be "outstretched and undulating . . . a vast ocean of meadowland." A Boston newspaper reporter similarly relied upon nautical metaphors to describe the landscape: "For miles and miles we saw nothing but a vast expanse of what I can compare to nothing else but the ocean itself. . . . We saw at intervals, groves of trees, which looked like islands in the ocean." The immigrants labored valiantly to remove the grasses and cultivate the soil. Plows that served admirably in the East proved inadequate to the task of breaking the sod and removing the sturdy grasses in Illinois, however. At the rate of an acre a day, with one farmer guiding the oxen and a second farmer struggling to keep the plough in the furrow, landowners made halting progress in clearing the land. Draft animals sometimes died in harness from the terrible strain. Farmers considered the breaking of thirty to forty acres of sod the first year a great triumph.[4]

The plight of the farmers improved dramatically—and agriculture in Illinois boomed—because of advances in technology. The first breakthrough resulted from the work of John Deere, a blacksmith from Vermont who moved to Illinois in 1837 and developed a plow specifically designed for the challenging conditions confronting prairie sodbusters. Deere replaced the iron plowshare with a stronger, self-cleaning steel plowshare that reduced resistance and made it possible for farmers to complete their work in much less time and with considerably less effort.

As a consequence, they cultivated more land and produced higher yields. In the 1840s, Deere moved his factory from Grand Detour to Moline, because of the readier access to steel, and in subsequent decades manufactured other types of machinery and farm implements.

Farmers likewise benefited from the contributions of Cyrus Hall McCormick's mechanical grain reaper. In 1840 farmers could harvest about three acres of wheat a day with a scythe and cradle, but this increased to fifteen acres a day after the introduction of the mechanical reaper. The farmers prospered not only because of the diminished labor costs but also because speedier harvesting reduced the rotting of the additional crops made possible by the use of John Deere's plow. Foreseeing the phenomenal increase in wheat production in Illinois, in 1847 McCormick moved his business from Virginia to Chicago and initiated a series of innovations that enabled him to outdistance rival manufacturers. Within three years, his new factory produced more than one thousand reapers. An industrial and marketing genius, he used labor-saving machinery to accelerate the mass production of his product and courted the consumers

The original McCormick's reaper revolutionized agriculture in Illinois and other Midwestern states. To be nearer his principal markets, Cyrus McCormick built a massive factory in Chicago. *Illinois State Historical Library*

with creative advertising campaigns and deferred payment plans. Deere and McCormick stood at the forefront of an agricultural revolution, highlighted by the production of horse-drawn cultivators, threshers, reapers, and the like, all of which increased production and efficiency.

Agricultural productivity increased also when farmers drained the marshy lands of east central Illinois. Because of the considerable capital outlays required, at first only wealthy landowners launched drainage projects. Laying drainage tile proved the most effective measure but remained prohibitively expensive until local companies in Joliet and dozens of other localities throughout the state began manufacturing the tile. The "drying out" of central Illinois farms began in the antebellum years and accelerated in 1879 and 1880 when the state legislature passed laws creating local drainage districts with the authority to levy assessments. In the twenty-year period that followed, these districts laid more than forty-nine thousand miles of tile—an amount sufficient to encircle the globe twice.

Improvements in transportation benefited farmers by shortening the amount of time needed to convey crops to market. With only a few exceptions, the state's roads consisted simply of packed earth, which often became impassable after heavy rainfalls. The ease of road travel fluctuated seasonally, being relatively dependable during the frozen winter and dry summer months but unpredictable and sometimes hazardous during the wet seasons of spring and autumn. The first macadamized road appeared in the 1830s between St. Louis and Belleville, and others soon followed in the densely populated southwestern part of the state. In 1848 the first plank road opened for business over a ten-mile stretch between Chicago and neighboring Riverside. The planks, eight feet long and three inches thick, rested on graded roadways. The collection of tolls allowed the privately owned roads to earn dividends ranging from 30 to 40 percent, and soon other plank roads from Chicago reached Naperville, Sycamore, Elgin, and Oswego. Steamboat landings on the Illinois River built plank roads to improve their customer access, and by 1851 entrepreneurs had invested a million dollars in six hundred miles of highways. Expensive to construct and difficult to maintain, the plank roads proved only a temporary solution; they disappeared later in the nineteenth century as the state assumed primary responsibility for road provision.

Better water transportation also proved important. At a time when the Appalachian Mountains still constituted a formidable barrier to east–west commerce on land, Illinois farmers typically dispatched their crops on flatboats on the tributaries that flowed into the Mississippi River and then southward to market in New Orleans. Unable to paddle northward against the Mississippi's powerful current, the farmers dismantled their flatboats, sold the lumber, and made their way home on foot or on horseback. An estimated one-fifth to one-fourth of the flatboats bound for New Orleans ran aground and never reached the city, so farmers rejoiced when sturdier steamboats turned the Mississippi into a reliable two-way thoroughfare. Technological refinements such as deck-mounted engines and shallow drafts made many Illinois backwaters navigable for the first time. An estimated two hundred steamboats were traveling on the state's rivers by 1835, and the number more than doubled within a decade. In later years, the railroads allowed farmers to speed their crops to markets even faster.

The state's farmers grew a variety of crops, but two in particular—wheat and corn—attained special importance. Thanks in large measure to the impact of McCormick's reaper (farmers in the eleven counties producing the most wheat also purchased 25 percent of the reapers sold between 1849 and 1857), Illinois had become the leading producer of wheat by 1859. In later decades, the center of the nation's wheat production shifted westward to the Great Plains states, but the grain remained an important cash crop for Illinois farmers. Corn proved especially well suited to the state's soil and climate, and farmers produced phenomenal yields that likewise by 1859 had made Illinois the leading producer (which it remained, unlike for wheat, for generations). Corn found a ready market for human consumption as well as animal feed for the growing livestock industry.

A small number of ranchers accumulated large tracts of land and dominated the state's livestock industry. By 1850 more than one hundred "cattle kings" raised cattle on sprawling estates and also bought livestock from small farmers before driving massive herds to Chicago and occasionally to Eastern markets. The largest ranches, averaging 18,000 acres apiece, sprawled over 2,000,000 acres in central Illinois and along the Kankakee River. The bonanza farmers included men like Michael L. Sullivant, reputedly the world's most successful farmer, whose 80,000 acres occupied parts of Champaign, Ford, Piatt, and Livingston counties; William Scully, who owned 47,000 acres in Logan County; John T. Alexander, who owned a 26,500-acre barony in Champaign County; and Isaac Funk, owner of 26,000 acres in McLean County. Operating at first mostly with hired hands who raised corn and fattened the animals before roundup time, the cattle kings soon opted for tenancy by dividing their land into smaller units and entering into sharecropping arrangements with renters. By the time of the Civil War, Illinois ranchers shipped more beef cattle to New York City than did the farmers from all other states combined.

The impact of the cattle barons can be seen in the story of Isaac Funk. A German immigrant who had been a poor day laborer before coming to Illinois in 1824, Funk saved his earnings for years and then purchased a farm, Funk's Grove, near Bloomington. He bought cattle from ranchers from Missouri to Texas, drove the herds back to his farm in Illinois for fattening, and eventually transported cattle and hogs to market in Chicago. Like other bonanza farmers, he originally grew his own feed corn but later subdivided his land into smaller farms and signed contracts with tenant farmers to work the land. Unlike many of his contemporaries who expressed little interest in innovative practices, Funk became an early advocate of new scientific farming methods. He experimented with different breeds of cattle and feeding practices. Having amassed huge landholdings and a considerable fortune, he devoted his later years to a crusade for more scientific farming and to other varieties of public service.

The drive for better farming methods also came from a series of newspapers published by John S. Wright, a Chicago booster businessman who foresaw the city's growth being linked with improved agriculture in Illinois and the Midwest. In 1841 Wright commenced publication of the *Union Agriculturalist and Western Prairie Farmer,* which quickly became known simply as the *Prairie Farmer.* The newspaper published a steady stream of articles by experts on crop rotation, fertilizers, conservation, irrigation, plant diseases, animal husbandry, and pest control. To increase credibility with the newspaper's readership, Wright solicited articles from farmers themselves and included on the paper's masthead the invitation "Farmers, write for your paper." Subscriptions increased significantly, and Wright became widely known and respected as a loyal friend to the farmer. At a time when many rural people derisively dismissed the need for schools, Wright effectively lent his prestige to the movement for public education by publishing countless editorials detailing how more scientific knowledge had improved farmers' lives. Underscoring his commitment to education, he used his own money to build the first public school building in Chicago.

As agriculture boomed and speculation in farmland increased in the antebellum years, urban development proceeded apace as well. The arrival of thousands of newcomers to the northern and central areas of the state resulted in the establishment of new communities, especially in the 1830s and 1840s. Town founders and boosters advertised widely, both within the state and farther east, for new residents and businesses, and their publicity campaigns typically repeated certain basic themes. Newspaper and magazine advertisements emphasized the nascent community's proximity to the necessary timber for construction, access to transportation, sources of water, rich soil in the surrounding farmland, and so forth. They stressed how important it was that the community had an adequate hinterland, noting that increased distance from rival towns enhanced the likelihood of prosperity. New towns platted within two or three miles of their competitors seldom thrived; the distance between towns that survived in central Illinois counties by the early 1850s averaged between six and nine miles.

The configuration of prairie towns differed, of course, but their layouts conformed to some general patterns. Just as the Land Ordinance of 1785 had established a blueprint for the sale of farmland in rectangular tracts, businessmen usually platted frontier communities in lots arranged along streets intersecting at right angles to form rectangular blocks. Mercantile establishments and family residences often existed cheek by jowl, but homeowners quickly sorted themselves out according to social class. The more prosperous residents moved to higher ground to avoid flooding and other disadvantages associated with lower elevations. From their hillside perches, the well-to-do enjoyed pleasing views and breezes. In the absence of varying elevations, the more affluent situated themselves upwind of the towns' business and industrial sections. Such locations minimized the danger from fires, a serious concern in an age when wooden structures predominated in frontier communities, and also the stench from the large numbers of animals inhabiting the towns as well as from the butchering, tanning, and other noisome activities common to downtowns.

Reflecting their immediate surroundings and the circumstances of their founding, Illinois towns varied in their growth and development. Some communities prospered, grew rapidly into cities, and produced handsome returns for those who had invested in their futures. Others remained small isolated places that never surpassed a certain threshold of size and economic vitality. Others foundered and disappeared completely from the map. Favorable geography and the zeal of enterprising boosters might have accounted for the success of some communities, but in other instances it seems nothing more than chance determined the outcome of urban speculation. The discovery of lead deposits sent hundreds of people flocking to Galena, which in the early nineteenth century became the state's first boomtown; but the community's ascendance was essentially complete by the time of the Civil War. By contrast, Chicago offered little hint of greatness in the early nineteenth century and existed for years in the shadow of Galena, only to become the metropolitan center of the Midwest after the Civil War. The destinies of fledgling Illinois towns remained unclear in these formative years.

Most new towns originated for the sole purpose of economic development and grew according to the successes and failures of countless entrepreneurs. Population increased as individuals and families established residence. In some instances, by contrast, communities followed a more clearly defined path laid out by groups of settlers who arrived with collective aims. In the case of Galesburg, for example, fifty families belonging to the same Presbyterian church in a New York village pooled their resources and jointly purchased twenty square miles of land in the northwestern portion of the state for the establishment of a new community. George Washington Gale, the church's minister, drafted a design for settlement in 1835, and families moved there the following year. Town fathers carefully planned the layout, setting aside one square mile as the community center, and Gale founded Knox College in 1836 to encourage the flowering of culture. Galesburg became an isolated and homogeneous place during its first decade, but the coming of the railroad brought a wider variety of people. Soon the original settlers disappeared into a larger, more heterogeneous population.

In the new town of Bishop Hill, Swedish immigrants sought to create a utopian community in distant Illinois. Objecting to the impurities he saw

in the Lutheran Church in his native Sweden, Erik Jansson called for reform and a strict reliance upon the teachings of the Bible. Finding himself
and his adherents persecuted by government and church officials, Jansson
planned to establish a community in Illinois in which all residents owned
property communally and agreed to care for each other. In 1846 he and
four hundred followers settled in Henry County; they immediately encountered extreme privations as a severe winter commenced. Living in
crude log houses and makeshift shelters in cramped conditions without
heat, the settlers fell victim to a food shortage, and an estimated ninety-six
colonists died of starvation. Better times followed in subsequent years, and
the community prospered as the distribution center for a thriving agricultural hinterland. Communal ownership failed, however, and the original
body of settlers dissolved their formal ties. Much of Bishop Hill's Swedish
heritage remained intact, but the utopian vision that animated the original settlers dissipated.

The most famous instance of communitarianism in Illinois occurred as
a result of the Mormon immigration. In 1830 the founder of the Mormon
Church, Joseph Smith, and his followers left New York and settled in Kirt-
land, Ohio, and subsequently in eastern Missouri. In 1838 twenty Mormons died in the Haun's Hill massacre, and Smith and his lieutenant,
Brigham Young, led fifteen thousand Latter Day Saints across the Mississippi River to the safety of Quincy, Illinois. The following year Smith purchased land on the site of an abandoned village, Commerce, and founded
a new town called Nauvoo (Hebrew for "beautiful place"). Nauvoo became
a haven for Mormons, especially after the Illinois General Assembly passed
a series of laws that granted Smith's followers an unprecedented degree of
autonomy. Authorized to write their own laws (as long as they did not
conflict with state and federal statutes) and to maintain their own military
unit for self-protection (the Mormon Legion), the Mormons created a prosperous community that became the envy of their less affluent neighbors.
By 1845 Nauvoo had become the largest community in the state.

The insular Mormon community in Nauvoo soon aroused strong negative reactions from the people of western Illinois. Complaints arose about
the Latter Day Saints' intolerance of dissent, their putative practice of
polygamy, and the exemptions from Illinois statutes that enabled Nauvoo
to function almost as a separate state. The size and power of Nauvoo's
Mormon Legion, the largest military force in the nation other than the
U.S. Army, led to rumors of an intended takeover of the state by force. Sporadic outbreaks of violence between Mormons and their neighbors culminated in the murder of Joseph Smith and his brother, Hyrum, in 1844. An
embattled minority with few supporters in the state outside of Nauvoo,
the Mormons surrendered many of the privileges they had previously enjoyed. In 1846 Brigham Young led the first four hundred families westward
toward Utah and, with hostilities continuing around Nauvoo, most of the

Mormon emigrants departed Illinois across the frozen Mississippi River in February 1846 after many outbreaks of violence, including the killing of Joseph Smith. *Illinois State Historical Library*

remaining Latter Day Saints followed before the year's end. The monumental Mormon Temple, erected in Nauvoo after Young's departure, lasted only a few years before being destroyed by fire and a tornado—a symbolic end to the story of the Mormon enclave in Illinois.

The founding of new towns and substantial growth of existing communities in the antebellum years resulted in the emergence of several towns as candidates for the new state capital. The selection of Vandalia had not led as hoped to the economic development of the surrounding lands in the Kankakee River basin, and the capital city itself had languished. Moreover, the rapid increase of population in the northern counties lent credibility to the argument that the capital should be situated more centrally in the state. Alton, Jacksonville, Peoria, and Springfield all vied to become the new state capital, and Alton narrowly finished first in a referendum held in 1834. Springfield submitted the most attractive bid, however, pledging to donate land for the capitol site as well as fifty thousand dollars toward the construction cost. The search for a new capital sparked an intense political contest in the general assembly, and according to legend, Springfield benefited from behind-the-scenes deals struck by the astute Sangamon County legislative delegation (the members of which, including Abraham Lincoln, were known as the "long nine"). Springfield won the vote in the general assembly on the fourth ballot in 1837. Construction began later that year on the new capitol, an impressive two-story Greek Renaissance structure replete with rotunda, dome, and porticos. Two years later, despite the efforts of Vandalia's leading citizens to annul the general assembly's decision, wagons began conveying state property to Springfield. Eager to be near the state's center of government, Lincoln left his home in nearby New Salem and moved to Springfield.

In the 1830s Springfield and a host of other Illinois towns seemed likelier candidates for urban greatness than Chicago. At the time of its founding in 1833, the settlement on the lake that would become Chicago contained approximately 150 houses and slightly more than twice that number of residents; by 1837, at the time of its incorporation, its population had grown to 4,000. A visitor from Boston in 1839 archly commented on the crude frontier conditions prevalent in Chicago, where the streets stood empty of carriages and handcarts but hogs, geese, dogs, and hens moved freely about. Yet the splendid location gave promise of commercial greatness as a vital link between the East Coast and the developing Midwest, and Chicago's growth accelerated after the opening of a new harbor there in 1834. Cognizant of the impact of the Erie Canal, Eastern businessmen made their way to Chicago in search of investment opportunities. The sleepy trading post that had once been populated primarily by Indians, French, and métis was, like the rest of northern Illinois, changing under the force of a Yankee invasion.

Convinced of the city's boundless opportunities for growth, speculators in the mid-1830s frantically bought and sold real estate in Chicago. Riverfront lots sold for $3,500 in 1836 and downtown lots for $250, an increase of 500 percent in just four years. Real estate speculators met newcomers to the city as soon as they disembarked from ships at the docks. "I never saw a busier place than Chicago was at the time of our arrival," wrote a British visitor in 1835. "The streets were crowded with land speculators, hurrying from one sale to another. . . . A young lawyer, of my acquaintance, had realized five hundred dollars per day the five preceding days, by merely making out titles to land." Longtime residents of the city watched incredulously as plots of previously unused, rapidly subdivided marshland sold for tens of thousands of dollars. The real estate boom ended abruptly with the Panic of 1837, and countless speculators lost fortunes, but the setback proved temporary as Chicago continued to grow at a rapid pace.[5]

Chicago's meteoric rise fascinated a number of visionary entrepreneurs who left the safety and security of the East Coast and became the fledgling city's founding fathers. William Butler Ogden came to Chicago in 1835, accumulated a fortune in real estate, and became the city's first mayor in 1837. Serving later as a city councilman, he led the crusade for railroad construction and spearheaded a number of civic and educational projects.

Walter L. Newberry also made his fortune purchasing downtown lots in his adopted city, became one of the founders of the Chicago Public Library, and bequeathed funds for the creation of the Newberry Library. "Long John" Wentworth, a giant measuring six foot six inches, came to Chicago in 1836 after graduating from Dartmouth College, published the *Chicago Democrat,* represented Illinois in the U.S. House of Representatives, and remained an ardent booster of the city for more than fifty years. New Englanders Gurdon Saltonstall Hubbard, Gustavus F. Swift, and Philip D. Armour founded meat-processing plants and helped Chicago supplant Cincinnati as the nation's meat-packing center.

Chicago's booster businessmen heartily endorsed the centuries-old observation by Jolliet and Marquette that Lake Michigan and the Illinois River could readily be connected—and with great benefit to the city on the lake. A canal linking those two bodies of water would complete a maritime network that would enable sailing vessels to travel from the East Coast to the Gulf of Mexico, and Chicago would be fortuitously placed at its heart. The very first internal improvement project to be considered by the Illinois General Assembly concerned the construction of a waterway between Lake Michigan and the Illinois River, and in 1822 the state applied to the federal government for a land grant for this purpose. Congress provided only the right-of-way and narrow easements on both sides of the canal for towpaths. Five years later, the viability of canals having been demonstrated in the East and the potential for development of the Midwest having been recognized, the federal government granted the state a total of 290,915 acres in alternate sections for five miles on both sides of the canal path. There then ensued a debate over whether the canal should have a spacious channel suitable for steamboat traffic or a more modest channel that would accommodate only canal boats. Rising construction costs and the disappointing revenue generated by land sales finally convinced the public to settle for a shallow-cut channel. Governor Joseph Duncan borrowed a half million dollars for start-up capital, and work on the project began in 1836.

The construction of the Illinois and Michigan Canal, which stretched ninety miles from Chicago to La Salle, proved an epic undertaking. A severe labor shortage forced recruiters to hire thousands of poor workers to leave their homes in Ireland and migrate to Illinois. Toiling long hours in dangerous conditions for only twenty or twenty-five dollars a month, the predominantly Irish workforce blasted a channel with black powder and then removed debris with picks, shovels, and other hand tools. Because of the 115-foot reduction in elevation between Chicago and La Salle, fifteen locks had to be constructed along the canal. Financial problems hounded the enterprise virtually from the beginning, and contractors resorted to paying wages and meeting other fiscal obligations in scrip. Work on the canal stopped completely in 1842, in large measure because the funding of other transportation improvement projects had increased Illinois's debt.

The Illinois and Michigan Canal at Ottawa. The ninety-mile-long canal, which opened for business in 1848, stretched from Chicago to La Salle. Photograph dated April 9, 1865. *Illinois State Historical Library*

The canal finally opened in 1848 and generated enough revenue through the sale of land and cargo tolls to retire the debt by 1870. The volume of canal traffic peaked in the 1870s, and the canal remained an important transportation artery for the rest of the nineteenth century.

Along with the construction of the Illinois and Michigan Canal, the State of Illinois initiated a number of other internal improvement projects in an effort to keep pace with similar activities going on throughout the East, where state governments and private entrepreneurs were building roads, turnpikes, canals, and railroads. Henry Clay's rise in national politics derived largely from his "American system," which prescribed a program of internal improvements funded by the federal government. To compete economically with other states, members of the Whig party in Illinois, including Abraham Lincoln, proposed an ambitious agenda of infrastructure enhancement. The general assembly passed internal improvements legislation in 1837 that provided funds for the betterment of the state's rivers and roads, especially to improve the delivery of the U.S. mail. Most important, the 1837 measure committed Illinois to the creation of a statewide railroad network; and when private businesses could not raise the capital to undertake the project, the general assembly allocated $3.5 million for the completion of the Illinois Central Railroad.

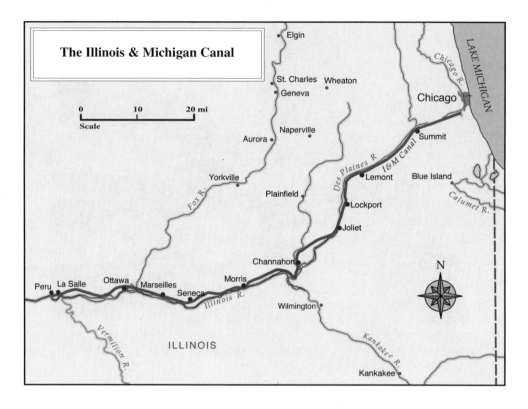

The blueprint of the proposed railroad network included several lines that collectively would link all the major regions of the state. The main north–south route would extend from Cairo at the confluence of the Ohio and Mississippi rivers to the Illinois River and then northwest to Galena. Anticipating the completion of the Illinois and Michigan Canal, the legislators saw no need for a railroad link to Chicago. The north–south trunk line would be intersected by two major east–west lines: the Northern Cross, running from Quincy through Springfield to the Indiana state line, and the Southern Cross, running from Alton to Mt. Carmel. The detailed plan provided for the later completion of additional branchlines. Construction began on the Northern Cross, but the Panic of 1837 intervened with devastating impact. Construction crews eventually completed a portion of the Northern Cross, but in 1839 work ceased on all other parts of the network. During the 1840–1841 session, the general assembly formally abandoned the railroad plans adopted so optimistically just a few years before. Communities founded along the proposed railroad route, places such as Montezuma, Moscow, Caledonia, and New Bedford, became ghost towns.

The Panic of 1837 left the state's grand internal improvements design in shambles. The second State Bank of Illinois—chartered in 1834 by a Whig-dominated general assembly—went bankrupt, costing thousands of investors their life's savings. Worse, the state had funded the bank by selling bonds and now faced the imposing task of paying off the bonds, the cost of the failed internal improvements, and the interest on both. Seeking to escape the burden of debt, residents of the state's northernmost counties opted for secession and asked congressional approval to join Wisconsin. Congress refused, and Illinois remained intact. By the early 1840s, a number of politicians fearing that the situation was hopeless urged Governor Thomas Ford to default on the state's financial obligations and declare bankruptcy. Ford refused. Instead, he devised a plan that raised taxes and gradually paid off the debt at an increasing rate as financial conditions improved. Fiscal solvency came slowly, but in 1880 the state paid in full the last of the bonds.

The state's fragile economic condition meant that railroad construction had to wait for external funding before resuming. In 1850 Illinois Senator Stephen A. Douglas shepherded a bill through Congress that granted the state 2,595,000 acres that could be sold to finance the construction of a railroad from Cairo to Dunleith near Galena, with a branch to Chicago. The general assembly awarded the contract for construction, along with the federal land grant, to a consortium of Eastern businessmen led by Robert Rantoul, which contracted to pay the state 7 percent of operating income. The Illinois Central Railroad Company employed Roswell B. Mason as chief engineer. He was a veteran railroad builder who had been involved in the construction of the Erie Canal. Work began in September 1851. Facing a severe labor shortage, Illinois Central contractors recruited heavily in New York City and in Ireland and eventually employed 100,000 laborers during the 1850s (as many as 10,000 laborers at one time). Extreme heat and rainfall led to the onset of various diseases (most notably cholera epidemics in 1854 and 1855) and caused delays, as did brawling and work stoppages caused by binge drunkenness. Nevertheless, Rantoul's company completed the 705.5-mile railroad (then the longest in the world) on time in 1856.

The completion of the Illinois Central Railroad not only tied the state's farmers more closely to national markets but also significantly enhanced the development of previously unsettled areas in central Illinois. Engaging in what the historian Paul W. Gates called its "colonization work," the company allocated considerable sums of money to an extensive advertising campaign to lure immigrants to the state. In 1856 alone, the railroad spent $16,900 on newspaper and magazine advertising, $11,700 on printing costs, and $14,400 on the salaries of recruiting agents. These agents initially traveled to Germany, Norway, Sweden, and Canada but increasingly concentrated their efforts along the eastern seaboard of the United

Construction of the Illinois Central Railroad lasted from 1851 to 1856. At the time of its completion, the railroad's 705.5-mile length made it the longest railroad in the world. *Illinois State Historical Library*

States. They targeted the teeming immigrant population of New York City by, for example, inserting panels extolling the virtues of Illinois in Gotham's Second, Third, and Sixth Avenue streetcars. By the end of the century, the company sold nearly 45,000 parcels of land from its grant of 2,595,000 acres. A host of communities, including Champaign, Centralia, Carbondale, Kankakee, Mattoon, and Effingham, sprang up at intervals along the tracks of the Illinois Central.[6]

No city benefited more from the coming of the railroads than Chicago, then in competition with St. Louis to become the nation's railroad center. The Michigan Central Railroad from Detroit reached Chicago in 1852, reducing the travel time from New York City to two days. By 1856 more than a hundred trains, serving thirteen different railroads, entered and left Chicago daily, and although the completion of the Illinois Central line established firm ties with the South, most new tracks laid in Chicago in the 1850s ran along an east–west axis. Also that year, the Chicago and Rock Island Railroad completed a bridge over the Mississippi River and for the first time advanced the city's reach beyond that formidable geographical barrier. Additional railroads and links to other lines extended beyond northern Illinois into Wisconsin, Minnesota, Iowa, Michigan, and Missouri, expanding Chicago's hinterland by hundreds of miles. Under the driving leadership of men such as William Butler Ogden, the railroads brought cereal grains, lumber, and other products to the city for processing. In the decade prior to the Civil War, railroad trackage in Illinois increased from 110 miles to 2,867 miles. Boasting eleven trunk lines by 1860, Chicago had emerged as the hub of America's expanding railroad network.

The rapid growth of Chicago and other communities, along with the development of agriculture in previously isolated areas of Illinois, meant that by the 1840s many people questioned the viability of the existing state constitution. A governing document that had been suitable to a sparsely settled state in 1818 now seemed antiquated after nearly three decades of social, economic, and political change. Chief among its defects, according to a population imbued with the precepts of Jacksonian Democracy, stood the excessive power delegated to the legislature and the absence of a veto for the governor. In 1842 a call for a constitutional convention narrowly failed, but in 1846 the proposal carried with 72 percent of the popular vote. The following year, 162 delegates met from June 7 to August 31 and composed a new constitution roughly three times as long as the original charter. The final product, an unwieldy bundle of compromises between Democratic and Whig partisans, garnered strong newspaper support, and on March 6, 1848, the state's voters ratified it by more than a three-fourths margin.

As a document ostensibly designed to enhance democracy, the 1848 constitution proved a mixed bag indeed. The new document reduced the size of the general assembly from 162 members to 100 and curtailed the length of legislative sessions by reducing the legislators' per diem payments after forty-two days of work. To avoid the kind of indebtedness incurred earlier through expensive public works schemes, the general assembly could fund only projects costing fifty thousand dollars or less; more costly projects had to be approved by a referendum of the state electorate. Article VI, Section I, narrowed the franchise to male citizens, obviating the earlier practice of allowing all white male inhabitants over the age of twenty-one to vote. The constitution restored the secret ballot, which had been established in 1818 but which had lost out to the practice of viva voce voting in the Jacksonian age. No movement to legalize slavery developed at the constitutional convention, yet delegates defeated a proposal to extend suffrage to African Americans by an overwhelming vote of 137 to 7 and instructed the general assembly to pass new laws proscribing black immigration and manumission. According to the new constitution, noted the historian James E. Davis, "Illinoisans opposed both slavery and political equality for blacks."[7]

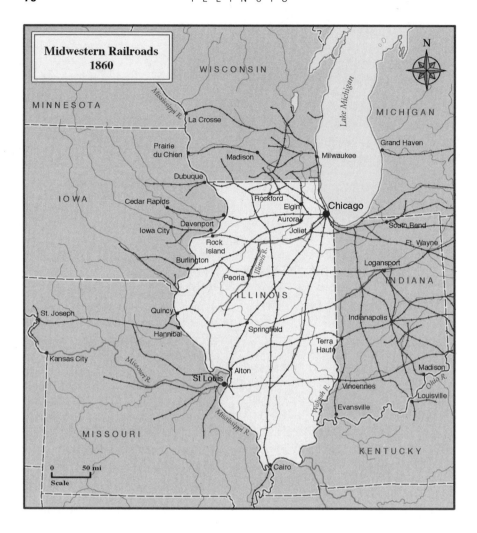

The ratification of a new constitution, inadequate as the new document may have been, underscored the remarkable changes that swept over Illinois once it had attained statehood. Whites hungry for land forcibly removed the remaining Indian tribes, and the remnants of French influence melted away. Large sections of the state previously left empty began to fill up, and a population predominately from the South struggled to accommodate newcomers from the Northeastern states and European nations. Speculation manias in land sales and urban development resulted from the redoubtable Yankee influence. Policy makers in Illinois recognized the importance of improved transportation and—despite financial setbacks that threatened the state's fiscal solvency—strained to finance internal improvements. The Illinois and Michigan Canal proved a boon to the state, but its importance quickly declined because of the railroads. As the frontier receded and the state became a magnet for large and increasingly diverse populations, some issues remained unresolved. Where, for example, did Illinois stand in the developing national crisis concerning slavery?

Galena

At a time when Chicago remained an isolated trading post, Galena thrived as the largest and most economically vital community in Illinois north of St. Louis. Fur traders and missionaries had built a few cabins along the Fever River (later renamed the Galena River) by the early nineteenth century, and Galena grew and prospered from the lead deposits located in the surrounding area. Essential in the production of rifles and bullets, lead proved more valuable than gold to early frontiersmen. The mineral could be difficult to locate and extract when concealed far underground, but the rich deposits in northwestern Illinois, eastern Iowa, and southern Wisconsin rested near the surface. In 1819 Richard M. Johnson, who later became U.S. vice president, brought a mining crew of a hundred men (including slaves) and unsuccessfully attempted to organize a large-scale extraction operation. Miners and prospectors from the eastern United States and many foreign countries participated in the "lead rush" during the 1820s, and by 1830 an estimated five thousand men labored in the surface mines around Galena. By the early 1840s, Galena-area miners excavated ore valued annually at more than one million dollars.

As a commercial center serving the miners, Galena grew along with the steamboat traffic on the upper Mississippi River. Steamboats carried the lead ore downstream to Alton and St. Louis and returned with the provisions needed in an isolated outpost. During the town's heyday, according to early settlers, gangs of stevedores simultaneously loaded pig lead onto and unloaded manufactured goods from as many as fifteen steamboats at a time tied up at Galena wharves. The community also served as a marketing and distribution center for the surrounding agricultural hinterland. Local entrepreneurs provided the capital for the extension of the steamboat system northward into Minnesota and, convinced that the future of their community rested with riverine commerce, initially spurned funds offered by the Illinois Central Railroad.

Visitors to Galena rhapsodized about its scenic vistas and natural beauty. Houses rose along the limestone bluffs overlooking the business district, which straddled the river. The preponderance of substantial homes bespoke the number of lawyers, doctors, craftsmen, and affluent merchants who had settled there. In 1839, at the time of its incorporation as a city, Galena boasted a land office, a branch of the state bank, three churches, a theater, and a municipal library containing eight hundred volumes. By 1845 Galena could justly claim to be the richest community in Illinois. When Ulysses S. Grant left St. Louis to work in his father's leather goods store in Galena in 1860, the community maintained a reputation for commercial vitality.

Later in the nineteenth century, however, Galena's fortunes began to decline. The depletion of the surface lead mines seriously damaged the local economy, and many prospectors headed for the gold mines of California or sought employment on railroad construction crews. Dreams of economic preeminence faded as the volume of traffic on the Mississippi River decreased and decades of erosion clogged the channel of the Galena River. Local businessmen rejoiced when the Iron Horse arrived in the mid-1850s, but they soon reconsidered when agricultural foodstuffs once collected in Galena instead headed by rail for Chicago. By the end of the century, population loss and financial retrenchment left Galena a picturesque but isolated community serving only the commercial needs of the immediate farming area.

Black Hawk

Black Sparrow Hawk, who later became known simply as Black Hawk, was born in 1767 in a Sauk village near the site where the Rock River flowed into the Mississippi River. In the late eighteenth and early nineteenth centuries, he and many of his people cultivated friendly relations with the Spanish and the British but developed an intense dislike for the Americans. In 1804 a group of Sauk and Fox chiefs negotiated a treaty at St. Louis with American military commander William Henry Harrison, which ceded fifty million acres of the tribes' lands east of the Mississippi to the United States. Black Hawk and other Sauks vigorously questioned the legality of the treaty, arguing that the chiefs had been inebriated at the time and that the tribes had never authorized them to finalize such agreements. The Americans disregarded these objections as more and more white settlers began moving into the area in question. During the War of 1812, Black Hawk sided with the British and fought against American forces at Frenchtown, Fort Meigs, and Fort Stephenson. Following the war, he enlisted the aid of the British in Canada and worked with the Winnebago prophet White Cloud to assemble an Indian confederacy against the Americans. As an influential war chief within his tribe, he argued that the Sauks should fight to retain their ancestral lands in northwestern Illinois.

Black Hawk as a young man.
Illinois State Historical Library

Most of the Sauks withdrew across the Mississippi to Iowa, but Black Hawk and several hundred others remained in their village.

In 1831, responding to a call for assistance from Illinois Governor John Reynolds, American forces arrived at Fort Armstrong on Rock Island, sending Black Hawk and his followers back to join their tribesmen in Iowa. The following April, erroneously believing that all members of the Winnebago, Potawatomi, and Mascoutin tribes would ally with the Sauks if violence ensued, Black Hawk returned with several hundred warriors, women, and children. The resulting Black Hawk War lasted through the remainder of the summer and, although the Indians achieved some scattered victories, the American armies of regulars and volunteers effectively exploited their many advantages. The hopelessly outnumbered Indians staved off defeat for weeks, evading their pursuers across much of northwestern Illinois and southern Wisconsin, but they eventually succumbed at the Battle of Bad Axe, where American troops slaughtered more than three hundred men, women, and children. The outcome of the war removed the last Indians from northern Illinois and opened the area to settlement by land-hungry whites.

Having been captured after the Battle of Bad Axe, Black Hawk became a prisoner at Prairie du Chien, Wisconsin, under the charge of Lieutenant Jefferson Davis and then at Fort Armstrong under the supervision of General Winfield Scott. At the request of President Andrew Jackson, authorities escorted the famous Sauk chief on a tour of the East Coast where he received a sword and a medal from Jackson himself. After confinement for a time at Fort Monroe, Black Hawk returned to Iowa, where he lived the remainder of his days as a subordinate to his longtime rival in the Sauk tribe, Chief Keokuk. He adopted a much more benign attitude toward the Americans in his later years, a change evident in the autobiography he published in 1833. He died at his lodge on the Des Moines River on October 3, 1838. A year later, grave robbers separated the head and several bones from his corpse; pieces of the skeleton were shown at exhibitions around the country. Curators at the Iowa Historical Society eventually recovered all of the bones, which were housed at the society in Burlington until it burned to the ground.

Slave State or Free?

History, geography, and demography combined to create an ambiguous legacy for slavery in Illinois. The first British inhabitants of the area allowed the French to retain their slaves, and the territorial governor's interpretation of the Northwest Ordinance allowed all slaveholders to do the same. White landowners relied upon the labor of indentured servants, some of whom were bound to their masters for as long as ninety-nine years, as a convenient substitute for slavery. The 1818 constitution established Illinois as a free state but stopped short of emancipation where the practice already existed. The Black Laws, adopted by the general assembly one year after the ratification of the constitution, limited the rights of slaves, free blacks, and indentured servants. The drive to call a second constitutional convention in the 1820s, which failed after heated debate divided the state's population, emanated from a desire to rejuvenate slavery. Each of the state's first four governors—Shadrach Bond, Edward Coles, Ninian Edwards, and John Reynolds—owned slaves at one time, and other influential state leaders in the early days of statehood affirmed slavery in terms of property rights. The initial population of the state by so many settlers hailing from the South reinforced the support of slavery, a condition altered somewhat but not eradicated by the increasing immigration of Yankees in the nineteenth century. At the same time, support for and opposition to slavery often cut across geographical divisions and ethnic backgrounds. Southerners sympathetic to slavery could be found in the state's northern counties while a small number of abolitionists lived in the southern part of the state known as Little Egypt. In yet another departure from the normal pattern, some German and Irish immigrants joined Old Stock Yankees in defending the peculiar institution. Even as passions escalated and the national crisis worsened, attitudes on slavery in Illinois remained difficult to sort out.

Although considerable proslavery sentiment persisted, a series of Illinois court rulings in the 1820s, 1830s, and 1840s chipped away at the foundations of slavery. In 1825 the state supreme court negated all indentures except those signed by masters and in 1836 freed the offspring of servants whose indentures originated in the territorial era. In 1841 the court prohibited altogether the sale of indentured servants, and the following year it struck down an existing law that empowered sheriffs to arrest and hire out on a monthly basis African Americans lacking proof of freedom. In 1843 the court ruled that any slaves brought into the state automatically gained their freedom. In *Jarrott v. Jarrott* in 1845, the court held that descendants of French bondsmen could no longer be deprived of their freedom and thereby removed the last vestiges of slavery in Illinois. An African American from Missouri who had been arrested in Sangamon County for failing to produce proof of his freedom challenged the constitutionality of the Illinois law requiring the capture and return of fugitive slaves. In 1849 the state supreme court upheld the suit and abrogated the fugitive law statute.

Much of the growing antislavery sentiment resulted from the pursuit and apprehension of runaway slaves, significant numbers of whom made their way north via the Underground Railroad. The secret freedom road in Illinois placed a premium on stealth, with participating whites hiding the fugitives during the days and spiriting them northward under cover of darkness. Terminals on the Underground Railroad operated at such Mississippi River towns as Alton and Quincy, from where passengers made their way through Bloomington and Knoxville to Joliet and Chicago before finally securing their freedom in Canada. The pursuit of runaway slaves, an unseemly business made worse by the controversial actions of slave trackers, aroused mounting opposition in the state. Illinoisans who opposed slavery recoiled when callous slave trackers broke into homes and ransacked property while combing the countryside for runaways, and the reckless behavior of these bounty hunters upset previously disinterested bystanders as well. In some highly publicized cases, trackers unable to locate the individuals they pursued simply abducted any African Americans they could find—including some who had never been slaves. Such wanton injustice led to retaliatory strikes by outraged Illinoisans intent upon freeing innocent black victims. In 1846 a mob freed two captured slaves in Chicago. Contemporary newspapers in the state, however, also recounted a number of incidents in which local authorities arrested whites for aiding fugitives. The Illinois General Assembly failed to pass personal liberty laws to nullify the Fugitive Slave Law of 1850, a course of action taken by several other Northern states, but enforcement of the federal statute remained sporadic. Local authorities frequently looked the other way when hearing of the presence of runaway slaves in the area or winked at sympathetic whites who contrived to blunt the fugitive slave law.

Free blacks who lived in antebellum Illinois occupied an awkward and often unsettled place in the society. A clear consensus had developed to exclude slavery from the state, but scant sentiment existed for racial equality. State laws denied free blacks the right to vote, initiate legal proceedings, testify in court, or serve in the militia. Limitations on education and property ownership further circumscribed their place in society. In 1853 the general assembly passed laws that seemed especially retrograde, prohibiting free blacks from establishing permanent residence in the state and preventing slaveholders from coming to Illinois for the purpose of manumitting their bondsmen. Reputedly only a handful of newspapers in the state endorsed the 1853 measure, and public opinion seemed to be running clearly in opposition to it, but no effective movement for repeal came until 1864. The environment for the relatively small number of free blacks in Illinois, who numbered just 5,436 in 1850 (less than 1 percent of the state's population), remained decidedly inhospitable.

Notwithstanding the daunting conditions they faced, some African Americans who managed to secure their freedom prospered in the state. One of the most remarkable free blacks in antebellum Illinois, "Free Frank" McWorter was born a slave in 1777 and managed to purchase freedom for himself, his wife, and several other family members. In 1830 he left Kentucky and settled in Pike County, Illinois, where he and his two sons subsequently bought eight hundred acres of land. Transcending his humble origins, he raised cattle, speculated in land, and eventually hoisted himself and his family into the middle class. In 1836 McWorter laid out a new community, New Philadelphia, which became a biracial center of trade for surrounding Hadley Township in Pike County. Resented by some of his less successful white neighbors, he suffered kidnapping threats and frequently encountered racism in his business dealings. At the same time, however, he won the respect of other whites who saw his success as an indictment of slavery and openly encouraged him in his business dealings.

Equally prosperous and more widely known, John Jones became the undisputed leader of Chicago's black community for more than a generation. Born to a mulatto mother and a white father on an eastern North Carolina plantation in 1816, Jones grew up with his legal status in question. Fearing that her husband planned to enslave her son, Jones's mother apprenticed him to a tailor. He worked for many years in Memphis, Tennessee, before returning to North Carolina in 1838 to obtain a certificate of freedom. In 1844 Jones came to Illinois, posted a bond of $250, and registered in Madison County according to state law as a free black. The following year, he moved to Chicago and opened a downtown tailor's shop that catered to the city's wealthy white residents. His successful business soon made him the richest and most socially prominent African American in the city, and he became an outspoken advocate for racial equality and an ardent abolitionist. His political activities increased after the Civil War, and with white support he won election to the Cook County board of commissioners.

The success of men like McWorter and Jones lent support to the fledgling abolitionist movement in the state. Although proslavery residents of Southern ancestry considered abolitionism yet another form of Yankee cultural imperialism and people throughout the state shied away from the antislavery fanatics whose zealotry gave the movement a bad name, a number of antislavery organizations appeared and rapidly gained membership throughout northern Illinois. In 1823, for example, the Reverend John Mason Peck and several members of his Baptist congregation took the lead in organizing the St. Clair Society for the Prevention of Slavery in Illinois. The Morganian Society, founded in Morgan County in 1824 to oppose the call for a constitutional convention, became a strong voice for moderate reform by arguing that studied enforcement of existing antislavery laws in Illinois would result in the eventual demise of the institution. Some abolitionist groups argued for more forceful action, and in 1837 the delegates at the Illinois State Anti-Slavery Convention in Alton adopted a resolution calling for the immediate abolition of slavery nationwide. By the late 1830s, Congregationalist churches in the state included a statement affirming abolitionism in their confessions of faith. Abolitionists clearly remained a minority of the population in Illinois, but their numbers were increasing and their influence growing.

Nothing galvanized the forces of antislavery more than the martyred death of one of their own, Elijah P. Lovejoy. A native of Maine, Lovejoy had come west as a young man and settled in St. Louis, where he founded a high school and edited a newspaper devoted to a variety of reform causes. He attended Princeton Theological Seminary, earned a divinity degree, and returned to St. Louis in 1833 as editor of the *St. Louis Observer,* a Presbyterian journal. Using the religious newspaper as a sounding board for his many and varied crusades, he railed against Roman Catholics, Baptists, Campbellites, alcoholic beverages, and with increasing frequency, slavery. His essays against the evils of slavery grew more strident as he condemned equally those who allowed slavery to exist and those who actually owned bondsmen. When he published editorials that excoriated the recent lynching of a free black man in St. Louis, a mob stormed his office and dismantled his printing press. Fearing for the safety of his wife and infant son, Lovejoy moved across the Mississippi River to Alton, Illinois, a community noted for its tolerance and liberal thought. Alton's reputation notwithstanding, proslavery residents greeted Lovejoy by throwing what remained of his printing press into the river.

Lovejoy assumed the editorship of the *Alton Observer* and quickly turned the newspaper into an organ for the abolitionist movement, but his bold antislavery message found no warmer welcome in Alton than it had in St. Louis. Some local antislavery men, most notably the Reverend Peck, refused to support Lovejoy's extremist brand of abolitionism and dissociated

themselves from his uncompromising editorials. Refusing to curb his rhetoric, Lovejoy pledged to speak out as a matter of conscience and in defense
of First Amendment rights. On several occasions, he dispersed groups of
thugs who threatened to tar and feather him, but on August 21, 1837, an
angry mob rushed his office and smashed his printing press. Financial contributions from Eastern abolitionists allowed him to purchase a new press,
but another unruly crowd quickly pushed the gleaming new press into the
river. Determined to make a stand in Alton, Lovejoy ignored the call by
other abolitionists to leave the city and defiantly ordered another printing
press. "If I fail," he announced grimly, "my grave shall be made in Alton."
Lovejoy and his supporters placed the new press in a huge stone warehouse on the riverfront, armed themselves, and prepared for the next on-
slaught. The assault came on November 7, 1837, and several men perished
in the ensuing gun battle. Shot five times, Lovejoy died in front of the
warehouse; the mob completed its work by destroying the printing press.
Local authorities failed to punish members of the mob who had stormed
the warehouse and instead indicted Lovejoy's cohorts for their role in the
affair. The incident provoked a flood of indignation nationwide. Membership in antislavery societies increased in Illinois, just as it did throughout
the North. Lovejoy's death symbolized to many the natural link between
violence and the peculiar institution of slavery.[1]

The failure of moral suasion and the continued growth of slavery convinced many abolitionists of the necessity for stronger measures. William
Lloyd Garrison, long the most influential of the abolitionists, inveighed
unceasingly against the crime of slavery but warned against involvement
in politics. Like many of their counterparts throughout the North, however, some abolitionists in Illinois began to question Garrison's preach-
ments against political activism. The Liberty party, founded in 1839 in
New York by a group of abolitionists disenchanted with the failure of the
nation's two major political parties to address the slavery question, provided the avenue for Illinois abolitionists to answer their political yearn-
ings. Citing biblical scriptures, party leaders described their efforts as a
moral crusade to eradicate the sin of slavery from American society. Contemporaries frequently commented on the Liberty party's religious trap-
pings. "The truth is," admitted one party spokesman, "that most of our
leaders and political speakers have been and are *ministers*—not statesmen
or politicians." The Liberty party in Illinois exerted a negligible influence
on state elections in the early 1840s but in 1846 achieved a slim electoral
majority in thirteen northern counties.[2] The Liberty party inveighed
throughout the 1840s against the "Slave Power," charging that Southern
slave interests maintained undue influence in the national government.
Accordingly, party loyalists (along with an increasing number of Northern
Whigs) saw the annexation of Texas in 1845 and the declaration of war
against Mexico the following year as part of a plot to spread slavery into

the expanding American frontier. Statehood for Texas and the addition of territory acquired from Mexico would mean disrupting the fragile balance of power between free and slave states in the national government. The outbreak of the Mexican War produced a surge of patriotism in Illinois. The general assembly immediately endorsed the actions of the U.S. Congress, and the state's young men responded eagerly to Governor Thomas Ford's call for volunteers to fight against Mexico. President James K. Polk had called for Illinois to contribute three regiments to the American fighting force, but enough men in the state volunteered to form nine regiments. Aghast at the widespread enthusiasm for the war, abolitionists saw the war as simply more evidence of the Slave Power's machinations.

Elected to the U.S. House of Representatives in 1846, Abraham Lincoln became one of the few politicians in Illinois to oppose the Mexican War. He vehemently denounced Polk for unjustly leading the nation into war and questioned whether the president had violated the U.S. Constitution in his haste to invade a foreign country. Lincoln's dissent made him unpopular in Illinois, and he declined to seek reelection in 1848. His assertion that expansionism would "enlarge and aggravate the distracting question of slavery" proved prescient, for the conclusion of the war immediately plunged the nation into a spirited dispute over the status of slavery in the territory won from Mexico. The Wilmot Proviso, which prohibited slavery in any territory acquired during the war, sparked intense debate within the Democratic and Whig parties in Illinois. The new Free Soil party, which developed after the Mexican War to oppose the expansion of slavery, gained control of the Illinois General Assembly after the 1848 elections and passed a resolution compelling the state's U.S. senators, Stephen A. Douglas and James Shields, to vote for the proviso; only two of the state's congressmen, Democrat John Wentworth and Whig Edward D. Baker, did so. The Wilmot Proviso failed to pass in Congress, and public opinion regarding its merit remained split in Illinois.[3]

The controversy over slavery and the territories raged on for several years and threatened to plunge the nation into fratricidal conflict. In an attempt to save the Union, Henry Clay conceived an omnibus measure called the Compromise of 1850, which included the admission of California as a free state, the organization of the Utah and New Mexico territories with no resolution of the slavery question, the settlement of the Texas boundary question, the abolition of the slave trade in the District of Columbia, and a more stringent fugitive slave law. Clay and diminutive Illinois Senator Stephen A. Douglas (known as the "Little Giant") politicked in Congress for eight months—managing contentious debates, drafting amendments to key passages, always seeking the middle ground between abolitionist forces and proslavery Southerners—but the painstakingly crafted legislative package failed to pass. With Clay bedridden and absent from the capital, Douglas continued the fight with a new and resourceful

strategy. Conceding the lack of a majority for the compromise, he reintro-
duced the five components of the bill separately and secured passage for
each part one at a time. Illinois Congressmen William A. Richardson and
John A. McClernand played important roles in the bill's passage in the
House of Representatives, but Douglas duly received the lion's share of the
credit for salvaging Clay's handiwork. Owing to the efforts of these legislators, Illinois became known as the savior of the Union when the Compromise of 1850 passed.

Flush with a newfound national prominence, Douglas returned from
Washington to defend the Compromise of 1850 to his Illinois constituents. For three and a half hours on October 23, 1850, in Chicago,
Douglas sparred verbally with a hostile crowd of four thousand who saw
the legislation as a cynical compact that surrendered too much ground to
the supporters of slavery. Denying any strong sentiment on either side of
the slavery question, Douglas identified as his only goal the restoration of
national harmony. (Critics of the measure pointed to the fact that Douglas's
first wife had owned more than one hundred slaves on a Mississippi plantation, considering this to be proof of his proslavery sympathies.) The
Little Giant defended the compromise as the instrument of popular sovereignty, a solution propounded by Michigan Congressman Lewis Cass that
argued for the right of the people in a territory to allow or exclude slavery
as they wished prior to application for statehood. Douglas prevailed in the
marathon oratorical contest, wringing from the crowd a set of resolutions
upholding the Compromise of 1850 as a requisite for preservation of the
Union. Subsequent speeches he delivered in Jacksonville and Springfield
produced positive outcomes as well. The general assembly rescinded its
support for the Wilmot Proviso and endorsed the Compromise of 1850.
The Free Soil party still fielded candidates in the 1850 and 1852 elections
in Illinois, but support for the third party ebbed as the majority of Democrats
and Whigs ratified Douglas's legislative achievement.

Having become the foremost spokesman for popular sovereignty, Douglas
likewise became the most ardent advocate for westward expansion. To
facilitate the development of the Great Plains, he offered a bill in 1854 to
organize the Kansas and Nebraska territories with popular sovereignty to
decide the question of slavery. These new territories lay within the
Louisiana Purchase, however, where the Missouri Compromise had outlawed slavery from latitude 36 degrees, 30 minutes, north to the Canadian
border. Passage of the bill with its provision for popular sovereignty in
Kansas and Nebraska aroused the hopes of Southern congressmen that
slavery could be established in an area where it had been outlawed for
more than thirty years, and as the price of their support for the measure
they demanded that this be made explicit. Douglas relented and amended
his bill to repeal the Missouri Compromise. Perhaps the Illinois senator assumed that slavery would not flourish in the soil and climate of the Great

Plains, but he clearly underestimated the extent of the public furor that followed in the North. Antislavery forces raged at the possible damage to be done by the Kansas-Nebraska Act and blamed Douglas, the man whom they had recently praised for his role in securing sectional peace.

What motivated Douglas to introduce such volatile legislation? Why risk upsetting the uneasy calm effected by the Compromise of 1850? There is no simple explanation to these questions, although several factors can be identified as key elements in his decision. Eager to enhance the economic development of the territories, Douglas and others sought the construction of a transcontinental railroad to stimulate settlement in the Great Plains. The provision of a vital transportation link to a vast isolated area would attract homesteaders and foster the building of towns. No railroad companies would undertake the massive project until the organization of the territories, however, and this, for entrepreneurial-minded politicians, lent a sense of urgency to the enterprise. Westward expansion, especially along a transcontinental railroad passing through Chicago, would mean economic benefits for Illinois. Because of his position as a principal stockholder in the Illinois Central Railroad, some of his critics charged, Douglas stood to profit personally if Chicago became a junction on the transcontinental railroad. Douglas's political rivals suggested that the Little Giant's presidential ambitions had led him to make a bargain with Southerners. They suspected that he offered the repeal of the Missouri Compromise in return for Southern support of his candidacy. Or perhaps, these various ulterior motives aside, Douglas truly believed in the principle of popular sovereignty and earnestly felt that the question of slavery ought most equitably to be left to the residents of an affected area. In all likelihood, a combination or perhaps all of these issues factored into Douglas's calculations.

With the support of his able lieutenant in the House, William A. Richardson of Illinois, Douglas successfully guided the Kansas-Nebraska Act through Congress. The state's other senator, James Shields, supported the measure, but in the House a majority of the Illinois delegation (four Whigs and one Democrat) voted in opposition. Throughout the North, antislavery forces excoriated the bill, and even moderates strongly questioned the repeal of the Missouri Compromise. A number of the leading antislavery politicians of the day, including Salmon P. Chase, Cassius Clay, and Joshua R. Giddings, came to Illinois to denounce what they termed Douglas's corrupt bargain with the Slave Power. In Ottawa, Illinois, opponents of the Kansas-Nebraska Act adopted a resolution providing for a statewide convention to be held later that year. Leading Democrats in the state expressed their fear that widespread dissatisfaction with Douglas's actions would lead to wholesale defections from the party.

As he had done four years earlier, Douglas returned home to explain his actions to the voters, but the results proved decidedly less satisfactory this time. He tried for more than two hours to address a huge crowd in Chicago, but hecklers kept him from delivering a defense of popular sovereignty. Despite the best efforts of the mayor and the police to maintain order, the rowdy onlookers continually interrupted Douglas with catcalls, epithets, and hisses. Exhausted and frustrated, Douglas finally yelled at the boisterous mob: "It is now Sunday morning—I'll go to church, and you may go to Hell!" He subsequently managed to speak to a gathering in Geneva only after a prominent local abolitionist interceded to calm the unruly throng. For nearly two months, Douglas spoke throughout the state in defense of the Kansas-Nebraska bill. The day after Douglas spoke in Bloomington, the former Whig congressman Abraham Lincoln offered a stinging rebuttal. Lincoln had retired from politics to devote full attention to his law practice, but the furor over the Kansas-Nebraska Act brought him back into the political arena. Douglas and Lincoln continued their colloquy across the state for most of October 1854.[4]

The fallout from the Kansas-Nebraska contretemps quickly became evident in Illinois politics. The issue of slavery and the territories, dormant for many years, was resurrected by Douglas's legislation and disrupted existing alignments in the state. The Democratic party, once a pluralistic coalition of voters representing a variety of different groups throughout the state, became as never before overwhelmingly Southern. Longtime Democratic voters among the Germans, French, Scandinavians, and Canadians deserted the party in large numbers. Prominent Democratic officeholders in the state such as Lyman Trumbull and Sidney Breese immediately declared their opposition to the spread of slavery and commenced the search for a new political home. Nativistic members of the disintegrating Whig party drifted toward the American (Know-Nothing) party, which exploited the fear of immigrants and Roman Catholics. Some former Whigs joined the Democratic fold, but those who objected most vehemently to the Kansas-Nebraska Act, the so-called Conscience Whigs, could not abide membership in the party of Stephen A. Douglas. Instead, they became part of the emerging Republican party, an amalgam of antislavery interests that formed in Wisconsin and Michigan in 1854. Antislavery gatherings that year in Springfield and Ottawa referred to themselves as Republicans, but early attempts to organize the party in Illinois proceeded fitfully. Seeking the Whig nomination for senator in 1854, Abraham Lincoln failed to attend a Republican convention held that year and declined to serve on a committee to which he had been appointed by the convention. (Lincoln failed to win election to the Senate and provided the necessary support for Lyman Trumble, who ran as an anti–Nebraska Democrat, to win the election.) Protesting the extension of slavery, a group of newspaper editors gathered in Decatur on February 22, 1856, and outlined plans for the first statewide meeting of the Republican party in Illinois. Convening in Bloomington on May 29, 270 delegates from seventy counties (almost none of whom hailed from southern counties) formally created the Illinois Republican party.

The Republican party in Illinois developed as a congeries of interests, and relatively few of its early members could be termed abolitionists. Free Soilers objected to the Kansas-Nebraska Act because of the harmful economic competition they thought slavery would cause for white farmers. Many newcomers to the Republican party sought the broader economic vision provided by the defunct Whig party and cared little, if at all, for anti-slavery doctrine. The party membership included abolitionists alongside outright racists; between the two extremes, observed a careful historian of the early Republican party in Illinois, stood a significant portion of the rank and file for whom Abraham Lincoln articulated a "gnawing moral anxiety moderate elements in America were coming to feel toward the institution of slavery." By no means advocates of racial equality, most members of the party expressed dissatisfaction with slavery, opposed unfair restrictions on the liberty of free blacks, and balked at the extension of slavery into additional territory.[5]

The election of 1856 produced encouraging results in Illinois for the fledgling Republican party. The Democratic candidate, James Buchanan, narrowly defeated Republican Charles C. Fremont in the presidential contest, but the Republicans won four congressional seats contested in the state that year. Abraham Lincoln passed at the chance to run for governor, arguing that the Republicans' best chance would be to nominate a former Democrat who could attract votes from the southern counties as well as from the north. William H. Bissell, a former Democrat from Monroe County, won the gubernatorial race over Stephen A. Douglas's perennial ally, William A. Richardson. Democrats maintained majorities in the general assembly and harassed Governor Bissell at every opportunity until he died in office in 1860. The Republicans understandably garnered most of their votes in northern counties while the heaviest Democratic vote came from the southern part of the state. The Republican stronghold centered in the area stretching northeast from Henry County to Lake County, and the healthiest Democratic vote came from the counties arrayed across southern Illinois from the Mississippi River to the Wabash River.

In 1857–1858, sectional tensions intensified in the aftermath of both the Dred Scott decision, in which the U.S. Supreme Court ruled that slavery could not legally be barred from the territories, and the struggle over whether Kansas would be admitted as a slave or a free state. Partisans on both sides of the slavery question looked with special interest at the senatorial election of 1858 in Illinois where the estimable Stephen A. Douglas would be seeking his third term. Having risen to national prominence because of the leading roles he had played in the Compromise of 1850 and the Kansas-Nebraska Act, pundits concluded, Douglas needed only to retain his Senate seat to become the frontrunner for the presidency in 1860. In the controversy over statehood for Kansas, Douglas had urged the rejection of the proslavery Lecompton Constitution, which he condemned as a mockery of popular sovereignty. Impressed by the Little Giant's principled stand, Eastern Republicans encouraged their Illinois counterparts not to contest his reelection. Unalterably opposed to Douglas's acquiescence to the spread of slavery, however, Illinois Republicans insisted on fielding a candidate.

The Republicans' choice for the U.S. Senate in 1858, Abraham Lincoln, had transcended humble origins and parlayed a keen intelligence and a fierce drive to succeed into a successful career in politics. After his family left Kentucky and resettled in Illinois, Lincoln toiled as an agricultural laborer, piloted flatboats down the Mississippi River, clerked in a general store, surveyed land, worked as a postmaster, and passed the bar exam after studying law on his own. From a simple country lawyer with virtually no formal education who had taught himself to read with borrowed books, he became a crafty corporate attorney whose clients included some of the wealthiest firms in Chicago. After serving four terms in the general assembly and one term in the U.S. House of Representatives as a Whig, Lincoln briefly retired from electoral politics before resuming his career as a Republican. He denied that he was an abolitionist but stated unequivocally his opposition to the expansion of slavery. In his speech to the

Abraham Lincoln in 1858, the year of the Lincoln-Douglas debates. *Chicago Historical Society*

Republican state convention at which he accepted the nomination, Lincoln made clear his differences with Douglas. "A house divided against itself cannot stand," he proclaimed. "I believe this government cannot endure permanently half slave and half free. I do not expect the Union to be dissolved—I do not expect the house to fall—but I do expect it will cease to be divided. It will become all one thing, or all the other."[6]

At the outset of the campaign, Douglas gave speeches to huge crowds in northeastern Illinois and Lincoln followed close behind offering rebuttals. Recognizing that their candidate's tardy appearances drew smaller audiences for addresses that seemed anticlimactic, the Republicans challenged the Democrats to a series of joint appearances for the duration of the contest. Douglas consented to debates in each of the seven congressional districts where he had yet to campaign. In the following weeks, Lincoln and Douglas squared off in Ottawa, Freeport, Jonesboro, Charleston, Galesburg, Quincy, and Alton. The thorough newspaper coverage that was afforded the Lincoln-Douglas debates provided ample opportunity for the two candidates to express their views to a national as well as a statewide audience. Alluding to the "house divided" speech, Douglas accused Lincoln of abolitionist sympathies. When Lincoln seemed to distance himself from some earlier statements, the Democrat charged him with tailoring his message to suit the particular audience. Of Lincoln and the Republicans, Douglas said: "Their principles in the north are jet black, in the center they are in color a decent mulatto, and in lower Egypt [southern Illinois] they are almost white." Lincoln stopped far short of advocating political and social equality for black men, but he did claim for them some if not all of the rights of free men. Furthermore, he contended that Douglas had broken a sacred contract by repealing the Missouri Compromise.[7]

At Freeport, Lincoln questioned Douglas closely about the status of slavery in the territories. Given the Supreme Court's recent ruling in the Dred Scott case that slavery could not be prohibited in a territory, how could the people there legally exercise their right of popular sovereignty? Could slavery in fact be employed anywhere, Lincoln asked Douglas, or should the authority of the Supreme Court be contravened? Douglas responded that the Court's decision referred only to the powers of Congress and not to the powers of a territorial legislature. The people in a territory could bar slavery simply by refusing to pass the laws necessary to support the institution. This so-called Freeport Doctrine appealed to antislavery voters in the North who feared that Douglas might be allied with the Slave Power. On the other hand, such fence-straddling disappointed Southerners who yearned for a straightforward statement upholding the right of slavery. The Freeport Doctrine aided Douglas in Illinois in 1858 but, as both of the principals in the senatorial race understood, would harm his chances in future national contests.

Lincoln won his share of moral victories in the debates that year but lost the election. The Republican won the state's popular vote, 125,430 to

N

WISCONSIN

LAKE
MICHIGAN

Dubuque
Galena
Beloit
Kenosha

Freeport
(Aug. 27)

Rockford

Chicago R.

IOWA

Mississippi R.

Chicago

Iowa R.

Rock R.

Des Plaines R.

Davenport

Fox R.

Rock Island

Ottawa (Aug. 21)

Kankakee

Kankakee R.

Galesburg (Oct. 7)

Pontiac

Illinois R.

Peoria

Bloomington

ILLINOIS

Champaign   Danville

Quincy (Oct. 13)

Urbana

Decatur

Springfield ★

Sangamon R.

Jacksonville

Charleston
(Sept. 18)

Terra
Haute

Kaskaskia R.

Embarras R.

MISSOURI

Vandalia

Alton (Oct. 15)

Edwardsville

Missouri R.

Little Wabash R.

Vincennes

St. Louis

INDIANA

McLeansboro

0   25 mi

Kaskaskia

Scale

Shawneetown

Ohio R.

Jonesboro
(Sept. 15)

KENTUCKY

Cumberland R.

Cairo

Tennessee R.

The Lincoln-Douglas Debates
1858

121,609, but the members of a gerrymandered general assembly cast 54 votes for the Democrat and 46 votes for the Republican. The particulars of state politics aside, the 1858 Illinois senatorial contest resonated throughout the nation for several reasons. The widely reported debates between the two able candidates provided a detailed explication of the issue that bitterly divided the nation. Politicians and editorial writers pronounced the clash in Illinois a preview of the upcoming presidential election. Douglas's political fate rested on the outcome of the 1858 struggle, and his reelection made him the frontrunner for the Democratic presidential nomination. Yet although the Little Giant became the clear favorite of Northern Democrats, the formulation of the Freeport Doctrine left his standing among Southerners in the party more fragile. At the same time, Abraham Lincoln emerged as a politician of national stature—a proven vote-getter who had held his own against the most eloquent of the Democrats and appeared to many observers to be the Republican party's presidential candidate of broadest appeal.

Much to Abraham Lincoln's advantage, the Republicans held their 1860 national convention in Chicago. Inside the Wigwam, the two-story wooden structure on Lake Street erected especially for the occasion, the loud, raucous galleries composed largely of Lincoln supporters cheered wildly at every mention of their favorite son. In Lincoln headquarters at the nearby Tremont Hotel, three-hundred-pound David Davis expertly managed the campaign. Entertaining state delegations, persuading, wheedling, bargaining, and cajoling, Davis and his subordinates argued that only "Honest Abe" could unite the disparate elements of the Republican party and defeat Douglas. Disparaging the candidacies of William H. Seward, Salmon P. Chase, and other leading contenders as too extreme in their opposition to slavery, the Lincoln men touted their man's moderation. Seward and Chase might be the strongest candidates in the East, argued Davis, but only Lincoln could carry Illinois and the other Midwestern states needed to win the election. The convention members agreed, on the third ballot, and Lincoln received the news by telegraph in Springfield that he had received the party's presidential nomination.

Stephen A. Douglas fared considerably worse at the Democratic national convention in Charleston, South Carolina. The slavery issue split the delegates along sectional lines, and Douglas adamantly rejected talk of secession by proclaiming the sanctity of the Union. Although he led the field of candidates through fifty-seven ballots, he failed to secure the necessary two-thirds majority for nomination. The convention recessed and reconvened in Baltimore, where Douglas finally received the nomination of the Democrats' Northern wing. The disenchanted Southern Democrats nominated their own presidential candidate, Vice President John C. Breckinridge of Kentucky. A fourth candidate, John Bell of Tennessee, the nominee of the newly formed Constitutional Union party, studiously avoided taking a stand on slavery and urged the preservation of the Union at all costs.

According to the custom of the time, Lincoln remained in Springfield during the campaign and awaited the arrival of newsmen from around the nation to interview him. Some influential Republicans, mostly former Whigs and well-to-do Eastern merchants, urged him to hedge on the party's opposition to the extension of slavery, but Lincoln insisted on standing firmly for free soil. He tried to convince slavery's ardent defenders in the South that he harbored no abolitionist sympathies, but his unwavering opposition to slavery in the territories ended any hope of reconciliation. If Lincoln won the election, Southern fire-eaters warned, secession would follow. Convinced he could not win at the head of a fractured Democratic party, Douglas spent the last month of the campaign touring the Southern states trying to suppress the sentiment for secession.

Lincoln won a substantial majority in the electoral college but received only about 40 percent of the popular vote. He outpolled Douglas by a count of 1,866,452 to 1,376,957 but received fewer votes than Douglas, Breckinridge, and Bell combined. In a sectional contest, Lincoln carried all the Northern states but received virtually no votes in the South, where his name did not even appear on the ballot in ten slave states. Breckinridge swept most of the slave states, and Bell won three border states. Douglas enjoyed broad-based support that transcended sections, but he frequently finished second to Lincoln in Northern states and to Breckinridge in Southern states; he received only twelve electoral votes: nine from Missouri and three from New Jersey's fusion slate. In Illinois, Lincoln won with 50.7 percent of the popular vote (winning approximately 70 percent of the vote in the northern part of the state and only 20 percent in southern counties) while the Republicans gained control of both houses of the general assembly and elected Richard Yates governor.

In the days immediately following the election, Lincoln watched from Springfield as national amity disintegrated. He offered a series of conciliatory statements in hopes of minimizing the number of Southern states opting for secession and declined to endorse the harsh tone of Governor-elect Yates's inaugural address, which argued against any concessions to the South. At the same time, however, the president-elect opposed the Crittendon Compromise, which proposed reviving the Missouri Compromise line and extending it to the Pacific Ocean; Lincoln refused to budge on his opposition to the extension of slavery. The state's Democrats met in Springfield and affirmed their loyalty to the Union but also urged compromise with the Southern states. The people of Illinois remained divided along sectional lines, and even those who supported the president-elect's stand against the extension of slavery hoped for a way out of the deepening crisis. With Lincoln's grudging approval, Governor Yates dispatched a state delegation to a peace convention in Washington, D.C., called by Virginia.

Illinois played a leading role in the dramatic events that led up to the Civil War. The state produced the two leading politicians of the late antebellum years—Stephen A. Douglas and Abraham Lincoln—and their debates in 1858 and 1860 helped frame the issues that divided the nation. The Republican party in Illinois grew rapidly in the late 1850s, assumed primacy in local elections in the northern counties, and secured control of state government in 1860, but the Democratic party remained a vital force, especially in the southernmost counties. As Abraham Lincoln prepared to leave Illinois in February 1861 for his inauguration in the nation's capital, the people of Illinois looked to the future with the same sense of uncertainty that was shared by other Americans throughout the nation.

Evanston

Around 1834 Abraham Hathaway built a log cabin several miles north of Chicago that is considered the first permanent house in Evanston. Ironically, considering the town's later association with the temperance cause, his abode became widely known as a roadside grocery that provided liquor for travelers. Throughout the 1840s, a small number of farmers and lumbermen lived in houses scattered around the Hathaway establishment. By 1850 Chicago and surrounding communities in northeastern Illinois contained no institutions of higher learning, the closest being Knox College in distant Galesburg. Representatives of the Methodist Episcopal Church resolved to establish a university in the area and, in January 1851, chartered Northwestern University. Although considerable sentiment existed originally for locating the university in Chicago, the institution's first president, the Reverend Clark T. Hinman, dissented and championed a suburban location suitably served by the railroads. Hinman and others expressed concern at the high cost of real estate in Chicago but, more important, rued the city's disreputability. Devout Methodists favored a bucolic setting, rather than a fast-growing city of mixed populations and social classes, for their center of sanctified learning. A site committee considered several locations along Lake Michigan, carefully noting the plans for future railroads to be constructed around Chicago. They chose a tiny settlement situated along the proposed Chicago and Milwaukee Railroad, which commenced operation on January 1, 1855. In October 1853 the university trustees purchased a 379-acre plot of land on which the school and much of the adjacent village was built. They named the community Evanston after a wealthy Chicago physician and one of the school's leading proponents, Dr. John B. Evans.

The Methodist influence on both the town and the university proved unmistakable from the start, no less so than in the unwavering commitment to the temperance crusade. The university charter adopted in 1855 explicitly forbade the sale of any intoxicating beverages (except for medicinal, mechanical, or sacramental purposes) within four miles of the campus. Surrounding suburban communities on Chicago's North Shore such as Wilmette, Winnetka, and Glencoe followed Evanston's lead by banning the sale of alcoholic beverages. In 1863 Evanston incorporated as a town because its residents believed the new legal status would improve the chances of retaining the four-mile limit. Just six years later, however, voters rejected the opportunity to attain city status for fear that the necessary legislation would jeopardize the four-mile limit.

Evanston quickly became one of Chicago's most affluent suburbs, a genteel bedroom community for well-heeled businessmen. Ranked first in per capita value of property among Chicago suburbs in 1870, Evanston lost some of its exclusivity as it grew in the late nineteenth and early twentieth centuries. Still, through the decades, an Evanston address retained its gloss even as the community grew and attracted a more heterogeneous population. At the same time, the community continued to be defined by its temperance ethos. In 1873 Frances Willard resigned as president of the Evanston College for Ladies. After a year at Northwestern University, she left to dedicate herself to the cause of temperance, becoming president of the Chicago Women's Temperance Union and in 1879 national president of the Women's Christian Temperance Union, a post she held for the next nineteen years. Fittingly, the union chose Evanston as the site of its national headquarters.

Stephen A. Douglas

Born on April 23, 1813 in Brandon, Vermont, Douglas moved with his family to upstate New York in 1830. Balking at the length of time required to become an attorney in New York, he headed west where admission to the bar required less formal training and apprenticeship. He lived briefly in Cleveland, Cincinnati, Louisville, and St. Louis before settling in Jacksonville, Illinois, in 1833. He later lived in Quincy before establishing his permanent residence in Chicago. Admitted to the bar in 1834, he quickly subordinated his legal work to politics. A loyal Democrat and passionate follower of Andrew Jackson, Douglas impressed his contemporaries with his energy, passion, and ambition. At the age of twenty-one, he became state's attorney for an eight-county district and in 1836 won election to the lower house of the general assembly. He relentlessly sought political

Stephen A. Douglas, the Little Giant of American politics, before the Civil War. *Illinois State Historical Library*

advancement, holding a series of elective and appointive offices in state government while running unsuccessfully for the U.S. House of Representatives in 1838 and the U.S. Senate in 1842. He finally won election to the House of Representatives in 1843 and remained a national legislator until his death eighteen years later. After serving two terms in the House, he won election to the Senate where he became one of the most influential public figures of the antebellum age.

Standing only five feet four inches tall, Douglas possessed a brashness and combativeness that earned him the nickname Little Giant. An eloquent speaker and fierce debater who packed the Senate galleries when he spoke, he never shied away from conflict and eagerly engaged the most controversial issues of the day. Announcing his unbridled faith in democracy and belief in America's destiny, he emerged as one of the foremost spokesmen of westward expansionism. His blueprint for the nation's future greatness revolved around the construction of a transcontinental railroad and the provision of cheap land to encourage Western settlement. As chairman of both the House and Senate territory committees, he authored and sponsored bills for seven territories (Oregon, Minnesota, Utah, New Mexico, Washington, Kansas, and Nebraska). As an ardent expansionist, he had no compunction about the ruthless removal of the American Indians whose presence in the West impeded the march of civilization.

Douglas never allowed the sensitive issue of slavery in the territories to dampen his enthusiasm for territory making. Determined to find a middle way between abolitionists and Southern proslavery advocates, he played a critical role in the passage of the Compromise of 1850. The furor over the Kansas-Nebraska Act, which he wrote and guided through Congress, severely damaged his standing among Northerners who recoiled at the repeal of the Missouri Compromise. Douglas continued to espouse popular sovereignty during the famed Lincoln-Douglas debates in 1858 but, despite winning re-election that year, lost the support of many Southerners who thought his defense of slavery inadequate. The Democratic party fragmented along sectional lines in 1860, thereby devaluing the presidential nomination he received that year. In his campaign, Douglas argued that the issue of slavery's extension paled before the need to preserve the Union, but he suffered a decisive loss to Abraham Lincoln. In the months before Lincoln's inauguration, Douglas tried to forge a compromise that would avert civil war but succeeded only in ruining his own health. He returned to Illinois dispirited that his beloved nation seemed on the verge of self-destruction. After delivering an impassioned plea for unity to the general assembly in Springfield and to a huge crowd in Chicago, he died on June 3, 1861, of typhoid fever.

Civil War

Despite Abraham Lincoln's attempts to mollify Southerners who expressed their unwillingness to accept him as president, the outcome of the 1860 election propelled the nation into crisis. In December 1860, South Carolina fulfilled its promise to secede from the Union in the event of a Lincoln victory, and several other Southern states joined the exodus. On February 8, 1861, representatives from Georgia, Florida, Alabama, Mississippi, Louisiana, and Texas joined South Carolinians in Montgomery, Alabama, to create the Confederate States of America. Having chosen Jefferson Davis as the first president, the Confederacy commenced operation as an independent nation. Lincoln remained conciliatory but at the same time declared his intention to preserve the Union. Twelve days after leaving Springfield, Lincoln arrived in Washington for his inaugural. Because of threats on his life, the president-elect slipped quietly into the capital at night. After assuming the oath of office, Lincoln hoped to assert the sovereignty of the United States in all of the states without provoking war—a delicate balancing act that ended in failure when Confederate forces fired on a federal fort on April 12, 1861. The bombardment of Fort Sumter in Charleston Harbor, a military attack upon an American military installation that culminated in the seizure of federal property, led Lincoln to issue a call for seventy-five thousand volunteers to suppress the rebellion.

The outbreak of the Civil War produced a jumble of emotions in Illinois. Stephen A. Douglas's impassioned entreaties to the state's Democrats to put the welfare of the nation before the interests of the party kept many potential dissidents loyal, but the Confederate cause attracted many followers throughout areas of southern Illinois. Confederate sympathizers in Williamson County met in Marion and discussed the formation of a new state, "Egypt," that would secede from the United States and ally with the new nation to the south (in retrospect, a likelier prospect if the neighboring slave states of Missouri and Kentucky had joined the Confederacy). Rumors abounded that dissidents would recruit brigades for the Confederacy, destroy bridges and train trestles, and otherwise undermine the war effort in Illinois. Such sentiment soon subsided under a wave of patriotism as leading Democrats such as John A. Logan initially wavered but then affirmed their fealty to the Union. At least in the first months of the conflict, concerns about the loyalty of southern Illinoisans sympathetic to slavery and secession proved unfounded. In the spring of 1861, Illinois filled the federal government's call for six regiments in just five days, and the surplus of volunteers gathering in Springfield included huge numbers of young men from the state's southern counties as well as from the northern regions.

Illinois Governor Richard Yates, an ardent nationalist and outspoken opponent of slavery, denounced the treasonous actions of the Southern states and began organizing volunteer regiments in numbers far exceeding the president's call to arms. After summoning the general assembly into special session, he persuaded the legislators to appropriate $3.5 million for military expenditures. (The special appropriation exceeded Illinois's constitutional debt limit, but the state supreme court upheld the extraordinary action.) Federal authorities in Washington requested that the governor send troops to protect strategically important Cairo, a key port city and railroad hub at the southern tip of the state, and Yates quickly dispatched 595 members of zouave drill teams and militia companies to fortify the community. The makeshift defense force, armed with all the rifles and shotguns that could be found in Chicago dry goods stores, converted empty fairgrounds sheds into temporary barracks and remained until thousands of regular troops arrived along with a flotilla of gunboats.

The U.S. Navy chose Mound City, Illinois, near Cairo on the Ohio River, as its principal freshwater depot. Already possessing shipbuilding enterprises, an iron foundry, and a massive waterfront warehouse, Mound City bested Cairo and Carondelet, Missouri, in the competition for government contracts. The navy leased the shipbuilding factory for forty thousand dollars a year and converted steamboats originally built for transporting cotton to New Orleans into gunboats. Innovative engineers affixed mortars to rafts and keelboats for use against Confederate warships on the Mississippi River, and unemployed steamboat men operated the makeshift watercraft. A riverfront hospital and a national cemetery containing 5,555 Civil War graves came to serve as testament to Mound City's importance in the conflict.

The first volunteers in Illinois received their military training at Camp Yates in Springfield, a cramped and altogether inadequate site at the old state fairgrounds. After the disastrous defeat of Union forces at First Bull Run on July 21, 1861, and the U.S. government's urgent call for an additional half a million volunteers, Illinois began constructing several new training sites. In the following months, military recruits received their training at a number of sites throughout the state, including Chicago, Peoria, Joliet, Quincy, Freeport, Ottawa, and Belleville. Camp Butler, located on

An artist's rendition of Union forces at Fort Prentiss near Cairo, Illinois, guarding the strategically important site at the confluence of the Ohio and Mississippi rivers. *Illinois State Historical Library*

a forty-acre tract six miles east of Springfield, quickly became the largest and busiest training site in the state. The urgent need for fighting men limited the length of the training sessions to an average of thirty or forty days; thousands of new soldiers moved through Camp Butler at a brisk pace and moved on to join other units at distant battlefields. As the war progressed and the Union needed facilities to incarcerate captured Confederate soldiers, Camp Butler and other training sites around the state erected stockades and doubled as military prisons. Camp Butler remained principally a training facility, however, where 114 of the 167 regiments of Illinois infantry, artillery, and cavalry deployed in the war were organized or discharged.

Volunteer regiments, often organized in specific localities, tended to be homogeneous groups. Members of ethnic groups frequently recruited their countrymen into units, and Irish, German, and Scottish brigades abounded. An indeterminate number of blacks enlisted in white regiments, either by passing as white or by serving as support personnel. State and local authorities initially turned away African Americans trying to enlist, but in October 1863 Governor Yates approved the creation of the state's first black regiment, the Twenty-ninth U.S. Colored Infantry. Railroad workers, Galena lead miners, farmers who belonged to the state agricultural society, and Protestant ministers organized their own regiments. The president of Illinois State Normal School left the college and organized a teachers' regiment. Given the dearth of experienced military personnel, the selection of regiment leaders proved haphazard. Mexican War veterans often assumed command, but in their absence, volunteers usually selected one of their own to become an officer. Typically, the organizer of a regiment simply assumed command. Patriotic zeal commonly substituted for experience and professionalism.

Voluntarism proved a great success in 1861, so much so that the state turned away more than one-fourth of the companies formed through local initiative and compelled many eager Illinoisans to enlist in Missouri regiments. By October 1861, Illinois regiments outnumbered those from New York. Governor Yates boasted of the surplus numbers of men who eagerly came forward to enlist, but by the spring of 1862, meeting the state's quotas had become noticeably more difficult. The enthusiasm for military service had ebbed throughout Illinois, for a number of reasons. The expectation of a speedy victory over the Confederates had been dashed, replaced by a rising sense of disillusionment. The poor performance of Union forces, underscored by substandard military leadership, resulted in a series of inglorious defeats in engagements throughout the nation. While Confederate armies compiled notable victories with alarming frequency, a large number of Illinois regiments received disappointing assignments guarding prisoners and patrolling the grounds in and around Cairo. Kept from seeking glory on the battlefield, many young men preferred to remain at home and take advantage of the abundant money-making opportunities in a thriving wartime economy. The governor desperately sought to avoid imposing a draft to fill the state's quotas, but the flood of volunteers had dwindled to a trickle after a year of fighting.

Beginning in the summer of 1862 and continuing for the duration of the war, Illinois compensated for the decline in volunteers by offering cash bounties to prospective enlistees and by instituting a draft. Eager to "escape the disgrace of conscription," Governor Yates and other state officials coordinated an extensive campaign of community pressure to maintain adequate numbers of volunteers. Illinois found it unnecessary to implement a draft in 1862, but the need for such measures in other states resulted in the passage in 1863 by the U.S. Congress of the first conscription act in the nation's history. Democrats and other critics of the war immediately criticized the conscription act, especially the commutation clause by which men could avoid the draft by paying three hundred dollars. The fact that men of means could avoid military service, unlike those unable to pay the commutation fee, led to charges that the war had become a poor man's fight.[1]

The conscription law, which mandated a house-by-house canvass by draft officials to identify eligible recruits, sparked new levels of resistance among the Illinois populace. "Opposition was encountered in almost every house," according to the federal official in charge of conscription, and originally passive resistance to the war now became much more widespread and intense. Evasion usually entailed the refusal to give enrolling officers information about residents or the providing of fictitious names, but resistance to the draft sometimes turned violent. In Chicago a mob attacked a conscription official, pelting him with bricks and leaving him lying unconscious in the street with scalp lacerations and a skull fracture. Enrollment officers in Olney temporarily suspended operations when a mob of five hundred resisters threatened to destroy the local draft office and demanded that the conscription rolls be handed over; an enrollment officer escaped to St. Louis with the lists of potential draftees, and the military had to be summoned to restore order. The most formidable opposition to the draft materialized in Williamson County, where officials declared martial law in Marion and dispatched two hundred cavalrymen to protect enrolling officers. Cursed, assaulted, shot at, and forced to relinquish their records, enrollment officials struggled to complete their tasks and frequently did so only with military escorts.[2]

In northern Illinois, especially in the Chicago area, the threat of the draft sent thousands of men fleeing the state. Governor Yates thought the problem of "skedaddlers" serious enough that he asked the War Department to declare martial law in northern Illinois to stanch the flow of men to Canada. The U.S. government responded by establishing a new system, which obligated all men leaving the state to obtain a passport and post a bond. Increased scrutiny by military and civil personnel resulted in the arrest of an estimated one hundred skedaddlers in Chicago on one day in 1862. The passport system, which Illinois officials judged effective, remained in effect until Washington policy makers no longer found the draft necessary.

Although many Illinoisans bitterly opposed conscription and resisted registration, the state met its induction quotas in the fall of 1863 and the spring of 1864 and thus avoided having to draft anyone. Lincoln's request in July 1864 for 500,000 more soldiers exhausted the supply of volunteers, however, and the state conducted its first draft on September 19, 1864. The president issued a call for another 300,000 troops on December 19, and again Illinois had to rely on the draft to meet its allotment. Although the two Illinois drafts identified a total of 32,279 conscripts, government officials inducted only 3,537 men. The others avoided service through a variety of methods, the largest number having failed their physical examinations. Some men paid the three-hundred-dollar commutation fee until the government closed that loophole in February 1864; afterwards, substitution still remained possible, and the price soared in a competitive market.

Some men paid as much as twelve hundred dollars to secure a substitute, and others sought to minimize expenses by purchasing draft insurance policies. For the nominal fee of two hundred dollars, for example, the Chicago Draft Insurance Company pledged to provide an able-bodied substitute for any policyholder who fell victim to the draft.

Despite the unpopularity of the draft and the state's increasing difficulty in meeting its quotas, Illinois provided 259,092 men to the Union Army and Navy during the course of the Civil War (approximately 15 percent of the state's population). African American regiments, organized for the first time in 1863, officially contained 1,811 men. All-white units included 150 infantry regiments, 17 cavalry regiments, 2 light artillery regiments, 8 independent artillery batteries, and 2,224 sailors and marines. Military officials reported 34,834 Illinois military men killed during the war (a casualty rate of 13.4 percent), of whom 22,786 died of diseases resulting from unsanitary living conditions, 5,874 perished in combat, 4,020 succumbed to wounds suffered in battle, and 2,154 died of other causes. Tens of thousands more returned to their homes after the war limping, on crutches, or bearing less visible wounds.

Although Illinois soldiers participated in a number of military campaigns spread throughout the nation, most of the state's regiments saw action in the western theater of the war. At the outset, Illinois troops took the field in Missouri to help counter the threat from secessionist forces. Next the state's regiments moved to western Kentucky and engaged Confederate forces at Fort Henry on the Tennessee River and Fort Donelson on the Cumberland River, under the leadership of General Ulysses S. Grant, a resident of Illinois who had initially commanded the Union's defensive forces at Cairo. Illinois troops under Grant's command at Shiloh paid a terrible price in one of the war's bloodiest battles, accounting for fully one-third of the Union force's 13,047 casualties in that engagement. An Illinois cavalry unit played a prominent role in the battle at Gettysburg, and the state's soldiers also fought at Vicksburg and Chattanooga; more than fifty Illinois regiments participated in General William T. Sherman's victorious march through Georgia in the last weeks of the war.

Illinois furnished 177 generals to the Union Army, none more prominent than Ulysses S. Grant. A native of Ohio and graduate of West Point who fought in the Mexican War, Grant left the army and worked with scant success at a series of jobs in St. Louis before moving to Galena, Illinois, to work in his brother's leather shop. When the Civil War began, he led a volunteer company from Galena to Springfield and, after serving as a quartermaster for several months, received a general's commission thanks to the intervention of an influential friend, Congressman Elihu Washburne of Galena. From his post at Cairo, Grant led Union forces to victory at several locations in the war's western theater. His successes in the West at a time when U.S. armies fared poorly everywhere else brought him to the attention of President Lincoln. Desperate for the brand of aggressive lead-ership Grant had exhibited at Fort Donelson, Shiloh, and Vicksburg, Lin-coln made him the supreme commander of all Union armies. In 1864–1865, Grant relentlessly pursued and attacked Confederate armies in a series of battles that soaked the Virginia countryside in blood. Critics called him a butcher for his merciless application of total warfare, but Grant brought the fratricidal struggle to a close and became the preemi-nent Union military hero.

On the home front, hundreds of thousands of loyal citizens out of uni-form made substantial contributions to the Union war effort. Illinois pro-duced relatively few manufactured goods in comparison with more heavily industrialized states in the Northeast. Its primary contribution came in the provision of farm products. To offset manpower shortages, farmwives and males either too young or too old for military service worked more often in the fields. In addition, the purchase of labor-saving equipment made in Chicago and Moline with income from rising prices and enlistment boun-ties allowed agricultural production to increase and to meet the army's in-creased demand for food. Crops and livestock reached markets faster than ever before because of the expansion of the state's railroads; although the shortage of manpower and materials slowed the construction of new lines, existing tributaries added twelve hundred miles of track during the war. In the prevailing spirit of patriotism, the Illinois Central Railroad lowered its prices so that farmers could make their mortgage payments, and it cham-pioned the cause of crop diversification by urging farmers to plant differ-ent crops that offered the prospect of higher prices.

Fund-raising efforts proliferated throughout the state, much of the money raised going to improve sanitary facilities in military encampments and training posts. A fair held in Chicago in 1863, at which attendees bought donated articles such as torn banners and other war relics, raised $86,000 for sanitation. A second fair, held in 1865, which auctioned the original draft of the Emancipation Proclamation provided by President Lin-coln for $3,000, broke all existing records by raising $240,000. Dozens of other communities across the state followed suit by holding their own auc-tions, bazaars, and benefit concerts, most of them organized by women.

Illinois women contributed to the war effort in a variety of ways, most notably in their efforts to improve sanitation and the quality of medical care provided the soldiers. Some women went to work as nurses and aides in army camps and the makeshift hospitals established near battlefields, ministering to the wounded and infirm. Mary Ann Bickerdyke, a Galesburg widow with nursing experience, attained considerable fame as the "cy-clone in calico" who spearheaded the crusade for more sanitary conditions in military hospitals. During the course of the war, she accompanied Illi-nois detachments and worked in infirmaries established near nineteen bat-tlegrounds. Despite resistance from army officers and surgeons who resented the intrusion of an aggressive female, Bickerdyke succeeded in initiating much-needed reforms. Before her intervention, wounded soldiers in their blood-soaked, soiled uniforms typically lay on the same filthy sheets until their medical conditions changed or their tattered linens had to be destroyed. Conditions improved dramatically and fewer secondary infections developed when military authorities complied with her demands that laundries be provided at hospitals and that orderlies begin scrubbing beds and floors. The caustic and assertive Bickerdyke made few friends when she questioned the competence of army physicians and clashed with high-ranking officers, but even her staunchest critics conceded the importance of her contributions.[3]

Women who were less adventurous than Bickerdyke worked for better sanitation and health care while remaining at the home front. Rolling bandages, collecting and assembling hospital supplies, and soliciting funds for medical care, they provided indispensable assistance to medical personnel. Aid societies founded by women, often under the auspices of churches and religious organizations, affiliated with or transformed into state and local sanitary commissions. Women also took the lead in caring for the soldiers' dependent families, a critically important contribution in the years before the founding of the Red Cross when no government agencies provided such aid. In Chicago, churchwomen founded a shelter for wounded soldiers and paroled prisoners. At war's end, the Soldiers' Rest Home in the Windy City also fed and temporarily housed returning servicemen.

Reform-minded Illinoisans concerned with issues of public health and sanitation blanched at the treatment of Confederate soldiers in the state's military prisons. As many as thirty thousand Confederate prisoners occupied Camp Douglas, situated at the southern edge of Chicago, at one time. The inmates suffered through an especially harsh winter in 1861–1862, plodding through ice and snow in the bitter winds blowing from frozen Lake Michigan. Severe overcrowding, inadequate sanitation, and the consumption of Chicago's untreated water resulted in an outbreak of typhoid fever; the ingestion of milk from diseased cows led to a diphtheria epidemic and a soaring mortality rate. According to Union officials, more than four thousand Confederate prisoners, approximately 15 percent of the total inmate population, died in Camp Douglas.

Although conditions at Camp Douglas elicited considerable protest from reformers, its reputation paled in comparison with that of the prison constructed at Rock Island, Illinois. Situated in the Mississippi River between Illinois and Iowa, Rock Island had been vacant since 1836 when the government closed a fort there. In 1863 construction began on an arsenal that, at the time of its completion four years later, became the world's largest. (The Rock Island Arsenal produced ordnance used in every American military involvement between the Civil War and Operation Desert Storm.) The Rock Island Prison, known as the "Andersonville of the

North," received the first Confederate prisoners on December 3, 1863. Of the twelve thousand prisoners incarcerated there, approximately two thousand died before the war's end—a 16 percent fatality rate not appreciably different from Camp Douglas's 15 percent, but far below that of Andersonville Prison, the South's infamous facility where the death rate exceeded 30 percent. Unfortunately for Rock Island's historical reputation, however, Margaret Mitchell consigned the fictional Ashley Wilkes to "unimaginable torments" there in her epic Civil War novel, *Gone with the Wind*. Writing that Yankee jailers gave only one blanket to every three prisoners and callously denied them adequate medical care, Mitchell erroneously reported that three-fourths of the inmates at Rock Island never saw the South again. Her hyperbole notwithstanding, conditions at the Rock Island Prison roughly approximated those at Camp Douglas and most other Northern prisons of the time.[4]

Lurid tales of unspeakable conditions and widespread suffering in its military prisons, though often exaggerated, fed the persistent antiwar sentiment in the state of Illinois. Latent sympathy for the Confederate cause, suppressed in the war's early months, surfaced increasingly as casualties mounted and the swift victory confidently predicted for Union forces failed to materialize. "Secession is deeper and stronger here than you have

Union soldiers and Confederate prisoners pose for a photograph at Rock Island Prison. The prison became infamous because of Margaret Mitchell's inaccurate descriptions of the treatment of Confederate prisoners there in *Gone with the Wind*.
Illinois State Historical Library

any idea," Governor Yates wrote to Illinois Senator Lyman Trumbull. "Its advocates are numerous and powerful, and respectable." The southern counties remained a secessionist stronghold, but substantial numbers of dissidents hailed from other areas of the state as well. Antiabolitionist rhetoric warning of job competition from emancipated slaves found receptive audiences among city laborers, especially among the Irish and other ethnic workers in Chicago. Arguing that Illinois possessed closer economic ties to the South than to the Northeast, some dissenters called for secession by Midwestern states and the establishment of an independent Northwest Confederacy. Outspoken antiwar Democrats became known as Copperheads, named after the poisonous snakes that strike suddenly from hiding, and they mounted bolder rhetorical attacks against the government as opposition to the war effort increased among the population.[5]

Governor Yates's avid prosecution of the war outraged antiwar Democrats, who used the occasion of a constitutional convention to further their cause. The state's population having doubled since the ratification of the 1848 constitution, the electorate in 1860 approved the drafting of a new governing document. As a result of the statewide elections held in 1861, the convention included forty-five Democrats and only twenty-one Republicans. Convinced of their omnipotence and determined to revise state government completely, the Democrats refused to work cooperatively with the general assembly. Claiming legislative authority in Illinois, a majority of the constitutional convention members voted to ratify an amendment to the U.S. Constitution, discussed the appointment of a new U.S. senator, and sent urgent communications to military commanders in the field.

Believing it had usurped the authority of the general assembly, the constitutional convention targeted Governor Yates as well. The Democrats advanced proposals to halve the length of the governor's term and to create a commission to assume the governor's wartime powers. They charged that Yates had authorized the expenditure of more funds for military purchases than was allocated in Washington, but their efforts to uncover a scandal implicating the governor backfired. Widely known for his indefatigable efforts on behalf of Illinois soldiers, Yates traveled to the bloodiest battle sites where the state's regiments fought and supervised the delivery of medical supplies to the front. Soldiers' families appreciated his attention to the needs of Illinoisans in uniform and resented attacks upon his solicitousness. The governor complied with the constitutional convention for a month but became exasperated with its intrusions and finally broke off all communication. Aware that public sentiment had shifted against their actions, the convention delegates announced a new plan to raise funds for improved medical care of the soldiers.

After repeated misadventures, the convention finally produced a new document that proved as controversial as the delegates' earlier behavior. The proposed constitution sought to curtail railroad construction, abolish bank charters, gerrymander the general assembly to the detriment of the populous northern counties, and unseat Republican officeholders in the middle of their terms while allowing some Democratic bureaucrats to finish theirs. A decisive majority of the delegates voted affirmatively, but most of the Republicans simply refused to sign the document. Widely condemned by Republican newspapers and denounced by banks and other business interests, the constitution failed to pass in a special June 1862 referendum by a vote of 141,103 to 125,152; Illinois soldiers concurred in their absentee ballots by a vote of 10,151 to 1,687.

Although the Illinois electorate rejected the new constitution, dissatisfaction with the Republicans' conduct of the war intensified in late 1862. President Lincoln's pursuit of a middle course left him open to reproof from both wings of his party, from Senator Orville H. Browning and the conservatives as well as from Senator Lyman Trumbull and the radicals. The president's decision to countermand General John C. Fremont's order freeing the slaves of Missouri rebels proved highly unpopular in Illinois, and the *Chicago Tribune* continually urged Lincoln to be bolder in his opposition to slavery. Governor Yates repeatedly prodded the president to employ sterner measures against the rebels and to hasten the emancipation of the slaves. At last yielding to his own predilections and to the entreaties of the Republican party's abolitionist wing, the president resolved to raise the issue of emancipation after a significant Union military victory and to make the struggle to reunite the nation a war to end slavery. His issuance of the Emancipation Proclamation after the triumph of the Union army at Antietam, Maryland, in September 1862 freed slaves behind Confederate lines and recast the war to preserve the Union as a struggle for freedom. Critics hoping for more than a war measure based upon presidential authority lambasted Lincoln's decision to stop short of eradicating slavery in the border states and areas of the Confederacy under Union occupation. His late-blooming appetite for abolitionism whetted, in the last months of the war the president pressed for the end of slavery in loyal states where it still existed (such as Maryland, Delaware, Kentucky, and Missouri) and championed the Thirteenth Amendment, which officially terminated slavery.

The Emancipation Proclamation infuriated the majority of Illinois Democrats, who limited their support to restoring "the Union as it was, the Constitution as it is, and the negroes where they are." The rapidly increasing number of freed slaves ("contrabands") spreading through Illinois by train from Cairo, argued the Democrats, offered merely a taste of future developments if the Union prevailed. The result would be increased competition for jobs between white labor and free blacks. Discussion of the growing fear and uncertainty engendered by the Emancipation Proclamation permeated the campaign trail in the weeks preceding the November 1862 election. The Democrats won a majority in the general assembly that year (thir-

teen to twelve in the senate, fifty-four to thirty-two in the house of representatives) as well as eight of Illinois's fourteen seats in the U.S. Congress.[6]

The 1863 legislative session opened with the Democratic majority issu-
ing a series of resolutions, which lambasted Lincoln for having issued the
Emancipation Proclamation, advocated an armistice that would allow the
South to rejoin the Union with slavery preserved, disclaimed the war as an
abolitionist plot hatched in New England, and called for the cessation of
military recruitment. To replace Republican Orville H. Browning in the
U.S. Senate, the general assembly elected a Peace Democrat, William A.
Richardson. In the state house of representatives, Democratic majorities
enumerated fifteen grievances against Yates and Lincoln and selected representatives to represent Illinois at a peace convention in Louisville, Kentucky. Yates vetoed an apportionment bill passed by the general assembly
and, before the measure could be passed over his veto, invoked an obscure
statute to prorogue both houses of the state legislature.

Peace Democrats let loose a storm of protest against Governor Yates for
proroguing the general assembly, just as they assailed President Lincoln for
his assumption of extraordinary executive powers during the war. Claiming that disloyalty in the North seriously curtailed the war effort, Lincoln
declared a national emergency and took steps to silence dissent. In 1862
he suspended the writ of habeas corpus and countenanced the arrest and
trial in military rather than civilian courts of Democrats who had been
critical of the administration. On June 17, 1863, a crowd of Democrats estimated at forty thousand gathered at Camp Yates a mile from the state
capitol to call for the immediate end of the war without military victory. A
cross section of Illinois Democrats, the gathering included some of the
state's wealthiest and most influential citizens; they condemned the rampant violations of constitutional rights perpetrated by Lincoln and Yates
and called for a national convention to reconstruct the Union. Republicans responded with their own mass meeting on September 3, 1863, at
which the governor and several Union generals argued the necessity of
continuing the war. President Lincoln sent a lengthy, closely reasoned letter dismissing the possibility of compromise and confirming his intention
of prosecuting the war to a successful conclusion.

No matter how large or respectable the opposition to the war in his native state, President Lincoln continued to defend the suspension of habeas
corpus and other extraordinary measures designed to stifle dissent. In 1863
the U.S. Congress bowed to pressure from the military and specifically affirmed the president's right to suspend the rights of individuals. The suppression of dissent included the press, and government officials silenced
newspapers that imprudently criticized the president or the military leadership. Union soldiers sacked the office of the *Bloomington Times* and threw
the type from the *Chester Picket Guard* into the street. Local officials closed
the *Jonesboro Gazette* for six weeks while soldiers searched for deserters in

the surrounding area. In the most celebrated instance, General Ambrose Burnside halted publication of the *Chicago Times* because of editor Wilbur F. Storey's incessant criticism of President Lincoln. When Lyman Trumbull and other leading Republicans condemned the action and vigorously defended the freedom of the press, Lincoln lifted the ban on the *Times* two days later. The president's capitulation pleased civil libertarians, but a number of prominent Republicans rued his decision and regretted that an example had not been made of the seditious Chicago editor.

Tension between Union loyalists and Confederate sympathizers persisted throughout the war. Guerilla bands from Missouri roamed the southwestern counties of Illinois, sometimes skirmishing with Union troops. Nightriders from both sides conducted campaigns of terror against their enemies, engaging in murder, arson, and pillage. Union soldiers dispersed Confederate mobs and pursued draft resisters and deserters. In less than six months, according to one study of dissent in Illinois during the Civil War, the authorities apprehended two thousand deserters, eight hundred in Williamson, Perry, Saline, and Jackson counties alone. At one point, the frequency of desertion in Cairo reduced the number of men left in a regiment there to thirty-five.

Both Union loyalists and Confederate sympathizers joined secret societies to advance their causes. Union leagues proliferated throughout the North in an effort to support Republican candidates at election time and to shore up morale through the use of propaganda. In Illinois as elsewhere throughout the North, Copperhead organizations often operated secretly to obstruct the draft, practice sabotage, and otherwise instigate dissent. The Knights of the Golden Circle, a secret society that originated in the South, changed its name to the Order of the American Knights in 1863 and to the Sons of Liberty in 1864. That year, some members of the Sons of Liberty purportedly conspired with Confederate spies to launch an armed rebellion in Illinois, Indiana, Ohio, Kentucky, and Missouri. The most zealous members of the conspiracy envisioned the ultimate creation of an independent nation in the Midwest, while the less ambitious simply plotted to free Confederate prisoners in the North, burn cities, and destroy rail lines to ease the pressure on the South. In Illinois, Confederate forces hiding near Mattoon and members of the Sons of Liberty planned to attack Camp Douglas, link up with freed prisoners of war from Rock Island and Camp Butler, and seize the state house in Springfield. The plan never unfolded, however, and membership in the Sons of Liberty evaporated as the war steadily turned in favor of Union armies. Several reputed leaders of the conspiracy, including former mayor of Chicago Buckner S. Morris, stood trial for treason. A military tribunal acquitted Morris but sent one man to prison for his role in the Northwest Conspiracy.

The most violent clash between dissidents and the war's supporters occurred in Charleston, Illinois, a noted center of Confederate sympathy.

Union soldiers stationed nearby and others returning home on leave objected to some Copperheads' open expressions of disloyalty, and in early
1864 there resulted a number of violent confrontations in Coles and Edgar
counties. On March 28, 1864, furloughed members of companies C and G
of the Fifty-fourth Illinois Infantry exchanged insults with a group of Copperhead Democrats in the Charleston Courthouse Square. Subsequent investigations failed to establish the precise sequence of events or pinpoint
the exact exchange of taunts that led the combatants to the use of
firearms. In any event, the two groups suddenly began shooting at each
other within the courthouse and outside in the adjacent square. When the
fighting subsided, the list of casualties included nine dead (six Union soldiers, two Democrats, and a Republican civilian) and twelve wounded
(four soldiers and eight bystanders), making the Charleston Riot in all likelihood the most lethal Civil War home front disturbance except for the
New York City Draft Riot of 1863. U.S. troops from Mattoon arrived by
train to restore order, initially seized fifty prisoners, and eventually de-
tained fifteen Democrats for various offenses; local juries later acquitted
two Copperheads brought to trial for murder.

The outburst at Charleston in March 1864 underscored the level of divisiveness in Illinois and in other parts of the North as Abraham Lincoln prepared to run for reelection. Although hopes for a Union victory seemed entirely more realistic than had appeared one or two years earlier, the war
continued in all its ferocity. In fact, as the 1864 campaign began, Union
armies engaged in the Wilderness Campaign experienced some of the dead-
liest fighting of the war. Northern partisans who had earlier cheered General
Grant's inexorable pursuit of his Confederate foes blanched at the horrifying
casualty figures amassed in Virginia and excoriated Lincoln for continuing
to support the general they now called the Butcher. As the degree of war
weariness intensified, many civilians called for peace at any price or at least
some exploration of the possibility of compromise with the South. The situation looked bleak for the president in Illinois, where the Democrats in the
general assembly blocked a law proposed by Joseph Medill, owner of the
Chicago Tribune, to permit Union soldiers to cast absentee ballots from the
field. In private correspondence, Lincoln wrote of his belief that he would
likely fail to carry Illinois and lose the 1864 election.

General George B. McClellan, the Democratic nominee for president,
confirmed his loyalty to the Union cause, but his party approved a platform that roundly denounced the war. Disgruntled Republicans critical of
Lincoln's wartime leadership, especially German Americans, lined up behind General John C. Fremont, who ran independently after having been
denied his party's nomination. Even though Lincoln faced formidable
opponents, the military events of the fall of 1864 worked in his behalf. A
sudden burst of Union victories—by David Farragut at Mobile, William T.
Sherman in Atlanta, and Philip Sheridan in the Shenandoah Valley in

Virginia—made clear the Confederacy's desperate and rapidly deteriorating situation. Fremont eventually withdrew from the race, and the Republicans argued persuasively that a vote for McClellan "would be a vote for the rebellion when it was about to fail, a vote for slavery when it had been abolished, and a vote for disunion when reunion had almost been achieved." Lincoln defeated McClellan by 2,203,831 votes to 1,797,019 and won Illinois by a margin of 30,736 votes. The Republicans scored a number of victories in the state, electing Major General Richard J. Oglesby governor and gaining control of the general assembly. The Republican general assembly awarded Richard Yates a seat in the U.S. Senate, ratified the Thirteenth Amendment (written by Lyman Trumbull) abolishing slavery, and expunged the Black Laws from the Illinois statute books.[7]

Robert E. Lee's surrender to Ulysses S. Grant at Appomattox Courthouse on April 9, 1865, signaled the end of the war and launched a joyful celebration throughout the victorious North. President Lincoln encouraged citizens to override the vindictive Republicans who sought to punish the South and suggested instead treating the vanquished Confederates with leniency so that the necessary healing and reconciliation could begin immediately. President Lincoln, however, died before he could implement this plan. He was fatally shot at Ford's Theater in Washington, D.C., by an embittered Southern sympathizer, John Wilkes Booth. Millions mourned as a funeral train covered with black cloth slowly carried the martyred president's corpse back to Springfield for burial in Oak Ridge Cemetery. In almost all quarters, disapproval of the president yielded to sorrow and admiration. Even the *Chicago Times,* perhaps the president's most virulent critic during the war, acknowledged the calamity befalling the nation: "It is hard to conceive of the occurrence of any event which would be so shocking to the sensibilities of the country, occasion sorrow so profound, and create apprehensions and forebodings so painful, as the event which today absorbs all minds and agitates the public heart to its lowest depths."[8]

On May 24, 1865, three weeks after Abraham Lincoln's burial, Illinois regiments joined the other Western armies in a final review before thousands of onlookers in Washington, D.C. The troops triumphantly paraded by the review stands along Pennsylvania Avenue, as the Eastern armies had done the day before. In Illinois in subsequent weeks, many veterans marched again in parades and participated in local celebrations honoring their contributions. Soldiers and civilians alike had made tremendous sacrifices in the preceding four years and could take satisfaction in the role they had played in the preservation of the Union. Many no doubt sought the return of the conditions prevalent a few years before, but the end of the war brought unprecedented changes as Illinois felt the overwhelming impact of industrialization, immigration, and urbanization. A largely agricultural society was poised on the threshold of modernization, about to become a modern technological state.

Cairo   ~~KOYO 6666418~~

Early boosters predicted that Cairo, situated at the confluence of the Ohio and Mississippi rivers, would become a
major entrepôt for the steamboat trade and would surpass
Cincinnati, Louisville, and St. Louis in size and importance. Because of its proximity to southern Illinois's vast
coalfields, these same enthusiasts foresaw Cairo becoming
the Pittsburgh of the West. Impressed by the city's geographical blessings, boosters even recommended that the nation's capital be
moved there from Washington, D.C. Such optimism proved unfounded,
however, and Cairo remained a relatively small community plagued by
regular flooding and modest economic development.

Slow population growth and speculative failure characterized its early
years. In 1818 a Baltimore businessman purchased land and incorporated
the city of Cairo, but when he died a year later the site reverted to the government. In the late 1830s, the Cairo City and Canal Company acquired the
property and began to build levees, warehouses, stores, and other facilities
in expectation of its becoming the southern terminus of the Illinois Central
Railroad. When economic depression forced the halt to railroad construction in 1840, the community sank swiftly into decline, and in one year the
population fell from about two thousand to one hundred. In 1846 share-
holders in the Cairo City and Canal Company sold their depleted stock to a
new company, the Cairo Property Trust, whose stockholders in New York
City, Syracuse, Philadelphia, and Boston eagerly anticipated the resumption
of work on the Illinois Central Railroad. Without rail connections northward, Cairo languished as a river port. Many boats bypassed the city because
of low water, inadequate docks and wharves, epidemics, steamboat disasters,
and ice in the winter months; its reputation as a lawless haven for drifters,
vagrants, and criminals minimized population growth as well.

The Illinois Central Railroad finally reached Cairo in 1856, and the local
economy registered some improvement. New enterprises opening there included a railroad depot, a whiskey distillery, several slaughterhouses, eight
hotels, and a flour mill. Nevertheless, investors continued to complain
about the limited population growth (permanent residents numbered only
2,188 in 1860) and the dearth of industry. Citizens of Cairo chafed at what
they considered unfair treatment by the northern counties of the state.
Considerable sympathy existed for the Confederate cause, and the editor
of the *Cairo Weekly Times and Delta* suggested that the city would be better
off as the capital of the new state of Southern Illinois. Because of the considerable support for the Confederacy in Little Egypt and the strategic importance of Cairo, the governor of Illinois sent thousands of troops to the

city at the outbreak of the Civil War. The termination of river trade with the South and the government's failure to pay the troops stationed in Cairo severely damaged the community's economy; the situation worsened with the imposition of martial law because of rampant drinking, prostitution, gambling, and violence. The reopening of the Mississippi River in June 1862 then revivified the local economy and launched a war boom that lasted for several years. By the end of the Civil War, Cairo's population had grown to 8,569 (6,486 whites and 2,083 blacks). Local speculators hoped that this sudden growth presaged greater expansion in future years, but the number of residents remained relatively constant, and the sale of lots declined in the late 1860s. Even the arrival of several additional railroads after the Civil War failed to stimulate growth, and the results of the 1870 census showed that population had fallen to 6,267.

John A. Logan

Despite the fact that his loyalty to the Union remained in doubt for some time after the beginning of the Civil War, by the end of the conflict John A. Logan stood second in reputation only to Ulysses S. Grant among Illinois military men. Born in Jackson County, Illinois, on February 9, 1826, Logan attended schools in Jackson and Randolph counties and then served as a second lieutenant in the Mexican War. After studying law at the University of Louisville, he served as a prosecuting attorney in southern Illinois for several years before winning election to the general assembly as a Jacksonian Democrat in 1852. Logan achieved notoriety in Springfield as the champion of legislation that barred free blacks from the state. Elected to the U.S. House of Representatives in 1858, he quickly allied himself with Southern congressmen and became a fierce defender of slavery. In 1860 Logan vainly supported Stephen A. Douglas for president but won reelection to the House by a landslide.

After the Civil War began and Douglas passionately urged Illinoisans to remain loyal to the Union, Logan said nothing at all. When his brother-in-law enlisted in a company from southern Illinois that fought for the Confederacy, Logan failed to denounce his relative's decision. After two months of silence, interpreted in many quarters as support for the South, Logan finally affirmed his loyalty to the North and helped recruit a regiment in the Union army. The esteemed congressman's belated avowal of loyalty undoubtedly played a role in offsetting secessionist sentiment in Little Egypt.

Logan's exploits during the war won him acclaim as a fearless warrior and able leader. After being severely wounded at Fort Donelson, he won promotion to the rank of brigadier general. Promoted again to the rank of major general, he served with great distinction at Vicksburg and in the

John A. Logan, an influential politician from southern Illinois, opposed Lincoln before the Civil War but remained loyal to the United States and became a Union general. *Chicago Historical Society*

Georgia campaign under William T. Sherman. Called Black Jack because of his dark complexion and bushy moustache, Logan returned to southern Illinois in 1864 to campaign as a War Democrat for Abraham Lincoln's re-election. Illinois politicians cited his speeches as a key factor in that year's success for the incumbent president and other Republican candidates. Logan rejoined Sherman's army and participated in the final Union offensive through the Carolinas and Virginia.

After the war, Logan completed his political odyssey by switching to the Republican party and helping to found the Grand Army of the Republic, a powerful veterans' organization closely allied with the GOP. Elected to the U.S. House of Representatives in 1866, he consorted with Radical Republicans, censured former Confederates, and served as a manager during the impeachment trial of President Andrew Johnson. Elected to the U.S. Senate in 1871, he became one of the foremost spokesmen in Congress for veterans' interests. In 1884 he sought the Republican nomination for president but finished behind James G. Blaine and had to settle for the second spot on the ticket. He campaigned vigorously as the vice presidential candidate, but Blaine lost that year to Grover Cleveland. Reelected to the Senate in 1885, Logan served slightly more than a year before his death on December 26, 1886. Democrats denounced Logan as an opportunist and perennial office-seeker without principle, whereas Republicans praised him as a successful military commander and one of the nation's most prominent politicians of the Gilded Age.

A Modernizing World

In the years comprising roughly the last one-third of the nineteenth century, Illinois underwent a remarkable transformation from a sparsely populated frontier to the nation's third leading industrial state. The arrival of great numbers of immigrants made the population more heterogeneous than ever before. As factories, streetcar lines, and commercial emporiums sprawled across expanding cityscapes, the countryside saw remarkable changes as well. A veritable agricultural revolution accompanied the industrial revolution as scientific advances created a new commercialized farming. Phenomenal economic growth brought inestimable benefits to producers and consumers, but it came unevenly in boom-and-bust cycles. Daring entrepreneurs amassed great fortunes and lived opulently, while nearby there huddled the impoverished workers whose labor fueled the massive industrial engine. Real wages rose and a significant number of workers ascended into the comfort and security of the middle class, but recurrent labor unrest and agrarian discontent underscored both the shortcomings of the emerging industrial system and the yawning inequality between the upper classes and the masses. The cost of modernization could be measured in the turmoil and upheaval that beset Illinois in the last decades of the nineteenth century.

Following the end of the Civil War, residents of Illinois dealt with a number of issues that had been left unresolved during previous years. The exigencies of the war had kept the general assembly from immediately taking advantage of the Morrill Act of 1862, for example. Under the auspices of the bill introduced by Senator Justin Morrill of Vermont, every loyal state received 30,000 acres of public land for each of its senators and representatives in the U.S. Congress. Revenue from the sale of land, which for Illinois totaled 480,000 acres, could then be used for the construction of a college of agriculture and mechanical arts. Several private colleges in the state wanted to divide the federal endowment, and an equal number of communities competed to be the site of a new land grant college. Boosters from Logan, McLean, and Morgan counties made especially generous bids to the general assembly but lost out to Champaign County, which subsequently built the college on unsettled land between the hamlets of Champaign and Urbana. The first male students attended classes at Illinois Industrial University in 1868; by 1871 a few women's names had appeared on class rolls. The university's first president, John Milton Gregory, expanded the curriculum to add languages, literature, natural sciences, and the fine arts to agriculture, mechanical, and other vocational courses. In recognition of these changes, Illinois Industrial University became the University of Illinois in 1885.

The end of the war also turned attention to what many people considered the inadequacy of the state capitol in Springfield. The steady expansion of government activities, brought into bold relief during the war when agencies operated out of hallways and tiny rooms in the capitol, made the compact statehouse on the city's downtown square effectively out of date less than thirty years after its construction. Arguing that tiny provincial Springfield had proved deficient as well, in 1865 Chicago, Peoria, Decatur, and Jacksonville submitted bids to the general assembly to be designated the new state capital. The good citizens of Springfield fought back, offering two hundred thousand dollars toward the cost of building a new capitol on a seven-acre plot donated by the city to the state. Responding to complaints about the lack of good overnight accommodations as befitted a capital city, Springfield boosters hurriedly completed the stately Leland Hotel. In 1867 the general assembly voted to accept Springfield's offer, and construction on the new statehouse began. In 1874, even as construction continued, state officials began occupying portions of the new capitol, with completion of the building (at a final cost of $4.5 million) coming eventually in 1884. The state bought the old capitol building, which had provided office space for Sangamon County in the interim, and restored it in 1961.

Just as the old capitol building seemed hopelessly outdated for a growing, modernizing state, so too did the Illinois constitution. Lamenting the failure to approve a new constitution in 1862, Governor Richard Oglesby called for another attempt after the war. In 1867 the general assembly mandated a public referendum, and the following year an apparently apathetic electorate approved the proposition by a scant 704 votes. Of the eighty-five delegates who traveled to Springfield in December 1869 for Illinois's third constitutional convention, Republicans outnumbered Democrats forty-four to forty-one. The ranks of both parties included a number of independents, however, and for the most part a spirit of bipartisan cooperation prevailed. In contrast to earlier constitutional conventions, delegates originally from New York and the New England states outnumbered men with Southern backgrounds. Reflecting the changes then sweeping the state, attorneys outnumbered farmers in the convention hall.

After five months of deliberation, the delegates unveiled the new constitution in May 1870. On July 2 the voters ratified the document, which became operational on August 8. The new constitution expanded the power of the executive, allowing for the first time the reelection of the governor and requiring a two-thirds majority for overriding a gubernatorial veto. As a countermeasure to the kind of political sectionalism in which almost no northern Democrats or southern Republicans in the state ever won election to the general assembly, three representatives would be elected from each district and voters could cast all three of their ballots for the same candidate. To safeguard against the kind of financial collapses that plagued the state in the 1830s, the constitution mandated referendum approval for receipt of loans in excess of $250,000 and established a debt limit of 5 percent on the state's taxable property. Overriding the opposition to voting rights for African Americans, the delegates granted universal suffrage to all male citizens above the age of twenty-one who had lived in Illinois for at least one year. Despite the efforts of Elijah M. Haines, a delegate from Lake County, the document failed to extend suffrage to women. Responding to complaints by farmers' organizations about the usurious rates charged by railroads and warehouses, the delegates set up the nation's first system of state regulation. A clear improvement over the 1848 constitution, the massive 1870 document later came into some criticism for being a "straightjacket on progress," but it served the state well enough to remain its governing charter for the next hundred years.[1]

A new constitution and a new capitol building did little to improve the tenor of the state's politics in the postbellum era, however. The Republican party maintained supremacy in Illinois by "waving the bloody shirt," keeping the enmity of the war years alive by claiming to be the party of union and smearing all Democrats as Copperheads. In 1868 General John A. Logan assumed command of the Grand Army of the Republic (GAR), a Civil War veterans' organization of more than four hundred thousand members founded by an Illinois physician, Dr. Benjamin Stephenson. The GAR became essentially an arm of the Republican party and an important instrument in discrediting the political opposition. The Republicans' demagoguery paid off, as they controlled the general assembly for the last quarter of the nineteenth century and elected every governor from 1865 to 1892. The outnumbered Democrats elected only one U.S. senator, John M. Palmer, between 1865 and 1912.

During the last decades of the nineteenth century, the years Mark Twain sardonically referred to as the "Gilded Age," Springfield became notorious as a welcoming home for special interests that wielded extensive influence over an ineffective state government. The public complained bitterly about the unchecked activities of lobbyists in the state capital, the avarice and immorality of legislators, and the ineffectiveness of lackluster governors. A number of reforms instituted by the 1870 constitution somewhat mitigated the influence of monopoly-seeking corporations by limiting legislative power, but Springfield remained an inviting location for businessmen and politicians looking for a quick dollar. The rapidly expanding industrial economy that created so much opportunity also bred moral laxity in state governments from Maine to California, and Illinois proved a microcosm of the national situation.

To be sure, Illinois at the end of the Civil War stood on the verge of spectacular economic growth and development. Its economy having long been dominated by agriculture, Illinois began to experience significant industrial growth in the 1860s. During that decade, capital investment in manufacturing rose by 243 percent and the labor force increased by 261 percent. According to the 1870 census, the value of agricultural products and manufactured goods in Illinois stood nearly equal. By 1890 the state ranked third nationally in industrial production, with less than one-third of the workforce engaged in agricultural pursuits. In 1900 Chicago alone boasted seven of the twenty-two factories in the country employing more than four thousand workers each. The Windy City's sprawling Union Stock Yards, steelworks, agricultural implement factories, railroad switchyards and car shops, garment sweatshops, and lumber mills employed thousands of workers. Chicago became the industrial behemoth of the Midwest.

The Great Chicago Fire of 1871, one of the most devastating episodes in the nation's history, only temporarily slowed the metropolis's inexorable expansion. In the midst of a searing drought, during which virtually no rain fell for more than three months, a fire broke out on Sunday, October 9, 1871, in a barn behind the O'Leary family's cottage on DeKoven Street. The fire spread rapidly through the wooden buildings, sidewalks, and streets of the Near West Side aided by a strong wind that blew sparks and burning cinders toward the city center. The raging conflagration cleared the South Branch of the Chicago River and reached the heart of downtown by early the next day. By late Monday night, when a cold driving rain finally doused the firestorm, the entire business district and much of the North Side extending out to the city limits had been leveled. The fire left three hundred people dead and another hundred thousand homeless; it had incinerated eighteen thousand buildings and replaced block after block of stately structures with ash and rubble. Stunned local officials estimated property losses at two hundred million dollars, 30 percent of all taxable real estate in Chicago.

Recovery commenced immediately. On Tuesday other cities sent food, blankets, and clothing on special trains, and distribution began under the supervision of the Chicago Relief and Aid Society. More than five million dollars in cash contributions, some from as far away as Europe, arrived in the following weeks. President Ulysses S. Grant wrote a personal check for one thousand dollars and urged others to be as generous. After the initial

A view of the devastation following the Great Chicago Fire of 1871, looking east on Randolph Street from the Chicago River. The tall structure still standing in the middle is the courthouse. *Illinois State Historical Library*

shock subsided, Chicagoans found reason for cautious optimism. The North Side and the central business district had been decimated, but the South and West sides had for the most part avoided serious damage. The stockyards, lumberyards, grain elevators, lakefront docks, railroad facilities, and hundreds of factories remained largely intact. Chicago listed as a major asset its close financial relationship with New York City bankers and traders who had good reason to restore the profitable East–West trade network that had flourished over preceding decades. Chicago's geographical advantages remained unchanged, Great Lakes maritime commerce continued, and the volume of railroad traffic resumed almost immediately and soon increased. The Windy City's buoyant civic and business leaders proudly affirmed Chicago's destiny and exhorted entrepreneurs to invest in the triumph that would surely rise out of tragedy. They found no shortage of risk takers.

Chicago's remarkable recovery left even the most optimistic boosters dumbfounded. Many residents of the city relocated elsewhere after the fire, but a greater number arrived seeking economic opportunity. During the 1870s, despite the Great Fire and the economic disruptions caused by the Panic of 1873, Chicago's population nearly doubled. By 1880, with more than 500,000 people, Chicago passed St. Louis in population and became the nation's fourth-largest city. The Windy City's population passed the million mark ten years later. It was now second in size only to New York City, and the astounding growth rate continued; its population rose to 1,700,000 in 1900 and 3,200,000 in 1910. As Chicagoans proudly boasted, their city had indeed risen like a phoenix from the ashes.

Chicago's resurgence after the Great Fire resulted from its assertion of primacy in several key industries, often spearheaded by the bold leadership provided by a few hard-driving businessmen. In the years following the Civil War, for example, Chicago became the nation's leading meat-processing center. Stockyards had previously been located haphazardly throughout the city, but in 1865 the Illinois General Assembly consolidated the business

The southwest section of the Union Stock Yards with a portion of the Packingtown meat-processing plants in the background. *Illinois State Historical Library*

when it created the Union Stock Yards and Transit Company southwest of the central business district. On one hundred acres of land, twenty-three hundred pens could hold twenty-one thousand cattle, seventy-five thousand hogs, twenty-two thousand sheep, and two hundred horses all at the same time. Along with the pens and chutes for the livestock, the massive archipelago contained a bank, a hotel, a board of trade, a post office, and a network of railroad spurs; Packingtown was virtually an autonomous city. In no other city could livestock producers conduct their business as efficiently as they could in Chicago with its excellent railroad connections, commodious stock pens, and centralized meatpacking facilities. In 1880 the city produced meat products worth ninety-eight million dollars, up dramatically from nineteen million ten years earlier, and profits soared also because of refinements in refrigeration. The meatpackers used natural ice in railroad cars to ship beef unspoiled to lucrative Eastern markets.

A few men dominated Chicago's meatpacking industry in the late nineteenth century. Nelson Morris, a German immigrant, came to Chicago in 1852, began working in a packinghouse, opened his own business, and made a fortune supplying beef to the U.S. Army during the Civil War. Two other leading meatpackers, Gustavus F. Swift and Philip D. Armour, made their mark after the Great Fire. Swift arrived from Boston in 1874 and perfected the disassembly line that made the butchering of cattle and hogs much more efficient. The owner of a grain commission business in Milwaukee, Armour first opened a branch in Chicago, then opened a packinghouse in 1875. Constantly seeking new markets, these men sold their beef overseas and developed the technology for preparing canned meat. Professing to use all parts of the animal except the squeal, they sold hides to leather companies and hair to mattress firms. From the other animal parts they made fertilizer, glue, soap, lard, margarine, buttons, candle tallow, and a host of other products.

Chicago also became one of the centers for the production of agricultural implements. Cyrus McCormick moved to the city in 1847 and opened a factory that manufactured 450 mechanical reapers that year. Continued refinements to the production process by 1876 allowed the factory, the largest in the city, to complete a harvester every twelve minutes. A marketing genius as well as an inventor, McCormick realized that the key to continued expansion of the business rested in convincing cash-poor farmers to buy the comparatively expensive reapers, which in 1860 retailed for an imposing $120. He pioneered in the use of two staples of modern American business, advertising and credit. Commission salesmen armed with advertising circulars, demonstration models, and warranties went to the farmers and told them how they could own the machines for only $30 down and the balance to be paid at harvest time. Farmers saw McCormick's product as a necessity rather than a luxury, and the firm sold 150,000 reapers in 1890 alone.

Midwestern farmers sent their wheat crops via railroad to Chicago, which by the time of the Civil War had bested St. Louis for primacy in the grain trade. The steam-powered grain elevator, perfected by Chicago merchants in the 1850s, transferred grain quickly and efficiently from railroad cars to warehouses for storage. Economic middlemen stored millions of bushels of grain in the massive elevators—some reaching 120 feet high—before sending the grain by railroad or ship to New York City. A group of grain traders created the Chicago Board of Trade, streamlining the buying and selling process and creating the grain futures market. By the late nineteenth century, Chicago controlled the nation's wheat market.

The iron and steel industry, essential for industrial expansion, thrived as well. Freighters carried iron ore from Minnesota's Mesabi Range through the Great Lakes to steelmaking enterprises scattered along the southern tip of Lake Michigan in northeastern Illinois and northwestern Indiana. In 1865 the North Chicago Rolling Mills produced the nation's first steel rails, and the city continued to roll more steel rails than any other city. The southeastern corner of Chicago, twelve miles south of downtown, housed a belt of steel mills wedged in between Lake Calumet and Lake Michigan alongside the Calumet River. After the federal government appropriated funds for the improvement of Calumet Harbor in 1869, the production of iron and steel increased significantly. In 1900 Chicago ranked third nationally in iron and steel production; in 1914, thanks largely to the continued growth of the industry in the Windy City, Illinois stood third in blast furnace production.

Chicago dominated the Midwestern lumber market also. Responding to the increasing demand for lumber to be used in homes, barns, fences, and railroad ties, lumberjacks floated logs from forests in Wisconsin, Michigan, and Minnesota down rivers to sawmills on Lake Michigan and then transported the finished lumber on barges to Chicago. By 1867, on average, more than two hundred vessels arrived per day. Local merchants bought the lumber, resold it, and shipped it by rail to customers throughout the Midwestern and Great Plains states. Chicago lumber merchants shipped one billion board feet of lumber in 1880 and enjoyed a monopoly as far west as Nebraska and Kansas. By the twentieth century, competitors in the Pacific Northwest and Southeast reduced the market for Midwestern lumber, but Chicago businessmen maintained a brisk trade for house construction in the metropolitan area.

The development of many of Chicago's industries, particularly grain, lumber, and meatpacking, relied upon the links forged by the railroad between the city and its hinterlands. In addition, a network of interurban electric railways connected the city to dozens of communities in northeastern Illinois, northwestern Indiana, and southeastern Wisconsin. An industry that both contributed to and benefited from the marriage of rural and urban America, the mail-order catalog business originated in the Windy City. Potter Palmer, Marshall Field, and Levi Leiter built the city's first department stores and revolutionized the business of retailing, but their downtown emporium tapped only the urban middle-class market. Aaron Montgomery Ward worked for two years at Marshall Field's before he quit and opened a business in 1872 that would serve an overlooked group of consumers—rural farm and small-town families. Convinced they were being bilked by rapacious middlemen, who bought consumer goods in cities and then sold them to isolated rural families at outrageous markups, farmers welcomed the opportunity to buy reasonably priced items from Ward's mail-order catalogs. In 1893 Richard Sears and Alvah Roebuck founded Sears, Roebuck and Company in Chicago and quickly outpaced their competitors with more aggressive sales techniques, larger inventories, and progressively bigger catalogs (the 1900 edition had more than a thousand pages). Sears, Roebuck and Company's nine thousand employees moved into a new forty-acre headquarters on Chicago's West Side in 1906, a suitable home for the world's leading retailer.

The Windy City's foremost businessmen, the intrepid entrepreneurs who amassed great fortunes in the decades following the Great Fire, formed a close-knit elite known as much for their opulent lifestyles as their financial acumen. The elite lived together in luxurious South Side neighborhoods not far from downtown. Marshall Field, George Pullman, and Philip Armour built palatial mansions on Prairie Avenue near Eighteenth Street, while others settled farther south on Michigan Boulevard between Jackson and Thirty-fifth Streets. Potter Palmer constructed a gaudy, quarter-million-dollar house on the Near North Side. They lunched at the Union League Club, socialized at the Onwentsia Country Club or the Saddle and Sirloin Club, and promenaded in their expensive carriages down Grand Boulevard on Sundays. They escaped the heat of summers in the city by going to their retreats in suburban Lake Forest and traveled by train to California to avoid the winter's icy blasts. In death they rested in Graceland Cemetery's ornate tombs, so striking that visitors regularly came to marvel at the architecture. Their lives became testaments to the triumph of the city on the lake.

Chicago's phenomenal industrial growth obscured the fact that several other Illinois cities significantly increased their manufacturing outputs as well. A number of communities in the northeastern corner of the state produced impressive amounts of iron and steel, including Joliet (which ranked third nationally in iron and steel production in 1900), Chicago Heights, and Waukegan. A second center of iron and steel production developed across the Mississippi River from St. Louis in Granite City, East St. Louis, Alton, Belleville, and Edwardsville. By the end of the nineteenth century, approximately one-fourth of the nation's liquor came from Peoria distilleries, and the National Stock Yards in East St. Louis thrived because of its excellent railroad connections with Western cattle kingdoms. Moline ranked second to Chicago in the manufacture of farm implements, and Rock Island, Rockford, Peoria, Springfield, and Freeport also became leading production centers. Relying upon the state's bountiful supply of clay, Illinois factories produced dishes, jugs, and other forms of pottery; brick makers used the clay to satisfy the demand for fireproof building materials throughout the country. By the 1870s the rising demand for cheap fuel to stoke the iron and steel furnaces led to the development of coalfields in the central and southern areas of the state.

Industrialization created a demand for labor, and Illinois's population increased because of both immigration and natural growth from 2,539,891 in 1870 to 3,826,352 in 1890. Much of the state's population shifted from

TABLE 1—Foreign-Born in Illinois by Nationality

Country of Origin	1870	1890	1910
Great Britain	192,960	95,113	85,176
Ireland	——	124,498	93,451
Germany	203,758	338,382	319,182
Holland	4,180	8,762	14,402
Sweden	29,979	86,514	115,422
Norway	11,180	30,339	32,913
Denmark	3,711	12,044	17,368
France	10,911	8,540	7,966
Belgium	——	——	9,399
Switzerland	8,980	——	8,660
Italy	——	8,035	72,160
Austria	2,099	8,087	a
Bohemia	7,350	26,627	163,020
Hungary	——	3,126	a
Russia	——	8,407	149,016
Poland	——	26,627	b
Others	39,390	54,995	117,179
TOTAL	**514,498**	**840,096**	**1,205,314**

a—included in Bohemia's total

b—included in Russia's total

Adapted from Ernest Ludlow Bogart and John Mabry Mathews, *The Modern Commonwealth, 1893–1918* (Springfield: Illinois Centennial Commission, 1920), 17.

rural to urban locations, especially Chicago. From 1870 to 1890, the percentage of the state's population living in the Windy City grew from 11.6 to 28.7 percent. During the same twenty years, the percentage of the Illinois population living in rural areas fell from 76.6 to 55.3 percent. The increase in the number of immigrants, particularly the foreign-born, proved especially noteworthy. Most of the 515,198 foreign-born persons in Illinois in 1870 hailed from northern and western Europe, including nearly 225,000 from the British Isles, 203,000 Germans, and 45,000 from Scandinavian nations. Twenty years later, the number of first-generation immigrants from the British Isles (including Ireland) had grown only to 260,000, the Germans to 338,000, and the Scandinavians to 126,000. By contrast, the number of immigrants from southern and eastern Europe had increased dramatically with Poles, Russians, Hungarians, Italians, and Bohemians leading the way. These patterns continued well into the twentieth century (see table 1).

About three-fourths of the foreign-born lived in Illinois's cities, and most of them settled in Chicago. In 1870 more than half of the city's residents were foreign-born; in 1890 first- and second-generation immigrants constituted more than three-fourths of the population. Arriving in a land with a surplus of rural population and a need for urban labor, these newcomers inevitably gravitated toward a rapidly growing city with a multitude of employment opportunities in its assembly lines and blast furnaces. Usually possessing little money and few skills, unable to converse in English and unfamiliar with American customs, the European peasants applied for work in Chicago's steel mills, meatpacking plants, and other mass-production factories seeking unskilled labor. They stacked wheat, forged metals, butchered hogs, and stitched clothing, thereby creating the industrial workforce required by the expanding city.

Workers in the late nineteenth century who played a large role in the remarkable success story of industrialization in Chicago and other Illinois cities often parlayed their opportunities into better lives for themselves and their families. An expanding economy provided jobs at attractive wages, and the rapid growth of white-collar employment opened new avenues for upward mobility. An expanding public education system aided newcomers to assimilate into the workforce. By pooling modest incomes, taking in boarders, joining mutual aid societies and other fraternal organizations, and living strictly within their means, working families saved money and paved the way to middle-class respectability for subsequent generations. Finding work as butchers, grocers, peddlers, barbers, shopkeepers, and the like, immigrants thrived in their supportive ethnic neighborhoods scattered throughout the cities. For a great number of Illinoisans fortunate enough to enjoy good health and uninterrupted employment, the industrial economy provided plenty of opportunity and served as a springboard to genuine success.

Not all workers prospered in the highly competitive industrial system, however, and many complained of their inability to share in the benefits engendered by the dynamic economy. Usually toiling twelve or fourteen hours a day, six or sometimes seven days a week, for low wages in unhealthy, unsafe workplaces, these workers relished the opportunity to earn a living but clearly saw how their exploitation resulted from employers' insatiable drive for ever-higher profits. State and federal government officials routinely shunned the powerless and sided with the entrepreneurial class, and workers had little recourse in their struggle to improve working conditions. After all, concluded the politicians, why intervene and run the risk of hampering a booming economy that created jobs? Organization of the workers into trade unions proved difficult with a polyglot workforce, and foremen often combined workers speaking different languages in the same space so that communication became difficult if not impossible. In an age of labor surplus, factory owners could easily fire any striking workers, hire replacements, and continue to operate without making any concessions to labor groups.

Defying all the forces arrayed against them, laborers in Illinois united in an effort to improve their lives. Railroad workers founded brotherhoods in several cities, and the nation's first coal miners' union originated in West Belleville. An omnibus union, the General Trades Assembly, met for the first time in Chicago in 1864. The drive to force an eight-hour workday gained momentum, and a number of organizations devoted to the reform appeared after the Civil War. In 1867 the Illinois General Assembly passed the nation's first eight-hour law, which guaranteed that workers could not be fired for refusing to work more than eight hours a day. The measure fell short of labor's expectations, however, as management found other excuses for terminating the employment of unwanted workers. By the mid-1870s, the Knights of Labor established its first locals in Illinois. Originally founded in Philadelphia in 1869, the Knights of Labor sought to organize all workers regardless of skill and called for the eight-hour day, limitations on child labor, equal pay for both sexes, and other bold reforms. The organization's Illinois membership peaked in the mid-1880s at fifty-two thousand members, about two-thirds of them working in Chicago.

Labor's situation worsened precipitously in 1873 when the nation suffered its most severe financial contraction yet. Scores of national and state banks failed, prices fell, and Eastern financiers contracted the currency to cut their losses. Businesses in Illinois and elsewhere tightened their belts by reducing production, lowering wages, and laying off workers. Chicago's unemployment rate reached an astronomical 40 percent, and workers fortunate enough to retain their jobs absorbed lacerating pay cuts that sometimes approached 50 percent. Accustomed to periodic downturns in the economy, workers expected that the worst effects of the Panic of 1873 would soon dissipate, but instead conditions continued to deteriorate. After three years of unrelieved misery, a rising tide of dissent became evident in Illinois cities. Socialists, anarchists, and other radicals assailed the efficacy of capitalism and called for revolution. Desperate workers who would have labeled such inflammatory talk as heresy a few years before began to listen more attentively, and the more respectable elements of society became distrustful of the laboring classes. Talk of class warfare no longer seemed so far-fetched.

In 1877 the simmering discontent erupted into violence nationwide in the railroad industry. With many railroads already in receivership, the Baltimore and Ohio Railroad implemented a substantial wage reduction that led many brotherhoods to declare strikes. Violence in Baltimore, Pittsburgh, and other Eastern cities raised the level of apprehension in Illinois, which contained more miles of track than any other state in the nation. The general assembly prepared for labor agitation, modernizing the Illinois National Guard in May and passing a law in July that made illegal the obstruction of any railroad traffic. Undeterred by the legislature's preemptive actions, railroad workers in East St. Louis walked off the job on July 21, 1877, and their compatriots followed suit in Chicago, Aurora, Carbondale, Peoria, Effingham, and other cities around the state. Strikers and local police clashed at several locations but most violently in Chicago, the nation's premier railroad hub. Spurred on by radical mobs, the striking railroad workers there laid siege to depots, attacked roundhouses, and overran freight yards; in pitched battles with police, nineteen people died and more than one hundred suffered injuries. Some mail and passenger service continued, but all freight traffic ground to a halt.

Determined to protect private property, Governor Shelby Cullom proclaimed the actions of the strikers a form of domestic insurrection and dispatched the National Guard to Chicago. He also appealed for assistance to President Rutherford B. Hayes, who sent six companies of the U.S. Army from Indian Territory to Chicago. Cowed by the show of force, the mobs of strikers and their supporters dispersed. When violence erupted in East St. Louis, Governor Cullom personally assumed command of two National Guard regiments there to restore order. State courts cooperated by issuing a series of injunctions, and soon the trains resumed operation throughout Illinois.

In the coal-mining town of Braidwood southwest of Chicago, miners voiced their support for the railroad shutdown and declared a strike of their own. Having endured pay reductions constantly since the onset of the Panic of 1873, fifteen hundred embattled miners walked off the job when the owners rejected their request for a modest wage increase. The mine owners imported African American strikebreakers, and when the strikers tried to drive the scabs out of town on July 27, 1877, Governor Cullom sent a National Guard battalion to protect the rights of property. The strike finally ended in November when the union dissolved, some strikers returned to work under prevailing conditions, and other miners drifted away in search of employment elsewhere.

By 1879 economic conditions had finally improved, but a residue of bitterness remained between capital and labor. The return of prosperity blunted the appeal of various groups of socialists in Chicago, who nevertheless successfully lobbied for the establishment of a state bureau of labor statistics. Sporadic outbreaks of violence punctuated strikes when management enlisted the service of strikebreakers or persuaded local and state officials to use force in defense of property rights. In 1883, for example, Governor John M. Hamilton sent state militia to Collinsville to disperse striking coal miners. The militia followed the fleeing strikers into neighboring St. Clair County, killed one miner, and arrested twenty-six others. Governor Richard J. Oglesby dispatched state troops to quell labor disturbances frequently during his third term in office (1885–1889), most notably against striking quarry workers in Lemont, to protect property in the Chicago stockyards, and to defeat striking railroad switchmen in East St. Louis, where sheriff's deputies killed four men.

The number of industrial disputes increased dramatically in 1886 when workers called more than a thousand strikes in Illinois. Contemporaries noted that immigrants rather than the native-born participated more frequently in labor violence and radical politics. Chicago became a center for the anarchist movement, which condemned the exploitation of the workers and called for the use of force as the only realistic antidote. The brand of fanaticism advocated in anarchist publications, most of which were distributed by German immigrants, specifically prescribed political assassination as the precursor to revolution. The anarchists' zeal doubtless attracted few converts from the immigrant masses, but capitalists and local officials feared the potency of their message at such a volatile time.

The anarchists found an inviting target in the sprawling McCormick harvester plant on Chicago's West Side. Recurrent wage reductions during the preceding years had led to frequent strikes, and management responded by imposing lockouts and employing strikebreakers and Pinkerton Detective Agency operatives. In 1885 after a protracted strike, owners reluctantly granted a 15 percent wage increase but the following February locked out workers who had participated in the strike and replaced them with nonunion workers. Union workers and scabs confronted each other daily for the next several months as tensions rose. On May 3, 1886, during yet another altercation, police riot squads shot and killed two unionists in front of the reaper plant. August Spies, an anarchist editor who witnessed the shootings, rushed back to his office at the *Arbeiter-Zeitung* and in the next day's edition of the German and English bilingual newspaper called for a protest meeting to be held at Haymarket Square. In a circular he wrote and later distributed, Spies exhorted workers to "rise . . . and destroy the hideous monster that seeks to destroy you."[2]

In this interpretation of the Haymarket Riot on May 4, 1886, police and members of the crowd exchange gunfire as the excited orator rails against the evils of industrial capitalism. *Illinois State Historical Library*

At Haymarket Square, a wholesale produce market west of the Chicago River, an estimated three thousand persons attended the mass meeting on May 4, 1886, and listened to a series of speeches by anarchists and labor leaders. Mayor Carter Harrison attended for a while and, convinced that the peaceful gathering posed no threat to public safety, left early along with many others in the dwindling crowd. On his way home, he stopped at a nearby police station and reported to Inspector John Bonfield that police had no reason to become involved. Bonfield disagreed. An implacable opponent of radicalism, the policeman saw an opportunity to provoke a confrontation and ordered the 180 men in his command to march toward Haymarket Square. The crowd had shrunk to a few hundred when the police detachment arrived and gave the order to disperse. Someone lofted a homemade bomb into police ranks, killing seven and wounding seventy-six others. The police fired into the gathering and clubbed members of the crowd who fled the scene. Like the identity of the bomb thrower, the number of bystanders who were killed and wounded remains undetermined.

In the aftermath of the Haymarket incident, public sentiment shifted strongly against the strikers and their radical supporters. The Chicago newspapers inflamed passions with sensationalist stories about imminent anarchist plots to topple the government. The police and Pinkerton detectives rounded up and questioned dozens of well-known political radicals before bringing charges against eight men for murder. In a trial that lasted nearly two months and attracted national attention, the prosecution made no effort to specify who threw the bomb but instead identified the accused as members of a conspiracy—even though some of the defendants had left the meeting before the bomb exploded and others had not even attended at all. Equating sedition with murder, the jury found the eight men guilty of harboring dangerous ideas if not of having acted on them. Judge Joseph E. Gary condemned seven men to death and sentenced the other to a fifteen-year prison term. Public opinion applauded a verdict that protected the people from violent foreigners and radicals. Skittish members of the Chicago establishment, still fearing that a threat to public safety persisted, wanted federal troops closer by. At the request of the general assembly, the U.S. Army built Fort Sheridan on Lake Michigan, twenty-seven miles north of the metropolis.

Questioning the fairness of the trial, a number of respectable citizens joined political dissidents in circulating petitions for clemency. The Illinois Supreme Court affirmed death sentences for the Haymarket rioters, and the U.S. Supreme Court declined to hear the appeal. Governor Richard Oglesby commuted to life imprisonment the sentences of two of the convicted men, and one man awaiting execution committed suicide in his cell; on November 11, 1887, the Cook County sheriff hanged the remaining four. More than a hundred thousand people nationwide joined an amnesty movement for the three defendants serving prison sentences, thereby launching a crusade that ended successfully after several years of effort. John Peter Altgeld, who in 1893 became the state's first foreign-born governor, reviewed the Haymarket trial records and found undeniable evidence of bias and procedural irregularity. Without warning, he pardoned the three prisoners on June 26, 1893, and brought the affair to a close. Altgeld received praise from some quarters for his courage, but overall the massive public expression of outrage surpassed the support he said he expected. Newspapers vilified the governor as a dangerous subversive and collaborator in revolutions. Members of a Danville mob justified their lynching of two men by citing their concern that, if the courts found the suspects guilty, the governor likely would have pardoned them. The pardon no doubt cost Altgeld his reelection in 1896.

Labor agitation continued in Illinois, cresting again in the Pullman strike in 1894. George Pullman, inventor of the railroad sleeping car, built a company town about fifteen miles south of downtown Chicago in hopes of creating a more salubrious environment for his workers. At first, visitors from around the world commended the company town, called Pullman, for its comfortable homes, healthy environment, and good schools, but the praise then turned to criticism of the owner's paternalism, high-handedness, and greed. "Here is a population of eight thousand souls," wrote economist Richard T. Ely after a visit to Pullman in 1885, "where not one single resident dare[s] speak his opinion about the town in which he lives. One feels that one is mingling with a dependent, servile people." Pullman's penny-pinching ways became intolerable for the residents when the Panic of 1893 devastated the local economy. As the depression worsened, the magnate laid off thousands of workers and drastically cut wages but steadfastly insisted on maintaining rents, service charges, and the cost of items in company stores. In May 1894 local workers, many of whom had joined the American Railway Union (ARU), went on strike. When ARU switchmen refused to handle any trains carrying Pullman cars, the local dispute became a nationwide showdown involving 125,000 workers in twenty-seven states and territories. Railroad workers in Decatur, Joliet, and several other Illinois communities joined in the boycott.[3]

ARU president Eugene V. Debs initially ordered his charges not to break federal law by interfering with mail trains, but the railroad owners added mail cars to Pullman trains to ensure the involvement of sympathetic officials in Washington, D.C. The General Managers Association of the twenty-four lines serving Chicago obtained a court injunction prohibiting the union from halting mail trains and asked for the intervention of the U.S. Army. President Grover Cleveland ordered federal troops from Fort Sheridan to Chicago, ignoring the impassioned objections of Governor Altgeld and Mayor John P. Hopkins. Two thousand army regulars arrived on July 4, 1894, and violence broke out almost immediately in several locations around the city. Mobs battled soldiers in the streets, rioters destroyed hundreds of railroad cars, and several strikers lost their lives during the two weeks that the troops remained in Chicago. The ARU capitulated, and the strike ended in total victory for Pullman. Convicted of conspiring to violate a court injunction, Debs served six months in the McHenry County jail.

A three-member strike commission appointed by President Cleveland to investigate the affair interviewed more than one hundred participants, including Pullman and Debs, before issuing a report surprisingly condemnatory of Pullman and the railroad managers. The commission criticized Pullman for bilking his town's residents and for refusing to negotiate with the strikers. It also recommended future action by the federal government to keep labor disputes from turning into violent disorders. The commission's sensible findings notwithstanding, the outcome of the Pullman strike remained clear: management had scored another clear-cut victory over disgruntled workers. The ARU dissolved, and the thousand Pullman workers left unemployed after the failure of the strike joined the growing legions of impoverished as the Panic of 1893 continued to be felt in Chicago and elsewhere.

Bloody strikes in Illinois coal mines reflected the degree to which labor unrest still plagued the state in the 1880s and 1890s. The arrival of Slavic and Italian immigrants created stiff job competition for the English, Irish, Welsh, and Scottish miners who had predominated earlier in the nineteenth century. To keep wages low, mine companies not only exploited the labor surplus but also began importing black strikebreakers who had been earning lower wages in Southern states. The United Mine Workers (UMW), which at first attracted few followers in Illinois after its founding in 1890, saw its membership rise after it won a showdown against the Illinois Coal Operators Association in 1898. After a strike began in Mount Olive and spread to Pana and Virden, coal-mine executives imported black strikebreakers from Birmingham, Alabama, and armed guards from St. Louis to protect them. A deadly exchange of gunfire led to the deaths of seven miners and four guards, and Governor John R. Tanner sent in the National Guard, but this time to bar the strikebreakers from the mines. Deprived of government protection, the mine owners agreed to a settlement that gave the miners an eight-hour day, a six-day week, and a new pay scale of forty cents per ton. (In the wake of the UMW's unprecedented victory, John Mitchell of Braidwood became the union's national president.) In 1899 striking miners killed five black strikebreakers in Pana and another five in neighboring Carterville. The struggle for fewer hours, higher pay, and safer working conditions continued in the Illinois mines.

Discontent likewise pervaded the state's rural areas as commercialized agriculture supplanted subsistence farming. During the Civil War, the federal government had purchased all the crops Illinois farmers could grow, which created an unprecedented prosperity. Farmers mortgaged their land to expand their holdings, purchased the new labor-saving machinery that the state's factories were manufacturing in abundance, and increased yields as much as possible. Demobilization of the army at the end of the war coupled with the declining demand for food in Europe glutted markets and drove prices down; overextended farmers could not pay their bills. Frustrated farmers complained that even though they had become more productive than ever, market forces cruelly left them in a worsening economic condition. They grappled with a lingering agricultural depression that made bumper crops and generous paydays a distant memory.

A pernicious combination of economic forces squeezed many Illinois farmers off their land. The rising cost of farmland and technology left only the wealthiest landowners able to compete in the new market economy. Those with ample means bought new machinery, fenced their land with barbed wire, rotated crops, laid tile to improve drainage, applied new scientific farming practices, and produced higher yields than ever before. By 1870, however, almost one-third of farmers in Illinois worked on someone else's land and owned less than three hundred dollars' worth in personal property—and the number of the landless was increasing. Some despondent farmers deserted their land and headed west in the unlikely hope that they could escape the influence of a powerful national market economy; others, including many young people, went to the cities seeking jobs in expanding industries and the opportunities for entertainment and excitement that were absent on the isolated farms.

Farmers in Illinois and throughout the Midwest saw economic policies forged in the nation's Eastern cities as a significant part of their problem. As debtors trying to meet their financial obligations, including fixed interest rates, they opposed the deflationary monetary policy favored by bankers. Farmers argued that they suffered doubly—as producers and as consumers—from high tariff rates. As producers they had to sell their crops in protected markets abroad, and as consumers they paid artificially high prices for manufactured goods thanks to import tariffs protecting domestic industries. From the Illinois prairies, it seemed that national economic policies conceived in Washington, D.C., took shape when Republican presidents and congressmen colluded with plutocrats whose vision seldom extended west of Wall Street. Wealthy businessmen underwrote Republican political campaigns, farmers believed, in return for which GOP officeholders maintained fiscal and taxation policies that served mercantile interests exclusively.

Farmers also felt mistreated by the railroads. The remarkable growth of a network of railroads in Illinois had initially proved a godsend for farmers, and with three-fourths of the state's farms within five miles of a railroad line by 1870, foodstuffs made their way rapidly to national markets. Yet the rapacity of the unregulated railroads robbed the farmers of much of their hard-earned profit. Charging more for short hauls than for long ones and making customers of small branchlines pay higher rates than those who used trunk lines, railroads profited from discriminatory rates that hurt small landowners especially. Farmers had eagerly helped finance the building of the railroads, sometimes by mortgaging their own property to purchase railroad bonds. Not too many years later, they suddenly found themselves losing money while shipping their products to market. The farmers lost money again when the railroads conspired with the owners of warehouses, grain elevators, and meatpacking plants. The railroads, for example, delivered all the wheat raised by farmers in seven Midwestern states (including Illinois) to a small number of gigantic grain elevators in Chicago, where the owners took advantage of their monopoly to pay the farmers less than they deserved. In many instances, knowing the farmers could take their produce nowhere else, the elevator owners brazenly dissembled when weighing and recording the grain.

Finally, farmers protested the alarming increase in tenancy. During the decade of the 1880s, the percentage of Illinois farms operated by tenants increased from 31.4 to 34 percent. Most worrisome, the farmers charged, the conditions of tenancy were becoming more onerous with the rise of absentee ownership and "rack-renting." William Scully, a wealthy Irish landowner infamous for charging exorbitant rents and evicting tenants without just cause, became the prototype of the ruthless alien investor when he acquired thousands of acres of land in central Illinois in the 1870s. Unlike most landlords who accepted a share of the grain or corn as payment for debts, Scully demanded cash rent and, in the face of disappointing yields or fallen prices, extended no leniency to the tenants on his three hundred Illinois farms. Vulnerable tenants called for the general assembly to take some action to protect the state's farmers against the ruthless excesses of absentee landlords that came to be known as "Scullyism."[4]

Faced with a number of serious economic problems, increasingly isolated as substantial numbers of rural folk moved into the cities, and keenly aware of their declining status in modernizing America, farmers formed associations that served both as social outlets and as political institutions designed to advance agrarian interests. In 1867 a young clerk in the U.S. Department of Agriculture, O. H. Kelley, founded the Patrons of Husbandry on behalf of farmers. Hundreds of local clubs known as granges began as social and educational organizations. Employing elaborate secret rituals, they admitted women as well as men. The first grange in Illinois met in the *Prairie Farmer*'s Chicago office, and soon the farmers' clubs honeycombed the state. Granges bargained on behalf of members to obtain farm machinery at a discount, and the mail-order firm of Montgomery Ward and Company created a grange supply house specifically for the group. Although the constitution of the Patrons of Husbandry proscribed political action, the grangers lobbied in Springfield for favorable legislation and supported candidates who pledged to aid the farmers. The Independent Farmers Organization, under the leadership of William C. Flagg, worked in tandem with the granges to effect political reform.

In 1870 the general assembly enacted a series of laws to govern the activities of the railroads, establishing maximum passenger fares, developing a formula for calculating freight rates, and creating a state board of railroad and warehouse commissioners. The railroads failed to comply with the new regulations, and the courts ruled the commission's regulation of freight rates unconstitutional. In 1873 the general assembly passed a new law that empowered the commission to establish reasonable rates subject to the railroads' ability to demonstrate the efficacy of higher rates. Litigation again ensued as the railroads and warehouses claimed the freedom to set their own rates safe from government interference. A test case developed when Ira Munn and George Scott, owners of a Chicago grain elevator, refused to obtain a grain storage license. In the 1877 landmark case of

Munn v. Illinois, the U.S. Supreme Court upheld the Illinois Supreme Court's decision affirming the state's regulatory power. In subsequent years, other states passed regulatory laws patterned after the Illinois model.

In the mid-1870s, the Greenback party supplanted the granges in Illinois as the principal vehicle for agrarian protest. Farmers caught in the deflationary spiral of the late nineteenth century thought that an increase in the treasury notes ("greenbacks") issued to finance the Civil War would bring some relief. In the wake of the Panic of 1873 and the passage of the Specie Resumption Act of 1875, which authorized the U.S. Treasury to resume specie (gold) payments in 1879, many farmers joined local Greenback clubs and ultimately the Greenback party. Greenback candidates achieved some success in local and state elections but never attained the strength necessary to influence the outcome of national contests. Adlai E. Stevenson, of Bloomington, who later became vice president of the United States as a Democrat, won election to the U.S. House of Representatives as a Greenbacker in 1874. Mark "Brick" Pomeroy, the state's most influential spokesman for soft money policies to aid farmers, claimed that 639 Greenback clubs existed in Illinois by 1878. In his Chicago-based journal, *Pomeroy's Democrat,* he dismissed both the Democratic and Republican parties as having been captured by the "money power" and blamed the economy's plight on the sinister influence of Jewish financiers. Disenchanted with factionalism within the Greenback party, Pomeroy left Chicago in 1879. Beset by dwindling resources and declining membership, the Greenback party continued to field candidates in Illinois through the 1884 election.[5]

By the 1880s, with the demise of the granges and the Greenback movement, the Farmers' Alliances became the principal advocates for agrarian interests. Like the granges, the alliances sponsored community activities and welcomed the participation of women as well as men. As a panacea for the farmers' ills, the alliances proposed the subtreasury plan. Designed to address the debilitating shortage of cash and credit in rural areas, the plan called for the federal government to build warehouses where farmers could store their crops until prices rose and to lend the farmers treasury notes based upon the eventual sale of the produce. Before repaying the loans, along with storage fees and nominal interest charges, the farmers could live off the treasury notes. The government would also provide low-interest loans to farmers seeking to purchase land. These inflationary measures by the federal government, farmers argued, could help agrarian interests in much the same way that high tariffs and land grants aided big business.

By the time that the various alliances had coalesced into the People's (Populist) party in the early 1890s, many Illinois farmers supported bimetallism as the optimal means of currency inflation. That is, they favored the free and unlimited coinage of silver as well as gold to increase the amount of money in circulation. In 1895, preparing for his reelection campaign the following year, Governor Altgeld convened a Democratic convention in Springfield that adopted as part of its platform a plank endorsing "free silver." William Jennings Bryan, a native of Illinois and graduate of Illinois College who had served in the U.S. Congress representing Nebraska, unexpectedly attended and gave a rousing speech for the silver cause. Bryan's Springfield oration turned out to be a preview of the "Cross of Gold" speech he delivered the following year at the Democratic National Convention in Chicago. Bryan left the Windy City in 1896 with the party's nomination for president, a feat he duplicated a few weeks later when the Populist party convention met in St. Louis. The standard-bearer for both the Democrats and the Populists, Bryan cast the 1896 election as a holy crusade for free silver against the forces of privilege.

Bryan's messianic campaign ended in failure. His Republican opponent, Ohio Governor William McKinley, issued a steady stream of platitudes extolling industrial growth, fiscal orthodoxy, and political moderation. McKinley's landslide victory (he won by more than 600,000 popular votes and by 271 to 176 in the electoral college) reflected both the inadequacy of free silver as a defining issue and Bryan's inability to forge a coalition between distressed farmers and urban workers. Tenants and owners of small farms may have endorsed free silver, but more prosperous farmers saw their welfare inextricably tied to national markets and feared that severe currency inflation would bankrupt the railroads and damage urban markets. Workers, who feared that free silver would devalue their wages, considered the Populist vision retrograde and saw the nation's future linked with industrial growth. The outcome of the election in Illinois mirrored these national developments. Bryan received just 43 percent of the vote while losing to McKinley in the state. Republican John R. Tanner unseated John Peter Altgeld as governor. To the dismay of agrarian radicals, the 1896 election signaled the triumph of modernism.

The sweeping changes overtaking Illinois created few opportunities for the state's modest African American population. After the Civil War, despite the repeal of the Black Laws and the passage of the Thirteenth, Fourteenth, and Fifteenth Amendments, a relatively small number of black expatriates from the South chose to resettle in the Land of Lincoln. The vast majority who did relocate came with few resources and limited skills; many arrived with no possessions other than what they carried or wore on their backs. Experienced only as field hands, they lacked the money to buy farms. Having been prohibited, as slaves, from receiving any education, they competed with thousands of European immigrants for back-breaking, low-paying jobs in mines and factories. Some black families found prospects so inhospitable that they returned to the South, while a small number found the legacy of slavery in Dixie so distasteful that they remained despite the insecurity. Census takers in Illinois found only twenty-eight thousand African Americans in 1870 (1.1 percent of the population) and eighty-four thousand in 1900 (1.8 percent of the population).

African Americans in Illinois enjoyed few civil rights. The 1870 Constitution guaranteed all males the right to vote, but because of their limited numbers, blacks exercised little political power. An 1872 "equal education" law passed by the general assembly promised all children regardless of color "the right and opportunity to an equal education," but local school officials, especially in central and southern Illinois, met the requirement by operating separate schools for black and white children. A Colored State Convention called by some of the state's most prominent African Americans in 1880 tacitly accepted segregated schools but complained about the employment of unqualified teachers in black schools. Convention delegates affirmed their allegiance to the Republican party but demanded greater representation in state and local governments. As the *Chicago Tribune* reported that year, many Republican leaders hesitated to pursue racial equality too strenuously for fear of making Illinois a haven for African Americans fleeing harsher treatment in the post-Reconstruction South.[6]

The last years of the nineteenth century witnessed an increase in violence against blacks, especially in the South, where the onset of Jim Crow went hand in hand with the application of more stringent measures of social control. White mobs took the law into their own hands and killed African Americans most often in Southern states, but a few highly publicized lynchings occurred in Illinois as well. In 1893 a mob of approximately one hundred whites from Mount Zion stormed the Macon County Courthouse in Decatur and hanged Samuel J. Bush, a black man accused of raping two white women. Governor Altgeld condemned the actions of the mob as "cowardly and diabolical," but a local grand jury ignored the testimony of several dozen witnesses and issued no indictments. In 1903 a white mob in Belleville hanged a black man, then doused his body in kerosene and set him on fire. Later that year in Danville, a mob hanged a black man from a telephone pole before returning the corpse to the county jail and burning it. The grizzliest lynching occurred in Cairo in 1909, when whites hanged an African American man accused of raping and murdering a white woman. After members of the mob riddled the dead body with bullets, they cut out the man's heart and sliced it into pieces for souvenirs. Finally, they burned and displayed his corpse as a warning to the city's black community.[7]

Lynch mobs killed two black men during the Springfield race riot of 1908, the era's most dramatic outbreak of racial violence. The riot began on August 14, when a white mob marched on the jail intent upon lynching a black man accused of raping a white woman. Discovering that the police had relocated black prisoners elsewhere for their protection, the mob moved into Springfield's African American community to vent its fury. Newspaper reporters heard white rioters yelling, "Lincoln freed you, now we'll show you where you belong!" After two days of mayhem, the black business district and blocks of residences lay in smoking rubble. Two

African Americans and four whites died before the National Guard restored order. Fearing comparable incidents of violence, authorities in communities throughout the state summoned police reserves and increased patrols. On August 31 black and white longshoremen in Chicago fought a pitched battle before club-wielding police finally separated them, and white mobs roamed the city afterward terrorizing black pedestrians. In Alton, with tensions elevated over the question of integrating public schools, white mobs severely beat African Americans spotted in and around downtown.[8]

Heightened racial violence along with unrest in the factories and on the farms underscored the rapid changes sweeping across Illinois in the post–Civil War years and the difficulties experienced by the state's people in adjusting to these alterations. Economic transformations, rapid population growth, massive immigration, and a changing ethnic mix made the late nineteenth century a tumultuous time in the state's history. Uneasy with the unsettling pace of change and not altogether satisfied with all aspects of the modern world emerging at the time, many Illinoisans called for additional changes to ameliorate the undesirable elements of industrial society. It remained unclear how effective this rising spirit of reform could be in tempering the worst abuses of industrialism.

Riverside

The entire Chicago area, including the many suburbs that ringed the city, had been laid out on a quadrilateral system, and growth occurred primarily by adding square block after square block to the existing settlements. This arrangement in many contiguous communities made property transactions both simple and convenient, but it created a monotonous sameness that led architects and planners to call for variations. In most cases, profit-seeking developers acquired large tracts of land outside the existing cities, subdivided the real estate, then sold rectangular lots to potential landowners with a minimum of planning. A major exception to this pattern—Riverside, Illinois—gained widespread acclaim as one of the nation's first planned suburbs.

After the Civil War, an Eastern speculator and promoter, Emery E. Childs, assembled a group of investors to form the Riverside Improvement Company. In 1868, having purchased a sixteen-hundred-acre tract of land where the Chicago, Burlington, and Quincy Railroad crossed the DesPlaines River nine miles west of downtown Chicago, the company asked the landscape architecture firm of Olmsted, Vaux, and Company to develop a residential suburb on the site. The forty-six-year-old Frederick Law Olmsted, who had risen to the top of his profession after designing New York City's Central

Park, visited the site and immediately foresaw its potential as an alternative to the bland, cookie-cutter suburbs that had already grown up around Chicago. Captivated by the site's gently rolling hills covered by groves of oak and hickory trees, which stood out in stark contrast to the flat prairies surrounding it, Olmsted designed a community planned in minute detail. He divided the land into generous lots, measuring 100 feet by 225 feet, and mandated that homes be set at least 30 feet back from the streets. Renouncing the layout of streets in the conventional gridiron pattern, he designed curving roadways that followed the natural contours of the landscape. His plan contained, in addition to essential services, a lake, extensive parkland straddling the meandering DesPlaines River, a downtown civic center, recreational facilities, schools, and other amenities. The consortium of investors approved his plan, and excavation work commenced that year.

The development of the suburb continued in fits and starts, however, as the Riverside Development Company encountered a series of financial crises. At the end of the year, the company defaulted on its payments to Olmsted and Vaux and offered the designers a number of lots in the suburb as payment for their work. The Great Fire of 1871 brought the sale of real estate in Riverside to a sudden halt, and the development company ceased all operations. Olmsted and Vaux dissociated themselves from the development and, expecting the worst, unloaded the last of their lots in Riverside for a nominal amount of money. By 1877 residents had moved into forty-five homes, and a board of trustees had created a village organization to administer the affairs of the nascent community. Construction of new homes continued at a leisurely pace for the next several years.

Despite its chaotic origins and failure to reward its original investors, Riverside's bucolic charm and careful planning contributed to its distinctiveness among Chicago's western suburbs. The community contained homes built by famed architect Frank Lloyd Wright and additional landscaping by Jens Jensen. In 1970 the U.S. Department of the Interior designated the entire village of Riverside a National Historic Landmark.

Joseph Glidden

Like many other Illinois farmers in the nineteenth century, Joseph Glidden left his home on the East Coast and traveled westward in search of cheap land. Born on January 18, 1813, in Sullivan County, New Hampshire, he and his parents left their farm for another in Orleans County, New York. After attending local schools, he matriculated at Middlebury Academy in Genessee County and at a seminary in Lima, New York. Glidden taught for several years in area schools before becoming a farmer and heading west in 1840 in search of land. In 1842 he settled in DeKalb County, Illinois, and

Joseph Glidden, whose invention of barbed wire revolutionized American agriculture.

purchased six hundred acres of land on the outskirts of DeKalb village. He remained a resident of DeKalb until his death on October 9, 1906.

Glidden encountered a problem common to farmers in Illinois and other prairie states—the absence of timber, large stones, or other materials for use in fencing. At a time when the number of farms was increasing substantially, imported wood proved too expensive and smooth wire failed to contain livestock. Fascinated by the potential of an armored wire fencing he saw at the DeKalb County Fair in 1873, Glidden determined to invent a more effective product. He twisted pieces of wire into barbs, then strung the barbs intermittently along two parallel strands of wire to form a durable fence that turned back any animals that bumped against it. Having successfully tested the wire on his own farm, Glidden received a patent for his invention in 1874 and began marketing the product the same year. He and his business partner, hardware merchant Isaac Ellwood, formed the Barb Fence Company of DeKalb and began selling the fencing at Ellwood's store as fast as they could make it. Hundreds of other inventors developed variations of "armored wire," and a patent war raged until the U.S. Supreme Court upheld Glidden's claims in 1892.

News of the fast-selling product spread quickly and attracted the interest of the owners of the Washburn and Moen Manufacturing Company of Worcester, Massachusetts. Eager to return to his first love, farming, the sixty-three-year-old Glidden agreed to sell the Worcester firm his half-interest in the company. The Washburn and Moen Company paid Glidden sixty thousand dollars and granted him a royalty of twenty-five cents on each hundredweight of wire manufactured for the next fifteen years (80.5 million pounds in 1880 alone). The transaction made Glidden a very wealthy man.

In the years following the sale of his patent, Glidden became DeKalb's leading entrepreneur and benefactor. He purchased more farmland; built and operated the community's leading hotel, the Glidden House; bought and then published the local newspaper, the *DeKalb Chronicle;* and assumed the vice presidency of a local bank. A devoted Democrat, he served one term as county sheriff and another as village mayor. Along with several other leading citizens, he successfully lobbied the general assembly to found a new state normal school in DeKalb and then donated sixty-four acres of his own land for the campus of the institution that later became Northern Illinois University.

Glidden's invention provided a durable and inexpensive means of enclosing vast expanses of open land and thereby exerted a great influence on the development of American agriculture. For the first time, Midwestern homesteaders could protect their pastures and crops from grazing cattle. Farther west, barbed wire ended open-range ranching by enabling large-scale ranchers to control their herds within large stretches of private property.

The Spirit of Reform

Only a few miles from the most opulent mansions on Chicago's South Side, thousands of men and women inhabited the cramped flophouses, missions, and vacant stoops of the city's infamous skid row. After visiting a boarding-house where transients paid two cents a night to huddle together on wooden shelves with no blankets, middle-class reformer Robert Hunter observed that the "animalism and despicable foulness and filth made one almost despair of mankind." Near the gilded homes of the "Sifted Few," Chicago housing officials commonly found as many as five people sleeping in the same bed in rickety tenements. Families residing in the city's teeming immigrant quarters suffered overcrowding, unsanitary living conditions, and disease, whether they were fortunate enough to be employed or not. Reformers lamented the natural tendency of the lower classes to seek refuge from their travails in the ubiquitous saloons dotting the cityscape, more than five hundred of them in the Stock Yards neighborhood alone. In Chicago's Levee, the red-light district a mile south of downtown, brothels, gambling dens, taverns, dance halls, arcades, and pawnshops offered wholesale vice to people from all over the city. Corrupt local officials winked at the immorality just as they largely ignored the deplorable conditions in which so many of the city's residents lived. Were such abominations inevitable in industrial cities? Could nothing be done to improve the lives of those excluded from the bounty of a generally affluent society?[1]

A variety of religious groups became active in the effort to ease the suffering of the growing number of poor people in Chicago and other Illinois cities. Protestant evangelists such as Dwight Moody and Billy Sunday adapted tent revivals, which had attracted huge throngs in rural America, to urban settings and established urban missions to preach the old gospel of sin and salvation. While Moody, Sunday, and other fire-and-brimstone ministers converted wayward souls by the thousands in Chicago, Roman Catholic missions also appeared throughout the Windy City. Young Men's

Christian Association (YMCA) and Young Women's Christian Association (YWCA) centers, originally designed to preserve the health and virtue of youngsters seeking their fortunes in the big city, offered a variety of services to travelers and residents in a wholesome environment. The Salvation Army, imported from England, gradually deemphasized its fervent evangelism and concentrated more on the provision of social services—as did many Protestant, Catholic, and Jewish agencies founded in Chicago's ethnic neighborhoods.

Secular varieties of reform proliferated alongside the burgeoning religious organizations. Imbued with a sense of optimism, a reverence for order, and a belief in the reliability of scientific inquiry and experimentation, progressives (as they called themselves) took aim at a number of nettlesome problems confronting the residents of Illinois communities in the late nineteenth and early twentieth centuries. Aging infrastructures needed to be restored, and expanding populations called for the delivery of more services. Rapid industrialization took a heavy toll on people's lives, altering the nature and pace of work, throwing more people into closer contact, and placing heavier demands on old institutions. Progressive reformers confronted the challenge of fashioning up-to-date solutions to problems created by modern technology.

A persistent technological problem concerned the provision of potable drinking water for Chicago's growing population, for example. Chicagoans had long dumped garbage, sewage, and all manner of industrial waste into the Chicago River, which then flowed into Lake Michigan, the source of the community's drinking water. The city piped its drinking water in from far offshore, but even so a brown, foul-smelling liquid (along with the occasional fish) still often poured out of the taps in Chicago homes. The water ranged from unpleasant to downright unhealthy. In 1889 the Illinois General Assembly approved a plan by engineers to construct a canal that would reverse the flow of the Chicago River and carry the effluent-laden water southward away from the lake. Following the course of the Illinois and Michigan Canal and extending twenty-eight miles southwest of the city to Lockport, the Chicago Sanitary and Ship Canal commenced operation in 1900. The massive waterway, standing 160 feet wide and 30 feet deep in places, solved the problem perfectly—at least as far as Chicagoans were concerned. Communities in downstate Illinois and Missouri complained about being the dumping ground for Chicago's garbage, but scientists responded that rivers flowing considerable distances cleansed themselves. Satisfied civil engineers adjudged the project an unqualified success.

Civil engineers collaborated with reformers to solve another vexing problem, the inadequacy of Illinois thoroughfares. The state's dirt roads, which turned to mud after heavy rains and winter thaws, proved entirely incapable of handling the increasing volume of automobile traffic. (Although Henry Ford and other Detroit-based companies soon established

their dominance, automobile factories existed in Chicago, Danville, Elgin, Kankakee, Rockford, Waukegan, and other Illinois cities in the industry's infancy.) Governor Charles S. Deneen (1905–1913), the first governor to address the issue in a systematic way, created a state highway
commission and appointed the state's first salaried engineer. During his
administration, the general assembly imposed a registration fee for license plates and designated the proceeds to a road-building fund. Governor Edward F. Dunne (1913–1917) strongly supported the good roads
movement, innovatively commuting parts of prisoners' sentences when
they worked on road-building gangs. But the great leap forward came under the administration of Governor Frank O. Lowden (1917–1921). The
Lowden administration drew up a plan to "pull Illinois out of the mud"
by funding the construction of four thousand miles of hard roads with a
sixty-million-dollar bond issue. Lowden oversaw the grading of roadways, while the paving occurred under his successor, Governor Len Small
(1921–1929). By the end of Small's administration, Illinois boasted of
more than seven thousand miles of paved roads. Usually a staunch opponent of reform, Small made an exception for the politically popular good
roads movement.[2]

Small's reform-minded predecessors in the governor's mansion had
also sought to bring greater honesty and efficiency to the operation of
state government. Progressives in Illinois blanched at the administrative
chaos that frequently prevailed in Springfield and that inhibited the operation of government bureaucracies. Governor Deneen agreed that an
entrenched system of patronage and spoilsmanship caused much of the
inertia and, like other progressives in Illinois and elsewhere, recommended the installation of a merit-based civil service system. Entrenched interests in Springfield blocked Deneen's attempts to impose a
comprehensive civil service system on Illinois government, but he
guided through the general assembly a law that replaced the state's seventeen welfare agencies (with their twenty-two hundred employees)
with a five-member board. Empowered to discharge incompetent employees, this board instituted a new hiring policy that was tied to performance on civil service examinations. Sympathetic to the goal of
streamlining state government, Governor Dunne appointed a commission, chaired by Professor John Fairlie of the University of Illinois, that
recommended the wholesale consolidation of multitudinous state agencies into a handful of departments.

With Deneen and Dunne having laid the groundwork for a thorough
reorganization of state government, Governor Lowden completed the
process during his first two months in office. The Civil Administrative
Code of 1917, which Lowden artfully steered through a progressive general
assembly, immediately won national acclaim as a model of state government reform. Patterned closely on Fairlie's outline, the code dissolved

more than one hundred state bureaucracies and left in their stead nine departments—agriculture, finance, labor, mines and minerals, public health, public welfare, public works and buildings, registration and education, and trade and commerce. The heads of these departments served in the governor's cabinet along with the head of the civil service commission, which oversaw hiring and firing practices in the nine units. Amendments in the code added and subtracted departments in subsequent decades, but the basic structure created by the 1917 code remained in place. Illinois progressives hailed the reorganization of state government as one of the reform movement's foremost triumphs.

Structural reform in Springfield notwithstanding, many progressives believed that the lion's share of modern industrial society's problems emanated from the mistreatment of the labor force. Because of the ineffectuality of the Knights of Labor, the American Federation of Labor, and other nascent trade unions, workers continued to endure low wages, long hours, and unsafe conditions as the nineteenth century gave way to the twentieth. University of Chicago economist Paul H. Douglas, who later fought for workers' interests as a U.S. senator, carefully documented the rock-bottom wages paid in Illinois's mass-production industries. In 1900, Douglas found, steelworkers laboring in the state's blast furnaces and rolling mills earned an average annual wage of $561.00, which translated to roughly $10.50 per week; workers in farm implement factories received $531.00 annually, or roughly $10.20 per week. According to his study of Chicago's meatpacking industry in 1904, workers on average received annual wages of $473.00, or $9.10 per week. Coal miners earned as much as $5.00 a day, thanks largely to aggressive unions, but they could wring few concessions from the mine owners regarding safer working conditions. Moreover, the mines operated sporadically—for example, for only 181 days in Sangamon County during the year ending in June 1913.

Women wage earners fared worse. In 1913, when single women needed to earn at least $8.00 a week to live in a city, the Illinois Manufacturers' Association reported that fifty-seven thousand women in Chicago received less than $5.00 weekly. In Peoria the lowest-paid women made as little as $3.50 per week, in Springfield $2.75 per week. The worst jobs for women were probably in Chicago's garment industry, where sweatshop owners ruthlessly exploited immigrant girls, using the piecework system and requiring long workdays in dark, airless shops. In their testimony before a state investigating commission, executives from one of the most notorious firms admitted that one of their female employees made as little as $2.60 per week but noted that she could earn more if she worked a whole week. Instead, the thirty-six-year-old Russian immigrant, a mother of three children, chose to work only forty-seven hours a week.

Employees in most Illinois industries continued to spend long hours on the job. In the steel mills, where implacable resistance by management had decimated the unions, workers often labored more than seventy hours a week. In the needle trades, men and women generally worked ten-hour days in a six-day week; clerks at Chicago's downtown retail stores also worked sixty-hour weeks. The most fortunate workers in such privileged industries as printing, breweries, and tobacco toiled forty-eight hours per week, and sometimes less.

Safety in the workplace became a grave concern for the public, and nowhere more so than in Illinois's coal mines. Miners claimed with considerable justification that theirs was the most hazardous occupation in the state. Dynamite explosions, fires, and faulty scaffolding in tiny mine shafts posed constant, lethal threats; coal dust and other toxic fumes took a deadly toll at a more gradual pace. A fire that killed 259 men in 1909 at Cherry Mine No. 2 in Bureau County, the most lethal mine disaster in Illinois history, graphically demonstrated the perils faced daily by the miners. Spurred on by public outrage at the tragedy, members of the general assembly gathered to examine inadequate mine-safety legislation. By the end of the special session, legislators had drafted a new set of regulations. As a bonus, the general assembly soon added the state's first workmen's compensation law.

To the dismay of the middle class, child labor remained a commonplace in industry. In some instances, children took jobs away from able-bodied adult workers. Long hours and hard work in unsafe conditions left physically immature young people susceptible to illness and accidents. Employment at an early age meant forgoing education and the opportunity for play, losses that immigrant families routinely judged acceptable in order to supplement meager household incomes. Well-intentioned reformers bent on eradicating child labor often encountered staunch resistance in immigrant neighborhoods where a family's survival depended upon financial contributions from all of its members.

It is not surprising that most workers resided in substandard housing. With little money to spend on transportation, they lived near their jobs in neighborhoods replete with poorly constructed tenements and tiny single-family dwellings. Real estate owners in Chicago crammed hastily built wooden structures onto standard lots measuring twenty-five by one hundred feet, leaving postage stamp–sized yards and minimizing light and ventilation. Tenements frequently covered three-fourths of the lots on which they stood. Few immigrant dwellings contained indoor toilets; family members had to use backyard privies, the contents of which frequently filled to overflowing. In some of the Windy City's most crowded working-class neighborhoods, such as the heavily Italian enclave southwest of downtown, the population density exceeded ninety persons per acre. An investigator of Chicago housing found the population density in the Polish quarter "three times that of the most crowded portions of Tokyo, Calcutta, and many other Asiatic cities."[3]

Reformers rued the high population densities, unsanitary living conditions, and other social ills that resulted from immigrants being crowded into Chicago's tenements.
Illinois State Historical Library

The horrible conditions in Chicago's working-class neighborhoods became a national scandal because of the muckraking exposés published in the early twentieth century. In the most sensational of these volumes, *The Jungle,* socialist Upton Sinclair described the horrors of Chicago's meatpacking industry as well as the miserable living conditions endured by the immigrants working in the stockyards. Hoping to discredit the capitalist system by detailing the ruthless exploitation of the hapless immigrant masses, Sinclair nevertheless found that his graphic descriptions of unsanitary practices on the killing floors most profoundly affected readers. "I aimed at the public's heart," Sinclair sadly remarked, "and by accident, I hit it in the stomach." The meatpackers denied the accuracy of the picture portrayed in *The Jungle,* but a congressional investigation confirmed the stories of filth and indifferent inspection in the meat industry. An outraged public demanded action—and Congress passed the Meat Inspection Act and the Pure Food and Drug Act—but the living conditions of workers in Packingtown remained abysmal.[4]

While Sinclair's novel generated more reaction nationally than locally, William T. Stead's *If Christ Came to Chicago* became an overnight best-seller and the topic of intense ongoing conversation in Chicago. A British journalist who came to Chicago to attend the Columbian Exposition in 1893, Stead strayed from the exhibits and tourist attractions to investigate the city's seamy underside. His 460-page book told lurid stories of gambling, prostitution, alcoholism, and crime among the city's poor. In one of the book's most famous passages, the scandalized Englishman described the famed Everleigh Club, an elegant brothel that entertained the cream of Midwestern society and paid its female employees as much as one hundred dollars weekly. Outraged Chicagoans decried Stead's audacity in airing the city's dirty laundry, and calling the book "a directory of sin," the *Chicago Tribune* recommended that it be banned. Content to confine vice within the carefully delimited boundaries of the Levee, the city's politicians ignored the book and the calls for reform it generated.[5]

Nor did Chicago's politicians evince much interest generally in the finer points of city governance. Members of the ruling clique in city hall—the aldermen collectively known as the gray wolves—accepted bribes, sold their votes to the highest bidder, and otherwise lined their pockets at every turn while ignoring the common good. Grafters, or "boodlers" as they came to be known in the Windy City, peddled their influence in the utilities and traction industries especially. The need for mass transportation and gas and electric services in rapidly expanding municipalities gave city councils the opportunity to grant valuable franchises to private companies—and to demand handsome remuneration in exchange for these considerations. Periodic scandals erupted as greedy city councilmen created dummy utility corporations and awarded them franchises.

Chicago's "traction wars" of the late nineteenth century revolved around the attempt made by Charles Tyson Yerkes to gain a monopoly over the city's electric streetcar business. The ruthless Yerkes, who came to Chicago after serving time in a Philadelphia prison and who became the model for the unscrupulous protagonist of Theodore Dreiser's novel *The Titan,* improved transit service by consolidating several lines, extending routes throughout the city, and modernizing equipment. He built the

Union Loop, the elevated line that encircled the downtown and gave Chicago's central business district its lasting nickname. Nevertheless, he became a hated figure locally for he watered stock, ignored the comfort and safety of passengers, raised fares, and saturated the city council with bribes. Yerkes finally lost his battle in the city council for a ninety-nine-year franchise when two equally unprincipled politicians, aldermen Michael "Hinky Dink" Kenna and "Bathhouse" John Coughlin, refused his $150,000 bribe and voted against him. In explaining the vote, Coughlin declared his preference for petty graft over such huge sums. "There's little risk and in the long run it pays a damned sight more," he opined. Yerkes sold his Chicago holdings and left for London.[6]

The rampant corruption in city government led to a series of reform movements in Chicago and elsewhere during the late nineteenth century and early years of the twentieth century. Progressives believed that the task of improving the quality of city governance began with throwing the rascals out of city hall. In the minds of respectable middle-class reformers, grasping politicians won elections and helped themselves to boodle after duping the uninformed, often apathetic electorate. If reformers could educate the voters, many of whom were unlettered immigrants susceptible to the schemes of political charlatans, then ameliorative legislation could be passed and the best men elected. Determined to vanquish political machines, they formed organizations of their own to advance good government. (Chicago machine politicians derisively referred to these reformers as "goo-goos.") In 1896, for example, more than forty thousand indignant Chicagoans joined the Municipal Voters' League to clean up local government. Backed by local newspapers, the league conducted investigations, supported independent reform candidates for office, and became a formidable force in local politics.

Throughout the Progressive Era, members of the Municipal Voters' League and other reformist groups fought to control city government. They helped in a number of instances to install progressive mayors in city hall who fought the good fight against the gray wolves in the city council. Carter Harrison II, who served as mayor from 1897 to 1905 and from 1911 to 1915, succeeded in improving such services as water purification, sewage disposal, and fire protection. Some reformers complained that Harrison ignored vice and cut political deals with some of the city's shadier aldermen, but they praised the mayor for defeating Yerkes in the traction wars. Harrison led the fight against the merger of corrupt utility companies, thereby lowering bills for Chicago customers, and made the streets safer by forcing the street railroad companies to elevate their tracks above street level. Edward F. Dunne, who later served as governor of Illinois, sported even better reform credentials than Harrison but achieved decidedly less. His advocacy of the municipal ownership of public transit fell short, and his crusade against the saloons turned many of the city's immigrants against him. Fred Busse settled the traction issue temporarily by awarding twenty-five-year franchises and commencing the electrification of the streetcar lines, and he appointed businessman Charles H. Wacker to chair a commission on city beautification. Under the direction of famed architect Charles H. Burnham, the Wacker Commission undertook a series of projects that transformed Chicago's lakefront and downtown.

Progressives believed that improved urban life could result from the physical transformation of the cities. Lamenting the haphazard growth of metropolitan areas in the past—unregulated growth at the whim of investors that left cities well suited for business but not for living—they employed professional city planners to alter existing land use as well as to devise new growth strategies. In 1909 architect Burnham presented his Chicago Plan, a 164-page blueprint for remaking the Windy City. "Make no little plans," Burnham said. "They have no magic to stir men's blood." He made no little plans for Chicago, offering instead a bold and sweeping proposal that refashioned the city's downtown and the surrounding real estate extending out to a sixty-mile radius. His vision included landscaped boulevards instead of crowded city streets, a twenty-mile-long park alongside Lake Michigan, acres of new parkland strewn throughout the city, reclamation of the noisome Chicago River, and completion of a new downtown civic center filled with massive buildings constructed in the classical architectural style.[7]

Burnham's grandiose design never came fully to fruition, but city fathers, suitably impressed, incorporated much of the Chicago Plan. He died in 1912 having seen little change incorporated into Chicago's cityscape, but in subsequent years the Chicago Planning Commission (under Wacker's driving leadership) doggedly completed many of his projects. Burnham's passionate appeal to beautify the city's seedy lakefront, to turn a neglected residue of industrial growth into a showplace, became reality with the creation of Grant Park, Navy Pier, Northerly Island, and Lake Shore Drive. Following Burnham's lead, the city relocated railroad terminals, built bridges, and completed a network of roads that completely altered traffic patterns. His Chicago Plan legitimized city planning and made him the foremost proponent of the City Beautiful Movement, which changed the faces of downtowns in countless American cities.

At the same time that Chicago became a pacesetter in the twentieth century's first version of urban renewal, another variety of reform took the Windy City and much of the nation by storm. Middle-class reformers, many of them women, opened settlement houses in some of the city's worst neighborhoods in an effort to improve the lives of the immigrant poor. In 1887 Jane Addams, a native of Cedarville, Illinois, and her friend, Ellen Gates Starr, visited the world's first settlement house, Toynbee Hall, established in London by Oxford University students three years before. In 1889 Addams and Starr opened Hull House in an old mansion on South Halstead Street in Chicago. In a densely populated, primarily Italian neighborhood on Chicago's Near West Side, the Hull House staff initiated a host of programs for the downtrodden immigrant population. Addams and her cohorts taught English language courses, operated kindergartens and a day care center, sponsored music and dance classes, supervised a gymnasium and the city's first public playground, scheduled presentations by guest speakers, and served inexpensive meals in a large dining hall. In short, the country's best-known settlement house became a haven for the poor in the midst of an otherwise hostile urban environment. Other settlements soon followed, including Charles Zueblin's Northwestern University Settlement (1891), Graham Taylor's Chicago Commons (1894), and Mary McDowell's University of Chicago Settlement (1894) near the stockyards. By 1900 fifteen settlement houses were operating in Chicago.

Settlement houses attracted a coterie of talented, reform-minded women to Chicago and, in turn, bred a number of other reform movements. Mary McDowell, the founder of the University of Chicago Settlement House, fought a long and successful campaign to keep the city from dumping garbage in the immigrant neighborhoods. She became a leader in the local labor movement and won election as president of the Chicago branch of the Women's Trade Union League (WTUL). Mary Dreier Robbins succeeded McDowell as the head of the local chapter and went on to win the national presidency of the WTUL. Julia Lathrop helped draft the Illinois juvenile court law (the first in the world), created the first juvenile court in Chicago, and became the first woman member of the state board of public charities. Florence Kelley worked for the 1893 Illinois law that curbed the employment of children in sweatshops, and she became the state's first factory inspector. Such talented Hull House alumni as Grace Abbott, Sophonisba Breckenridge, Alice Hamilton, and Louise DeKoven Bowen created a myriad of institutions at both local and state levels to aid the city's unfortunates and then went on to prominent national positions in social welfare agencies.

Working in settlement houses, creating and staffing new government agencies, joining organizations or acting individually, women assumed a prominent role in the progressive movement. Even though the 1870 state constitution maintained voting as an exclusively male prerogative, women became increasingly active politically in the last decades of the nineteenth century. Suffragists chipped away for years at the resistance to women's voting and made gradual progress. Black women's clubs, such as the Alpha Suffrage Club and the Frederick Douglass Woman's Club, lobbied aggressively for female suffrage. In 1891 Illinois women obtained the right to vote in school board elections, although they could not cast ballots for county superintendents of schools or the state superintendent of public instruction; in 1909 they received the right to hold school offices not created by statute. In 1913 the general assembly passed a law making Illinois the first state east of the Mississippi River to grant women the right to vote in municipal and presidential elections. Six years later, the state ratified the Nineteenth Amendment, which provided for women's suffrage in all elections.

During the decades that they worked for the vote, women contributed to the reform effort through their work in a multitude of women's associations. Impervious to divisions based upon race, ethnicity, class, and religion, the historian Maureen A. Flanagan noted, women in Chicago developed a vision of the city "that promoted a concept of urban life and good government rooted in social justice, social welfare, and responsiveness to the everyday needs of all the city's residents." Whereas male reformers primarily sought to wrench political power away from corrupt politicians and to restore honesty, efficiency, and order to municipal government, their female counterparts broadened the field to engage all the city's residents in a grassroots effort. Women reformers agitated for better housing, schools, workplaces, streets, and urban service; they broke new ground in calling for parks, playgrounds, beaches, kindergartens, and day care centers. They spoke for women, children, immigrants, African Americans, and other groups traditionally excluded from mainstream society. Although women reformers' vision remained unfulfilled in certain cases, their achievements frequently changed the face of urban life.[8]

Women's associations became inextricably involved with several reform causes as part of their desire for better municipal housekeeping. That is, they applied their own housekeeping expertise in a larger attempt to make the city a healthier, cleaner, and safer place in which to live. Such an orientation inevitably led to an interest in housing reform, and women's groups took the lead in the crusade to make adequate lodging available to all classes in the city. At the outset this meant conducting detailed surveys of the housing stock and widely disseminating the information gathered. In 1895, for example, the residents of Hull House published *Hull House Maps and Papers,* the first detailed study of inadequate housing in a Chicago neighborhood. Women's groups argued for municipal ordinances that would raise health and safety standards in the city's tenements and for the construction of model housing units by government—a reform that met considerable opposition from real estate interests as an unwarranted intrusion by government into the private market. Wider provision of low-income housing by government awaited the Great Depression of the 1930s.

Women's concern with public health and safety also led to calls for enhanced involvement by municipal government, and again Hull House led the way. Addams, McDowell, and others condemned Chicago's longtime practice of awarding franchises to private companies for the collection of garbage. They argued that the awarding of exclusive contracts led to bribes and kickbacks in city hall as well as to shoddy service in the neighborhoods. Under the relentless scrutiny of the Woman's City Club (WCC), the city council opted in 1914 for municipal garbage collection and disposal. Following the Iroquois Theater Fire of 1903, in which 602 men, women, and children perished, women activists blamed corrupt politicians and building inspectors for failure to enforce fire safety standards. In 1912 the city council finally created the Bureau of Fire Protection and Public Safety within the fire department. Reformers enjoyed less success in their efforts to upgrade the quality of the city's air, a formidable task with Chicago so reliant upon the burning of coal for heat. Tired of seeing their laundry darkening on the line and a thin layer of grit settling on the food they served their families, women launched a fight against smoke pollution. Working with the WCC, the Anti-Smoke League called on city government to adopt smoke abatement ordinances and to enforce them vigorously. Significant business interests prevailed, however, and the city council stopped short of enacting any restrictions on smoke emissions.

As political activists, women in Chicago also became embroiled in the attempt to reform the public school system. Reformers' interest stemmed from two separate issues, the improvement of instruction for the community's children and better treatment of teachers (the vast majority of whom were women) by school administrators (mostly men). With regard to the former issue, they advocated increased spending for the schools and the application of John Dewey's principles of progressive education; to achieve the latter, they favored higher salaries and a greater voice for teachers in the educational bureaucracy. Because of these priorities, women reformers backed the Chicago Teachers' Federation (CTF) in an ongoing struggle against a conservative board of education dominated by wealthy businessmen. In 1907 newly elected Mayor Fred Busse forced the resignation from the board of education of progressive board members thought to be on good terms with the CTF and affirmed his support of Superintendent Edwin Cooley, a conservative with strong ties to the business community who had repeatedly cut teachers' salaries. When ill health forced Cooley to retire in 1909, however, the school board selected Ella Flagg Young as his replacement. A cohort of Dewey's at the University of Chicago and principal of the Chicago Normal School, Young became the first woman to head the public school system of a major metropolis.

Reformers cheered when Young raised teachers' salaries, involved faculty in curricular and other pedagogical matters, initiated a penny-lunch program for elementary school students, and worked cooperatively with the CTF, but the board of education increasingly failed to act upon her recommendations. Complaining that she had been "the victim of a political intrigue" among school board members, Young resigned in 1913 and ignited a public furor that raged for months. Jane Addams, the WCC, and other women's groups enlisted the support of Mayor Harrison, against the board, and Young rescinded her resignation. An uneasy peace prevailed until 1915 when, while Young was on vacation, the board adopted the antilabor Loeb Rule, which both prohibited teachers from joining any organization whose executive officers were not teachers and required teachers to sign pledges not to join unions. Young retired and left Chicago. In later decades, women continued to lead the battle for reform of public education.[9]

Progressives devoted to the improvement of education cared also about the state's institutions of higher learning, and they found in Governor John P. Altgeld a champion of their cause. Like many other reformers, Altgeld thought it especially important that Illinois increase its support of public colleges and universities. The governor conceded that private institutions such as Northwestern University and the University of Chicago could make useful contributions, but he thought them elitist and undemocratic—"creatures of monopolistic wealth," he called them. Advanced learning for the masses must be the responsibility of government, he believed. Determined to enhance the state's financial contributions to the University of Illinois, he successfully championed an unprecedented legislative appropriation of $422,000 for the Champaign-Urbana school in 1895. Equally committed to improving teacher training programs, Altgeld advocated increased support for the state's normal schools. He lobbied in the general assembly for more liberal appropriations for existing normal schools in Carbondale and Normal and helped secure funding for the establishment of new normal schools in DeKalb and Charleston. In all, Altgeld did more for higher education than any of his predecessors in the governor's mansion.[10]

Some reformers seeking the improvement of society through better education sought the same result through the elimination of alcoholic beverages. The Woman's Christian Temperance Union (WCTU), headquartered for many years in Evanston, attracted a large following among women in rural and small-town Illinois, who argued that the elimination of saloons would cure a host of societal evils such as gambling, prostitution, high crime rates, and family dissolution. A different situation prevailed in Chicago and other large cities, however, where the huge immigrant population vigorously opposed the passage of legislation designed to limit personal freedoms. Strong opposition to the temperance movement existed also in Peoria, where the distilleries comprised a powerful economic interest. In Rockford, temperance opponents pointed out that the city could ill afford to close down the taverns; in 1895, they estimated, the city received more than thirty-eight thousand dollars in saloon license fees. Undeterred, progressives charged that saloon interests colluded with local politicians in an unholy alliance that governed many of the state's larger communities.

Prospects improved for the temperance movement around the turn of the twentieth century. Wracked by internal dissension and dealt a crippling blow in 1898 by the death of its renowned leader, Frances Willard, the WCTU surrendered its leadership in the antialcohol crusade to the Anti-Saloon League (ASL). Recognizing the unlikelihood of making the entire state dry immediately, the ASL concentrated its considerable efforts on securing local option legislation. Every year between 1901 and 1907, the

A newspaper cartoon applauds the Anti-Saloon League's "turning up the heat" on the state's liquor interests. *Illinois State Historical Library*

WELL, IS IT HOT ENOUGH FOR YOU?

ASL introduced local option bills in the general assembly, and the 1907 version finally passed. No local option referendum ever appeared on a ballot in Chicago, which in the ensuing years remained as wet as ever, but much of the rest of the state dried up. In 1910 dry advocates boasted that no saloons operated in 40 of the state's 102 counties or in 1,059 of its 1,500 townships. By the time that Illinois ratified the Eighteenth Amendment in 1919, which established Prohibition nationwide, 55 counties and 1,425 townships had already eradicated saloons under the 1907 local option statute. Under the aegis of the Eighteenth Amendment, officials closed seven thousand saloons in Chicago, three hundred in Peoria, and two hundred and twenty in Springfield.

The tension between Chicago and much of the rest of the state over the alcohol question underscored the ambivalence felt by many immigrants about progressive reform. In many instances, as historian John D. Buenker has shown, immigrant politicians avidly supported reform measures in city councils and state legislatures. Realizing the potential benefits for their constituents, new-stock lawmakers voted for bread-and-butter reforms aimed at better housing, safer workplaces, and a healthier environment. At the same time, however, immigrants brought with them to America various customs and religious practices that conflicted with the type of moralistic reform urged by old-stock middle-class progressives. In Illinois this meant that delegations to the general assembly from Chicago and other cities with heterogeneous populations frequently failed to support reforms popular elsewhere in the state. Whereas middle-class reformers and various education groups backed a proposal for the distribution of free and uniform textbooks to public school students, for example, Roman Catholic and Lutheran clergymen led the opposition. Immigrants approved of free textbooks but balked at the imposition of uniform tracts that would preach conformity to native values and customs. The same groups disagreed about the desirability of legalizing and regulating professional athletics. Urban immigrant legislators introduced a series of bills into the general assembly to create a state athletic commission and to legalize prizefighting; coalitions of rural and small-town politicians defeated them all.

Old-stock middle-class reformers sympathetic to the plight of immigrants in Chicago formed the Illinois Immigrants' Protective League (IPL) in 1908. A list of the IPL's founders included Jane Addams; Margaret Dreier Robbins, WTUL president; Grace Abbott, who later became director of the federal Children's Bureau; Sophonisba Breckenridge, social worker and University of Chicago professor; and Julius Rosenwald, chairman of the board of Sears, Roebuck and Company. The IPL initially concentrated upon the protection of immigrants, especially single women and young girls, when they first arrived in Chicago. Aware that approximately 20 percent of women who left New York City's Ellis Island for Chicago never arrived at their destinations, IPL members found that many ended up in saloons, brothels, and labor camps as victims of the white slave trade. In addition to meeting newcomers at railroad stations and guiding them to safe and suitable lodging, IPL members provided them with assistance in finding work, enrolling in school, and dealing with the police and other authorities. Often, they worked in tandem with settlement houses and other local social welfare institutions. Middle-class, Protestant, old-stock IPL members reported struggling with their own ethnocentrism and admitted their own ignorance of immigrant customs, but they played an important role in aiding immigrants at a time when government offered no such social welfare services.

Like immigrants, African Americans encountered many hardships in industrial cities where segregation prevailed. Unwelcome at Hull House and other settlement houses in Chicago, the residents of black neighborhoods frequented the Negro Fellowship League, the Wendell Phillips Settlement, the Emanuel Settlement, the Clotee Scott Settlement, and the Frederick Douglass Center. These settlements provided domestic and manual training, youth recreational programs, lectures, and employment information. Ida B. Wells founded the first black women's club in Chicago, which became the headquarters for the Illinois Federation of Colored Women's Clubs (IFCWC) in 1899. Black club women developed programs in child and elderly care throughout Illinois, including the Phyllis Wheatley Club for Youth in Chicago, the Amanda Smith Home in Harvey, and the Lincoln Colored Home in Springfield. The Big Sister Club of Decatur worked with juvenile courts to rehabilitate black delinquent girls and to help place them in suitable homes. By 1922 the IFCWC, with more than eighty clubs statewide, was the largest organization in Illinois advancing the interests of African Americans.

In the aftermath of the Springfield race riot in 1908, reformers founded national organizations that opened branch offices in Chicago and other Illinois cities. The National Association for the Advancement of Colored People (NAACP), founded in 1909 in New York, opened a chapter in Chicago two years later and grew out of the efforts of white activists such as Jane Addams and Emil Hirsch and African American leaders George Hall and Charles Bentley. The biracial organization concentrated on legal and legislative activities concerned with securing equal rights for blacks. By contrast, the National Urban League, founded nationally in 1911, sought to provide job opportunities for African Americans in industrial settings and to provide social welfare benefits for struggling black immigrants in cities. The Chicago branch opened in 1917, and in the early years of the twentieth century, like the NAACP, the Chicago Urban League relied almost entirely on philanthropic contributions from Julius Rosenwald and other white progressives. These organizations played a larger role as the African American population increased significantly in later years.

Whether seeking to improve the lives of African Americans, or those of immigrants or other groups in Illinois communities, reformers invariably proceeded along similar lines. Educating the public and then seeking change within existing institutions, they imposed middle-class values and pursued measured solutions. To be sure, some critics who articulated a full-blown critique of capitalism dismissed the possibility that conservative American society could produce the kind of change necessary to create a truly humane and egalitarian society. A number of political dissidents joined the Socialist party in the early twentieth century, for example, and socialist candidates won election to public office in fifty-four Illinois communities between 1900 and 1920. They enjoyed the greatest electoral success in small and medium-sized towns, although a coalition of Yankee, German, and Scandinavian socialists maintained control of local government in Rockford for more than thirty years. More common was the experience of Upton Sinclair, however, who saw progressives with limited reform objectives co-opt the radical message of his socialist tract, *The Jungle*. Reformers saw the protection of meat-eating consumers as a more sensible and realizable goal than the dismantling of the American economic system. They were, after all, reformers and not revolutionaries.

The spirit of reform that animated Illinois communities during the period of American history known as the Progressive Era produced a number of salutary changes. Some of the problems that emerged during the period of rapid industrialization proved immune to reformist solutions, but there was much that changed to improve the lives of the working class. Women played leading roles in a variety of movements, becoming forceful and frequently successful advocates for change. Reformers often enlisted government as the agent of change, establishing a procedure that intensified during the twentieth century. The spirit of reform ebbed as the nation became embroiled in World War I, but the number and complexity of problems generated by industrialism assured that the drive for improving society would resume in later years.

Harvey

Turlington Harvey was born in upstate New York on May 10, 1835, and moved to Chicago at the age of nineteen with, according to legend, only one copper penny in his pocket. He went into the lumber business and eventually owned mills in Michigan and Wisconsin along with ninety lumberyards in and around Chicago. He became a local hero when he rebuilt tenements for workers rendered homeless by the Great Fire of 1871. Harvey became a good friend of the famed Protestant evangelist Dwight L. Moody, who had conducted services for Confederate prisoners at Camp Douglas and later spearheaded the social gospel movement that preached salvation in the industrial cities of the late nineteenth century. The devout Harvey became one of the principal benefactors of Chicago's social gospel movement, contributing considerable sums of money to the Moody Bible Institute and underwriting the YMCA.

Hoping to create a new community that would advance the principles of Christianity, Harvey looked for a site outside Chicago where he could found a new city. In 1891 he purchased seven hundred acres at the intersection of the Illinois Central and Grand Trunk railroads, approximately twenty miles south of the Loop, and incorporated the village of Harvey. Having built the first steel cars used by the railroads, he located his massive American Fire-Proof Steel Car Company factory in the heart of the new town. To lure other businesses into the planned industrial sector of his new community, Harvey offered free land and generous subsidies. Most important, he felt, was that Harvey, Illinois, might provide employers the opportunity to situate their enterprises in a wholesome environment where industrious and pious workers could raise their families.

Under the guidance of Harvey, Moody, and other prominent religious figures who served as members of the Harvey Land Association, the new village began as a temperance town as well as a planned industrial community. Although Harvey rejected the comprehensive social engineering employed in nearby Pullman and insisted that the residents of his town be afforded considerable autonomy, he remained adamant that temperance be unceasingly enforced. Firmly committed to the benefits of sobriety for the working class, Harvey included restrictive covenants prohibiting the sale of alcoholic beverages in every deed of sale to homeowners.

The "Magic City," as advertising circulars called the new village, prospered in its early days. Thousands of visitors to the 1893 Chicago World's Fair traveled by train to tour the famed experiment in Christian urban living. Harvey's population increased to five thousand within the first two years, and ten factories opened during the same time. Boom times ended with the Panic of 1893, however. Land values plunged and Turlington Harvey saw his financial holdings evaporate. The citizens of Harvey narrowly upheld temperance for a few years in a series of public referenda but, freed of their founder's influence, soon voted to license saloons. The temperance clauses of the original Harvey property deeds were declared unconstitutional by the Cook County courts. References to Harvey as a temperance community had disappeared from local newspapers and broadsides by the early 1900s. The community continued to grow but became just one of many municipalities wedged into the sprawling suburban network extending south of Chicago. Residents quickly forgot Harvey's origins in an earlier era's spirit of reform.

Jane Addams

Jane Addams was the most famous American woman of the early twentieth century and one of the most important reformers of the Progressive Era. Born in Cedarville, Illinois, on September 6, 1860, she grew up in an affluent home. Her father, John Huy Addams, served several terms as a state senator. After graduating from Rockford Female Seminary (later Rockford College) in 1881, she attended Philadelphia's Woman's Medical College for six months before dropping out because of poor health. On her second trip to Europe, she observed the first settlement house designed to aid London's poor, Toynbee Hall. Back in the United States, she left Cedarville and settled in Chicago. Single, college-educated, independently wealthy due to a large family inheritance, and living in a society that offered few choices to women in her circumstances, she faced the question of what to do with her life.

In 1889, along with a college friend, Ellen Gates Starr, she founded Hull House in one of the city's teeming immigrant neighborhoods. Addams recruited other wealthy, well-educated young people to take up residence among the urban poor in order to ease the burden of poverty, accelerate the assimilation of the immigrant masses, and publicize the regrettable living and working conditions spawned by industrialization. Although not the first settlement house opened in the United States, Hull House became under Addams's tireless leadership a model that was copied by countless institutions in cities throughout the nation. She clearly explicated the philosophical underpinnings of the settlement house movement in a number of magazine and newspaper articles as well as in her widely read book, *Twenty Years at Hull House* (1910).

Jane Addams of Hull House, one of the leading reformers in the United States for more than four decades. *Illinois State Historical Library*

From her post at Hull House, Addams became an influential figure in the era's reform movement. An eloquent public speaker and prolific writer, she championed a number of progressive causes while attending to the day-to-day operations of Hull House. An avid supporter of working men and women, she helped found the WTUL, attempted to mediate the Pullman strike in 1894, and aided the labor activities of Florence Kelley, a Hull House resident who became Illinois's factory inspector. Unafraid to mix it up in the political arena, Addams worked hard for woman's suffrage, served several terms on the city's school board, led reform elements in an effort to unseat her ward's corrupt alderman, and seconded Theodore Roosevelt's nomination for president at the Bull Moose party convention in 1912. Although Hull House excluded African Americans, Addams expressed her personal sympathy for the plight of black Americans and helped found the NAACP in 1909.

A determined advocate of international peace and staunch opponent of militarism, Addams spoke out repeatedly against U.S. involvement in World War I. One of the founders of the Woman's Peace party in 1915, she was elected the first president of the Women's International League for Peace and Freedom (WILPF) in 1919 and supported the antiwar activities of the National Committee on the Cause and Cure of War throughout the late 1920s and early 1930s. Her pacifism generated considerable criticism and tarnished her previously unblemished reputation. In 1931, however, she received the Nobel Peace Prize for her work with the WILPF. Addams died on May 21, 1935, in Chicago, having won international renown for her peace advocacy as well as for her social welfare activism.

An Artistic Renaissance

Chicago's phenomenal growth after the Great Fire of 1871 notwithstanding, the image of a crude frontier community stubbornly persisted. The city's population and industrial production increased dramatically, but residents of the nation's Eastern cities saw little evidence of cultural refinement in the remote prairie outpost. Chicago suffered from no shortage of factories, railroad yards, or hard-driving capitalists, supercilious Easterners observed, but where was the evidence of high culture expected of every great city? Visitors from New York City, Boston, Philadelphia, and other Atlantic seaports disparaged the Windy City for its dearth of opera houses, libraries, museums, and comparable institutions. What contributions, after all, were Chicagoans making to the advancement of Western civilization? The city's leading citizens saw the need to change these unflattering popular perceptions, and their efforts began to pay real dividends in the last decades of the nineteenth century. Chicago became the cultural capital of the Midwest and the center of an artistic renaissance.

Nothing helped more in the quest to brighten Chicago's tarnished image than the Columbian Exposition of 1893. Throughout the nineteenth century some of the largest and wealthiest cities in the world had held a series of expositions (also called world's fairs) to showcase new technology and promote their own urban triumphs. Such extravaganzas included the 1851 Crystal Palace Exposition in London; the 1876 Centennial Exposition in Philadelphia, which commemorated the centenary of the American Declaration of Independence; and the 1889 Paris Exposition, which unveiled the Eiffel Tower. When the U.S. Congress authorized cities to compete for the honor of hosting an exposition honoring the fourth centenary of Christopher Columbus's discovery of the New World, Chicago seemed a most unlikely choice. New York and European skeptics quickly dismissed Chicago's candidacy as preposterous, for how could such an upstart with so little history of its own pretend to mount an appropriate salute to four hundred years of American history? New York City, Washington, D.C., and St. Louis quickly emerged as frontrunners in the competition, but leading Chicagoans and their allies throughout Illinois were feverishly working to capture the honor. Thanks to the impressive ten-million-dollar bid that the city managed to submit and the indefatigable behind-the-scenes politicking of Illinois Senator Shelby Cullom, President Benjamin Harrison signed the law in 1890 that awarded the exposition to Chicago. Spurned suitors from New York City, Washington, D.C., and St. Louis were aghast.

In a remarkably short period of time (less than three years from start to finish), Chicago transformed an uninviting 633-acre tract of flat marshlands south of downtown in Jackson Park into one of the greatest world's fairs in history. Frederick Law Olmsted, the famed landscape architect who had created New York City's Central Park, drained the Jackson Park swamps and fashioned lakefront fairgrounds that contained a lagoon surrounded by exhibit halls and a basin to hold facsimiles of Christopher Columbus's three vessels. Chief architect Daniel Burnham enlisted some of the world's foremost architects to design the seventeen major buildings and the more than one hundred lesser structures that covered the landscape. Massive convention halls composed of steel frames covered with

A panoramic view of the eastern portion of the World's Columbian Exposition, which attracted more than twenty million visitors from May 1 to October 30, 1893. *Illinois State Historical Library*

white plaster glittered in the sun and sparkled at night in the light of hundreds of electric bulbs. Even the most jaded visitors commented on the beauty of the White City, as it came to be called. One awestruck writer called the result of the Olmsted-Burnham collaboration "very likely the most beautiful thing ever created on the western hemisphere."[1]

During the six-month life of the fair, from May 1 to October 30, 1893, an estimated twenty-seven million people from all over the world attended. They saw presentations of the most advanced technology that existed at the end of the nineteenth century as well as futuristic renderings of life in the twentieth century. The exposition featured exhibits from seventy-two nations, nineteen of which constructed their own buildings. Thirty-eight U.S. states sponsored buildings as well. Other structures housed exhibits devoted to machinery, agriculture, mining, electricity, transportation, forestry, aquatics, and a host of other subjects. The Women's Building featured exhibits on women working inside the home, in the paid labor force, and in various reform causes; the Children's Building included an actual nursery along with the usual array of exhibits. Visitors rode on moving sidewalks, performed high-level mathematics on electric calculating machines, watched moving pictures on Thomas Edison's brand-new kinetoscope, and took breathtaking rides on the Ferris wheel. Designed by George Washington Gale Ferris, a Galesburg engineer, the 140-foot-high contraption towered above the fair just as the Eiffel Tower dominated the Paris Exposition. Rotating on a forty-five-ton axle, the Ferris wheel could carry as many as two thousand passengers at once—sixty riders in each of its thirty-six glass-enclosed cars. During each ride, a band provided musical entertainment from one of the cars.

Adjacent to the White City, the mile-long Midway Plaisance provided lowbrow escapism for visitors tiring of the awesome achievements of science and technology. A series of attractive exhibits re-created the lives of different cultures from around the world, including villages of Eskimos, South Sea Islanders, Laplanders, African Bushmen, and German burghers, among others. In the Streets of Cairo exhibit, visitors sidestepped camels as they lined up to see the authentic gyrations of exotic belly dancers from North Africa. Repulsed by the lasciviousness of the belly dancers, evangelist Dwight Moody surrounded Jackson Park with tent tabernacles and conducted a great revival that attracted thousands seeking Christian renewal. Although intended strictly as a modest sideshow, the Midway attracted huge crowds that sometimes dwarfed the numbers of fairgoers filing through the more refined White City exhibits. The masses visiting the Midway saw the death-defying escapes of young Harry Houdini, boxing exhibitions staged by heavyweight champion Gentleman Jim Corbett, and such eye-catching grotesqueries as a two-headed pig and a dwarf elephant standing thirty-five inches tall. They also listened to new ragtime music played by an African American pianist, Scott Joplin. The Midway, commented one dazzled observer, was "everyone with the brakes off."[2]

An overwhelmingly popular and financial success, the fair nevertheless sparked some disapprobation. The most trenchant criticism came from black fairgoers, who registered displeasure both at the condescending depiction of African culture and at their exclusion from the planning and operation of the exposition. Blacks complained that the attitudes of paternalism and cultural superiority evident in the depiction of the African village left the unmistakable impression that African Americans descended from a savage and barbaric civilization. Such a tragic result could have been avoided, they argued, if African Americans had been enlisted in the preparation of the exhibit—a problem repeated throughout the White City as well as on the Midway. President Benjamin Harrison initially included no minorities on the fair's 208-person board of national commissioners and later, after receiving a protest delegation at the White House, named one African American an alternate commissioner. Of the thousands of people employed at the exposition, only two African Americans held clerkships; the remaining black employees served as porters, custodians, or unskilled laborers. Incensed at such treatment, black newspapers led by activist Ida B. Wells raised the money for the publication of a pamphlet, *The Reason Why the Colored American Is Not in the World's Columbian Exposition*. Widely distributed at the fair in English, Spanish, German, and French, the pamphlet contained an introduction by the revered abolitionist Frederick Douglass. Although dissidents such as Wells achieved few of their goals, their protests sparked discussions about racial inequality that had not been heard previously.

Overall, the Columbian Exposition became a promotional triumph that brought Chicago national and international acclaim. The wellspring of goodwill generated by the fair evaporated quickly, however, as the Panic of 1893 descended upon the country. Widespread unemployment swept across Chicago, and hundreds of homeless people moved into the abandoned structures of the White City. In 1894 a fire broke out when striking railroad workers battled U.S. Army troops in Jackson Park, and most of the plaster-covered buildings in the White City burned to the ground. The only world's fair building to survive the nineteenth century on the original site of the exposition, the Fine Arts Palace in altered form became the Museum of Science and Industry. Artifacts and exhibits left behind formed the heart of the Field Museum's extensive collection. The Midway Plaisance connecting Jackson Park and Washington Park alongside the University of Chicago likewise served as a remembrance of the world's fair. If relatively little of the physical structures remained, the impact of the Columbian Exposition should not be minimized. By underscoring the perfectibility of the city through planning and the expert use of technology, the urban configuration in Jackson Park launched the City Beautiful Movement. Success also confirmed the vision held by Chicago boosters of their home and improved the way people around the world perceived the Windy City.

Visitors to the Columbian Exposition who strayed from Jackson Park north to the Loop had the opportunity to view the pathbreaking architecture that had also been drawing attention to Chicago. In the city's first few decades, when no vernacular American architecture existed, builders simply replicated the classical Greek and Roman styles popular in older American cities. In the frenetic rebuilding that occurred after the Great Fire of 1871, however, many local businessmen took advantage of the occasion to commission daring architects and engineers to build more innovative structures. The resultant Chicago School of Architecture married form and function by creating robust, practical buildings that also possessed pleasing aesthetic qualities. Men such as Louis Sullivan, William Holabird, Martin Roche, Dankmar Adler, John Wellborn Root, and the ubiquitous Daniel Burnham made Chicago's downtown not just a collection of large buildings serving the city's mercantile interests but also an architectural showplace.

The reputation of the Chicago School of Architecture soared along with the completion of dazzling skyscrapers in and around the Loop. Astronomical real estate prices in the city's downtown—reputedly the highest in the world at the time—created a scarcity of affordable building space, and businessmen sought a way out of the conundrum by building higher and higher structures. Technological problems barred the way, chiefly the weight of the heavy stones and bricks used for construction. The use of such dense material put increasing stress on foundations as structures increased in height, limiting construction to eleven or twelve stories. William Le Baron Jenney, an engineer who had served with General William T. Sherman during the Civil War, solved this problem in 1885 when he built an office building for the Home Insurance Company. He used steel girders to form a sturdy skeleton and then filled in the sides of the building with less substantial material. This "iron cage and curtain wall" technique distributed the weight equally throughout the building, rather than concentrating it all on the foundation, and theoretically allowed skyscrapers to be extended higher without limit. Thinner walls increased interior floor space, and the use of steel beams rather than masonry permitted the inclusion of more windows. Later advancements in building technology such as reinforced concrete, caissons, wind bracing, and fireproofing made skyscrapers sturdier and safer.

Even as they built increasingly taller skyscrapers, Chicago architects continued to bring an aesthetic sensibility to their creation of all manner of buildings. Architects immediately proclaimed the sixteen-story Monadnock Building, completed in 1891 by architects Burnham and Root, one of the nation's premier commercial buildings—"an achievement unsurpassed in architectural history," according to a leading critic of the day. Louis Sullivan, who emerged as the leading figure in the Chicago School, completed such masterpieces as the Carson Pirie Scott Store, the Auditorium, and the Old Stock Exchange. A student of Jenney, Sullivan in turn became the mentor of

The interior of Frank Lloyd Wright's Unity Temple in Oak Park, which became internationally renowned and an icon of modern architecture. *Library of Congress, Prints & Photographs Division, HABS ILL, 16-OAKPA, 3-5*

Frank Lloyd Wright. From the studio he opened in Oak Park in 1889,
Wright trained a number of aspiring young architects. Believing Victorian-
style houses unsuited to the gently rolling Illinois tablelands, Wright built
hundreds of low-rise homes, businesses, churches, university buildings, and
shops that rested comfortably on the Midwest's flat plains. The Robie
House in Chicago and the Dana House in Springfield epitomized the simple
yet elegant designs characterizing his residential buildings. Wright's Prairie
School exerted as strong an influence on residential architecture as the
Chicago School did on the downtown skyline; together, they helped to
form the rudiments of an indigenous American architecture.[3]

As the Chicago School of Architecture gained worldwide renown, the
city made great strides in its growing support of the fine arts generally.
Wealthy businessmen and their wives became generous patrons of the arts
even though the Windy City produced few artists of distinction. The most

conspicuous exception was Paris-trained sculptor Lorado Taft, who became famous for his statue of Black Hawk perched above the Rock River, his *Fountain of Time* on the Midway Plaisance, his *Fountain of the Great Lakes* in Grant Park, and his *Alma Mater* on the University of Illinois campus in Urbana. The Art Institute of Chicago assembled a rich collection of paintings and took its place among the nation's finest art museums. Incorporated shortly after the Great Fire, the Art Institute initially rented space in a downtown building before moving into a nearby structure of equally limited proportions. Regardless of the modest facilities for display, benefactors and curators spent considerable sums of money to acquire paintings by the Dutch artists Rembrandt, Rubens, and Frans Hals. The city helped the institute's trustees to acquire a suitable home for such an impressive and growing collection by working cooperatively with the directors of the world's fair to construct a new facility. The Columbian Exposition used the museum, built on Michigan Avenue several miles north of the fairgrounds, and then ceded ownership to the Art Institute after the summer of 1893.

The city funded the daily operation of the art museum, while philanthropic-minded millionaires donated their own possessions and provided the money to purchase collections or individual works of art. Bertha Palmer, wife of real estate magnate Potter Palmer, gave her collection of Impressionist paintings, and steel tycoon Martin Ryerson provided paintings, sculpture, and prints of Western art. In 1906 the Art Institute purchased El Greco's 1577 masterpiece *The Assumption of the Virgin*, a landmark acquisition that sparked much comment in European art circles. Thanks to the generosity of the Friends of American Art, a consortium of patrons formed in 1909, the institute obtained some of the most famous paintings by Winslow Homer, John Singer Sargent, James McNeill Whistler, Gilbert Stuart, John Singleton Copley, and Mary Cassatt.

In 1913 the Art Institute brought to Chicago the controversial International Exhibition of Modern Art, an exhibit of Cubist, Impressionist, and Postimpressionist art that had been shown in the Sixty-ninth Regiment Armory in New York City when none of the city's galleries would provide space. The Armory Show, which introduced the American public to the work of such European artists as Renoir, Manet, Gauguin, Matisse, Picasso, and van Gogh, caused a furor in New York City that nearly resulted in riots. Midwesterners reacted no less strongly. A puzzled Chicago writer asked if the exhibit "originate[d] in an insane asylum." Local art critics dismissed Marcel Duchamp's *Nude Descending a Staircase* as a "blast in a shingle factory" and a "tornado in a lumberyard." In the midst of a statewide vice investigation, Illinois Lieutenant Governor Barrett O'Hara and other members of his commission viewed the exhibit to consider its effect on public morality; they decided against censoring the show. Curious visitors came in record numbers—the Art Institute reported an attendance of 188,650 during the brief engagement—even

while clergymen and civic leaders condemned modern art for its pruri-
ence and ugliness. The headlines merely served to enhance the Art Institute's reputation in the international art world.[4]

Chicago's elite likewise provided the wherewithal for the creation of a
world-class music emporium. Impatient at having to await the arrival of
traveling music companies, devotees of classical music hoped to form a
permanent orchestra in Chicago. Theodore Thomas, a highly respected
conductor of one of the traveling orchestras that frequently visited
Chicago, had grown weary of the peripatetic life and gladly agreed to assemble a permanent orchestra for the community. At first, the Chicago
Symphony Orchestra performed in the Auditorium, the dazzling am-
phitheater designed by Louis Sullivan. The cavernous auditorium proved
too large for the relatively small symphony orchestra, however, and the
musicians became demoralized when audiences regularly failed to fill all of
the hall's forty-eight hundred seats. When Thomas threatened to resign,
trustees built a new venue designed by Daniel Burnham. The Orchestra
Hall, with twenty-five hundred seats, was constructed with dimensions
more suited to the performance of classical music and opened to widespread acclaim in 1904. "We are now in the same room as the audience,"
remarked a satisfied Thomas.[5]

The establishment of a permanent opera in Chicago paralleled the experience of the symphony. Opera aficionados relied upon traveling troupes
from New York City and New Orleans (many of which reported substantial
financial losses in the Windy City) and clamored for the creation of a local
company. In 1910 the Chicago Grand Opera Company, composed primarily of singers and musicians from the Manhattan Opera Company,
opened for business in the Auditorium. During its first twenty years, the
opera company became best known for the sensational performances of
prima donna Mary Garden. Born in Scotland, raised in Chicago, and
trained in Paris, the flamboyant soprano scandalized many Chicagoans
with her sensuous renderings of French and Italian operas. The public up-
roar caused by her undulating "Dance of the Seven Veils" from Strauss's
Salome resulted in the opera's cancellation after just two performances. Renamed the Chicago Civic Opera, the local company left the Auditorium in
1929 and moved into the newly completed twenty-million-dollar Chicago
Civic Opera House. The Chicago Civic Opera also launched a ten-week
summer season at Ravinia Park in suburban Highland Park, where the
Chicago Symphony Orchestra staged a series of public concerts.

The state's colleges and universities contributed to the cultural renaissance through their support of creative work and scholarship. Both the
University of Chicago and Northwestern University launched ambitious
building projects to accommodate their growing student enrollments. The
Chicago Institute of Social Science, part of the University of Chicago, later
incorporated as the Chicago School of Civics and Philanthropy and be-

came a training ground for social scientists and the precursor of the institution's pathbreaking school of social work. Determined to be more than a cow college, the University of Illinois hired a distinguished faculty in literature and the fine arts. The state's five normal schools—at Normal, DeKalb, Carbondale, Charleston, and Macomb—brought a heightened cultural awareness to isolated corners of Illinois. Various private colleges scattered throughout the state, such as Knox College, Shurtleff College, Illinois College, McKendree College, and James Millikin University, did the same. The 1890s also saw the founding of several technological schools that incorporated the teaching of literature and the arts into their fundamentally vocational curricula. The Armour Institute of Technology (which later became the Illinois Institute of Technology) and the Lewis Institute opened in Chicago in 1893 and 1896, respectively, while the Bradley Polytechnic Institute of Peoria began enrolling students in 1897.

Along with a flowering of the fine arts in the late nineteenth century came an increased interest in the culture and history of the state. In 1889 the general assembly founded the Illinois State Historical Library in Springfield, which collected books, manuscripts, and other primary documents related to the state's past. In 1903 the general assembly made the Illinois State Historical Society, organized four years earlier in Springfield, an adjunct of the state historical library. The historical society immediately began holding annual meetings for the reading of papers dealing with state history and commenced publication of its *Transactions* and its quarterly journal. In 1909 the University of Illinois joined in the effort to promote an appreciation of the state's history, formally affiliating with the state historical library and forming the Illinois Historical Survey under the direction of the graduate school. Spearheading the effort at the university, Professor Clarence W. Alvord of the history department assumed the editorship of the *Collections of the Illinois State Historical Library* and the *Mississippi Valley Historical Review*. He also became the general editor of the five-volume *Centennial History of Illinois*. To commemorate the memory of its leading historical figure, the state acquired Abraham Lincoln's Springfield home in 1887 and one of his New Salem residences in 1917.

The late nineteenth century also saw the spread of libraries throughout the state. In 1872 the general assembly passed a law enabling communities to use tax revenues for the construction and maintenance of public libraries. The Chicago Public Library, which had been decimated by the Great Fire of 1871, received generous donations of books from around the world and gradually replenished its collection. In 1897, after shifting locations from one temporary site to another, the public library moved into permanent quarters downtown. The Newberry Library of Chicago, a private reference library containing books, pamphlets, manuscripts, and maps of historical significance that had commenced operation in 1887, moved into its new building across from Bughouse Square in 1893.

Smaller communities throughout the state built public libraries thanks to the philanthropy of Andrew Carnegie, the Scottish immigrant who devoted a portion of the vast fortune he made in the steel industry to the construction of libraries. In many instances, these public libraries became the cultural centers of villages and towns scattered across Illinois. Some of these libraries acquired books written in foreign languages to reflect the ethnic composition of their patrons. One-third of the volumes in the Belleville Public Library were written in German, for example.

The rapid proliferation of libraries reflected a rising interest in literature. Although great numbers of young Midwesterners aspiring to be writers went to New York City and other East Coast cities, many chose the more accessible destination of Chicago. Hailing from small towns in Illinois, Indiana, Ohio, and Iowa, these writers frequently sought to escape the numbing small-town conformity and dreary environments that stifled their creativity. At the same time, they moved to the nearest metropolis offering the cultural opportunities and anonymity lacking in their hometowns. In Chicago they could browse through the avant-garde art exhibited in the Armory Show, attend Isadora Duncan dance performances, listen to Theodore Thomas conduct the symphony, talk with great literary figures such as William Butler Yeats and Amy Lowell when they visited, or simply argue with other intellectuals in Chicago's many taverns. Seldom blessed with much money, they lived in rundown bohemian neighborhoods populated by other struggling writers and artists. Their unconventional behavior would have been unacceptable in the cloistered small towns of the Midwest and may have raised eyebrows among conservative members of the middle class, but living in the big city allowed them greater freedom and a wider array of behaviors.

Chicago's principal bohemia, a smaller version of New York City's Greenwich Village, centered around the corner of Fifty-seventh Street and Stony Island Avenue on the city's South Side across from Jackson Park. Writers rented cheap studios in one-story buildings that had been hastily built as shops catering to the crowds visiting the Columbian Exposition. Floyd Dell, a native of Barry, Illinois, and editor of the *Friday Review of Literature,* rented a studio on Fifty-seventh Street while his wife, Margaret Curry, resided around the corner on Stony Island. (Typical of the casual living arrangements favored by the bohemian set, the spouses lived apart.) Their studios served as gathering places for the city's writers, some of whom later achieved success and others of whom vanished into obscurity. Struggling young writers also congregated at the colorful Dill Pickle Club, where owner Jack Jones, a former safecracker, paid poets to recite their verse. "I give them the high-brow stuff until the crowd goes thin," Jones confided to Sherwood Anderson, "and then I turn on the sex faucet."[6]

At first Chicago's growing literary reputation rested upon the publication there of several magazines that gained national readerships. *The Dial,* published in Chicago by Francis Fisher Browne from 1880 until 1919 when it moved to New York City, published the work of such local authors as Hamlin Garland as well as writers from throughout the country. Harriet Monroe, an art critic for the *Chicago Tribune,* founded *Poetry* magazine in 1912 after receiving generous financial backing from such old Chicago families as the McCormicks, Palmers, and Lowdens. Determined to offer literature that would be accessible to a broad readership and not just to the local literati, Margaret Anderson founded the *Little Review.* (Aspiring poets pinned their work to the outside of the tent where the nearly impoverished Anderson lived, near Ravinia Park alongside Lake Michigan.) For many years the editors of *The Dial, Poetry,* and the *Little Review* carried on a lively series of exchanges regarding their selections for publication and the trends developing in American literature.

By the turn of the century Chicago had become known as the home of a group of talented poets and novelists whose gritty realism and spare writing won large audiences. The poets wrote mostly in free verse, while the naturalistic novelists produced stark prose that described everyday life without adornment. Devoid of romanticism, their work often dealt with themes common to Chicago, Illinois, and the Midwest. The noted writer and critic H. L. Mencken commented: "Find me a writer who is indubitably an American and who has something new and interesting to say, and who says it with an air, and nine times out of ten I will show you that he has some sort of connection with the abattoir by the lake." Thanks to the moral and financial support provided by Harriet Monroe, the work of three poets—Carl Sandburg, Vachel Lindsay, and Edgar Lee Masters—advanced the reputation of the Chicago literary set.[7]

A second-generation Swedish immigrant from Galesburg, Carl Sandburg worked as a journalist and socialist organizer in Wisconsin before coming to Chicago in 1913. He published his first collection of poems shortly afterward and wrote prolifically during the next several decades. His famous 1914 ode to Chicago referred to his adopted home as the "city of big shoulders" and the "hog butcher for the world." In such volumes as *Cornhuskers, Smoke and Steel,* and *Good Morning, America,* he extolled the virtues of the working class, protested society's mistreatment of the poor, and glorified the Midwestern countryside. Some readers thought his casual use of colloquialisms and attention to the commonplace crude and inelegant, but more found his descriptions vivid and compelling. While continuing to write poetry, Sandburg worked as a newspaper reporter and editorialist for the *Chicago Daily News,* participated in radical politics, played the guitar, sang folk music, and authored a number of children's books. He received Pulitzer Prizes for his collected works of poetry and for a portion of his epic six-volume biography of Abraham Lincoln.

A young and intense Carl Sandburg in 1908, when he and many other gifted young writers and artists came to Chicago. *Illinois State Historical Library.*

Vachel Lindsay, a native of Springfield, gave up hopes of becoming an artist and turned instead to writing poetry. For years he lived as a vagabond, reciting his poems in exchange for food and lodging. Lindsay's situation improved in 1913 when Harriet Monroe's *Poetry* published his celebrated "General William Booth Enters into Heaven" and other poems. Monroe thought Lindsay's poetry the best she published during the era. A mystic and selfless humanitarian with a great love for his state, Lindsay hoped to instill a greater patriotism among his countrymen, but he gradually grew more disillusioned and emotionally disturbed, and the quality of his writing declined in later years. He committed suicide in the family home near the governor's mansion in Springfield.

Edgar Lee Masters became a keen observer of small-town life after having grown up in the Illinois communities of Petersburg and Lewistown. A successful attorney in Chicago for many years before he began writing, Masters eventually published thirty volumes of poetry and prose. His *Spoon River Anthology*, a collection of epitaphs in free verse, told the life stories of many deceased people in a fictional Midwestern small town—some of whom bore a striking resemblance to people who had actually lived in Petersburg and

Lewistown. His frank depiction of the Midwestern bourgeoisie, dealing with the tragedies as well as the triumphs of the people, proved shocking to many readers accustomed to a more genteel Victorian prose. In describing the hypocrisy and small-mindedness of most residents, he also celebrated the heroic struggles of the enlightened minority who nurtured culture and fought against the forces of prejudice and ignorance.

The merciless dissection of small-town life reached its apotheosis with Sherwood Anderson's *Winesburg, Ohio,* the account of a fictionalized community as seen through the eyes of local residents. Born in Camden, Ohio, Anderson came to Chicago at the age of seventeen and lived there briefly before serving in the U.S. Army during the Spanish-American War. After the war, he married and undertook a series of dead-end jobs in small Ohio communities. Dissatisfied with his middle-class life, he left his wife, returned to Chicago, began working as a copywriter for an advertising firm, and launched his writing career. His third novel, *Winesburg, Ohio,* consisted of twenty-three related sketches that illuminated crucial episodes in the otherwise humdrum lives of the citizens. Written in the straightforward realistic style that was characteristic of the Chicago writers, the book won widespread acclaim and set a standard of excellence that critics felt Anderson never equaled in his subsequent work.

Theodore Dreiser, who many critics considered the greatest naturalistic novelist of the early twentieth century, spurned the subject of small Midwestern towns and wrote instead about the harshness of life in Chicago. Born in Sullivan, Indiana, Dreiser initially visited Chicago at the age of sixteen and remained in its thrall the rest of his life. His first novel, *Sister Carrie,* told the story of a young working girl who came to Chicago, lost her virtue, and survived only by becoming the mistress of a number of wealthy businessmen. The sordid tale, portraying the protagonist as a predator as well as a victim, scandalized the reading public and forced Dreiser to battle the censors for the rest of his career. Indeed, the original version of *Sister Carrie* appeared only in 1981. His second novel, *Jennie Gerhardt,* the tale of a young woman who is seduced by a famous politician and bears his child out of wedlock, received an equally inhospitable reception from affronted critics. Dreiser's trilogy based upon the life of Chicago transit czar Charles T. Yerkes *(The Financier, The Titan,* and *The Stoic)* portrayed the immorality and avarice that built the metropolis. His most commercially successful novel, *An American Tragedy,* blamed materialistic society for the ruthless pursuit of wealth by the protagonist, who was convicted and executed for the murder of his girlfriend. *An American Tragedy* was banned in Boston.

The Chicago writers not only lived unconventionally and wrote salacious stories in unorthodox styles, but many of them became political radicals whose activism in behalf of unpopular causes further alienated members of genteel society. They became, according to H. L. Mencken, a "red ink fraternity."[8] Even those writers whose liberalism stopped far short of radicalism found themselves alienated from the political mainstream. Carl Sandburg, whose poetry extolled the virtues of the downtrodden, worked for many years as a reporter for a socialist newspaper and ardently campaigned for socialist candidates. Margaret Anderson hosted at her fabled north shore tent a rogue's gallery of radicals that included anarchist Emma Goldman and Big Bill Haywood of the International Workers of the World. Sherwood Anderson openly consorted with journalist John Reid, who converted to Communism and moved to the Soviet Union, and ran afoul of authorities during World War I for his criticisms of American policies. Floyd Dell, who moved to New York City to edit *The Masses,* stood trial for sedition because of the radical journal's uncompromising antiwar editorials.

While the arts and letters flourished in Chicago, the city also served as the heart of the nascent motion-picture industry. In the first two decades of the twentieth century, pioneering filmmakers in the Windy City produced thousands of movies, which were shown in the nickel theaters starting to appear in cities across the nation. By 1910, for example, an estimated twelve thousand theaters operated in Chicago alone. William Selig, who owned both indoor and outdoor studios in the city, made countless action films set in the Wild West starring Tom Mix and other cowboy actors. The Essanay Film Manufacturing Company employed Charlie Chaplin, Francis X. Bushman, Wallace Beery, and the era's other leading actors in its lucrative productions. Chicago's predominance in filmmaking ended when the studios left for the sunny climes of southern California. Selig concluded that filming his cowboy movies would be easier in Los Angeles, where the salubrious climate made year-round outdoor production feasible. He also headed for the West Coast to avoid patent infringement lawsuits brought against him by Thomas Edison's lawyers. Selig's competitors soon followed him westward, and by the end of World War I Hollywood had supplanted Chicago as the filmmaking capital of the world.

World War I brought to a close a brief period of literary ferment in Illinois, termed the "Robin's Egg Renaissance" by Sherwood Anderson, and ended an era of cultural development that fulfilled the hopes of many of the state's leading citizens. Although Illinois's reputation still largely revolved around outstanding accomplishments in industry, agriculture, and transportation, the remarkable success of the Columbian Exposition and the city's noteworthy achievements in art, music, literature, and architecture brought Chicago grudging recognition as a world-class cultural center. The formation of impressive institutions and the singular successes of talented individuals improved the state's image. Residents of the East Coast could no longer dismiss the state as a remote and isolated cultural wasteland.

Oak Park

In 1833 recent immigrants from Yorkshire, England, Joseph and Betty Kettlestrings, bought a quarter-section of land between Chicago and the Des Plaines River that had only a few years previously been the home of Sauk and Fox Indians. They soon turned their small frame house into a tavern for weary travelers making the journey to and from the Chicago market. Population followed the construction of the Galena and Chicago Union Railroad, the first railroad running west from Chicago, and the Kettlestrings began selling off parcels of their land in the 1850s. In the wake of the Great Fire of 1871, many Chicago residents left the city and built in the surrounding area. At the time of the fire, the settlement known as Oak Park had a population of about 500; it counted 4,589 residents in 1890. Despite its steady growth in the last decades of the nineteenth century, the community remained unincorporated and a part of Cicero Township until 1902 when Cook County created the village of Oak Park. At that time, the suburb's ten thousand people lived primarily in single-family residences intermingled with clusters of apartment houses. Like other suburbs that grew up in the shadow of Chicago, early residents of Oak Park hoped to create a refuge from the sinfulness of the nearby metropolis. An 1872 law passed by the general assembly banned the sale of alcohol in the village, and Oak Park remained dry for the next hundred years.

A leafy bedroom community adjacent to Chicago, Oak Park became known as the home of Frank Lloyd Wright and, not coincidentally, for the splendid architecture of its houses and public buildings. Wright built his home and studio on Oak Park's Chicago Avenue in 1889 and remained there for the next twenty years as he founded the Prairie School of Architecture. During that time he designed dozens of structures in the village and the adjacent suburb of River Forest, including his first public building, a Unitarian Universalist church called Unity Temple. The area surrounding his home and studio, which contained the largest concentration of prairie-style homes in the world, later became a national historic district. A partial list of Oak Park residents who also shaped American culture in the twentieth century would include Nobel Prize–winning novelist Ernest Hemingway, best-selling author Edgar Rice Burroughs, psychotherapist Carl Rogers, and the founder of the McDonald's fast-food-restaurant chain, Ray Kroc.

In the second half of the twentieth century, Oak Park struggled to reconcile its reputation as a progressive community with the rising tensions developing over the issue of open housing. Local leaders, who proudly called Oak Park the "World's Largest Village" and embraced the humanistic legacy of Frank Lloyd Wright and Ernest Hemingway, recoiled when the overwhelmingly white population of the suburb violently resisted racial integration after World War II. In 1951 white mobs twice firebombed the home of Percy Lavon Julian, a renowned scientist who sought to become the first African American to live in Oak Park. Sympathetic white community groups defended Julian, who remained a resident of the suburb until his death in 1975. Village trustees approved a policy designed to foster racial diversity, and Oak Park became one of the first Illinois communities to adopt an open housing ordinance. Over the last quarter of the twentieth century, according to the historian Andrew Wiese, Oak Park remained one of the few U.S. suburbs to maintain a generally integrated housing market. In 2000, with the preponderance of Chicago's suburbs virtually all-white or all-black, 78 percent of Oak Park's fifty-two thousand residents were white and 22 percent were African American.

Louis Sullivan

Born in Boston, Massachusetts, on September 3, 1856, Louis Sullivan had by the age of twelve decided that he wanted to become an architect. Accordingly, at the age of sixteen and without having received a high school diploma, he enrolled in the building and architecture program at the Massachusetts Institute of Technology (MIT). Hungry for practical experience, he left MIT and began working as a draftsman and an apprentice for a Philadelphia firm. In 1873 he joined his parents in Chicago and, eager to participate in the building boom after the Great Fire, became a draftsman in the office of architect William Le Baron Jenney. To obtain additional formal training, he studied for several months in 1874–1875 at the Ecole des Beaux Arts in Paris. After extensive travels through France and Italy, he returned to Chicago in 1875 and opened his own business as a freelance draftsman and decorative designer. In 1883 he and Dankmar Adler formed a partnership that lasted for the next fourteen years.

The firm of Adler & Sullivan became a leader in the Chicago School of Architecture and mostly designed commercial buildings in the Windy City but also completed projects in Seattle, Washington, Pueblo, Colorado, and Buffalo, New York, among other places. Sullivan's reputation was enhanced after the completion of Chicago's Auditorium in 1889. In subsequent years he designed a number of ornamented skyscrapers, which superseded the utilitarian solutions to structural problems devised by other builders by employing what he called a poetic architecture. He exaggerated the verticality of the skyscraper and added other stylistic flourishes to make large buildings into works of art. Critical of the classic revival architecture that had predominated at the Columbian Exposition, he designed the Transportation Building in a very different style—and brooded when the public failed to embrace his innovation. A prolific writer who published extensively on the history

Louis Sullivan, the father of modern American architecture. *Chicago Historical Society*

and philosophy of architecture, Sullivan composed a theory of design based upon Ralph Waldo Emerson's Transcendentalist ideas and Walt Whitman's poetry. His buildings, he affirmed, sought an American architectural style that bespoke a naturalistic sensibility in an urban setting.

After he dissolved his partnership with Adler, Sullivan endured a prolonged period of personal and financial hardship. He auctioned his personal library and household furnishings to pay for his wife's floundering acting career in New York City, before the marriage ended in divorce in 1916. Falling behind on his rent payments, he vacated his office in the Auditorium Building Tower and worked out of his cramped living quarters. Slowed by a series of chronic illnesses during the last years of his life, Sullivan received a dwindling number of commissions—most notably for the design of the Carson Pirie Scott Store and several small-town banks.

Hailed as the prophet of modern architecture, Sullivan became known to the lay public for his dictum that form follows function. A founding member of the Western Association of Architects, which later merged with the American Institute of Architects (AIA), he accepted a number of lifetime achievement awards from European societies and posthumously received the prestigious AIA Gold Medal. His influence lived on through the career of Frank Lloyd Wright, who served as Sullivan's draftsman from 1888 to 1893. In forming the Prairie School of Architecture, Wright adapted his mentor's organic principles and ornamental design while constructing the foundation for the International Style aesthetic.

World War I and the Red Scare

Fought a century after Illinois became a state, World War I initiated a series of changes that reverberated for decades. Massive demographic shifts accompanied and sometimes sparked economic and social changes of long-lasting duration. In the rush to mobilize for a global war, government created a host of bureaucracies and imposed a set of ordinances that left the citizenry regulated, organized, and managed as never before. Bombarded with patriotic slogans and fed a steady diet of propaganda that demonized the Central Powers, many of the state's residents responded with an intolerance and nativism that persisted long after the end of the war. Although American involvement in World War I lasted barely nineteen months, the crusade to "make the world safe for democracy" proved far more portentous than the population had anticipated in 1917.

Separated by the Atlantic Ocean from the fratricidal rivalries that periodically plunged the great nations of Europe into war, the United States had studiously avoided involvement in Old World political disputes for much of the nineteenth and early twentieth centuries. Delighted to be exempt from the toxic mixture of competition, fear, and mistrust that pervaded Europe after 1870, Americans attributed the prolonged period of peace and prosperity they enjoyed to their "splendid isolation" in the Western Hemisphere. When the Great War erupted in 1914, most Americans hoped to avoid involvement and applauded when President Woodrow Wilson urged his countrymen to be "impartial in thought as well as in action." Neutrality seemed the wisest policy, especially because of the divergent views about the European war expressed by the nation's many and varied ethnic groups. Although a majority of Americans favored the British and the French, the loyalties of the large German, Austrian, and Irish immigrant communities left the nation uneasily divided. Wilson's reelection in 1916 owed in large measure to his success at keeping the nation out of war, but soon tensions arose over the Germans' unrestricted use of U-boats (submarines) in the Atlantic. Wilson's brand of impartiality overlooked British violations of American neutrality that broke international law and interfered with free trade but held 'Germany strictly accountable for the loss of American lives. At the president's urging, Congress declared war against Germany on April 6, 1917.[1]

As throughout the rest of the nation, the majority of people in Illinois endorsed Wilson's decision to ally with Britain and France—but support for war proved far from unanimous. On the one hand, American casualties of German submarines, stories of German atrocities against civilian populations in Europe, and fear of Prussian imperialist designs lent credibility to the picture of Germany as a militaristic nation driven by ideals inimical to American democracy. The strength of historic, linguistic, and cultural U.S. ties with Britain reinforced the public leanings toward the Allies. On the other hand, German immigrants argued that an effective British propaganda machine had created a distorted view of their homeland. In their view, the Central Powers had been the victims of a series of secret alliances stitched together by Britain and its allies, and Germany had fought no more barbarously than its enemies. A noted Anglophile, Woodrow Wilson was practicing a bogus neutrality and was steering the nation into an unnecessary war that offered little hope of achieving the lofty goals he articulated.

Because of the large number of immigrants from central Europe, a considerable amount of support for the Central Powers existed in Illinois. With 319,199 immigrants from Germany and 163,065 immigrants from Austria in 1910, Illinois contained more residents from those nations than any other state. One million people of German origin lived in the state, one-tenth of the national total. Chicago's 399,977 first- and second-generation German immigrants in 1914 made it the sixth-largest German city in the world. When World War I began that year, German flags appeared and bands played German patriotic songs throughout the Windy City's North Side. Groups of Northsiders sang "Die Wacht am Rhein" (The Watch on the Rhine) on downtown street corners, and the German American National Alliance staged a massive rally to express fealty to the fatherland. The *Illinois Staats-Zeitung,* the most widely read German language newspaper in the state, warned that American intervention in the "European holocaust" might lead to "a war of the races" in the United States.[2]

On April 1, 1917, a delegation of twenty-five prominent German Americans from Chicago traveled to Washington, D.C., in a fruitless attempt to dissuade President Wilson from seeking war against the Central Powers. In the congressional debates following Wilson's war message, no legislator spoke more passionately in opposition than Illinois congressman-at-large William E. Mason. "It is a dollar war," Mason charged. "It is a war between kings for money and for territory. It does not involve a single human life that interests a great republican democracy like the United States." Congressman Fred A. Britten of Chicago also dissented vigorously and introduced an amendment that would have made military service abroad entirely voluntary. Of the fifty U.S. congressmen who voted against the war resolution, five hailed from Illinois.[3]

The state government, though in the hands of the Republican party, quickly closed ranks behind President Wilson's Democratic administration and pledged its support to the war effort. Governor Frank O. Lowden, a Republican with presidential ambitions of his own, wholeheartedly backed Wilson and called for the people to put political and ethnic loyalties aside in pursuit of a common goal. "There is only one test of patriotism in a war like this," intoned Lowden. "Either we are for the government or we are against it." The general assembly, which promptly endorsed the governor's remarks, adjourned in July 1917 and did not reconvene until after the end of the war. As a result, Lowden administered the state's affairs with total impunity and directed virtually all of his efforts for nineteen months to supervision of the war effort.[4]

In the spring of 1917, Lowden moved swiftly to mobilize the state's military forces. Because of the use of American soldiers along the Mexican border the year before, the Illinois National Guard stood readier to respond than it otherwise would have. By the end of the summer, twenty-five thousand National Guardsmen from the state traveled to Camp Logan, Texas, where they became part of the U.S. Army's Thirty-third Division. The state's naval battalion included 814 enlisted men and 40 officers. Lowden called for volunteers to form a supplementary state militia and soon assembled 38 companies for service within Illinois. Voluntary enlistment in the U.S. Army proceeded at a dilatory pace. Military recruiters stationed outside of Cub's Ball Park in Chicago on April 12, 1917, failed to record a single enlistment out of the 18,000 spectators who attended the game that day. Similarly disappointing recruiting efforts nationwide led to the passage of a federal selective service act on May 18, 1917. By the time the war ended, slightly more than 315,000 Illinois men between the ages of 18 and 45 served in the army, navy, or marines—approximately 60,000 more than had served during the Civil War.

The U.S. Armed Forces utilized several training facilities in Illinois. The army converted Fort Sheridan into an officers' training camp and built Camp Grant near Rockford for enlisted men. The Great Lakes Naval Training Center, which opened in 1904 in Lake County, north of Chicago, expanded to accommodate as many as fifty thousand seamen and became the world's largest facility. (Under the direction of John Philip Sousa, the Great Lakes Naval Band became internationally renowned.) The University of Illinois established a new school of military aeronautics to provide preliminary instruction in aviation. Having successfully completed the program, novice pilots then went to Chanute Air Field in Rantoul or Scott Air Field near Belleville for in-flight training. By the end of the war, Scott Field had graduated fourteen squadrons, and members of twenty-two squadrons had received at least some of their training at Chanute Field.

U.S. soldiers undergo bayonet drills at Fort Sheridan, north of Chicago, during World War I. *Illinois State Historical Library*

Unlike the practice during the Civil War, when servicemen from the same localities remained together in units throughout their training and combat, the U.S. War Department freely integrated men from different states in the various divisions. As a result, only a minority of Illinois soldiers served in divisions in which men from their state formed a majority. Units usually became even more heterogeneous as time passed and the army randomly assigned replacements. The One Hundred and Forty-ninth Field Artillery Regiment from Illinois was part of the Rainbow Division, for example, so named because it consisted of National Guard units from twenty-six states. The Thirty-third Division, which contained a large number of Illinois soldiers, served at various times under American, British, and French command. The War Department failed to keep state-by-state casualty records, so the exact number of Illinois servicemen who perished in World War I remains unknown.

As military preparedness proceeded rapidly, the federal government assumed extraordinary powers to win the war. Officials in Washington, D.C., decided not to levy price controls or to ration consumer goods, choosing instead to appeal to the citizenry for increases in conservation. The U.S. Congress did sharply raise corporate taxes, however, and implemented measures to curb financial speculation. Moreover, concerned that private industry would not deliver vital services, the government nationalized the railroads, coal mines, telephones, telegraphs, and the shipping industry.

In cooperation with the federal government, Illinois assembled an organizational structure for administering civilian affairs. On May 2, 1917, the general assembly passed a law creating the State Council of Defense (SCD) to act as the official clearinghouse for all government agencies, institutions, and municipal officers involved in war work. Appointed by the governor for open-ended terms, the fifteen members of the SCD possessed expertise in industry, labor, transportation, and natural resource regulation. Charter members of the council appointed by Governor Lowden included utilities tycoon Samuel Insull as chairman, Lieutenant Governor John G. Oglesby, meatpacker J. Ogden Armour, Illinois Federation of Labor (IFL) president John Walker, IFL secretary Victor Olander, and Chicago businessman Charles Wacker. With the exception of Walker and Olander, all the council's members represented the interests of big business. When the trade union representatives and industrialists squared off at the council's first meeting, Lowden admonished both sides to cooperate for the common good. "This war can be won by neither labor nor capital alone," the governor said. "Gentlemen, you have got to work together!"[5]

The SCD supervised all war-related activities in Illinois from its headquarters in Chicago, a six-story office building donated by Samuel Insull. Its eleven standing committees—auditing, coordination of societies, food production and conservation, industrial survey, labor, law and legislation, military affairs, publicity, sanitation and public health, survey of manpower, and women's organizations—monitored dozens of county and local agencies while directing the work of more than fifty thousand civilian volunteers. To encourage cooperation among neighboring states, the SCD organized a confederation of defense councils in thirteen Mississippi Valley states, which was chaired by Insull.

A women's drum corps in review at Great Lakes Naval Training Center, north of Chicago, during World War I. *Illinois State Historical Library*

The residents of Illinois felt the SCD's presence in a myriad of ways. To boost support for the war, more than five thousand volunteer speakers known as Four-Minute Men delivered brief speeches at theaters, churches, lodges, and other community centers detailing the reasons for U.S. participation. The Four-Minute Men spoke to an estimated eight hundred thousand persons per week, and other states soon deployed their own squads of patriotic orators. To coordinate relief work, the SCD worked closely with the American Red Cross, the YMCA, the Knights of Columbus, and other philanthropic organizations. To raise money, the council aided in the sale of liberty bonds totaling $1.3 billion. In all, more than three hundred thousand volunteers across the state staffed newly created government positions, rolled bandages, boxed medical supplies, knitted sweaters, and accomplished a host of the other mundane chores that are necessary to a successful war effort.

The SCD's women's committee performed a number of useful and innovative functions during the course of the war. The committee dispatched more than three hundred speakers across the state to inform women's groups about what they could do to support American servicemen. Their presentations dealt with such topics as the need for thrift, the purchase of liberty bonds, and how to conserve food, clothing, and fuel. Committee members also helped to place women in the workforce and sought to establish day care centers at workplaces to help mothers who toiled in industrial occupations. The Americanization Department attempted to accelerate the acculturation of immigrants, in particular endeavoring to ease their transition into the workplace; the subcommittee on colored women tried to provide many of the same services to African Americans who had recently moved to Illinois from Southern states. At the same time, the committee lobbied for child labor legislation that would continue to protect young workers after the end of the war.

The SCD worked closely with the Illinois branch of the Federal Food Administration to ensure that the state's farmers would meet the increasing demands for agricultural products. Food riots in European cities and worrisome shortages in some East Coast communities in the United States underscored the urgency of agricultural production in the fertile states of the Mississippi Valley. "Food will win the war!" cried Washington bureaucrats faced with the need to feed Europe and a labor force depleted by military enlistments. In fact, the United States faced two interrelated problems: how to increase agricultural production and how to conserve precious foodstuffs. Officials in Illinois, as in the other Midwestern states composing the American granary, sought to increase agricultural yields while at the same time devising conservation programs.[6]

The acute labor shortages on Illinois farms challenged state and national policy makers to devise innovative solutions. The SCD created a number of agencies to enhance production, including the Food Production Committee, the Farm Labor Administration, and the Seed Corn

Administration. The War Garden Advisory Committee exhorted city dwellers to grow much of their own food in their backyards or nearby empty lots. The Patriotic Food Show Committee sponsored a conference at the Coliseum in Chicago to educate homemakers about the efficient preparation of meals. Although officials opened farm-labor-recruiting stations in public buildings and newspaper offices throughout the state, the call for volunteers living in urban areas to work on farms produced a "land army" of insufficient size to offset the rising demand for labor. The Illinois office of the United States Boys' Working Reserve worked closely with local school boards to establish agricultural courses in the high schools and to award academic credit to students for farmwork. An estimated forty-five thousand boys participated in the high school program statewide, and the Boys' Working Reserve placed twenty-one thousand students on farms for full-time or part-time work. The contributions of these emergency programs proved inadequate, however, and the government had to award draft deferments to men engaged in agricultural work.

To oversee food conservation efforts, the Federal Food Administration divided Illinois into fifteen districts and appointed an administrator to supervise activities in each. A statewide conservation campaign generated a favorable response as 850,000 families signed pledge cards affirming that they would restrict consumption of specific items. Restaurants as well as households observed meatless and wheatless days. Trade agreements limited the sale of sugar, wheat flour, milk, ice, and other commodities to wholesalers and retailers. Although the rates of voluntary compliance remained high, the Federal Food Administration created a department of investigation and enforcement in 1918. The department attributed most violations to ignorance or oversight but turned the cases of deliberate transgressions over to the Justice Department for prosecution.

Along with food shortages, the SCD and federal government agencies had to deal with the potential problem of inadequate supplies of fuel. The dependence of war industries, railroads, and home heating upon coal as the principal source of fuel made it imperative to establish an effective policy for use and conservation. Coal prices tripled in the first sixty days of the war, and mine owners eager to maintain high profit levels resisted the SCD's subsequent attempts to regulate production levels and rates. The owners then repudiated an agreement negotiated in July 1917 between Secretary of the Interior Franklin K. Lane and an ad hoc committee of seven Illinois coal operators that set a maximum price for coal. Assailing the widespread profiteering by the mine owners, Governor Lowden appointed Orrin Carter, chief justice of the Illinois Supreme Court, as the state's fuel czar. With the counsel of a committee composed of three members of the SCD, three members of the Illinois Coal Operators' Association, and three representatives of the United Mine Workers, Carter could fix prices and determine production levels.

The Illinois coal operators balked at Carter's unprecedented power in an industry historically free of government regulation. Lowden's representatives at a meeting of thirteen Midwestern states persuaded the other delegates to endorse a proposal for cooperation between the states and the federal government for control of the coal industry. Again, the coal operators renounced the agreement for allowing a government presence in the mines. On August 21, 1917, President Wilson announced a schedule of rates composed by the Federal Trade Commission, and Lowden declared his willingness to seize and operate the state's mines, if it was necessary, to enforce federal edicts. The SCD and fuel administrators appointed in each county enforced federal mandates on the production and consumption of coal, including prices and the rationing of quantities for industrial use. Even though the system worked reasonably well, fuel shortages during the bitterly cold winter of 1917–1918 periodically necessitated the imposition of lightless nights and heatless days.

In addition to supervising the provision of food and fuel, the SCD spearheaded the drive to increase the state's industrial productivity. By 1917 many industries in Illinois had already converted to war production because of the orders for munitions and armaments placed by European combatants. Under the aegis of the SCD, the Commercial Economy Administration established guidelines for the efficient use of resources, which gave primacy to war material over consumer goods. In 1917, for example, the agency warned Illinois residents against Christmas shopping and other unpatriotic acts that would squander precious resources in wartime. The SCD created the War Business Committee to seek government contracts for Illinois corporations, an effort supplemented by the Illinois Manufacturers Association's War Industries Bureau. These ad hoc organizations claimed to have attracted more than five hundred million dollars in wartime contracts to the state, roughly one-fourth of the total in 1918. The procurement of wartime contracts benefited dozens of Illinois companies, most notably John Deere, Armour, Swift, Western Cartridge, American Steel Foundries, and the Northwestern Barbed Wire Company.

In its final report, the SCD identified as the most important factor in the state's contribution to the war effort the "uninterrupted social and industrial peace." The SCD's civilian personnel committee worked in tandem with the U.S. Employment Service and the Illinois Department of Labor to locate workers for war industries, while its labor committee mediated labor disputes. John Walker, Victor Olander, and other IFL leaders strongly endorsed the position of the American Federation of Labor (AFL) president Samuel Gompers that the interests of American workers would best be served by the defeat of German autocracy. Taking their cues from the AFL's national office, local unions invested dues in Liberty Bonds. In large measure because of pay increases and improved working conditions, the state's workers conducted few strikes. Local officials settled work stoppages by streetcar workers in Springfield and by railroad switchmen in Chicago, and union leaders stifled talk of a general strike by coal miners. Labor violence erupted infrequently, most often when black strikebreakers willing to work for low wages replaced striking white workers; the race riot that broke out in East St. Louis in 1917 resulted from such a situation. In most cases, however, effective mediation and trade unions' decisions to honor no-strike pledges maintained the peace. Union leaders and the rank and file viewed themselves as partners in the nation's wartime crusade and generally reacted positively to the government's efforts to shape public opinion.[7]

The intense propaganda campaign directed in Washington, D.C., effectively shaped public opinion, demanding conformity and curtailing civil liberties in a fashion that resounded strongly in Illinois as elsewhere. By executive order, President Wilson created the Committee on Public Information (CPI) under the chairmanship of journalist George Creel. The CPI distributed more than seventy-five million pamphlets, thousands of posters, and several full-length motion pictures that all argued for German culpability in the outbreak of war and the need for American intervention on the side of the Allies. Creel denied that his agency practiced manipulation or censorship, contending that the CPI sought only to provide the public with accurate information about events in Europe; yet in fact, accuracy and objectivity in government reporting proved casualties of the war. In sensationally written material and in films with titles such as *The Beast of Berlin* and *To Hell with the Kaiser*, the CPI employed half-truths, exaggerations, and distortions to shape public opinion against the "dreaded Hun." German Americans complained bitterly that Creel and the talented cadre of writers and scholars he recruited simply manufactured tales of Teutonic atrocities out of whole cloth.

In Illinois, where government officials worried about the strength of the German community, a steady stream of speakers crisscrossed the state denouncing the enemy and extolling the democratic ideals that impelled American involvement in the war. Governor Lowden called Germany "the cruelest military autocracy the world has ever known" and termed the American war effort the "holiest cause" in history. Former President Theodore Roosevelt told a large Springfield audience that no patriot could question America's entry into the war, and his successor in the White House, William Howard Taft, later reassured a crowd in the Illinois capital that the United States had launched a religious crusade to eradicate German sins. Speaking in Chicago, Senator Elihu Root bluntly dismissed the right of dissent in wartime and asserted that opposing views could not be tolerated when the government had determined upon a course of action.[8]

The SCD avidly directed the propaganda effort in Illinois. Under the energetic direction of Republican progressive Harold L. Ickes, the organization's neighborhood committees distributed more than two hundred thousand pieces of patriotic literature and held countless mass meetings. The

SCD worked with communities to expand local Fourth of July celebrations to include presentations on wartime patriotism and the sacredness of the Allied cause. State authorities feted traveling representatives of the British, French, Belgian, and Rumanian governments and held a conference of newspaper editors to outline ways in which the press could sustain the war effort. Public schools introduced patriotism as a part of their curricula, and the University of Illinois's history, political science, english, and economics departments created a new course, "War Issues," that presented a straightforward defense of the Allied cause. The SCD urged the discontinuation of German language instruction in the schools, an effort enthusiastically endorsed by Governor Lowden. "You do not get the true American spirit if you are educated in a foreign tongue," Lowden explained. "The English tongue is the language of liberty, of self-government and of orderly progress under the law." In Chicago, where the school board never formally banned the teaching of the language, enrollments in German classes dropped so precipitously that schools simply stopped offering them.[9]

Although the vast majority of persons of German ancestry unwaveringly supported the American war effort, they still felt the full brunt of the intense propaganda campaign. State and federal officials placed German Americans under surveillance and tallied bond subscriptions as an index of loyalty. (When the district attorney discovered disappointingly low bond sales in heavily German areas of Cook and DuPage counties, he instructed Lutheran ministers to preach patriotism to their congregations.) Local officials anglicized German street names and forbade the playing of music by Bach, Beethoven, Mozart, Brahms, Wagner, and other German composers in public places. Restaurant owners changed the names of sauerkraut and frankfurters to liberty cabbage and liberty sausages. German shepherd dogs became Alsatians. In their quest to ferret out subversives, employers in war industries fired workers with German surnames; so did the Chicago Athletic Club. After hooligans defaced the statue of author Friedrich von Schiller, the Chicago government placed the Johann von Goethe monument into storage for the duration of the war.

Fearing persecution, Illinoisans of German ancestry affirmed their support of the war, kept a low profile, or disguised their heritage. In the rush to superpatriotism, some German Americans took the initiative to dispel doubts about their loyalty. Chicago's Germania Club changed its name to the Lincoln Club, and the Bismarck Hotel became the Hotel Randolph. In similar fashion, trustees of the city's German Hospital rechristened it the Grant Hospital, and the Kaiser Friedrich Mutual Aid Society was replaced by the George Washington Benevolent Aid Society. To deny their German ancestry, many people changed their surnames or claimed a different nationality. The number of respondents in Illinois who identified themselves to census officials as German declined from 191,000 in 1914 to 112,000 in 1920.

Although German Americans remained the principal targets of wartime persecution, other groups suffered as well because of unpopular positions they took during the conflict. The federal government passed laws such as the Sedition and Espionage acts that limited dissent and imposed stiff penalties for those judged to have incited disloyalty or unduly criticized the Washington administration. Pacifists who opposed all wars found their positions precarious, especially those who applied for conscientious objector status to avoid conscription. Even Jane Addams, who strenuously argued against the charge that pacifism in any way eroded patriotism, found herself under attack from staunch defenders of the war effort. Pacifist opposition to the war centered in Chicago where women, Quakers, academicians, and political radicals challenged the Selective Service Act.

In June 1917 dissidents in Chicago formed a branch of the People's Council of America for Democracy and Peace, a national organization devoted to the attainment of a quick and democratic resolution of the war. When authorities in Minneapolis reneged on its agreement to host a People's Council convention in September of that year, the organization hastily arranged to convene instead in Chicago, where Mayor William Hale Thompson offered the Auditorium as a meeting site. Whereas Mayor Thompson affirmed the group's right of free speech, Governor Lowden saw the situation in a very different light. Lowden instructed Chicago's chief of police to disperse the gathering, but Thompson, arguing that "law-abiding citizens" had every right to assemble peacefully, countermanded the governor's order. The People's Council delegates met for two days before National Guardsmen summoned by Lowden from Centralia, Carmi, Harrisburg, and Salem could get to Chicago. Having successfully transacted their business, the members of the People's Council departed, leaving Mayor Thompson to face a storm of protest. Amid resounding plaudits for the governor, Chicagoans hanged the mayor in effigy in Grant Park and talked openly of his impeachment. If Thompson had been acting out of political considerations (he was seeking the Republican nomination for the U.S. Senate in 1918), his attempt to appeal to the state's German American voters seemed to backfire with much of the electorate.[10]

Radical political groups made an inviting target in the highly charged wartime atmosphere. The Socialist party, founded in 1901 by Eugene V. Debs and others, issued a steady stream of antiwar pronouncements from its national headquarters in Chicago. In June 1917, the local post office revoked the mailing privileges of the *American Socialist,* the official party organ; in September, justice department officials raided the Socialist headquarters, seized party records, and suspended publication of the *American Socialist.* In 1918 the federal government indicted several Socialist party leaders—Adolph Germer, national party secretary; J. Louis Engdahl, editor of party publications; the Reverend Irwin St. John Tucker, a prominent evangelist; and Victor Berger of Milwaukee, who had recently been elected to Congress—for conspiracy to obstruct the war under the Espionage Act. Following a three-week trial, the jury found all the defendants guilty. Arrested, tried, and convicted after giving an antiwar speech in Canton, Ohio, Debs received a sentence of ten years.

Federal officials also targeted the Industrial Workers of the World (IWW), a syndicalist labor organization that had been founded in Chicago in 1905. Although the IWW attracted most of its following from miners and agricultural workers in Western states, the organization maintained its headquarters in Chicago and enjoyed some popularity in several northern Illinois communities. In June 1917 Rockford police arrested the secretary of the IWW local and more than one hundred men who participated in a march opposing the draft. Officials in neighboring Freeport and Belvidere arrested dozens of men suspected of IWW connections, and a federal grand jury in Freeport indicted 134 men for draft evasion. In the mass trial of the accused draft dodgers in U.S. district court, Judge Kennesaw Mountain Landis sentenced 117 men (including 62 aliens) to a year and a day at hard labor. The government deported 37 aliens after they served their sentences for "conviction of a crime involving moral turpitude."[11]

On September 5, 1917, authorities raided IWW offices in Rockford, Chicago, and several other cities nationwide. On the basis of records seized in the dragnet, a federal grand jury returned a blanket indictment in U.S. district court that charged 166 IWW leaders with committing ten thousand crimes (mostly illegal strikes, boycotts, and sabotage) as part of a plot to subvert the war effort. Defense attorneys charged that Judge Landis prevented them from introducing exculpatory evidence so that their clients failed to receive a fair hearing in court. Although the trial lasted for more than four months, the jury returned a guilty verdict in a brisk fifty-five minutes. Landis meted out harsh sentences (as long as twenty years in some cases) and imposed fines ranging from five thousand to twenty thousand dollars. The IWW leaders lost their appeals and immediately began serving their prison terms—with the notable exception of the organization's secretary treasurer, Big Bill Haywood, who jumped bail and fled to the Soviet Union. Demoralized and bereft of leadership, the IWW fell into rapid decline. In 1923, in recognition of the blatantly unfair trial afforded the defendants, President Calvin Coolidge commuted the sentences of wartime prisoners still serving time for violation of the Espionage Act.

Suppression of dissent sometimes resulted in violence. In Havana, fifteen armed men sacked the home of Edward Speckman, a German American who had been overheard making unpatriotic remarks. In Staunton, agents of the xenophobic American Protective League tarred and feathered Severino Oberdan, an Italian immigrant accused of secretly belonging to the IWW, and John Metzen, an attorney from Chicago who had defended IWW members in court. On April 5, 1918, a mob in Collinsville hanged Robert Paul Praeger, a German American with socialist sympathies, who nonetheless had affirmed his support of the war and had tried to enlist in the armed forces. The trial of the eleven men charged with the murder ended in acquittal, and numerous incidents of coerced patriotism such as flag kissing continued to occur in nearby Madison County communities. The nation's press condemned the Praeger lynching as the "most notorious act of mob violence" during World War I. Governor Lowden chided the actions of the Collinsville mob but also called for more rigorous prosecution of sedition and treason.[12]

Victory over the Germans and their allies sparked a joyful celebration in Illinois, and huge throngs throughout the state warmly welcomed home the soldiers who had fought at Chateau Thierry, Belleau Woods, the Argonne, and other celebrated European battles. Still, a residue of bitterness and hostility remained within the victorious nation. In the aftermath of the armistice that ended the conflict, confrontations flared between ethnic groups. Having endured questions about their loyalty during the war, German Americans lamented the harsh peace forced upon their fatherland by the victorious Allies. Although the vast majority of German immigrants had behaved in an exemplary fashion during the war, nativists still in the throes of superpatriotic zeal continued to denigrate the "Huns." Irish Americans, who demonstrated for Irish independence from Great Britain, took to the streets to protest when the postwar treaty left their homeland under despotic British rule. Italian Americans seethed when President Wilson abrogated secret wartime treaties that had ceded land to Italy. Old World hostilities unleashed by the war sparked battles between Poles and Lithuanians in Chicago's stockyards. Anti-Jewish pogroms in Poland led to hand-to-hand fighting between huge mobs of Jews and Poles in Chicago. Ethnic tensions boiling in the cauldron of war were slow to cool down.

An economic recession caused by rising unemployment and stagnant wages exacerbated racial as well as ethnic and class tensions. Returning servicemen intensified the competition for jobs that had been filled by others during the war. Recruited by companies starved for workers and lured by stories of social equality, thousands of African Americans left the South and headed to the Promised Land of the Northern industrial cities. The *Chicago Defender,* a black newspaper widely read throughout the South, told African Americans that they would be safer and more prosperous above the Mason-Dixon Line. Between 1910 and 1920, the black population of Chicago doubled; fifty thousand Southern blacks arrived in the years 1916–1919 alone. Having received well-paying jobs during the war in the meatpacking plants, steel mills, Pullman car shops, and other factories, blacks desperately sought to retain them. In one of America's most segregated cities, shoehorned into a narrow strip of land on Chicago's South Side known as the Black Belt, they yearned for more living space. Determined to keep African Americans out of the ethnic neighborhoods bordering the Black Belt, whites bombed twenty-six homes purchased by African

Americans in 1918–1919. Competition for space and jobs created a combustible mix in the months following the end of World War I.

Racial animosities spilled over in July 1919, when whites stoned to death a black boy in Lake Michigan who had swum too close to a white-only beach. When white policemen refused to arrest the guilty parties, frustrated blacks clashed with white crowds and an isolated incident turned into a full-blown riot lasting for six days. White gangs wandering through the city beat African Americans they encountered, while blacks pummeled whites foolhardy enough to enter the Black Belt. Whites drove through the South Side and shot black bystanders from their speeding cars. Because of his political rivalry with Governor Lowden, Mayor Thompson refused at first to request additional force from the state to quell the disturbance. Thompson finally relented, however, and National Guard troops gradually restored order. The toll of the rioting left the populace stunned: fifteen whites and twenty-three African Americans dead, more than five hundred persons injured, and more than three thousand residents left homeless by vandals and arsonists. Race riots erupted in several other U.S. cities that summer, including Knoxville, Tennessee, Omaha, Nebraska, and Washington, D.C., but none equaled the ferocity and destruction of the Chicago clash.

Stung into action by the Chicago riot and by the episode in East St. Louis two years earlier, Governor Lowden convened a race relations commission in Chicago to identify the causes of the disorders and to propose ways of preventing future outbreaks. Comprising six prominent African Americans and six influential whites, the commission spent eighteen months investigating race relations in Chicago and published its final report in 1922. Citing as causes of the riot the rapid growth of African American population, competition for jobs, housing conflict, and discrimination in public places, the commission listed fifty-nine recommendations designed to improve race relations in Chicago and elsewhere in the state. Equal rights and opportunities would produce racial harmony, the commission adduced, just as segregation and discrimination would surely lead to recurrent problems.

As the racial violence in the summer of 1919 clearly demonstrated, the tensions of the preceding years failed to dissipate promptly at the end of the war. Seven months after the armistice that ended the fighting in Europe, the Illinois General Assembly passed a sedition law patterned closely after earlier federal legislation. Both chambers of the newly formed general assembly endorsed the American Legion, an organization devoted to "kill[ing] radicalism by spreading Americanism."[13] Fear and hatred of the Germans metamorphosed into an aversion to all manner of foreign doctrines and influences. In the immediate postwar period, the Red Scare encompassed fear of the IWW, socialists, and international Communism (the latter viewed as a particular threat because of the Bolsheviks' triumph in the Russian Revolution and the creation of the Soviet Union). After the Socialist party splintered in 1919, separatists formed the Communist Labor party and Communist Party U.S.A. (CPUSA) in Chicago; the national offices of the CPUSA remained in Chicago until 1927 when they moved to New York City.

To purge the nation of insidious radical influences, U.S. Attorney General A. Mitchell Palmer planned the roundup of dangerous aliens in an operation carefully choreographed by the labor department, the commissioner of immigration, and the justice department. The Palmer Raids, conducted in Chicago on January 1, 1920, and throughout the rest of Illinois the following day, involved the arrests of CPUSA, Communist Labor party, and IWW members. Federal and local authorities arrested several hundred radicals in Chicago, nearly two hundred in Rockford, six in East St. Louis, and one in Moline. Law enforcement authorities turned aliens over to immigration officials and U.S. citizens over to the state's attorney's office for possible grand jury action.

A 1918 demonstration for an independent Lithuania in Chicago's McKinley Park shows the strength of ethnic loyalties during U.S. participation in World War I. *Illinois State Historical Library*

From June through August 1920, twenty members of the Communist Labor party stood trial in Chicago for sedition. In an atmosphere of fear and retrenchment, the prosecution's argument that party membership alone indicated a desire to overthrow the government proved compelling to the jurors. Famed criminal attorney Clarence Darrow's eloquent defense of civil liberties seemingly made less of an impression than the prosecutor's impassioned summation, which concluded with a recitation of all verses of the "Star Spangled Banner." The judge sentenced the defendants to jail terms ranging from one to five years; the Illinois Supreme Court upheld the sentences and the U.S. Supreme Court declined to hear the case. Shortly after the defendants began serving their sentences, however, Governor Len Small pardoned the prisoners. Small reported that his mail reflected a fairly equal division in the opinions of his constituents concerning the pardon. About half the letter writers praised the governor for his courage, likening his principled action to Altgeld's pardon of the Haymarket rioters, while the other half condemned him for desertion of 100 percent Americanism. Clearly, wartime passions died hard, even in the wake of an American victory.

America's brief participation in World War I left an ambiguous legacy in Illinois. Wartime mobilization resulted in increased industrial and agricultural productivity, and the leading roles played by the SCD and the federal government contributed to the centralization of authority. Questions about the efficacy of American neutrality gave way to a unified effort to support the armed forces, yet deep divisions within the society remained throughout the war and afterward. Demands for conformity and loyalty produced shocking levels of bigotry, violence, and xenophobia. Nor did such passions subside immediately after the end of the war in 1919. At the conclusion of the conflict, Illinoisans shared with other Americans the desire for a respite from wartime upheavals and a return to "normalcy."

East St. Louis

In 1797 James Piggott built two cabins on the Illinois side of the Mississippi River across from St. Louis and began operation of a ferry service. Farmers in the American Bottom used Piggott's ferry to transport their grain, livestock, and lumber to St. Louis markets. The settlement that grew up around Piggott's cabins, known initially as Illinoistown, changed its name to East St. Louis in 1861. After the Civil War, a number of industries in St. Louis relocated across the river to East St. Louis, which became one of the nation's premier meatpacking centers after the opening of the National Stock Yards in 1871. Already the terminus for a few railroads, East St. Louis became a major Midwestern railroad hub in the postbellum decades when twenty-seven trunk lines radiated from the city. In 1874 the Eads Bridge opened across the Mississippi River, rendering the ferry obsolete and making East St. Louis an important gateway in the expanding national trade network. With more than three hundred coal mines located nearby, the city's ready access to fuel attracted such industries as iron, steel, aluminum, lumber, glass, soap, and beer. One of the fastest-growing cities in the country, East St. Louis's population doubled every ten years between 1890 and 1920.

By 1917 East St. Louis had become a gritty industrial city where workers lived under a canopy of soot in rickety shacks close to factories. The affluent classes who did business in the city lived in St. Louis or other nearby communities. When World War I created labor shortages, local businessmen recruited an estimated ten thousand African Americans from the South. Forced to live in already overcrowded slums and willing to take jobs at low wage levels rejected by trade unions, blacks came into conflict with white workers. Resentment against black strikebreakers in an aluminum ore factory led to sporadic violence, and a worried Governor Lowden assigned National Guard troops for several weeks to keep the peace. When the National Guard withdrew, whites armed themselves, invaded black neighborhoods, and launched an orgy of murder and arson. National Guardsmen swiftly returned but either stood idly by and watched or joined in the fray on the side of the whites. In all, thirty-nine African Americans and nine whites died, hundreds suffered injuries, and arsonists destroyed 250 buildings and 40 freight cars in the railroad yards. A grand jury indicted 144 men, including 5 policemen, but obtained no convictions. A postriot study enumerated several causes for the riot, including economic competition and corrupt local political institutions that provided inadequate law enforcement and winked at intolerable slum conditions.

Throughout the remainder of the twentieth century, especially in the years after World War II, East St. Louis suffered steady population and economic decline. Of all U.S. cities with populations exceeding fifty thousand, East St. Louis was the second poorest in 1920. Later, between 1950 and 1965, the city's population dropped by half. The loss of thousands of jobs precipitated by the exodus of the packinghouses, steel plants, and other factories decimated the local economy. Even as whites fled the city and African Americans became the overwhelming majority of the population, a corrupt political machine remained in control of city hall. Black political reformers finally ousted the crooked politicians in the 1970s but won a hollow prize for their efforts. By the end of the twentieth century, abandoned buildings lined empty streets where factories once operated night and day, and the city hitched its economic hopes to the chintzy allure of the gambling casinos in riverboats anchored downtown.

Samuel Insull

Born in London, England, on November 11, 1859, Samuel Insull came to the United States at the age of twenty-two and became Thomas Edison's personal secretary. In 1889 he became an executive in the General Electric Corporation, the world's first electrical-equipment manufacturer. Three years later, he resigned the vice presidency at General Electric to become the president of the Chicago Edison Company (which changed its name to Commonwealth Edison in 1907). Instead of charging fixed monthly rates for electricity consumers, Insull installed meters that enabled his subordinates to monitor usage patterns. Applying the theory of economies of scale, he replaced small generating plants with mammoth, centrally located power stations, which allowed him to reduce production costs. By merging with dozens of rival energy companies in and around Chicago, he offered low rates to industries and homes. Through an intricate web of holding companies, he linked several corporations together in one of the most sophisticated financial networks in American history. Having provided electricity for Chicago's elevated train system and interurban lines, Insull acquired the public transit system as well. A cagey businessman, he bribed Chicago city councilmen and state legislators to secure franchises and safeguard his monopolies against regulatory laws. By the time that the United States entered World War I, the successful entrepreneur's electricity empire included not only Chicago and surrounding suburbs but also large portions of Wisconsin, Indiana, and Ohio.

In 1917 Illinois Governor Frank O. Lowden chose Insull, one of the nation's most successful and admired businessmen, to head the newly created State Council of Defense. Concerned that his native England would fall to German armies, Insull became an early and ardent advocate of American intervention on the side of the Allies. To ensure that the SCD began operating quickly and efficiently, he donated an office building to serve as the agency's headquarters as well as his own employees to serve as the office staff. Determined to convince the American public of the need for fighting, Insull created the Four-Minute Men program to deliver propaganda speeches in Illinois communities. Government officials and the press praised Insull's administrative skills and recognized the indispensable role he played in mobilizing Illinois resources for war.

Insull's financial empire continued to prosper after World War I. In 1929, when his companies supplied nearly one-eighth of the nation's electricity and gas, Insull stood as the most powerful man in Chicago and one of the most influential businessmen in the country. The Great Depression of the 1930s brought a stark reversal of fortune, however, and the man who had been regaled as a wise industrial statesman suddenly became seen as a prime example of the grasping businessman whose excesses had

Samuel Insull (center), the discredited utilities tycoon whose
loss of a financial empire signaled the onset of the Great
Depression. *Chicago Historical
Society*

undermined American affluence. His holding companies survived the
stock market crash of 1929, but reduced power consumption and declining
public transit ridership brought crushing financial losses in 1931. When
Insull's corporations failed to make interest payments on holding company bonds and lapsed into bankruptcy in 1932, investors lost $638 mil-
lion. As much of his $150 million fortune evaporated, Insull fled to Europe
one step ahead of an army of angry creditors. Arrested and extradited from
Greece, the humiliated tycoon stood trial three times in 1934–1935 on
charges of mail fraud, embezzlement, and bankruptcy law violations. Acquitted each time, Insull returned to Europe, where he died of heart failure
in a Paris metro station on July 16, 1938.

Prosperity and Depression

At the end of World War I, Illinois seemed poised to enjoy a period of prolonged prosperity. Its population of 6.5 million people, about one-third of
whom resided in Chicago, lived in one of the nation's most affluent
states. A surge in industrial productivity during the war had left Illinois
behind only New York and Pennsylvania in total manufacturing output.
The state ranked first in meatpacking and the production of agricultural
implements, third behind Pennsylvania and Ohio in iron production, and
fourth in the manufacture of electrical equipment (electrical motors, batteries, and telephone and telegraph equipment). A brief postwar agricultural recession notwithstanding, the state stood among the leaders in annual crop and livestock production. Problems of conversion after the war
proved nettlesome, and some industries seemed better suited than others
to achieve sustained economic growth. Still, the United States emerged
from the Great War as the preeminent economic nation, and Illinois possessed the natural and human resources necessary to share in the nation's
bounty. The defeat of German autocracy and imperialism left American
capitalism well positioned to compete in international markets. Like their
counterparts elsewhere in the country, Illinoisans viewed their future economic prospects with optimism.

Believing that Illinois's already bright future would be enhanced by the
improvement of state government, progressives called for the modernization of the 1870 constitution. In 1917, at the urging of Governor Frank O.
Lowden, the general assembly overwhelmingly endorsed a constitutional
convention, and in a 1918 referendum the state's voters concurred. The
membership of the convention, which Lowden summoned into session on
January 6, 1920, consisted of two delegates from each of the state's senatorial districts (eighty-five Republicans and seventeen Democrats). The convention then met in fits and starts, however, recessing for fourteen months
at one juncture and working only a total of 140 days. After two years and

nine months of sporadic deliberation, more than twice the length of time devoted to the enterprise by any previous constitutional convention, the delegates finally produced a document. The electorate rejected this constitution by a margin of 921,398 to 185,298, a margin of five-to-one, while Cook County voters did so by a ratio of nineteen-to-one.

The proposed constitution perished principally because of sectionalism. Just as the most recent reapportionment of the state's legislative districts gave downstate rural areas disproportionate majorities, the formula for membership of the constitutional convention left Cook County underrepresented. Fearful of being dominated by Chicago interests, downstaters resisted the redrawing of electoral districts to reflect the state's population distribution, defeated proposals to include initiative and referendum provisions, and prohibited municipalities from acquiring public utilities. The proposed constitution granted Chicago some home rule powers but not on revenue matters. The Chicago newspapers, which had championed a constitutional convention in the hope of addressing sectional inequities, editorialized against the final product. Governor Len Small and Chicago Mayor William Hale Thompson spoke against the constitution, as did Clarence Darrow, Harold Ickes, and other leading Chicago progressives. Cook County voters used the power of their numbers to defeat the constitution in a statewide referendum, but malapportioned legislative districts continued to blunt Chicago's home rule aspirations.

Progressives failed to modernize the state through constitutional revision, but they scored a resounding victory in the decades-old battle against the demon rum. Following the preparatory work done by the WCTU and the Anti-Saloon League, the exigencies of wartime provided the impetus for America's most conspicuous foray into social engineering. Reformers made temperance a wartime issue, arguing persuasively for the conservation of precious resources and against the harmful effects of alcohol on American workers and soldiers. The preponderance of German brewers—Schlitz, Busch, Pabst, and others—aided the dry cause. Wets objected to infringements on personal liberties, and immigrant groups identified the drive to outlaw beer and wine as an assault against their various cultures. Success for the temperance cause came with the ratification of the Eighteenth Amendment to the Constitution, which outlawed the manufacture, sale, and importation of alcoholic beverages, and passage of the Volstead Act, which outlined the means for enforcement. Problems soon arose, however, as Congress appropriated paltry sums for enforcement and the treasury department assigned few agents to the task. The so-called noble experiment foundered, and eager consumers spent increasing sums of money on bathtub gin and bootleg beer.

Chicago became an international symbol for the failure of Prohibition. Corrupt policemen and judges looked the other way, receiving handsome payments for their myopia, as Irish and Italian gangs vied to provide the il-

legal alcohol to a thirsty public. Rival gangs formed and dissolved temporary alliances across ethnic lines, and the Beer Wars resulted in countless hi-
jackings and an estimated two hundred murders between 1920 and 1924.
Gangland slayings peaked at seventy-six in the year 1926. Police officials, aldermen, and judges routinely attended the garish funerals of mobsters slain
in public shootouts. Mayor William Hale "Big Bill" Thompson flaunted his
opposition to Prohibition and openly consorted with gangsters.

Chicago's bootlegging gangs played a deadly Darwinian game of survival of the fittest whereby the most ruthless competitor rose to the top
by eliminating his rivals. James "Big Jim" Colosimo, onetime chief of the
city's gambling and prostitution enterprises, failed to gain control of the
emerging bootlegging trade and in 1920 fell victim of a gangland execution probably ordered by his nephew by marriage, Johnny Torrio. Barely
surviving an attempt on his own life, in 1925 Torrio fled to Italy and surrendered leadership of his gang to a gunman recently imported from New
York City, Al Capone. With the murder of seven members of the Moran
gang in the St. Valentine's Day massacre of 1929, Capone vanquished the
last of his rivals and solidified his control of the city's underworld. After
expenses, including payoffs to policemen, politicians, and judges, the

Members of Bugs Moran's gang killed by Al Capone's gunmen in the St. Valentine's
Day massacre, February 14, 1929. Chicago was known in the 1920s as a haven for
gangsters. *Illinois State Historical Library*

Capone organization cleared an estimated seventy million dollars in 1930. When a reform mayor sought to sever the ties between local officials and organized crime, Capone moved his headquarters to suburban Cicero and continued to conduct business as usual in Chicago. The intercession of federal officials eventually sent Capone to prison for income tax evasion, where he died of syphilis after serving seven years, but organized crime continued to flourish in his absence.

An atmosphere of lawlessness pervaded Chicago during the Roaring Twenties. Largely unaffected by the gangland violence, which seldom claimed victims among the general public, Chicagoans tolerated illegal activities to acquire alcohol. An extraordinarily popular figure who received warm ovations from the crowds at Chicago Cubs baseball games and at area racetracks, Al Capone repeatedly referred to himself as a businessman who simply provided the public a product it demanded. "If people didn't want beer and wouldn't drink it," he commented, "a fellow would be crazy for going around trying to sell it. I've seen gambling houses, too . . . and I never saw anyone point a gun at a man and make him go in." Big Bill Thompson, who served as mayor from 1915 to 1923 and again from 1927 to 1931, made no secret of his opposition to Prohibition. Citizens not surprisingly became jaded in an environment where politicians, gangsters, policemen, and judges profited from lax law enforcement.[1]

Bootlegging flourished in Illinois's rural counties as well. Moonshine from makeshift stills slaked some local thirsts, but more commonly trucks or automobiles imported liquor from larger urban areas. Responding to rumors linking bootleggers and operators of gambling operations to the Chicago underworld, rural vigilantes united to curtail corrosive big city influences. In the state's southern counties, where Prohibition advocates often exercised considerable influence, antiurban feeling, nativism, and ethnocentrism contributed to rising tensions. The Ku Klux Klan (KKK), resurgent in the 1920s in Midwestern states as well as in the South, inveighed against the foreigners and Catholics involved in the downstate bootlegging trade. As the self-appointed defenders of public morality, members of the KKK donned their hoods and burned their crosses on behalf of Prohibition.

In Williamson County, which had a long history of violence in the coal mines, the KKK vowed to eradicate bootlegging and gambling activities managed by persons with Italian surnames. The Klan hired S. Glenn Young, a former federal agent with a reputation for violent tactics and self-promotion, to spearhead the battle against the foreign invaders. Young led a group of Klansmen, who had been deputized by a U.S. Treasury agent, in a series of raids on roadhouses and liquor outlets. After Klansmen fought pitched battles with bootleggers and brandished machine guns in courtrooms to intimidate witnesses, Governor Len Small sent the National Guard into "Bloody Williamson" to restore order.

Ku Klux Klan funeral procession for S. Glenn Young in 1925. Before National Guardsmen restored order in "Bloody Williamson" County, twenty men had been killed in the battle to control the illegal liquor business. *Illinois State Historical Library*

Young, two Klansmen, and a deputy sheriff died in a gun battle in a Herrin cigar store. By the time the last National Guardsmen withdrew, twenty men had been killed and illegal liquor continued to flow unabated.

Violence flared in Williamson County throughout the decade. When members of the United Mine Workers struck near Herrin on April 1, 1922, the mine owner fired the men, replaced them with nonunion miners, and hired armed guards to protect the strikebreakers. Angry strikers laid siege to the mine, captured and disarmed the strikebreakers, then brutally murdered nineteen of them. The strikers mutilated some of their victims at the site of the massacre and then established a temporary morgue where townspeople further disfigured the corpses. Local juries acquitted all of the 214 men charged with murder in the episode. Later in the decade, a war broke out between two rival gangs vying for control of the vice trade in Williamson and Franklin counties. Gang members murdered two mayors, a state highway policeman, and eleven others before hostilities ceased. In 1928 the state hanged Charlie Birger, the leader of one of the gangs, for capital crimes; the other gang, led by Carl, Earl, and Bernie Shelton, avoided prosecution. In subsequent years, the Shelton brothers expanded their criminal empire across much of southern and central Illinois.

While criminals fought for control of such illicit enterprises as bootleg liquor and gambling, mainstream businesses in the state enjoyed a prolonged period of economic growth. As a microcosm of what came to be called Coolidge Prosperity, Illinois communities recorded noteworthy economic advances on several fronts. A remarkable building boom transformed downtown Chicago as the addition of the Tribune Tower, the Wrigley Building, the Palmolive Building, and other skyscrapers enhanced its already impressive skyline. The Merchandise Mart, the largest commercial building in the world at the time of its opening in 1931, contained ninety-seven acres of floor space. The Stevens Hotel, later known as the Conrad Hilton, claimed that its three thousand rooms made this the world's largest inn. The construction of thousands of single-family dwellings expanded the housing stock in cities, suburbs, and towns of all sizes across Illinois. The state built a plethora of roads to carry the growing number of automobiles, trucks, and buses owned by a growing population; Illinois ranked first among the states, with more than seven thousand miles of concrete roadways. Utility companies blanketed the landscape with power lines, banks lent capital for the creation of new businesses, worker productivity increased, wages and salaries rose. Inflation remained low, the value of the dollar high. By and large, Illinoisans in the 1920s earned more dollars, worked fewer hours, and made enough money to purchase a greater number and wider variety of goods than ever before.

The dramatic rise in consumption resulted from new business practices in the 1920s that allowed the rapidly expanding middle class to acquire luxury items previously reserved for the rich. A minor force in American life before World War I, advertising became influential in the postbellum years as a means of stimulating consumption. Businessmen began to realize the potential of advertising, in no small measure because of the success of George Creel's Committee on Public Information (CPI) and other government agencies at shaping public attitudes during the war. Expenditures on advertising increased nationally from $1.4 billion in 1918 to $4 billion in 1929. According to the economist Stuart Chase, advertising agencies spent more money in 1925 to educate consumers than the nation's public school systems spent to educate pupils. Captains of industry came to rely on "captains of consciousness" to create the demand for products that business had already developed. President Calvin Coolidge proclaimed that the business of America was business, and Madison Avenue emerged as the nation's unofficial capital.[2]

Having created and defined markets, business executives further stimulated consumption through the expansion of credit and the innovative use of installment buying. While some members of the working class took advantage of the new "buy now, pay later" opportunities, the middle class benefited most from liberal credit policies. By 1926 American retailers were selling six billion dollars' worth of goods annually (that is, 15 percent of total sales) by installment. Consumers especially appreciated the opportunity to purchase expensive items with an affordable down payment followed by regular reimbursements. In 1925 American consumers bought 90 percent of pianos, washing machines, and sewing machines, 80 percent of phonographs, 75 percent of tractors, and 70 percent of furniture and gas stoves on installment plans. By the end of the decade, three-fourths of automobile owners purchased their cars on installment.[3]

The automobile stood at the vanguard of the economic expansion of the 1920s. Economists estimated that the automobile accounted for 90 percent of the petroleum consumed in the country, 80 percent of the rubber, 75 percent of the plate glass, 25 percent of the machine tools, and 20 percent of the steel. The number of automobiles licensed in Illinois increased from 478,438 in 1919 to 1,630,816 in 1929. In the latter year, 2,477 new car dealerships, 218 used car dealerships, 3,967 filling stations, 1,120 filling stations attached to other businesses, 656 tire and battery stores, and 415 brake, battery, and ignition shops operated in the state. Altogether, thirteen thousand proprietors of businesses catering to automobile owners employed more than forty thousand workers in Illinois. The appearance of roadside restaurants and cabins built on the outskirts of towns for motorists' overnight accommodations likewise resulted from expanding automobility.

Several Illinois firms manufactured automobiles in the 1920s, but only the Velie Motor Vehicle Company of Moline still operated by the end of the decade. An offshoot of a farm machinery business, the Velie Company enjoyed considerable success before becoming a casualty of the Great Depression. Such models as the Bush, the Classic, the Coey Flyer, the Drexel, the Elgin, the Ogren Six, the Portin-Palmer, and the Woods Electric originated in Chicago. The Glide was produced in Peoria, the New Era in Joliet, the Moline-Knight in East Moline, and the Roamer and the Halladay in Streator. Unsuccessful at converting to mass-production assembly-line techniques and unable to attract adequate funding for national advertising campaigns, these small local firms failed to compete effectively with Detroit's giants, Ford, General Motors, and Chrysler. During the same years that Detroit became the center for the manufacture of passenger cars, however, Chicago emerged as the leading producer of commercial vehicles such as trucks, buses, taxicabs, and hearses. The Yellow Truck and Coach Manufacturing Company, a General Motors subsidiary, operated plants in Chicago and Moline.

In addition to its economic impact, the automobile exerted a strong influence upon the lives of Illinois residents. Suburbanization accelerated, the population density of metropolitan areas declined, and the number of passengers on railroads and interurbans decreased. Once the key to the movement of people and goods through city streets, the horse virtually vanished from the urban scene. The greater mobility provided by the automobile altered the shopping habits of housewives, threatening the viability of mom-and-pop dry goods stores and augmenting the appeal of chain stores. Automobiles gave new mobility to criminals, teenagers, and others seeking to escape the clutches of watchful authority figures. Traditionalists rued the car's negative impact on family life as parents and progeny had the means to pursue their own interests independently. Guardians of public morality frowned on the privacy provided adolescents for their amorous activities. According to a juvenile court judge, the automobile had become a "house of prostitution on wheels." While acknowledging the concerns expressed by critics of the car, the *Chicago Tribune* concluded in 1924 that the product's benefits far outweighed its shortcomings. The ubiquitous automobile occupied a central niche in the developing affluence of American society.[4]

Yet although significant numbers of people benefited from economic growth, not everyone shared equally in the fruits of Coolidge Prosperity. While advertisers eagerly pursued the middle class's disposable income, unskilled and semiskilled workers found their economic situations as precarious as ever. Unemployment rates remained alarmingly high, reaching 15 percent at times during the 1920s. Having climbed substantially during World War I, real wages remained steady or inched ahead gradually from 1923 to 1929 in the steel, agricultural implements, meatpacking, and clothing industries. In the coal mines the average annual death toll from accidents approached two hundred, and falling prices drove wages down. Overproduction of bituminous coal, along with rising competition from other fuels such as oil, gas, and hydroelectricity, resulted in a 43 percent decrease in prices in Illinois during the decade; wages fell 23 percent as a result. Having worked only eight hours a day during the war, coal miners labored for nine and ten hours daily during the 1920s. A historian studying the economic conditions of workers in the 1920s concluded, "The struggle for economic security, not the struggle to keep up with the Joneses, dominated working-class life in the prosperity decade."[5]

If a checkered prosperity prevailed in the industrial sector, the situation on Illinois farms was more uniformly bad. The loss of European markets, the withdrawal of government subsidies, currency deflation, and increased competition from Canadian and Australian farmers caused a depression in rural America after World War I. Having weathered the postwar setback of 1920–1922, farmers expected that slumping agricultural prices would rebound to wartime levels. Instead, hard times continued throughout the remainder of the 1920s and into the 1930s. Compounding the situation, many small farmers had reacted to unusually high agricultural prices in 1917–1919 by buying more land, frequently at inflated prices. As demand and prices fell in the 1920s, farmers went deeply into debt and faced the threat of bankruptcy. In a time of general prosperity, banks and other lending institutions enforced a shocking number of farm mortgage foreclosures. As in earlier periods of agrarian crisis, large land-holders fared better than those who farmed fewer acres.

Beginning in the autumn of 1929, events laid bare the superficiality of prosperity throughout the nation. The collapse of the stock market in October of that year, more a symptom of the structural weaknesses of the economy than the Great Depression's proximate cause, signaled the onset of a downward economic spiral that afflicted the state for the next decade. The bull market of the 1920s, in which the prices of securities rose steadily, rested precariously on an unsure foundation of credit. Securities prices rose largely because of the whims of investors, not necessarily because the value of the stock reflected the economic health of the corporation. Purchasing stock on margin for a fraction of its purported worth, investors assumed that dividends would continue to increase, and they often lacked the wherewithal to pay their debts if prices fell. Investors lost more than forty billion dollars in the Great Crash of 1929, a cataclysmic event that left millions of people facing financial ruin.

The stock market collapse signaled the beginning of the Great Depression, but several factors combined to send the nation's economy into a prolonged tailspin. First, the United States operated in an unstable international economy that never fully recovered from World War I. The Allies, particularly England and France, owed the United States huge sums of money that they could repay only because American investors underwrote German indemnities and reparations to the Allies. European debtors were struggling even more because of high American import tariffs levied to protect domestic farmers and manufacturers from foreign competition. The collapse of the international economy, which had been kept afloat by American credit, reduced export opportunities for American businesses—a disaster at a time when saturated domestic markets led to dwindling consumption. In part, economists identified the descent of the United States into economic depression as part of a larger international crisis of capitalism.

The absence of diversification in American industry loomed as another major cause of the Great Depression. Economic expansion in the 1920s depended overwhelmingly on a few key industries such as automobiles and construction. When they faltered, other industries lacked the size and productivity to fill the void. Meanwhile, long-standing difficulties in mining, farming, railroads, and textiles made the situation worse, for high unemployment in these "sick industries" retarded purchasing power and depressed whole regions of the country. Developments in the industrial, farming, and mining areas of Illinois mirrored national patterns.

Most important, a fundamental maldistribution of income created poverty in the midst of plenty. A Federal Trade Commission study found that the richest 1 percent of the population possessed 60 percent of the nation's wealth. The federal government's regressive taxation policies during the 1920s had further reduced purchasing power. Productivity during the period of economic growth had far outpaced wage increases, and surpluses of industrial goods were overflowing the warehouses. American industry mass-produced goods at a dizzying pace, but not under conditions in which the American people could purchase them. As sales declined, executives countered dwindling profits with production cutbacks, reduced wages, and layoffs. Resultant unemployment increases only deprived workers of more disposable income, thus causing other rounds of contraction and more rapidly falling profits. A vicious downward spiral led the nation into symbiotic tragedies of plant closings, joblessness, and bankruptcies.

Although the residents of East Coast cities felt the impact of the deepening depression during the winter of 1929–1930, the number of unemployed in Illinois at first grew very gradually. By the winter of 1930–1931, however, alarm filled Illinois communities as conditions rapidly worsened. December 1930 payrolls in industry had fallen more than 30 percent from the December 1929 numbers; in January 1931 unemployment in the state exceeded seven hundred thousand. Government officials reported 1.1 million men and women unemployed by October 1931, and the number of jobless peaked at 1.5 million in January 1933. From 1925 to 1932, factory payrolls fell 53 percent in Peoria, 54 percent in East St. Louis, 58 percent in Aurora, 63 percent in Decatur, 70 percent in Quincy, 73 percent in Danville, 76 percent in Rockford, 80 percent in Rock Island, 86 percent in Joliet, and 93 percent in Moline. As factories and coal mines closed, freight revenues fell by 50 percent on the state's railroads; deepening poverty similarly reduced the number of passengers. As a result, the Illinois Central Railroad discharged half of its sixty thousand employees.

The situation in Chicago became so perilous that the city virtually ceased to function. Mayor Anton Cermak, elected in 1931 as the champion of the city's anti-Prohibition forces, faced intractable economic problems. The unemployment rate reached a harrowing 40 percent in 1932, and workers fortunate enough to retain their jobs often absorbed crippling pay cuts up to 50 percent. The city's tax delinquency list filled 260 newspaper pages. Public schoolteachers, who went unpaid for months at a time, provided lunches for more than eleven thousand children daily. Unemployed workers failed to meet their mortgage payments, and the number of homeless increased dramatically. A shantytown appeared at the very edge of the Loop on Randolph Street, and an estimated three hundred people established residence in a haphazardly constructed Hooverville at a South Side garbage dump. Fifteen hundred homeless Chicagoans slept on the lower level of the Michigan Avenue Bridge. As the Midwest's transportation hub, Chicago attracted thousands of transients to its already sizable stable of unemployed and indigent; throngs of uprooted men and women descended upon the city, hoping for work and lodging, but found only breadlines and cardboard shacks.

Desperate schoolteachers in Chicago during the Great Depression, sometimes not paid for months at a time, protested on behalf of public education. *Illinois State Historical Library*

The last to be hired and first to be fired, African Americans suffered disproportionately during the Great Depression. When factories trimmed their payrolls, foremen singled out unskilled black workers as the first to go. When upper- and middle-class white housewives cut expenses, they released their black maids, cooks, and butlers. By the summer of 1930, every bank in Chicago's Black Belt had closed its doors. For the first time in its history, the *Chicago Defender* began urging African Americans to remain in the South rather than come to the erstwhile Promised Land. Angry at ghetto businesses owned by whites who refused to employ black workers, African Americans in Chicago organized a "Spend Your Money Where You Can Work" campaign and boycotted chain stores for their high prices and discriminatory hiring policies. To aid Black Belt residents facing eviction for failure to pay their rent, groups of the unemployed formed flying squadrons that clashed with police and bank officials. Although no full-blown race riots ensued, hard times raised the level of interracial tension.[6]

Another disadvantaged minority consigned to the margins of Chicago life, Mexicans also found their financial security seriously jeopardized. Recruited by factory owners to allay the World War I labor shortage in Chicago, some Mexicans arrived from farms throughout the Midwest seeking wintertime work, but most came directly from Mexico via the railroads. They settled primarily in the neighborhoods of South Chicago, the Back of the Yards, and the Near West Side. By 1928 they comprised 9.4 percent of the city's steelworkers and 5.7 percent of the workforce in the packinghouses. Many Chicago employers, especially the meatpackers, promised the Mexicans steady employment but then used them essentially as strikebreakers. As the Great Depression worsened, U.S. immigration officials implemented a policy of repatriation. Collaborating with state and local welfare agencies, they rounded up Mexican workers and their families—regardless of citizenship status—and dispatched them back to their homeland. The Mexican population declined from twenty thousand in 1930 to sixteen thousand in 1940 because of repatriation and immigration restriction.

Outside the cities, economic conditions were worsening even more rapidly. Illinois farmers, who had been battling economic depression conditions since the conclusion of World War I, hoped in vain that prices for their crops would rebound. Their failure to make mortgage payments on the land led to an unprecedented number of foreclosures and evictions. With more than half of the state's coal mines closed, coal miners worked sporadically; the average coal miner by the mid-1930s secured employment for only six months per year. Seeing only poverty and isolation in the countryside, many rural folk (especially young people) abandoned their homes and sought work in the cities. In the vast majority of cases, they found the situation no better in urban settings.

When families proved incapable of handling the rising tide of misery, charitable organizations labored valiantly to provide relief. Secular and religious charities increased their fund-raising activities and began to expend more money for aid to the destitute. As effects of the depression became more visible, private charities increased their outlays to $7,925,388 in 1931 and $8,431,823 in 1932. In the next several years, however, private spending decreased (from $3,501,525 in 1933 to $1,403,489 in 1934 and $942,480 in 1935) because philanthropic contributions declined and government began shouldering more of the burden. The cumulative effects of depression took their toll on charitable giving, and the dearth of relief funds from private sources led to increased demands on public institutions. A deeply felt aversion to government involvement in the economy softened simply because policy makers could see no viable alternatives.

Local and county governments, the principal purveyors of public relief in Illinois before the Great Depression, possessed fewer resources as economic conditions worsened. By the fall of 1931 as unemployment rose and tax revenue plunged, counties began rejecting applications for relief and trimming allowances to help as many families as possible. The average monthly relief allotments for families by December 1932 varied widely by county, ranging from a token $1.83 in Alexander County (Cairo) to Cook County's comparatively luxurious $29.15. The average allowance for families receiving relief outside of Cook County stood at $12.81, an entirely inadequate monthly stipend by any measure. County officials turned hopeful eyes to Springfield, arguing that the state was responsible to provide for the general welfare when local resources came up short.

Governor Louis L. Emmerson, a conservative Republican banker from Mount Vernon, sought to rely on private charity and minimize government actions. Like President Herbert Hoover, Emmerson feared that providing relief to the unemployed—even as an emergency measure—would undermine their rugged self-reliance. In 1930 he appointed the Governor's Commission on Unemployment and Relief to devise ways of creating jobs and helping private agencies distribute relief. Still averse to the state government's disbursing money to the unemployed, he disregarded

The unemployed lined up for handouts on South State Street in Chicago during the grim days of the Great Depression. *Illinois State Historical Library*

the recommendation by the governor's commission to seek appropriations from the general assembly for relief. Compounding the state's financial problems, Chicago stood on the verge of bankruptcy. A reassessment of real estate requested by Mayor Big Bill Thompson resulted in Cook County being two years delinquent in paying its share of Illinois property taxes, which had been since the nineteenth century the state's chief revenue source. The general assembly met in special sessions in 1930 and 1931 to consider Cook County's tax collection problems and authorized Chicago to issue revenue bonds and to create the new office of assessor. The general assembly passed a state income tax proposed by the governor, but the courts ruled it unconstitutional.

In February 1932, reluctantly conceding that the unemployment problem in Illinois had become a crisis, Governor Emmerson asked the general assembly to create the Illinois Emergency Relief Commission (IERC) for the dispersal of state funds. Provided with $20 million for unemployment relief, the seven-member IERC established rules and regulations for the expenditure of funds by the counties; the IERC administered state aid directly in Cook County. The $20 million appropriation, planned to suffice for the entire year, however, lasted only through July. The state's voters approved a $25 million relief bond issue to be repaid from future gas tax revenues, and the IERC issued $17 million in bonds without referendum for relief in Cook County. The governor imposed a number of economy measures (asking state employees to relinquish one day's pay per month, for instance), but the state's deficit continued to mount. Beginning in August 1932 and continuing for the next year, Illinois relied almost exclusively on the federal government for relief funding.

His hands-off policies having been discredited by 1932, President Hoover proposed that the federal government create the Reconstruction Finance Corporation (RFC) with $500 million in capital and the authority to borrow an additional $2 billion. He hoped to stimulate employment through RFC loans to banks, building and loan associations, insurance companies, railroads, and other corporate giants, whose investment would create jobs and revive the economy. Critics railed against Hoover's trickle-down economics, especially when the RFC lent $90 million to the gigantic Central Republic Bank of Chicago but refused to lend the City of Chicago $70 million to pay its municipal employees and teachers. On July 21, 1932, Hoover signed an amendment to the RFC bill, the Emergency Relief and Construction Act, that provided $1.5 billion for public construction of income-producing projects, $300 million in loans to states for direct relief, and $200 million for the liquidation of ruined banks. From July 1932 to April 1933, Illinois received more funds ($48 million) than any other state under the auspices of the Emergency Relief and Construction Act. Economic conditions continued to deteriorate in Illinois, however, just as they did nationwide. Hoover's belated attempts to engage the federal government in the fight against the Great Depression proved too little, too late.[7]

In the 1932 presidential election, the nation's voters repudiated Hoover and instead chose Democratic candidate Franklin D. Roosevelt with his vague promise of a "new deal" for the American people. Roosevelt defeated Hoover in Illinois by 450,000 votes as the Democrats gained political control of the state. Henry Horner of Chicago trounced Len Small by 566,000 votes and became the state's first Jewish governor. The Democrats outnumbered the Republicans in both chambers of the general assembly, thirty-three to eighteen in the senate and eighty to seventy-three in the house, and in the delegation to the U.S. Congress by nineteen to eight. Hoover's failure to combat the economic depression effectively discredited the Republican party and made possible the Democratic landslide in 1932. Whereas Hoover and Emmerson had preached forbearance and acted cautiously to limit government involvement in the economy, Illinois voters cheered when Roosevelt proclaimed, "I assert that modern society, acting through its Government, owes the definite obligation to prevent the starvation or the dire want of any of its fellow men and women who try to maintain themselves but cannot."[8]

By the time that Roosevelt took office in March 1933, a financial crisis loomed in Illinois. As panic set in, desperate depositors withdrew all their money from banks and precipitated a series of bankruptcies. All of Rock Island's banks closed, for example, leaving the people with no access to their savings. Bank moratoriums in other states further eroded confidence in the financial system, and deposits in Chicago banks plunged $350 million in just two weeks. On the day of Roosevelt's inauguration, Governor Horner closed all of the banks in Illinois; the president shut all of the nation's banks two days later. The venerable Chicago Board of Trade ceased operations for the first time in its history. Federal legislation legalized the national banking holiday and empowered the secretary of the treasury to reopen financially sound institutions. Under guidelines established by the Emergency Banking Act, most of Illinois's seven hundred banks reopened within three months. Depositors regained confidence in the state's financial institutions, and the banking crisis subsided.

Roosevelt's unfolding blueprint for economic recovery entailed the federal government's simultaneous initiatives to revive both industry and agriculture. To rationalize supply and demand in the industrial sector, the New Deal initiated an unprecedented experiment in business-government cooperation. The National Industrial Recovery Act (NIRA) suspended antitrust laws and provided for the drafting of industrial codes regulating production, prices, and labor conditions. To administer the complex machinery created by the law, Roosevelt selected two Illinoisans—Hugh S. Johnson, retired military officer and former general counsel of the Moline Plow Company, as head of the National Recovery Administration (NRA);

and Chicago progressive Harold L. Ickes as chief of the Public Works Administration (PWA). Ickes also served as secretary of the interior. Despite charges by the Illinois Manufacturers Association and the Illinois Chamber of Commerce that the increased government presence in the conduct of business amounted to socialism, the general assembly passed legislation complying with NRA directives. Blue eagle emblems signifying participation in the NRA appeared in store windows across the state, but there was scant evidence of economic recovery. When the U.S. Supreme Court ruled the NIRA unconstitutional in 1935, most observers already considered the experiment a failure.

Roosevelt's agriculture policies produced much better results. The Agricultural Adjustment Act (AAA), the centerpiece of New Deal efforts to aid farmers, established voluntary production controls designed to reduce supply and thereby raise prices. Participating farmers received benefit payments financed by a tax on food processors. The combination of federal policy and severe drought created scarcity and drove prices up nearly to pre–World War I levels, so that when the U.S. Supreme Court found the AAA unconstitutional in 1936, Congress quickly passed similar legislation drafted to pass judicial muster. The Agricultural Adjustment Administration (AAA), which worked closely with the Farm Bureau Federation and benefited large landowners much more than small landowners and tenants, provided government assistance that allowed many farmers to survive the Great Depression decade. Some McDonough County farmers objected to the loss of freedom engendered by government marketing quotas, and they founded the Corn Belt Liberty League in 1938 to protest against the second AAA. This league attracted several thousand members in Illinois, Indiana, Iowa, and Nebraska, but most farmers rejected its message in favor of desperately needed government aid. By institutionalizing a system of federal government subsidies to agriculture and by encouraging investment in tractors and other forms of technology, the New Deal eased the transition from subsistence farming to agribusiness. In addition, the Rural Electrification Administration revolutionized farm life. The number of Illinois farms with electricity increased from 16 percent to 43 percent during the 1930s and continued to grow in subsequent decades.

More immediately, the Roosevelt administration struggled with the crippling unemployment that continued to plague the nation. The IERC, rechristened the Illinois Emergency Relief Administration (IERA), acted as the state's administrative arm of the Federal Emergency Relief Administration (FERA). Immediately following its creation by Congress in May 1933, the FERA began dispensing relief to the unemployed as well as work relief for the employable. Most FERA jobs involved unskilled construction and maintenance work, but some employables obtained white-collar work. During the bitter winter of 1933–1934, the Civil Works Administration (CWA) provided much-needed jobs in the state improving public buildings and streets and constructing airports, stadiums, and parks. Although the FERA and the CWA provided some form of relief every month for more than a million persons between March 1933 and July 1934, these federal agencies turned away more than six hundred thousand persons because of inadequate resources. Nevertheless, the infusion of federal dollars was a godsend to a state that was wholly unable to care for its indigent population.

Other New Deal relief programs helped as well. The Civilian Conservation Corps (CCC) in the state employed a hundred thousand unmarried males between the ages of eighteen and twenty-five during the 1930s. The CCC transported the young men from Illinois communities to rural camps in other states, where they planted trees, drained swamps, built dams and reservoirs, and refurbished parks and beaches for six-month stints, and then sent twenty-two dollars of their thirty-dollars monthly wage home to their families. The National Youth Administration (NYA) offered two services for young people: providing grants for college and high school students whose lack of money jeopardized their chances of remaining in school, and helping others who could not find jobs through vocational training and temporary financial assistance. As late as 1941, after the worst of the Great Depression was over, the NYA still enrolled more than fifty thousand youths in Illinois. The PWA failed to put significant numbers of people to work until late 1934 but eventually employed thousands of Illinoisans in large-scale construction projects. In Chicago, for example, PWA labor built the State Street subway, three public housing projects, and thirty new public schools.

The establishment of the Works Progress Administration (WPA) and the passage of the Social Security Act in 1935 refashioned the New Deal approach to relief. The WPA paid a security wage that was in excess of the relief stipend but less than prevailing wage rates and, like the FERA, mandated a means test for job applicants. For some of the millions of unemployable men and women, the federal government provided additional aid with Social Security. The New Deal's largest and most generously funded relief program, the WPA employed more than one million men and women altogether, and as many as two hundred thousand at any given time in Illinois. Designed to pay people for doing some kind of work and avoid if at all possible simply providing the unemployed with a dole, the WPA also contributed to the improvement of the state's infrastructure. Unlike the PWA, which allocated its funds on massive construction projects, the WPA typically employed more people and spent fewer funds on building materials. Although the agency occasionally tackled large-scale construction and landscaping projects (the completion of Chicago's Lake Shore Drive, for example), most of the WPA's work resulted in the provision or refurbishment of sidewalks, sewers, roads, bridges, viaducts, culverts, and other bricks-and-mortar projects. Along with the CCC and the

National Guard, WPA workers helped provide relief to the seventy-four thousand people in eight southern Illinois counties who were left homeless when the Ohio River flooded in January–February 1937.

Roughly half of the Illinois population received government relief at one time or another during the Great Depression, and the people understandably raised questions about the fairness and efficiency of social welfare dispensation. The allocation of billions of dollars to local sponsors required diligent supervision to guard against fraud and misuse of public funds. Harry Hopkins, President Roosevelt's chief relief administrator, established an unassailable record regarding such matters with the FERA and the CWA; but with the huge sums of WPA money available, the task became more difficult in 1935. As anti–New Dealers quickly pointed out, the ability to award relief to millions of Americans created the potential for the WPA to become a political machine for the Democratic party—a very real possibility, Republicans charged, when Hopkins was quoted as saying, "spend and spend, tax and tax, elect and elect." Hopkins worried especially about charges of electioneering by WPA officials and meted out harsh penalties to any agency employees who were guilty of electoral irregularities. Rumors of a politicized WPA persisted, however, and irate Republicans singled out Illinois as one of the worst offenders.[9]

The furor in Illinois revolved around a complex set of political, sectional, and personal issues. The contest for precious relief funds involved Republican suspicions of Democratic depredations, tensions between the Chicago masses and the downstate population, and the rivalry between two aggressive politicians, Governor Henry Horner and Chicago Mayor Edward J. Kelly, for New Deal largesse. The struggle between Horner and Kelly for the beneficence bestowed by WPA's Harry Hopkins affected social welfare provision in Illinois and altered the political landscape at both state and national levels.

The history of Chicago's vaunted Democratic machine began with Anton Cermak, the Czech immigrant from Braidwood who defeated Big Bill Thompson in the 1931 mayoral election. Cermak parlayed his leadership of the United Societies for Local Government, an anti-Prohibition pressure group popular with many of Chicago's ethnic groups, into political success as a ward committeeman and state representative. He united the city's German, Irish, Polish, Jewish, and Czech voters into an unbeatable coalition that dominated Cook County politics for the following half century. The mayor strongly opposed Roosevelt's nomination at the 1932 Democratic national convention but did not live long enough afterward to make amends. Fatally shot on February 13, 1933, by a crazed gunman who was probably firing at the president-elect, Cermak died nineteen days later. In the chaotic days following the martyred mayor's funeral, several Democratic factions vied for control of city hall. At the urging of party chairman Patrick A. Nash, the city council selected chief engineer of the Chicago Sanitary District Edward J. Kelly as the new mayor. The Kelly-Nash machine thereafter became one of the most notorious political machines in the nation.

Coming into office at the nadir of the Great Depression, Kelly quickly established himself as a forceful and—at least at first—popular mayor. He acted decisively, made necessary budget cuts in local government offices, successfully lobbied the Illinois General Assembly for special authority to collect unpaid taxes, secured precious federal dollars from nascent New Deal agencies, and expunged red ink from municipal ledgers. He presided over the immensely popular Century of Progress Exposition, a world's fair that in many ways paled in comparison to the Columbian Exposition but nevertheless provided necessary escapism to a beleaguered public desperate for distractions from depression conditions. Most important, Kelly set out to mend political fences with the Democratic administration in Washington, D.C., that Cermak had broken. "Roosevelt is my Religion!" Kelly proclaimed proudly as he became one of the president's foremost champions in state and national forums. While reformers inside and outside of the Democratic party railed at the close bond between the White House and Chicago's city hall, the generous and uninterrupted flow of New Deal funds to Cook County underscored the success of Kelly's efforts at reconciliation.[10]

Friendly to the Chicago machine from the outset, Harry Hopkins established a direct pipeline of WPA funds to Chicago, bypassing the rest of Illinois. After his landslide reelection in 1935 established Kelly as the most powerful politician in the state, a position threatened but never destroyed by electoral outcomes in subsequent years, Hopkins turned his back on the mayor's rivals in the Democratic party. Governor Horner complained that Hopkins ignored him, even refusing to return his telephone calls; Harold L. Ickes lamented Hopkins's blind worship of Kelly to President Roosevelt, but to no avail. Hopkins went out of his way to support the Kelly administration, funneling extra money to the Chicago office. In December 1936, for example, he phoned Illinois's WPA director to tell him, "The Treasury has found a little more money, and I don't want to put you and Ed [Kelly] in a hot spot. If there is any money here and it will do some good, I want you to have it." Meanwhile, Hopkins threatened on several occasions to curtail relief appropriations to Illinois unless the state agreed to increase its own contributions. Governor Horner felt that Kelly and Hopkins conspired against him, just as many downstate Illinoisans looked askance at the comparatively generous sums of relief dollars being funneled to Cook County.[11]

Kelly and Horner, once friends and neighbors in the Chicago neighborhood of Hyde Park, drifted apart in the 1930s. Bridling at the increasingly popular notion of the mayor's primacy in the state Democratic party, Horner insisted upon asserting his independence from the Chicago leadership. In 1935 Kelly pushed through the general assembly a bill allowing Chicago to license off-track betting on horse races, a measure that would provide funds desperately needed to pay teacher salaries. Horner vetoed the bill without warning, decrying the immorality of legalized gambling. Incensed at what he termed the governor's breach of loyalty to the party, Kelly marshaled the forces of the Chicago machine to deny Horner reelection in 1936. The Cook County Democrats chose Dr. Herman Bundesen, the obscure president of the Chicago Board of Health, to oppose Horner in the Democratic primary. Kelly and Bundesen criticized the governor for imposing an unpopular sales tax on the people of Illinois—despite the fact that Kelly had avidly supported the levy as a necessary fiscal measure. Horner campaigned against bossism, criticized inadequate voter registration statutes in Cook County that allowed electoral irregularities, and cast himself as the defender of downstate interests against the ravenous designs of Cook County politicians. The Roosevelt administration maintained, throughout the primary, a "neutrality" that favored the Kelly-Nash forces, adding to Horner's image as a scrappy underdog fighting the good fight against powerful adversaries. In a remarkable upset, the governor carried every county in the state except Cook County to win the Democratic primary and defeated the Republican candidate in the general election.

Horner's reelection left a residue of bitterness in Illinois politics. The governor resumed his vendetta against the Chicago machine, publicly announcing his intention to oppose Kelly's reelection in 1939. In the meantime, he guided through a special session of the general assembly a tough voter registration law for Cook County and vetoed a bill enabling Chicago to pay relief costs with sales tax revenue. He clashed again with Harry Hopkins, interrupting the flow of relief from Democratic Washington, D.C., to a Democratic administration in Illinois. In November 1938, however, Horner suffered a coronary thrombosis that left him bedridden for the remainder of his days in office. Unwilling to resign and turn the state over to Lieutenant Governor John Stelle, a Kelly-Nash ally, he struggled to conduct state affairs from his bedroom in the executive mansion. Incapacitated and politically powerless, he watched helplessly as Kelly retained the mayoralty in 1939. Horner died on October 6, 1940, a month before Republican Dwight Green succeeded him in the governor's mansion. Only the third Democratic governor of Illinois since the Civil War, Horner struggled because of his feud with Kelly and failed to link Springfield with Chicago to the benefit of his party.

In Cook County, by contrast, Democrats built a political organization in the 1930s whose hegemony continued for generations. The Kelly-Nash organization preserved the ethnic coalition forged by Anton Cermak and increased its political potency through a series of astute refinements. Mayor Kelly won the backing of the city's primarily Republican business community through the efficient delivery of municipal services, a vigorous downtown building program subsidized by emergency federal funds, and a hard-eyed willingness to slash expenditures for the sake of budget balancing. Most important, the additional revenue and votes supplied by the New Deal, organized crime, and African Americans enabled the Chicago Democrats to survive the Great Depression when the nation's other great political machines expired.

The New Deal contributed to the growth and sustenance of the Chicago Democratic machine in the 1930s through both financial resources and electoral support from thousands of beholden relief recipients. In fact, the primary contribution of federal largesse lay in the financial bellwether it provided the Kelly mayoralty during the debilitating depression years. Armed with federal money, the city avoided paying great sums for the support of the indigent and unemployed. Blessed with working capital, Kelly did not have to cut patronage and city services. At a time when the greatest threat to the Democratic machine came from financial disaster rather than an able opposition party, the New Deal funds assured Chicago's solvency.

During the threadbare depression years Kelly turned to organized crime as a second source of revenue. The mayor deplored the publicity attending gangland killings, and to a great degree his administration curtailed the rampant lawlessness of the Roaring Twenties, but gambling revenue was so important to the ward organizations that city hall made no genuine effort to enforce antivice statutes. In 1934 the *Chicago Daily News* reported that the machine raked in a hundred million dollars per month from illicit vice operations. The involvement of the Democratic machine with the legatees of the Capone mob was solidly entrenched at virtually every level of government. Many machine precinct captains operated gambling houses, and frequently their partners occupied prominent positions in the syndicate hierarchy. The police, controlled by Democratic ward committeemen, along with the judiciary shared culpability with the politicians. Sensitive to the personal liberties expected by his constituents and appreciative of an additional source of revenue, Kelly repeatedly defended gambling and other forms of vice.

While Chicago's poor African American community offered modest economic resources, Kelly saw a bounty of votes in the historically Republican Black Belt. The mayor set out to capture the African American vote and did so by appointing blacks to an unprecedented number of municipal posts, by selecting them as candidates for elective offices, and by distributing government funds—first municipal and later, in much larger quantities, federal—to the depression-stricken South Side. The mayor intervened on several occasions to defend the principles of desegregated housing and education. As a result of these concerted efforts, blacks supported Democratic candidates in all elections, consistently giving Kelly a greater percentage of the vote than he received in the city at large. Kelly's capture of the African American vote proved a monumental contribution to the Democratic machine in Chicago,

especially in the wake of significant demographic changes after World War
II. With the black population of Chicago increasing and whites fleeing to
the suburbs, the black vote became a precious commodity to white politicians seeking to maintain political control of the city.

The Democratic machine in Chicago also benefited from the support of
organized labor, despite the potentially disastrous Memorial Day massacre
of 1937. In this incident, Chicago police fired pistols into a crowd of fleeing picketers outside a steel plant, killing ten and wounding thirty more.
Kelly staunchly defended the actions of the police, but a well-publicized
investigation by a U.S. Senate committee chaired by Robert LaFollette Jr.
condemned the police action and the city's blatantly partial inquiry. The
mayor so feared retaliation at the polls by working-class voters that he
met with officials from the Congress of Industrial Organizations (CIO) to
discuss ways of improving relations. Kelly offered them future exemption
from police interference in return for official forgiveness of his role in the
Memorial Day whitewash. The CIO worked for the machine in subsequent elections, and, amazingly, a steelworker whose eye had been shot
out in the 1937 skirmish prominently endorsed Kelly in the 1939 mayoral
campaign. Thereafter, Chicago police assumed a more restrained stance
during labor-management confrontations, and the city's union leadership
became part of the Democratic machine.

Labor strife occurred as well in the southern Illinois coal mines, where
the United Mine Workers of America (UMW) and the Progressive Mine
Workers of America (PMA) struggled for the opportunity to represent embattled workers against the mine owners. The PMA, which probably enjoyed a larger membership in the early 1930s, accused the UMW and its
charismatic leader John L. Lewis of being too cozy with the mine owners
and of not representing miners' interests avidly enough. The UMW responded with charges that Communists dominated the PMA's leadership
ranks. In the two unions' bitter competition for worker allegiances, violence and vandalism became commonplace. State officials reported 313
crimes against persons and property in the Illinois coalfields from 1932 to
1934. Partisans of the two unions bombed the coal-carrying Chicago and
Illinois Midland Railroad sixteen times; they also dynamited mine shafts,
union halls, houses, cars, and relief stations and fatally shot strikers,
strikebreakers, and policemen. Governor Horner tried unsuccessfully to
mediate the dispute and had to send National Guard troops into several
counties to quell the violence. In 1937 the federal government indicted
PMA leaders for conspiracy and interference with interstate commerce,
and a grand jury found thirty-six of them guilty. With much of its leadership in prison, the PMA continued to exist but took a backseat to Lewis
and the UMW in Illinois. In subsequent years, Lewis negotiated a series of
contracts designed to extract the best pay raises and safety conditions possible for a dwindling number of workers in a declining industry.

Labor violence permeated Northern industrial states such as Michigan and Pennsylvania during the Great Depression, but with the exceptions of the coal wars of the early 1930s and the Memorial Day massacre in 1937, organizing efforts in Illinois proceeded peacefully. New Deal measures such as Section 7a of the NIRA, the National Labor Relations Act, and the Fair Labor Standards Act guaranteed the right of workers to organize and bargain collectively. Union organizers—with some license—told workers that President Roosevelt wanted them to join a union, and they did so in unprecedented numbers. The craft unions of the American Federation of Labor (AFL) and the industrial unions of the CIO conducted massive organizing drives that recruited impressive numbers of workers, particularly in the building trades, stockyards, and transportation industries. Blue-collar workers joined unions more rapidly than did their white-collar counterparts. By the end of the 1930s, the AFL and the CIO had succeeded in recruiting more than 25 percent of the state's industrial workers. The remarkable rise of the unions in the New Deal era led to a marriage between organized labor and the Democratic party and underscored the rising influence of the federal government in American life.

As throughout the rest of the nation, by the end of the decade the New Deal had failed to eradicate the Great Depression in Illinois. Unemployment remained nearly 15 percent in the late 1930s, relief rolls remained uncomfortably high, salaries and wages failed to rebound to pre-1929 levels, and there was little evidence of business expansion. Owing to the severity of the depression and the paucity of funds in state and national coffers, somewhere between one-third and one-half of the people in the state who were eligible for relief were instead left to their own devices. Still, the New Deal's impact on Illinois was considerable. If Roosevelt's programs failed to restore full prosperity, they stopped the downward spiral that threatened to destroy American capitalism. Newly created agencies saved the banks, the railroads, and the securities industry while shoring up other vulnerable areas of the economy. At the same time, federal dollars provided a modicum of relief to a ravaged population. Finally, the New Deal invested the federal government with unprecedented authority and changed the way citizens in Illinois viewed institutions and leaders in the nation's capital. For better or worse, the relationship between Springfield and Washington, D.C., would never be the same.

Decatur

In the early nineteenth century, as growing numbers of farmers moved into central Illinois, very few communities existed there to provide services and marketing facilities. Most villages served populations clustered along the rivers of southwestern and southeastern Illinois rather than the sparsely populated rural areas of the state's interior. To accommodate the increasing rural population, in 1829 the state created Macon County out of Shelby County. In the absence of a settlement of any size to become the county seat, a few settlers platted a village at the bend of the Sangamon River. They named the modest community of four square blocks after Commodore Stephen Decatur, the U.S. naval hero of the Battle of Tripoli. On July 10, 1829, investors bought only two lots at a public sale of land; no city government developed until 1836 when the population reached three hundred. Despite its location in the heart of a fertile agricultural region, Decatur experienced very little success in its early years because of its distance from the well-traveled transportation routes crossing central Illinois.

The coming of the railroads in 1854 finally accelerated growth and established Decatur as a processing point for agricultural products, a transportation link to larger markets, and a distribution center of retail goods to the surrounding hinterlands. The town also housed the maintenance shops of the Wabash Railroad, several farm implement factories, and a metal-working industry supplying parts for the railroads and plumbing equipment for homes built in the area. (In the twentieth century, the manufacture of auto parts replaced the declining railroad parts industry.) The city's population approached four thousand by 1860 and exceeded seven thousand by 1870. Suitably impressed, the Illinois Republican party held its state convention there in 1860. The convention endorsed Abraham Lincoln, who had tried cases in Decatur courtrooms when he traversed the eighth circuit court from 1838 to 1857, for president.

Between 1900 and 1930, Decatur's population nearly tripled as it became a national center for processing the raw materials of central Illinois for export. In the years between the world wars, as the wheat market contracted, soybeans emerged as the second leading crop (behind corn) produced by Illinois farmers. Agronomists and chemists at the state's agricultural experiment stations created new strains of soybeans that thrived in the soil and climate of central Illinois. Research scientists developed a host of food products made from the soybean, which was found to be high in protein, and discovered as well a number of industrial uses for the processed seeds. In 1922 the A. E. Staley Company opened the nation's first soybean-processing plant in Decatur, and in 1939 the Archer Daniels Midland Company established milling operations there. When World War II disrupted the importation of vegetable oils from Asian nations, Illinois farmers planted even more acres of soybeans, and Decatur became known as the soybean capital of the world. In the years after World War II, Decatur remained an important agribusiness center as a number of national corporations established subsidiary processing plants there. Population growth slowed in the last decades of the twentieth century, a condition attributed to the decline of the railroads and to the fact that Decatur failed to attract interstate highway connections. The completion of Interstate 72 creating links with Springfield to the west and Champaign-Urbana to the east and scientists' explorations into the potential use of farm products as renewable energy sources provided hope that Decatur could remain a vital agribusiness hub in the twenty-first century.

Red Grange

Born on June 13, 1903, in Forksville, Pennsylvania, Harold Edward "Red" Grange moved to Wheaton, Illinois, at the age of five with his father, brother, and sisters after his mother's death. A star athlete at Wheaton High School, he earned sixteen letters in four years (four each in football, baseball, basketball, and track and field). He became especially renowned for his performance in football, scoring seventy-five touchdowns and kicking eighty-two conversions during his high school career. He delivered ice during the summers to help support his family and later became known as the Wheaton Iceman.

In 1922 Grange enrolled at the University of Illinois and starred on a talented freshman football team that regularly defeated the varsity in scrimmage games. In 1923 he led the Fighting Illini to an undefeated season and Big Ten Conference co-championship, earning his first of three consecutive All America honors. Modest and self-effacing, he minimized his own accomplishments and praised the efforts of his teammates. The following year, Grange became a national hero to rival Babe Ruth, Jack Dempsey, and other athletic demigods of the Roaring Twenties when he played one of the most sensational games in college football history. Against a powerful University of Michigan team at the dedication of Illinois Memorial Stadium, he ran for touchdowns of 95, 67, 56, and 45 yards in the first quarter. He ran 12 yards for a touchdown in the third quarter and threw a touchdown pass in the fourth. In leading the Illini to a 39–14 rout of the favored Wolverines in front of sixty-seven thousand spectators, he accounted for 480 yards running and passing in forty-one minutes of play. He amazed the sporting world with another spectacular performance three weeks later, scoring three touchdowns and accumulating 450 total yards in a 21–21 tie with the University of Chicago. A Chicago sportswriter nicknamed him the "Galloping Ghost," and nationally syndicated columnist Grantland Rice wrote a popular poem to commemorate his achievements.

Immediately after completing his senior season, Grange withdrew from the university and signed a lucrative contract to play professional football with the Chicago Bears. At a time when most players in the struggling and slightly disreputable National Football League earned around one hundred dollars a game, Grange received a guarantee of two thousand dollars a game

Red Grange, known as the Galloping Ghost, became one of the most famous athletes of his time while playing football for the University of Illinois and the Chicago Bears. *Chicago Historical Society*

plus a percentage of gate receipts. Having recently been moved to Chicago from Decatur by owner George Halas, the Bears averaged only about five hundred spectators a game before Grange's arrival. His first game was against the Bears' crosstown rivals, the Chicago Cardinals, and attracted a crowd of thirty-six thousand. At the conclusion of the regular season, the Bears played seventeen games in six weeks on a phenomenally successful national tour. That year, Grange earned the unheard of sum of $250,000 from salary, gate receipts, endorsements, and cameo appearances in movies. In the late 1920s, he acted in several motion pictures and toured in popular vaudeville productions. Grange's celebrity lent the fledgling business of professional football a financial boost and an air of respectability.

Following his retirement, Grange served as an assistant coach for the Bears for several years before becoming an insurance broker. The first prominent athlete to become a sportscaster, he broadcast Chicago Bear games on radio and television for more than twenty years. Selected to the College Football Hall of Fame in 1951 and the Professional Football Hall of Fame in 1963, Grange also received the Walter Camp Distinguished American Award in 1981. He died on January 28, 1991.

CHAPTER TWELVE

World War II

The rise of the Axis powers—Nazi Germany and Fascist Italy in Europe and Japan in Asia—made conflict likely by the late 1930s and left Illinoisans ambivalent about American involvement in another global war. Virtually everyone deplored Adolf Hitler's brutal attacks against democratic institutions in the West and condemned Japan's imperialist designs on China and Southeast Asia. Public opinion overwhelmingly favored America's World War I allies, Britain and France, but polls also clearly showed the people's desire to avoid participation in war if at all possible. Remembering the carnage in the last war, isolationists across the political spectrum adduced a number of arguments for noninvolvement. Conservatives feared that war would strengthen the hand of a federal government that had already grown dangerously powerful during the Roosevelt administration. Conversely, liberals worried that giant corporations would reassert their dominance and dismantle New Deal reforms. Apprehensive that wartime passions would unleash another wave of nativism, German Americans dreaded a replay of 1917–1918. Irish Americans still nurtured their nationalistic aspirations and saw no reason that the United States should delay the dissolution of the British Empire. African Americans found the threat from domestic racism much greater than the threat from Hitler's declarations of Aryan superiority. A number of different groups opposed American involvement for a variety of reasons, making isolationism a powerful force in Illinois in the interwar years.

Opposition to U.S. involvement in the war flourished in the Midwest, and Chicago became the unofficial capital of isolationist forces. The Windy City's Robert E. Wood served as the national chairman of the America First Committee, and University of Chicago president Robert M. Hutchins became academe's leading antiwar spokesman. Elizabeth Dilling's organization, We, the Mothers, Incorporated, staged a march on Washington to protest passage of the lend-lease bill. Most of all, the

Chicago Tribune persistently and passionately inveighed against any whiff of internationalism. With the words "World's Greatest Newspaper" stenciled on its masthead, the staunchly Republican *Tribune* boasted the largest circulation in the Midwestern states. Robert R. McCormick, the newspaper's editor and publisher, devised an unwavering editorial policy that opposed the Lend-Lease Act, the peacetime draft, and all other preparedness measures that he claimed would nudge the nation closer to war. Touting Illinois and the Midwest as the bedrock of isolationism, McCormick warned that a war against Fascism would be the first shot in a successful Communist takeover of the United States.

President Roosevelt worried incessantly about the *Chicago Tribune's* influence in the nation's heartland. The *Chicago Daily News,* published by Frank Knox, a moderate Republican who later served as Roosevelt's secretary of the navy, provided an internationalist perspective, but its modest circulation offered scant competition to the McCormick paper. Angered at the shrill isolationism of the *Tribune,* interventionists exulted when a new morning newspaper with a liberal bent, the *Chicago Sun,* began publication on December 4, 1941. Having recently received a multimillion-dollar inheritance from his grandfather, Marshall Field III founded the *Sun* as a liberal Democratic alternative to Chicago's Republican newspapers. Before Field's paper could mount a sustained critique of the *Tribune's* isolationism, however, the Japanese attacked Pearl Harbor on December 7, 1941, and Congress responded with a declaration of war. The bitter foreign policy debate abruptly ceased as the most vehement isolationists, including McCormick and the *Chicago Tribune,* pledged their full support to the war against the Axis powers.

The conditions determining U.S. entry into World War II, so very different from the circumstances leading to hostilities against the Central Powers a generation earlier, instantly created a unity of national purpose. The perfidy of the Japanese attack on Pearl Harbor sparked a surge of nationalism and healed rifts between internationalists and isolationists. In contrast to other American wars, during World War II very little antiwar sentiment surfaced and few dissenters went to prison for unpatriotic speech. Hatred of Germany as America's principal enemy focused more on Hitler and the evils of Nazi doctrine than on the German people. The German American Bund, which had failed to attract a large membership in Illinois in the 1930s, lost all legitimacy during the war. The German language had already disappeared from most churches and schools, and expressions of loyalty to the Nazi regime became highly unpopular. More than twenty years after the end of World War I, German Americans had been fully acculturated in American society.

The Japanese in Illinois escaped the xenophobic frenzy of the World War I era, initially because so few of them lived there at the outset of the war. When the federal government removed Japanese Americans from the West Coast in 1942 and resettled nearly thirty thousand of them in Chicago, local authorities reported few unpleasant incidents. A number of businesses such as the Stevens Hotel, McGraw-Hill Publishing Company, and the Curtiss Candy Company quickly hired the Japanese newcomers. Unlike the Hearst newspapers in California, which shamelessly portrayed the Japanese as a fifth-column threat to West Coast security, almost all of the Chicago dailies urged forbearance and tolerance. Even the skeptical *Chicago Tribune* conceded in a 1945 headline: "Jap-Americans Sent to Chicago Making Good: Ten Thousand Prove They Are Good Citizens." At the end of the war, approximately fifteen thousand Japanese Americans remained in Chicago while roughly an equal number returned to the West Coast.[1]

Preparations for war, which accelerated after Pearl Harbor, had actually begun in Illinois after the fall of France in the spring of 1940. After their induction, members of the National Guard reported for training at Camp Forrest in Tennessee. Between the passage of the Selective Service Act in September 1940 and U.S. entry into the war in December 1941, sixty-three thousand men in Illinois joined the U.S. Army, Navy, Marine Corps, and Coast Guard. The old arsenal at Rock Island modernized its operations, new federal ordnance factories commenced operations at Elwood, Kankakee, and Savanna, and a shell-loading plant opened at Crab Orchard Lake, west of Marion. Private industry likewise began converting to the production of arms and other lend-lease goods for use by Britain. Governor Dwight H. Green and Chicago Mayor Edward J. Kelly traveled separately to Washington, D.C., to lobby for defense contracts on behalf of Illinois industries. By the end of 1940, manufacturers in Chicago, Rockford, Peoria, Springfield, East St. Louis, and other cities had received lucrative federal contracts. Indeed, months before U.S. entry into the war, the lingering economic depression in Illinois had begun to recede because of the increased spending on military goods.

After Pearl Harbor, the conversion of Illinois industry to military production proceeded at a furious pace. Appointed chairman of the War Production Board (WPB) by President Roosevelt, Donald M. Nelson of Sears, Roebuck and Company set ambitious production goals for his home state of Illinois. The federal government erected massive factories and retooled existing facilities for the mass production of planes, tanks, ships, and artillery. The one-square-mile, hundred-million-dollar Dodge factory in Chicago, reputedly the largest in the world, employed thirty thousand men and women in the manufacture of B-29 Superfortress bomber engines. Sprawling airplane factories in suburban Melrose Park and Park Ridge covered nearly as many acres. The Elgin Watch Company produced time fuses for antiaircraft shells, the Pullman Company built tanks and aircraft parts, International Harvester assembled gun carriages, and the Western Electric Company in Cicero developed and refined radar. Factories in the tiny town of Seneca, which became known as the Prairie Shipyard, manufactured landing craft and then floated the finished products down the Illinois and Mississippi rivers to the Gulf of Mexico. Because of the extraordinary productivity at ordnance plants in Rock Island, Illiopolis, Green River, East Alton, Elwood, and Kankakee, Illinois led all states in the production of ammunition.

To sustain such industrial productivity in the face of a manpower shortage, the state's industries relied as never before upon women workers. The number of women in the state's workforce rose from 854,276 in 1940 to 1,281,000 in 1944, nearly a 50 percent increase. During those years, the number of women engaged in manufacturing increased by 117 percent. By necessity, many toiled in the previously male preserve of heavy industry. Women typed memoranda and took temperatures, but they also operated drill presses, wielded jackhammers, and welded airplane parts. They worked in Chicago steel mills, Danville foundries, Wood River oil refineries, Seneca shipyards, the Rock Island arsenal, and fluorite mines outside Rosiclare. In communities across the state, gender barriers crumbled as women drove taxicabs and streetcars, collected garbage, read gas meters door-to-door, and played baseball professionally. (The All-American Girls Baseball League, launched by Chicago Cubs owner Philip K. Wrigley in 1943, fielded teams in Chicago, Peoria, Rockford, and Springfield, as well as other Midwestern communities.) Married women found that their dual roles as housekeeper and breadwinner could be stressful, especially without adequate day care for their children, but they enjoyed doing their patriotic duty and making extra money. Married and unmarried women alike reveled in the new freedom and economic independence they enjoyed during the war, and although some women eagerly returned to the home after V-J Day, many did so grudgingly. Women's expanded role in the 1940s laid the foundation for more sweeping changes in gender roles in later years.

Many revolutionary changes in the postwar world originated in weapons research being conducted covertly at the University of Chicago. The nation's atomic energy program, driven by the fear that German physicists' research was nearing completion, employed hundreds of scientists in a race to harness the power of the atom. In a secret laboratory hidden beneath the university's Stagg Field, physicists split the atom and produced the first self-sustaining chain reaction. Following this breakthrough, scientists successfully detonated an atomic bomb in New Mexico as a prelude to its use against Japan in August 1945. The government moved the reactor developed beneath Stagg Field to the Argonne National Laboratory twenty-five miles southwest of Chicago, where research into military and civilian uses of atomic energy continued after the war.

Preparation for war included the raising of armies as well as the production of weaponry, and Illinois responded promptly by establishing 361 local draft boards (180 in Cook County and 181 in the remaining counties) to supervise military recruitment. President Roosevelt appointed

Paul G. Armstrong, a Republican businessman from Chicago, World War I veteran, and former commander of the American Legion in Illinois, as the state director of selective service. During the course of the war, 958,000 men and 14,000 women over the age of eighteen from Illinois joined the armed forces, about two-thirds through the selective service system and one-third by enlistment. (Final casualty figures listed 22,192 Illinois soldiers and sailors dead and another 159 missing in action.) Until the last year of the war, when the military voiced urgent manpower needs, draft boards granted deferments to fathers, farmers, and men holding critical jobs in war industries.

During the course of the war, Illinois training fields hosted hundreds of thousands of men and women from all parts of the United States. Situated a thousand miles from the nearest ocean, the Great Lakes Naval Training Center became the largest naval training facility in the world. Although it had been closed between 1933 and 1935, Great Lakes trained more than a million sailors for duty during World War II (approximately one-third of the men in the U.S. Navy). In 1942 the segregated U.S. Navy opened Camp Robert Smalls, named for a former slave and Civil War naval hero, on part of the Great Lakes base for the training of African Americans. By the end of the war, between five thousand and six thousand blacks had graduated from one of the schools at Camp Smalls. Northwestern University's Abbott Hall operated a midshipmen's school, known as the "Annapolis of the West," that graduated several thousand men annually. Other naval personnel received training in the Chicago area at the Glenview Air Base, the University of Chicago, Navy Pier, and the Naval Armory.[2]

Other training fields throughout the state that had been lying dormant during the 1920s and 1930s suddenly sprang to life in 1941–1942. At Fort Sheridan men and women soldiers received training in artillery, motor transport repair, and baking; in 1944 it became a prisoner of war camp to incarcerate German soldiers. Camp Grant south of Rockford trained seven thousand paramedics at a time and became the second-largest medical replacement center in the country. Newly created Camp Ellis near Galesburg trained engineers and medical personnel while serving as the primary training field for the Illinois reserve militia. Chanute Field in Rantoul graduated as many as sixty-two thousand army air force technicians per year, and Scott Field near Belleville served as the army air force's primary communications school. The army converted the state fairgrounds in Springfield into an air force depot and provided advanced flying instruction at Camp George near Lawrenceville. Parks Air College, a commercial pilot school near East St. Louis, trained army fliers during the war.

The state's colleges and universities prepared their students for a variety of roles in the military. The University of Illinois, which General John J. Pershing called the "West Point of the West," conducted the nation's largest officer training program apart from the military academies. From

1942 to 1946, more than thirty thousand men participated in the Regional Officers Training Corps (ROTC) program on the Champaign-
Urbana campus. Northwestern University conducted a number of training
programs for the navy, and the Illinois Institute of Technology provided
instruction for both army and navy engineers. The University of Chicago
trained army and navy airmen at its Institute of Meteorology, one of only
five such schools in the country and the only one in the Midwest. Loyola
University formed a medical unit staffed by enlisted men and graduates
from its nursing school. The presence of so many servicemen on Illinois
college campuses compensated in part for the schools' depleted enrollments during the war.

In response to the urgent need for training facilities, the army leased
space in downtown Chicago skyscrapers and public buildings. The Army
Air Force Technical Training Command stationed fifteen thousand radio
operators and mechanics in the plush Stevens and Congress hotels. Converting luxury suites into barracks, army personnel did away with four-
poster beds and cancelled maid service. Crossing Michigan Avenue, these
trainees used Grant Park as a drill field. Instructors taught classes in the
Coliseum, medical corpsmen turned the Chicago Beach Hotel into an in-
firmary, and the United Service Organizations (USO) transformed the Auditorium Hotel into a servicemen's center. Relatively few servicemen enjoyed such pleasant surroundings, of course, for most inductees received
their training in more prosaic outposts far from Chicago's bright lights.

Activities at army training fields and naval stations inevitably disrupted
the lives of civilians in neighboring communities. Problems of law and order, compounded by jurisdictional clashes between military police and
county sheriffs, arose around military bases. Local authorities complained
about the frequency of drunken brawls involving servicemen, while army
officers decried the operation of brothels and the high incidence of vene-
real disease among the troops. Small towns like Rantoul, with a population of only sixteen hundred in 1940, proved unable to meet the demand
for housing created by the arrival of hundreds of noncommissioned officers and civilian workers to adjacent bases. Overcrowded schools, shortages of potable drinking water, and inadequate sewerage resulted from the
rapid influx of population. Rural and urban dwellers sometimes lost their
homes to make room for military field expansion or the construction of
munitions factories. Illinoisans accommodated themselves to these incon-
veniences, mindful of the commitment necessary for the war effort.

As in World War I, Illinois farmers faced the imposing task of increasing yields to supply the nation's armies and its allies. During the recent
depression when the laws of supply and demand had driven prices downward, government had imposed production limitations in response to declining export markets. With the removal of restrictions and the full application of fertilizers and other chemicals on all available land, farmers

produced bumper crops. Herbicides removed weeds without the costly and time-consuming use of machines, and insecticides eradicated deadly pests that threatened entire crops. Earlier development of hybrid seeds by Gene Funk of Bloomington, Lester Pfister of El Paso, and C. L. Gunn of DeKalb had produced record corn yields by the 1940s. According to data compiled by the U.S. Bureau of the Census in 1945, McLean County led all U.S. counties in corn production, Champaign County farmers led the field in soybeans, Henry County in hogs. Of the leading one hundred counties in total farm production that year, Illinois could claim thirteen— McLean, La Salle, Iroquois, Champaign, Livingston, Cook, DeKalb, Henry, Bureau, Kane, Vermilion, Ogle, and Sangamon. The state's farms exceeded the goals established by the War Food Administration, the federal agency established to preside over agricultural affairs.

Remembering the agricultural depression of the 1920s and 1930s that had followed the boom times of World War I, Illinois farmers worried that the higher prices and renewed prosperity they enjoyed during World War II would give way to mounting surpluses and dwindling profits with the end of hostilities. Wartime reduction in the number of landholdings caused some concern about the survival of the family farm. From 1940 to 1945 the number of farms in the state fell from 213,439 to 204,239 and the farm population from 978,907 to 759,429. Correspondingly, the average size of farms increased from 145 to 154 acres. With the World War I example in mind, however, this time the farmers behaved differently and generally improved their economic positions. Most farmers resisted the urge to buy huge tracts of land at inflated prices, instead using additional income to pay off existing mortgages. (From 1940 to 1945, farm mortgage indebtedness declined by more than 22 percent.) Most important, farmers' net income tripled. They complained about inflation, rationing, the scarcity of some consumer goods, and the shortage of agricultural labor that forced them to work longer hours, but farmers fared well during the war.

Their improved circumstances notwithstanding, some farmers resented the benefits won by urban laborers during the war. First and foremost, farmers recognized, sharply reduced unemployment rates in cities resulted simply from wartime labor shortages. The new workforce included women working outside the home for the first time, retired men returning to the job, teenagers given permission to leave school, and newcomers from other parts of the country. Thanks to the insatiable demand for war materiel, men and women readily found jobs with generous wages augmented by overtime pay. But higher wages for factory workers came, it seemed to rural folk and urban businessmen alike, also because labor unions took advantage of wartime exigencies on behalf of the rank and file. Despite a no-strike pledge taken by labor leaders in December 1941, unions conducted thousands of strikes in the United States during World War II—and work stoppages became commonplace in Illinois. From 1942 to 1945, more than fifteen hundred strikes broke out in the state. Labor relations in Illinois seemed even more volatile because of the number of cases of noncompliance referred to President Roosevelt by the War Labor Board (WLB) and the number of cases resulting in federal seizure of work sites. Of the forty instances nationwide in which deadlocked negotiations led to military seizure of property, six occurred in Illinois.

The state became known as the premier battleground of labor-management conflict during the war because of a number of highly publicized cases. In 1941 violent strikes at four International Harvester factories (three of them in Illinois) led President Roosevelt to create the National Defense Mediation Board to settle disputes in industries profiting from war contracts. The strikes involved more than fourteen thousand workers and resulted in a loss of 453,000 man-days of work. As a result of intercession by the mediation board, the Farm Equipment Workers' Union called off the strikes at the plants in East Moline, Rock Falls, and Chicago, but negotiations between management and labor continued for a year. International Harvester finally granted workers a healthy (by the standards of the time) pay raise (12.5 cents an hour), and the company enjoyed peace until another series of union demands led to a flurry of strikes in the last year of the war.

Strikes and violence broke out repeatedly in the historically tempestuous coal mines, where John L. Lewis of the United Mine Workers (UMW) repudiated his political alliance with President Roosevelt and denied the jurisdiction of the WLB. A major battle occurred in the spring and summer of 1943 when an estimated twenty-four thousand UMW members in seventy mines conducted work stoppages in the face of the president's threat to induct striking miners into the armed forces. On three occasions, the government seized the mines and operated them for weeks at a time. In June 1943, in response to Lewis's brazen defiance of the no-strike pledge, the U.S. Congress passed the Smith-Connally Anti-Strike Act over the president's veto to provide harsh penalties for union leaders encouraging activities harmful to the war's conduct. Relative peace descended upon the mines in 1944, but strikes resumed in the spring of 1945. The tense dispute took on an especially bitter edge because of the possibility that a strike-induced shortage of coal could interrupt war production or jeopardize public health. Because of adequate supplies of the commodity, that never happened.

Despite the decidedly lower stakes involved, the American public became equally enthralled with the clash between unionized workers and the mail order firm of Montgomery Ward and Company. The retailing giant's chairman of the board, Sewell Avery, argued that because of Montgomery Ward's noninvolvement with war work, the WLB could claim no jurisdiction in the company's dispute with the United Mail Order, Warehouse, and Retail Employees Union. The seventy-one-year-old Avery, a longtime opponent of the New Deal, ignored a WLB directive and staged a one-man sit-down strike when President Roosevelt announced that the government would seize and operate Montgomery Ward's Chicago plant. In a comical scene displayed in newspaper photographs the next day, two military policemen carried Avery out of the building. The union won a collective bargaining election, but the unrepentant Avery again refused to comply with government orders. When Montgomery Ward outlets in six other cities also clashed with the WLB, the army took possession of the stores in all seven cities. In the Chicago plant, soldiers ignored Avery and worked around him as he sat seething at his desk. No token occupation, government representatives operated the Montgomery Ward stores from December 28, 1944, to October 18, 1945.

Militant labor unions and a government determined to maintain wartime production levels meant higher wages and better benefits for workers. The war demanded sacrifices, however, and the nonmilitary population on the home front altered their lives substantially to aid the nation's cause. The Office of Price Administration (OPA), created by Congress in 1942, instituted rationing for a number of crucial commodities such as rubber, gasoline, coffee, and sugar. In 1943 the OPA issued stamps for the purchase of meat, butter, cheese, shoes, and various canned goods. Most citizens dutifully used their ration books and limited their purchases according to the rules, but a black market developed for those willing to pay extra for additional quantities of beef, sugar, or coffee. Automobile companies ceased production of new models and turned out tanks and airplanes; factories that had been making silk stockings now manufactured silk parachutes instead. Shortages of consumer goods, created when manufacturers retooled to produce war materiel, left workers with fat paychecks but unable to buy the items they could never have afforded during the Great Depression. As a consequence, despite their longings for new goods, workers often tightened their belts and padded their savings accounts. Patriotic Americans willingly deferred gratification until after the war as part of the shared sacrifice necessary for victory.

The state called for Illinois civilians to aid the war effort in a variety of ways, and millions of volunteers responded. In April 1941 the general assembly created the Illinois State Council of Defense, which in 1943 became the Illinois War Council, to organize the civilian population along the lines prescribed by the National Defense Advisory Commission in Washington, D.C. In total, 640 local councils organized themselves under the jurisdiction of the Illinois War Council and its executive director, Frank Parker. In August 1941 Fiorello La Guardia, director of the Office of Civilian Defense (OCD), designated the Chicago metropolitan area a defense unit separate from the rest of Illinois and named Mayor Kelly its chief administrator. The Chicago defense unit included most of Cook County, parts of Lake, DuPage, and Will counties, and Lake County, Indiana—an area of 1,171 square miles containing a population of more than 4.5 million people. Even though Chicago had been designated an independent OCD unit, the Illinois War Council maintained its headquarters in the Windy City; a subsidiary office opened later in Springfield, which dealt with some downstate defense matters.

Local councils opened civilian recruiting stations to enlist volunteer defense workers, ultimately enrolling more than half a million people outside of the Chicago metropolitan area. To train local directors, the Illinois War Council conducted a statewide defense school in Springfield on March 15, 1942. Under the supervision of the men and women taught in Springfield, members of local units engaged in a number of activities designed to protect their communities in the event of attack or sabotage—lookouts watched the skies for enemy bombers, air-raid wardens conducted drills, and auxiliary policemen, firemen, and medical personnel prepared for the delivery of emergency services. Though some mayors and other Illinois War Council officials scoffed at the likelihood of Axis air strikes in downstate Illinois and paid scant attention to local air-raid wardens, civil protection units devoted considerable time to honing skills in firefighting, bomb demolition, traffic control, first aid, and the use of gas masks. Although they never had to deal with air raids or invasions, civil defense personnel led relief efforts after a destructive tornado hit Marshall County in 1943 and the Illinois, Wabash, and Mississippi rivers flooded in 1944. Members of the American Legion and other World War I veterans became conspicuously involved in the formation of local defense units.

To augment food production, parent-teacher associations urged city residents to cultivate urban gardens, and the University of Illinois's College of Agriculture exhorted farmers to maintain their own "thrift gardens." In 1942 the Illinois War Council initiated a Victory Garden program to encourage people to grow their own vegetables in backyards, empty lots, and assorted receptacles on rooftops. The council's victory garden committee conducted workshops and published manuals to provide inexperienced gardeners with rudimentary information. The *Peoria Journal-Transcript* published a daily gardening column, and other newspapers offered series or individual articles on the subject. In 1943 Illinois officials counted 1,151,000 victory gardens, by far the highest total of any state in the nation. Agricultural experts estimated the total weight of produce from these gardens at a million tons (with a net value of $85 million). In 1944 the number of victory gardens increased to 1,275,000, with the value of produce exceeding $97 million. The gardens produced healthy surpluses, and more than two hundred communities (at least one in every county) established canning centers. In 1943 these community centers canned more than two hundred million quarts of food.[3]

An increased emphasis on conservation led to the systematic salvage of metals, rubber, paper, fats, and other everyday products that could be recycled and used as war materiels. Under the auspices of the OCD and the WPB, an extensive public relations campaign sought to educate citizens as to how the conservation of mundane objects of apparent insignificance could constitute a meaningful contribution to the war effort. Some delinquent farmers, plumbers, and junk dealers hoarded scrap metals, but compliance rates grew significantly with time. Elementary and high school students took the lead in salvage, bringing pots and pans, automobile bumpers, lamps, tools, and scrap metal to their schools. Women carried excess lard, bacon grease, and scraps of gristle and fat to their butchers, who in turn sent the refuse to military processing plants for use in making explosives. Such piecemeal scavenging added up to millions of tons of scrap metal, aluminum, paper, and other commodities by the end of the war.

Working in tandem with the U.S. Treasury, the Illinois War Council also provided yeoman service in the bond drives conducted during the war. In many cases, volunteers went door to door to secure pledges; in other cases, payroll savings plans created by Illinois businesses allowed workers to purchase bonds through regular payroll deductions. Such Hollywood celebrities as Judy Garland, Fred Astaire, Harpo Marx, James Cagney, and Claudette Colbert performed in bond rallies in Chicago and other cities. Most Illinoisans pledged modest sums, but Marshall Field III's

Illinoisans participated in scrap metal drives during World War II as part of massive conservation and salvage efforts on the home front. *Chicago Historical Society*

purchase of ten million dollars' worth of war bonds became widely regarded as the largest single bond sale in the nation. In each of the eight major bond drives conducted by the federal government, Illinois exceeded its quotas as established in Washington, D.C. In each of the last six campaigns, total bond sales in the state exceeded one billion dollars. During the war, only New York State surpassed Illinois and only New York City surpassed Chicago in total bond sales.

Owing to its large population and industrial prowess, Chicago became in the minds of national and state officials a prime target for Axis sorties or fifth column activities. Because Mayor Kelly repeatedly pointed out that northeastern Illinois was more accessible than the East Coast to enemy bombers from Europe via Greenland and Canada, the army declared the Chicago region a critical area and gave it a high priority rating for OCD protective equipment. "This is not 'playing soldier.' This is war!" the mayor proclaimed, and Chicago set the standard among large American cities for defense mobilization. The civilian defense office enrolled nine hundred thousand volunteers and organized the metropolitan area into divisions, communities, and blocks. Chicago included 7 divisions divided into 108 communities; the suburban region contained 8 divisions and 118 communities. The twenty thousand blocks in the entire Chicago area became the backbone of the decentralized system, and block captains (both men and women) emerged as the key administrators in the network. Chicagoans claimed that the democratically organized block arrangement was their city's signal contribution to civil defense.[4]

Under Kelly's aggressive leadership, Chicago led the nation's cities in the sale of war bonds, total number of military enlistments, and salvage collection. One-seventh of all plasma donated to the American Red Cross during the war came from Chicagoans. In fund-raising as well, the city stood second to none. In its 1942 Flag Day extravaganza, billed as the largest and longest parade ever held in the United States, 400,000 people marched 51 miles from Howard Street on the northern edge of Chicago to the Indiana state line, taking 17 hours in all. In conjunction with an all-day show held at Soldier Field, the parade raised $565,000. Chicago was the only city in the nation where servicemen and -women rode streetcars and buses free of charge. Finally, the lavish downtown Servicemen's Center became the outstanding feature of the city's hospitality to visiting soldiers.

Kelly opened the flagship Servicemen's Center in the heart of Chicago's Loop in August 1941. Open twenty-four hours a day and free of charge to all military personnel, "Mr. Kelly's Nightclub" occupied twelve floors of a building renovated by Works Progress Administration (WPA) labor and city workers. Kelly's wife supervised operations in the canteen, often putting in twelve-hour days, while her volunteer helpers ranged from society matrons to maids working their days off. Approximately thirty-five hundred women, many of them members of the USO, acted as hostesses. Quiet

floors near the top of the building contained rows of beds and a public library, while recreational facilities for dancing, bowling, and card playing
occupied the lower floors. An average of ten thousand soldiers per week
passed through the center on weeknights, as many as forty thousand during weekends. In 1942 Kelly opened a spacious outdoor facility on twelve
acres in Lincoln Park and a separate center for African American servicemen in the Black Belt. Even years after the war, soldiers from across the nation spoke glowingly of the hospitality they received in Chicago.

Other Illinois cities did their best to provide "northern hospitality" to
servicemen from around the country stationed at bases in the state. The
city of Rockford spent sixty-five thousand dollars to convert a deserted
high school building into a servicemen's center for use by soldiers at
nearby Camp Grant. Galesburg operated two servicemen's centers, one for
whites and one for blacks, which attracted huge crowds from Camp Ellis.
Springfield became the chief recreation center for men working at the Illiopolis ordnance plant as well as from Camp Ellis. Governor Green and
his wife hosted hundreds of servicemen at dinners and ice cream socials in
the governor's mansion. USO buses conveyed hostesses from Champaign-
Urbana, Pontiac, and other central Illinois communities to Chanute Air
Force Base in Rantoul for dances. Railroad centers such as Freeport and
Danville operated canteens in the terminals for the hundreds of thousands of soldiers and sailors in transit.

Along with the throngs of servicemen and -women stationed in or
passing through Illinois communities came thousands of African Americans from the South seeking jobs in defense industries, the vast majority
of them making their way to Chicago. Although the migration of Southern blacks to Northern cities during World War I has been termed the
Great Migration, the northward exodus of African Americans beginning
in World War II included many more people. In 1940 the U.S. Census Bureau reported that 277,731 of Illinois's 387,446 African Americans lived in
Chicago. The city's black population, second only to New York City, increased to an estimated 375,000 by 1945. During the same five years, the
number of blacks employed in Cook and DuPage counties increased from
80,350 to more than 220,000. As many as two thousand African Americans weekly immigrated from the South, arriving by train, automobile,
and bus. The strain on housing, education, and cultural institutions,
chronicled by sociologists Horace Cayton and St. Clair Drake in their classic study *Black Metropolis* (1945), raised serious concerns about the city's
ability to assimilate so many newcomers in such a short period of time.

From the outset of the war, blacks voiced concerns about discrimination
in defense production industries. How could the United States condone discriminatory hiring practices while fighting a war in defense of democracy
against Nazi doctrines of Aryan superiority? President Roosevelt's Executive
Order 8802, issued in June 1941 under the threat of a march on Washington

to protest such discrimination, created the Fair Employment Practices Committee (FEPC) to monitor employment in businesses receiving defense contracts. The FEPC established a regional office in Chicago and in January 1942 held hearings on racial and religious discrimination in Chicago area factories. The Illinois General Assembly passed a law against discrimination in all defense contracts based on race, color, or creed but failed to adopt a measure creating a state FEPC. African Americans found employment by the thousands in Chicago-area defense plants but usually in the least-skilled and lowest-paying jobs. Few blacks captured any white-collar positions, and the long-standing proscription against hiring African Americans in the city's State Street retail center remained in force.

The tens of thousands of blacks who came to Chicago during the war found jobs but soon discovered that the city had virtually no housing to offer them. A severe citywide housing shortage produced a minuscule vacancy rate of 1.5 percent in 1941, far below the 5 percent rate judged optimal by the Metropolitan Housing and Planning Council. Little construction occurred during the Great Depression, and wartime demands for men and material exacerbated the problem. The meager amount of public housing built in the late 1930s and early 1940s barely scratched the surface. When the Ida B. Wells project opened in 1941, the Chicago Housing Authority received 17,544 applications for only 1,662 units. Desperate for lodging, African American families crowded into one-room "kitchenettes." According to a 1944 city agency report, as many as six people occupied each of the Black Belt's 11,160 kitchenettes. Reinforcing the city's rigid racial segregation, white property owners signed restrictive covenants that prohibited selling or renting to blacks. In 1940 the Chicago branch of the National Association for the Advancement of Colored People (NAACP) won the landmark *Hansberry v. Lee* case that allowed a black family to purchase a home in the white Washington Park neighborhood. The *Hansberry* decision proved an isolated victory, however, and restrictive covenants continued to operate in nearly 80 percent of the city in 1945.[5]

Competition for scarce housing and conflict over employment brought racial tension to a flash point in the summer of 1943 in dozens of Northern cities. Across the nation, all told, 242 interracial battles erupted in forty-seven cities, including Buffalo, Harlem, Los Angeles, and most violently, Detroit, where the death toll reached thirty-four (twenty-five blacks and nine whites). Mayor Kelly, a popular political figure among the Windy City's black voters, assured the *New York Times,* "We are not going to have what happened in Detroit." Meanwhile, two hundred prominent Chicagoans met to discuss what action the city could take to forestall rioting. They urged the mayor to form a biracial committee similar to the one appointed by Governor Lowden after the 1919 race riot. At their request, Kelly appointed five African Americans and five whites to the Mayor's Committee on Race Relations (later renamed the Mayor's Commission on

Human Relations) and charged them with identifying and alleviating sources of racial friction. For its creation and for his firm guidance through the troubled war years, Kelly received widespread acclaim. As the first interracial commission of its kind, the Chicago model became the standard that was imitated by countless cities in the post–World War II era.[6]

In 1943 Governor Green created the Illinois Interracial Commission to address racial antagonisms throughout the state. To foster racial tolerance, the commission sponsored a series of conferences and worked closely with the state's teachers colleges in conducting workshops and seminars. At the urging of the commission, seven Illinois communities (Champaign, Danville, Evanston, Galesburg, Peoria, Rockford, and Springfield) created their own human relations councils. With very little funding and a limited mandate to maintain peace and productivity during the war, the Illinois Interracial Commission and the local councils understandably adopted a policy of gradualism. Uninterested in initiating sweeping social change, the commission made few headlines and launched even fewer forays against the racial status quo. When a racial incident that threatened to lead to violence occurred in Fulton County near Camp Ellis, the commission interceded to help secure a peaceful resolution. Otherwise, segregation and discrimination predominated throughout most of Illinois.

The relative quiescence of the war years, however, belied a growing dissatisfaction among the state's rising African American population. The 1940s, observed the historian Robert G. Spinney, proved a seedtime for future reform. Declaring their intention to wage a "Double V" campaign (signifying victory at home and abroad), more militant blacks than ever before protested racial inequality. The *Chicago Defender* repeatedly chronicled instances of discrimination against African Americans in uniform and demanded an end to segregation in the armed forces. James Forman and George Houser founded the Chicago Committee on Racial Equality (CCRE), the forerunner of the Congress of Racial Equality (CORE), which conducted sit-ins to desegregate restaurants in Chicago's Loop—a generation before sit-ins became a staple of the civil rights movement in the South. Although the full force of the quest for civil rights came much later, the initial stirrings of discontent appeared during World War II.

Challenges to traditional patterns of race relations suggested the degree to which World War II would be a watershed in Illinois history. The war's impact on soldiers and workers—both men and women—presaged wholesale change in the postwar years. A rejuvenated economy obliterated the massive unemployment of the Great Depression and, Americans fervently hoped, paved the way for a new era of prosperity. The return of peace, they believed, would mean the realization of hopes and desires long deferred. In fact, the postwar years ushered in spectacular economic growth and an age of unprecedented mass consumerism; it also brought a concatenation of problems both old and new to test the resilience of the state's people.

Deliriously happy Chicagoans celebrated downtown when they learned that World War II had ended with an Allied victory. *Chicago Historical Society*

Rock Island

Along with Moline, Illinois, and Davenport and Bettendorf in Iowa, Rock Island forms part of an extensive metropolitan area alongside the Mississippi River known as the Quad Cities. Various Indian tribes occupied the region long before the first European explorers arrived in western Illinois. When Marquette and Jolliet traveled down the river in 1673, they found Illini villages there; when Zebulon Pike's government expedition came in 1805, the Sauk and Fox tribes predominated. In 1816 the federal government built Fort Armstrong on Rock Island, a two-mile-long island of solid limestone in the Mississippi River, and a trading post and small settlement grew nearby. In 1835 the town called Stephenson became the county seat and six years later became known as Rock Island. During the 1840s and 1850s, Rock Island grew along with the burgeoning commerce on the Mississippi River. In addition to the increasing volume of steamboat traffic (as many as nineteen hundred docked there annually), rafts of logs floated down from northern woodlands for sawing at area mills. Huge riverine traffic jams occurred there as the steamboats crept carefully through the rafts, which extended a hundred yards in width and a third of a mile in length. In 1856 the Chicago and Rock Island Railroad completed the first railroad bridge across the Mississippi River, and both steamboat traffic and the lumber-milling industry declined sharply. During the Civil War, the federal government built a prison and an arsenal on Rock Island near the abandoned site of Fort Armstrong. Both Rock Island and Moline became important centers for the agricultural implements industry, with the International Harvester Company factories in the former and the John Deere Company plants in the latter.

During the late nineteenth and early twentieth centuries, as a rough-and-tumble river town, Rock Island became a haven for carpetbaggers, gamblers, snake oil salesmen, and an assortment of hucksters who gave the city a reputation for lawlessness. From his famous stone mansion on Twentieth Street, John Patrick Looney managed his monopoly of the city's gambling, prostitution, and illegal liquor trades. He bribed local officials, killed off rival gang members, and attacked prominent citizens and reform-minded politicians in his newspaper, the *Rock Island News*. Looney's bloody reign of terror ended in 1922 when he fled the city after his twenty-four-year-old son died in a street gun battle. Apprehended three years later in Mexico and convicted of various crimes, Looney spent his last years in the state penitentiary in Joliet. Paul Newman's character in the 2002 film *The Road to Perdition* was based upon Looney's life.

Rock Island became a boomtown during the world wars when thousands of workers migrated to the city seeking work in the arsenal and other war-related manufacturing enterprises. Change came most significantly during World War II, when the workforce at the arsenal grew from 2,735 to 18,675. While housing construction came to an abrupt halt in most Illinois communities during the war, Rock Island received special permission from Washington, D.C., to build emergency housing to offset the local shortage. As a consequence, builders erected hundreds of private homes and public housing units in 1942–1944. For the first time since the Civil War, the federal government sent prisoners of war to the Rock Island arsenal—much to the displeasure of the local population. Residents of the Quad Cities objected to the freedom of movement afforded the Italian prisoners who worked in the arsenal in 1944–1945. American Legion posts in the area asked that the prisoners be withdrawn, but to no avail.

Robert R. McCormick

One of the giants of American journalism, McCormick was born in Chicago on July 30, 1880. His father served as U.S. ambassador to several European countries, and his maternal grandfather was the publisher of the *Chicago Tribune*. He attended elite schools in England before graduating from Groton preparatory school in Massachusetts (as a schoolmate of Franklin D. Roosevelt) and Yale University. After a brief career in politics (he served a two-year term in the Chicago City Council and a five-year term as president of the Chicago Sanitary District), the conservative Republican became the publisher of the *Chicago Tribune,* a post he held for the next forty years. He put the paper on sound financial footing, offsetting the rising costs of newsprint by acquiring timber rights in Canada and building paper mills in Quebec and Ontario. Introducing narrative comic strips, a women's section, and other innovations, McCormick and his cousin Joseph Patterson elevated the newspaper from third in circulation among the city's dailies to first. The *Tribune* boasted the largest readership in the Midwest, and McCormick placed the words "The World's Greatest Newspaper" on its masthead.

McCormick initially opposed U.S. involvement in World War I but served with distinction in the American Expeditionary Force and rose to the rank of colonel. He quickly reaffirmed his isolationist beliefs after the war, opposing U.S. membership in the League of Nations and vehemently criticizing both the British Empire and the Soviet Union. Throughout the 1920s, *Tribune* editorials reflected his disdain for Prohibition and any expansion of government. In 1924 he founded Chicago radio station WGN (call letters standing for World's Greatest Newspaper) and launched a weekly newsmagazine, *Liberty,* which the *Tribune* finally abandoned in 1931 after losing almost fourteen million dollars. Circula-

Robert R. McCormick of the
Chicago Tribune, one of the
giants of American journalism.
Chicago Historical Society

tion continued to increase for the *Tribune,* and by the end of the 1920s the paper trailed only the *New York Daily News* nationally.

In the 1930s McCormick became the bitter enemy of Franklin D. Roosevelt and the New Deal. Opposing the National Recovery Administration (NRA) as being both fascistic and communistic, the *Tribune* portrayed Roosevelt, Adolph Hitler, Benito Mussolini, and Joseph Stalin in a political cartoon as the Four Horsemen of the Apocalypse. Staunchly opposed to giving Britain financial and moral support in the years leading to World War II, McCormick advocated appeasement of German territorial claims in Central Europe and defended Japanese expansionism in Asia. Three days before the attack on Pearl Harbor, the *Tribune* published a secret War Department plan outlining the nation's plans for fighting the Nazis in Europe. After the attack, McCormick threw the paper's support solidly behind the war effort but conducted an ongoing battle against the government over censorship issues.

McCormick avidly supported Republican candidates against President Roosevelt, backing Alf Landon in 1936, Wendell Willkie in 1940, and Thomas Dewey in 1944. Convinced that the Republicans would regain the White House in 1948, the *Tribune* published the inaccurate headline "Dewey Defeats Truman" in its early edition the morning after the election. The photograph of a beaming Truman holding aloft a copy of the newspaper became one of the most famous photos in American political annals. Frustrated with the Republican party in the 1950s, McCormick attempted unsuccessfully to create the American party as an alternative for conservatives. He died at his palatial estate in Wheaton on April 1, 1955.

CHAPTER THIRTEEN

Postwar Boom and Suburban Growth

At the end of World War II, the people of Illinois tempered their hopes for continued prosperity with concerns about the economic future of the nation. Stark memories of the unemployment, bankruptcy, and homelessness during the recent Great Depression left policy makers and economists every bit as concerned as workers were about the conditions that would prevail following demobilization. Had the wartime boom been a temporary interlude, they worried, and would the nation slide back into a nightmare of overproduction and underconsumption? In fact, a prolonged period of affluence ensued when the United States emerged from the war as the world's dominant economic power. Along with financial success came a host of demographic changes that altered the shape of Illinois and created challenges for the second half of the twentieth century. A rapidly rising postwar population stemmed in part from a significant influx of immigrants whose presence altered the makeup of certain areas of the state. Communities with unprecedented numbers of children faced the need to modify and expand educational facilities. Chicago's loss of people and the concomitant growth of its suburbs, along with the continuing decline of the rural population, raised important questions about resource allocation and altered the state's politics. Significant changes that transformed Illinois in the last years of the twentieth century can be seen in their formative stages in the years immediately following World War II.

Even before the Japanese surrender in August 1945, Illinois communities were struggling with the difficult transition from wartime to peacetime. Gold stars in windows, signifying the loss of a loved one in military action, and the appearance of honor rolls and monuments in city squares and public parks served as eloquent testimony to the human sacrifices that had been made to win the conflict. One of the most pressing problems facing Illinois involved the assimilation of veterans, a group comprising roughly one-eighth of the state's population. In 1943, a year before the

U.S. Congress passed the Servicemen's Readjustment Act (the GI Bill of Rights), Illinois Governor Dwight Green created the Committee on the Rehabilitation and Employment of Veterans. In 1944 the governor's committee issued a booklet, "It's All Yours, Veteran," that instructed discharged soldiers how to obtain state and federal benefits. The Illinois War Council allocated funds for veterans's aid, and local war councils established information centers for the same purpose. In 1945 the general assembly created the Illinois Veterans Commission (IVC) with an appropriation of $2,801,960 for 1945–1947. The IVC had established 146 branch offices by 1949, at least one in each of the state's counties.[1]

In addition to the GI Bill of Rights, which provided an extraordinarily generous set of benefits to the nation's veterans, Illinois proffered a number of emoluments and services. In 1946 the general assembly awarded bonuses financed by a $385 million bond issue to veterans, and survivors' benefits to the families of soldiers who had lost their lives in military service. Veterans received $10 per month for domestic service and $15 per month for service overseas, up to a maximum of $900, the same amount granted for survivors' benefits. The state offered scholarships to students attending the University of Illinois and the five state teachers colleges who could not complete their degrees in the time allotted by the GI Bill. Because federal tuition grants fell short of the complete cost of instruction and state colleges lacked the physical plants to accommodate the large numbers of veterans seeking undergraduate degrees, the state urgently increased funding for higher education. The general assembly also appropriated nearly $8 million for the addition of veterans' wings to hospitals in Jacksonville and Elgin and for the construction of new rehabilitation centers specifically for veterans in several communities.

Peoria gained national recognition for its pioneering work in easing veterans back into the societal mainstream. Based largely upon the field research of Dr. Harold Vonachen, medical director of the Caterpillar Tractor Company, the Peoria Plan of Human Rehabilitation became a model veterans' organization for other cities in Illinois and elsewhere. With grants from the state and the Community Chest, local businesses, labor unions, veterans' organizations, churches, the American Red Cross, and other social service agencies established the Veterans' Service Center as a centralized clearinghouse for the treatment of physically and emotionally disabled veterans. Counselors distributed information about the GI Bill and state benefits, medical personnel furnished health care, psychologists administered tests for vocational guidance, and psychiatrists provided therapy for survivors of traumatic wartime experiences. Personnel involved with the Peoria plan gave particular emphasis to the study and care of the physically disabled and achieved notable success with new occupational therapy methods that prepared many paraplegics for gainful employment. Within a short time, civilians also began using the service center's vocational and counseling services.

Veterans who returned to farming found the state of agriculture alto-gether better than it had been prior to the war. Despite general grumbling that farms had gotten bigger and that some farmers were being forced to expand their acreage or sell to absentee owners, most homesteads remained individually owned and family operated. Between 1940 and 1949, farmers reduced their mortgage indebtedness by half. Postwar demand for crops re-mained high, and rising prices encouraged farmers to acquire new technol-ogy. Illinois continued to be among the leading states in corn, soybean, and hog production, while a growing number of the state's farms increas-ingly began raising chickens, fruits, and vegetables. The federal government continued to be a benign presence, increasing subsidies when prices wa-vered in 1948 and extending social security protection to agricultural labor-ers in 1950. Illinois farmers' organizations such as the Farm Bureau Federa-tion quibbled with the U.S. Department of Agriculture over the particulars of subsidy payments for various commodities, but overall the 1950s re-mained a period of record productivity and high prices in agriculture.

Veterans bound for the cities sought government aid in finding suit-able housing, because there was a serious shortage in Illinois during and after World War II. Even though most GI loans awarded in the state went for lodging, private industry could not build affordable housing quickly enough to meet the demand. (Of the 65,353 loans granted by the Veter-ans Administration in Illinois between March 28, 1946, and November 15, 1948, 1,368 loans went for farms or farm equipment, 4,520 for busi-ness, and 59,465 for homes.) In 1945 the general assembly invested cities and counties with the power to acquire slums or blighted areas for the purpose of providing public housing and allocated ten million dollars to local housing authorities for these purposes. More than one hundred lo-cal housing authorities were in existence in Illinois by 1948, but owing to the traditional bias against government intrusion into the private housing market, construction of very few public housing units pro-ceeded. More commonly local authorities used public funds for slum clearance and commercial site development and left the construction of single-family units to private builders. Critical housing shortages led to innovative responses in some Illinois communities. The Williamson County Housing Authority used state funds to purchase four hundred homes from the Illinois Ordnance Plant and then sold them on long-term contracts to Herrin and Marion residents. Veterans in Rockford banded together to form a corporation, bought barracks at Camp Grant from the War Assets Administration, and converted them into private housing units. Peoria made use of state funds to construct a housing project consisting of three hundred trailers. Despite such efforts, how-ever, veterans were still facing severe housing shortages as late as 1949.

While housing remained a persistent problem, local draft boards and veterans' organizations reported that servicemen and -women experienced few problems finding jobs after the war. The Selective Training and Service Act of 1940 obligated employers to rehire all honorably discharged veterans who applied within ninety days after leaving the armed forces; businesses could not fire reemployed veterans without cause for a year. Local draft boards handled reemployment disputes, but the willingness of employers to welcome back former employees from military service minimized the number of such cases. The task of helping veterans with no claim to reemployment fell to the Illinois State Employment Service, which worked in tandem with veterans' organizations, college placement offices, and other groups to find jobs for veterans. The Illinois Labor Department's division of placement and unemployment compensation reported that a total of 320,000 veterans claimed unemployment benefits during the twelve months ending July 31, 1946, but the number had fallen to 88,000 by the end of the year. Initial problems of readjustment to civilian life, difficulties in finding decent housing, and the desire to relax a while before rejoining the workforce accounted for the gradual return to work by discharged military personnel. By the time that veterans completed their preparations for rejoining the workforce, a thriving economy invariably provided ample opportunities for employment.

Census of Manufactures data for the late 1940s revealed that Illinois remained the third-leading manufacturing state in the nation behind New York and Pennsylvania, and conversion from war materiel to consumer goods proceeded smoothly. Nearly three-fourths of all manufacturing gains came in Chicago, but industrial growth occurred in many other parts of the state as well. Illinois continued to excel after the war in such heavy industries as iron and steel, food processing, farm implements, and printing and publishing. In the 1940s, the state became the chief producer in the radio and electronics industries, with Chicago firms leading the way and plants in Springfield, Elgin, Bloomington, and Mt. Carmel also playing leading roles. Companies such as Zenith, Motorola, Admiral, and others best known for the mass production of televisions, radios, phonographs, and other electronic equipment flourished by landing postwar defense contracts for radar, guided missiles, and other robotic devices being produced in Cold War–era America.

Chicago's wartime construction and expansion of industrial facilities, unequaled in scope elsewhere in the country, actually continued for several years after the defeat of the Axis powers. Corporations purchased existing plants and modified them for the manufacture of altogether different commodities or adapted the products for peacetime uses. International Harvester purchased the Melrose Park engine factory, and Western Electric acquired the Studebaker engine plant—in both cases retooling factories that had made war materiel for the manufacture of completely different products thereafter. The Preston Tucker Automobile Corporation bought the Chicago Dodge engine plant, reputedly the world's largest factory at the time of its completion, for the manufacture of its new model automobiles, a venture that failed miserably when Tucker filed for bankruptcy in 1950. Although the aircraft industry fled Chicago after the war for Los Angeles and other West Coast localities, the Windy City acquired the runways and other facilities used by the Douglas Aircraft Company and built a second civilian airport to complement Midway Airport. The spectacular growth in subsequent years of O'Hare Field, which became the world's busiest airport, made Chicago a vital air transportation center. Just as the railroads had once put the city at the heart of the nation's east–west transportation network, the development of transcontinental airplane traffic after World War II reinforced Chicago's earlier prominence.

Industrial growth, full employment, and increased purchasing power combined to create a postwar economic boom of unprecedented dimensions in the United States. Workers brought home bigger paychecks, which gave them more money to spend on the cornucopia of goods being produced by American industry. Between 1945 and 1950, per capita real income rose 6 percent; in the 1950s, it increased another 15 percent. In addition to higher incomes and savings that had accumulated during previous years, shoppers enjoyed easy credit that made the deferral of gratification wholly unnecessary. Consumer credit grew from $5.7 billion in 1945 to $58 billion in 1961. Unable to purchase scarce items during the war years, consumers went on a postwar shopping spree that allowed them to satiate desires long deferred. Rather than stand in long queues with coupon books to receive their limited allowance of meat, sugar, canned goods, shoes, and other necessities as during the war, blue- and white-collar workers formed lines to buy televisions, appliances, and other luxury items. No longer manufacturing bombers and tanks, Ford, Chrysler, General Motors, and their few remaining competitors returned to the mass production of automobiles. Families purchased a car—sometimes two—and added a garage to the blueprint of the new home they planned to build or buy. Automobile ownership doubled in Illinois within ten years following the conclusion of the war.

The postwar advent of the automobile triggered massive suburban growth and transformed the Illinois landscape. At the same time, federal government policies underwrote metropolitan decentralization by providing a number of incentives for urban dwellers to vacate inner-city neighborhoods for the suburbs. Under the auspices of the Highway Act of 1956, which created the interstate highway system, the federal government provided 90 percent of the cost for the high-speed expressways that whisked commuters into and out of central cities. The Federal Housing Administration and Veterans Administration insured long-term mortgage loans, reduced average monthly payments for home buyers, and greatly enhanced the possibility of home ownership for the working class. The Internal Revenue Code allowed home owners to deduct mortgage interest and property taxes from their gross taxable income while providing no comparable perquisites for renters. "Simply put," concluded the urban historian Kenneth T. Jackson, "the Internal Revenue Code finances the continued growth of suburbia." Intentionally or not, policies forged in Washington, D.C., encouraged development of the countryside surrounding existing urban places.[2]

Having been made more accessible and affordable by government policy, suburbs also proved attractive to urban residents for other reasons. The existence of cheap and plentiful land on the metropolitan fringes allowed suburbs to offer large houses and yards on spacious lots. City dwellers accustomed to living in cramped apartments, row houses, and tiny bungalows appreciated the plethora of detached dwellings and low population densities common in suburbia. High taxes, rising crime rates, aged and deteriorating infrastructures, and overcrowded schools in the inner cities made suburbs look all the more inviting. So did the influx of newcomers that had begun during the war years and continued in the late 1940s and 1950s. Although people left central cities for a variety of reasons, the desire to escape racial change often figured in the calculations of new suburbanites (which came to be known as white flight). The drab architectural boredom of the expanding suburbs bothered some cultural critics, who complained about the monotony of countless similar ranch houses lined up on uniform-sized lots as far as the eye could see. Whatever their aesthetic shortcomings, however, single-family tract houses proved undeniably desirable to a population hungry for home ownership, more living space, good schools, and personal safety. The poor lacked the wherewithal to relocate, but vast numbers of the working and middle classes availed themselves of what they perceived to be a golden opportunity. Families loaded their possessions into moving vans, piled the children into their automobiles, and headed for the crabgrass frontier.

Suburbanization drained people and resources from communities throughout Illinois, but Chicago felt the impact of decentralization most severely. The Windy City's population peaked at 3.6 million in 1945 and then began declining in the postwar years. Between 1945 and 1958, the completion of the Congress Street Superhighway (later renamed the Eisenhower Expressway), the Edens Expressway, and the Calumet Skyway (later renamed the Chicago Skyway) improved the flow of automobile traffic for suburban commuters. A number of outlying municipalities experienced dramatic population growth, and developers created new communities where open rural landscapes had stood only a few years before. Between 1940 and 1960, Evanston's population grew from 65,389 to 79,283, Hinsdale's from 7,336 to 12,859, and Homewood's from 4,078 to 13,371. During the same two decades, Skokie's population exploded from 7,172 to 59,364. Throughout the "collar counties" surrounding Chicago—Cook, DuPage, Lake, McHenry, Kane, and Will—bulldozers carved out living spaces for hordes of suburbanites.

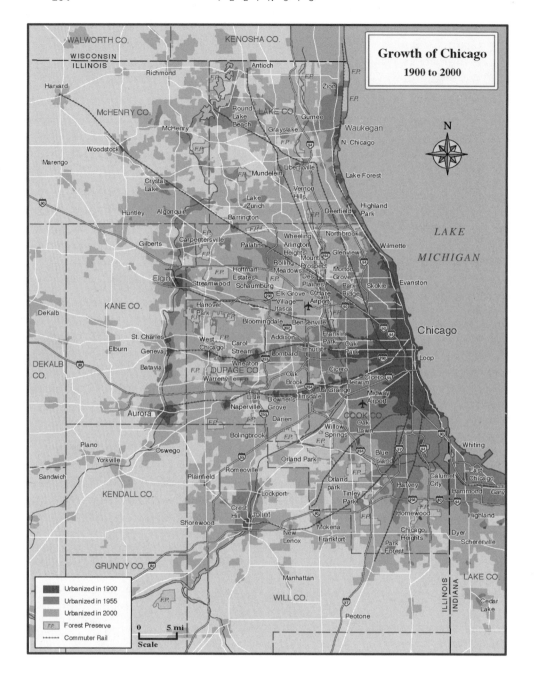

Growth of Chicago
1900 to 2000

Urbanized in 1900
Urbanized in 1955
Urbanized in 2000
F.P. Forest Preserve
Commuter Rail

0   5 mi
Scale

Retail followed population. Catering to the needs of consumers who balked at driving great distances to do their shopping, developers built new malls at the intersections of suburban thoroughfares. Like Old Orchard Shopping Center, which opened for business in Skokie in 1954, the new malls offered attractively landscaped settings and acres of free parking so that suburbanites could avoid navigating through heavy traffic and battling for scarce parking spaces when patronizing downtown stores. Anticipating that much suburban shopping would occur in the evenings after commuters had left their downtown workplaces, mall planners included plenty of lighting in parking lots. Retailing giants such as Marshall Field's noted declining sales in their flagship stores downtown and inserted satellite outlets in the shopping centers opening in suburban locations.

As the Chicago metropolitan area metastasized across northeastern Illinois, industries also deserted the inner city for the suburbs. Outlying sites offered land for expansion, and industrialists increasingly sought large, single-story plants rather than multistory facilities for the use of assembly-line production techniques. Large suburban tracts of land allowed businesses to avoid downtown congestion and provided ample parking for workers. Whereas factories once depended upon downtown railroad connections, automobiles and motor trucks operating on modern expressways provided another opportunity for relocation to the periphery. As a consequence of these changes, Chicago's share of manufacturing employment in the metropolitan region fell from 71 percent in 1947 to 54 percent in 1961; less than half of the industrial jobs remained in Chicago in 1965.

Nothing symbolized the loss of manufacturing in Chicago more than the demise of the meatpacking industry. Known for a century as "hog butcher of the world," from Carl Sandburg's apt phrase, the Windy City watched the meatpacking giants emigrate after World War II. With trucks supplanting the railroads and packinghouses employing new technology, the economies of scale provided by the Union Stock Yards no longer remained crucial to profit-seeking businessmen, who moved their plants to smaller towns in Midwestern and Southwestern states. All of the great meatpacking plants that had played such an indispensable role in the city's rise were closed by the mid-1960s, and the Union Stock Yards became a ghost town. Only empty cattle pens, vacant factories, and thirty thousand unemployed workers remained in the Back of the Yards neighborhood.

Less visibly, Chicago also lost its primacy in the field of atomic energy. After the pioneering research completed underneath the University of Chicago's Stagg Field during World War II, the government looked outside the city to create additional research facilities. The Argonne National Laboratory, built twenty-five miles southwest of Chicago in 1946, did pioneering work in the production of electricity, and the U.S. Atomic Energy Commission in 1966 selected a site in DuPage County for the construction of a three-hundred-million-dollar "scientific city" dedicated to atomic research. In the last decades of the twentieth century, the government situated its newest "atom smashers" in New York and California instead of Illinois. Scientists more often conducted cutting-edge atomic research in Sunbelt locations far from Chicago and its suburbs.[3]

Losing people, businesses, and jobs to the burgeoning suburbs, Chicago simultaneously underwent significant demographic changes that altered the racial and ethnic character of the city. The most significant, the mass migration of Southern blacks to the city that had begun during World War II, continued unabated in subsequent decades. The African American population of the city rose from 277,731 in 1940 to 492,265 in 1950 (an increase of 77 percent) and again to 812,637 in 1960 (an increase of 65 percent). Such remarkable population gains assumed even greater importance because of the concurrent flight of whites to the suburbs. Whereas African Americans accounted for roughly 8.2 percent of the city's population in 1940, their numbers constituted 13.6 percent in 1950 and 22.9 percent in 1960. As these numbers indicate, the population transformations of the 1940s and 1950s far outdistanced the impact of the World War I–era Great Migration.

Chicago's South Side ghetto creaked and groaned under the inexorable crush of the arriving multitudes—until it finally broke. The 1950 census reported population densities in some areas of the Black Belt to be three times that of the city as a whole, and the situation continued to deteriorate as an estimated three thousand blacks a month arrived from the South during the following decade. In the 1950s, an average of twelve city blocks per month changed from majority-white to majority-black ownership, that is, roughly 225 housing units per week. Whole blocks that had been occupied by white families for generations changed racial composition entirely within a matter of weeks. White families often carted off their belongings by day, and to avoid harassment by white mobs, African American families unloaded their furniture from moving vans by night.

As a result of the acute competition for living space in Chicago's South Side, a small colony of black settlement grew into what the historian Arnold R. Hirsch has called the "second ghetto" on the city's West Side. As upwardly mobile Jews and other Eastern Europeans left the West Lawndale neighborhood west of the Loop, African Americans raced in from outside the metropolitan area to seize suddenly available housing. Many new arrivals to West Lawndale came from the city's South Side, having been displaced by earlier urban renewal projects that had replaced dilapidated housing with public housing monoliths, hospitals, and university buildings. Chicago's use of the Illinois Redevelopment Act of 1947 and the Urban Community Conservation Act of 1953 (progenitors of the national housing acts of 1949 and 1954, respectively) uprooted thousands of poor South Side residents who ended up miles away in the emerging second ghetto. From 1940 to 1960 West Lawndale's white population plummeted from 102,048 to 10,792, while the number of black residents soared from 380 to 113,827. The West Side became Chicago's new port of entry for black immigrants, and the area's black population exploded from 13 percent in 1950 to 91 percent ten years later. The African American settlement spread steadily westward to the city limits and northward into the Garfield Park and Austin neighborhoods.[4]

Retreating whites yielded ground grudgingly in the 1940s and 1950s, years that Hirsch termed "an era of hidden violence." While local newspapers sought to maintain a facade of racial amity and studiously avoided printing stories that might sully Chicago's good name, interracial violence frequently recurred as African Americans moved into previously all-white enclaves. The "chronic urban guerilla warfare" began during World War II as whites stormed the residences occupied by "blockbusting" black families. From May 1944 through July 1946, white mobs attacked forty-six black residences and killed at least three persons. Full-scale riots ensued at Airport Homes in 1946 and at Fernwood Park Homes in 1947, when the Chicago Housing Authority attempted to move black veterans into temporary public housing projects in all-white neighborhoods; in both disturbances, police fought hand-to-hand with several thousand white rioters. Similar outbreaks occurred in the Park Manor and Englewood neighborhoods in 1949, at Trumbull Park Homes in 1953, and in Calumet Park in 1957. In each instance, squads of Chicago policemen protected African Americans from rampaging white mobs.[5]

A sustained effort by the Chicago press minimized reporting of most racial disturbances in the post–World War II years. The press even managed to downplay the slaying of two African Americans in 1956 with the Democratic National Convention in progress just a few miles away in the International Amphitheatre. But no amount of collusion between local officials and the media could stifle coverage of the 1951 riots in suburban Cicero. The all-white, heavily Eastern European people of the industrial suburb immediately west of Chicago, many of whom had fled the inner city to escape the influx of black residents, drew the color line indelibly and vowed to defend their property values. When an African American family attempted to move into one of an apartment building's twenty units, thousands of whites took to the streets in opposition. The burning and vandalism continued for several days and nights before hundreds of National Guardsmen, Cicero policemen, and Cook County sheriff's deputies restored order. Newspapers from around the country and the world editorialized against the savagery displayed in Cicero. A cynical spokesmen for the Congress of Racial Equality (CORE), hardened by years of such rioting in Chicago, observed that at least few blacks suffered serious injuries and no one died. Nonetheless, noted the historian James R. Ralph Jr., Cicero became "the preeminent symbol of northern bigotry" in the 1950s.[6]

Although the violence that flared periodically in Chicago never escalated into a riot comparable to the 1919 conflagration, race relations remained strained in the city throughout the postwar years. As boss of the powerful Cook County Democratic machine, Mayor Kelly received high marks from the city's African Americans, which proved a liability with Chicago's white electoral majority. By 1947 critics were complaining that the seventy-year-old Kelly, who suffered from a number of physical ailments, lacked the vitality to continue in the mayor's office. They also despaired at Chicago's tarnished image, a result of Kelly's inattention to municipal housekeeping. The city's better element blanched at scandals involving the school system and the police department and the official tolerance of organized crime. Most distressing to many of Chicago's white voters, however, Kelly threw his administration's support behind open housing and public school desegregation. Scandals of every stripe had surfaced over the years and the Democratic party had always survived intermittent flurries of public indignation, but party insiders would not tolerate city hall's imprimatur of racial integration. Afraid of alienating the party rank and file and losing control of city hall, chairman of the Cook County Democratic party Jacob M. Arvey and his cohorts persuaded Kelly not to run for reelection in 1947.

To burnish the Democrats' lackluster image, Arvey chose nonpartisan civic reformer Martin Kennelly to replace Kelly. A wealthy moving-van magnate, Kennelly had no experience in politics but had become well known locally as the chairman of a number of charitable organizations and businessmen's associations. As mayor the silver-haired Kennelly cut a dashing figure snipping ribbons, speaking at official functions, and giving bland speeches extolling civic rectitude. Unlike Kelly, whose actions on behalf of African Americans undercut his support among Democratic party leaders, Kennelly acted consistently in ways that pleased his white constituency. When violence erupted at Fernwood Park Homes and again in Park Manor and Englewood, the mayor declined to follow his predecessor's policy of using police to protect blacks seeking housing in segregated neighborhoods. He opposed an open housing ordinance and launched a campaign to eradicate gambling from the Black Belt while allowing it to flourish everywhere else in the city. Party leaders certainly endorsed Kennelly's abandoning the African American community but recoiled when he took his own good government rhetoric seriously enough to pursue civil service reform. His efforts to reduce the number of patronage workers on the city payroll resulted in the removal of approximately twelve thousand jobs from Democratic machine control, and his tenuous support among party workers evaporated. In 1951 party leaders reluctantly acquiesced to the popular Kennelly's reelection, in large measure because no other Democratic candidate seemed ready to challenge the incumbent. In 1955, however, an ambitious Democrat, Richard J. Daley, emerged from the bevy of mayoral hopefuls, and Kennelly immediately became expendable.

Daley's election in 1955 represented a victory for the machine over ostensibly more progressive candidates, Martin Kennelly in the Democratic primary and Republican Robert Merriam in the general election, and the city's reformers forecast disastrous times ahead for Chicago. At a time when money, businesses, and people were fleeing the city for suburban sanctuaries, few civic leaders felt confident that the new mayor—an unimpressive, inarticulate career politician from the grimy Bridgeport neighborhood—possessed the talent or the inclination to fashion an urban renaissance. The silk-stocking element surely cringed when Daley asserted his dominance over the traditionally unruly city council and consolidated power in his dual roles of mayor and party chairman. The Chicago Democratic machine, a fractious collection of squabbling politicians during the Kennelly years, became more disciplined and powerful under Daley; it developed into an electoral juggernaut sustained by patronage and favors that vanquished all opposition while operating at variance with textbook descriptions of democratic government.

Yet even as Daley directed the most powerful urban political machine in the nation, his name began cropping up among the lists of new-breed mayors who fought valiantly in the postwar years to stem the flow of people and resources to the suburbs. Chicago's civic elite, braced for the Democratic machine's plundering of city hall, admitted that the new administration seemed surprisingly good. The horse-betting parlors and whorehouses, ubiquitous before the war, failed to reappear, and the crime rate did not appreciably rise. Surrounded by his blue-ribbon management team, a group of idealistic young civil servants collectively known as the Whiz Kids, Daley initiated a series of reforms that significantly improved the city's delivery of services. He hired an additional twenty-five hundred policemen, eight hundred firemen, and five hundred sanitation workers, and his installation of new mercury arc streetlights made good his assertion that "there is not a big city in the world which has street lighting that can compare to Chicago's." These improvements necessitated an increase in property taxes, but he eased the tax burden when his representatives in Springfield secured legislation granting Chicago the authority to increase sales taxes and to tax public utilities.[7]

Daley quickly won the approbation of Chicago's business community by launching an ambitious building program concentrated in the Loop. The completion of the Prudential Building in 1955 marked the construction of the first downtown office building since 1934; the Inland Steel Building opened in 1957, followed by a host of others, including the world's tallest building, the Sears Tower. For all his connections with the city's corporate leaders and rhetoric about an architectural renaissance downtown, Martin Kennelly had in eight years done very little to revitalize the central business district. In the few instances in which Kennelly had initiated projects (the Prudential Building, the Congress Street Expressway, and a lakeside water filtration plant, for example), completion came after

the 1955 election, so the new mayor presided over the ribbon-cutting ceremonies and received the accolades. "The immense program of [public]
building that began in 1955 constituted the foremost example in the U.S.
of the spontaneous reconstruction of the urban core," concluded architectural historian Carl W. Condit. When Daley sought reelection in 1959, he
received the overwhelming support of Chicago's Republican business elite.
The local press called his landslide victory—he received more than 70 percent of the ballots cast and carried forty-nine of the city's fifty wards—a
triumph of good government. Daley's reputation deteriorated in the 1960s
and 1970s, but he genuinely appeared during his early years in city hall to
be a reformer whose innovative leadership benefited a robust Chicago.[8]

Despite the challenges presented by profound economic and demographic changes in the middle of the twentieth century, Chicago continued to be the undisputed social and cultural heart of the Midwest. As in
the late nineteenth century, the fine arts thrived in the Windy City. New
additions to the metropolitan skyline, many designed by Ludwig Mies van
der Rohe and other practitioners of the modernistic Bauhaus School of Architecture, maintained the city's reputation as an architectural mecca. The
Art Institute of Chicago, Field Museum, Adler Planetarium, Shedd Aquar-
ium, and Museum of Science and Industry continued to attract large appreciative crowds from around the world. Critics praised the books and
plays produced by local authors associated with what came to be called the
Chicago School of Literature. Writing in the naturalist tradition of
Theodore Dreiser, authors such as James T. Farrell, Nelson Algren, and
Richard Wright penned social protest novels in the 1930s and 1940s. In
later years Saul Bellow, Gwendolyn Brooks, and others employed a gritty
realism to tell stories of life in Chicago. Studs Terkel's oral histories provided a human dimension to analyses of sweeping societal change, and
Mike Royko's newspaper columns and books used wit and sarcasm to ex-
pose the peccadilloes of faceless bureaucrats and crooked politicians.

The desire for reform, especially a determination to improve the tenor
of politics and government, swept throughout Illinois in the late 1940s
and early 1950s. The infamy of the Democratic machine in Chicago,
influence-peddling and payoffs in Springfield, and corrupt courthouse politics in the southern counties combined to saddle Illinois with the reputation of one of the nation's most corrupt states. Veterans who had fought
overseas to vanquish totalitarian regimes and citizens on the home front
who had contributed to the same goal both believed that their sacrifices
on behalf of democracy would pay dividends in the postwar years. Good
government forces argued that elected officials should be held to higher
standards of conduct, and a number of idealistic men ran for elective office
for the first time to alter the political status quo. If nothing else, rising
public indignation convinced the state's power brokers that the old politics of business-as-usual would no longer be tolerated.

The crusade for political reform succeeded largely because of the influence of Jacob M. Arvey, a longtime machine loyalist and World War II veteran who assumed the chairmanship of the Cook County Democratic party after the war with enthusiasm and a profound sense of purpose. Still a partisan Democrat and intensely loyal to the Chicago machine, Arvey also saw politics as an avenue for improving the quality of public life. "When I was in the Army," he recalled, "I was determined that when I went back into politics it would be on my terms—with good candidates." Newly ensconced in a position where he could utilize his proven political skills to attain the lofty goals he set for himself and his party, he vowed to make the Democratic party in Illinois a vehicle for reforming government by running dynamic young men for key offices. By virtue of their numbers, the Cook County Democrats controlled the state party, and in 1948 Arvey selected two political neophytes, Paul H. Douglas and Adlai E. Stevenson, to run for U.S. senator and governor, respectively. Both men enjoyed reputations for political independence, and each had consistently excoriated the conduct of the Cook County Democratic machine. Neither Douglas nor Stevenson had compiled a solid vote-getting record in state politics, and they lacked seasoned political organizations and generous financial backing, but the two candidates won landslide victories in 1948 and, in the course of their careers over the next two decades, became important figures in American politics. Douglas served three terms in the U.S. Senate and became one of the most respected spokesmen for liberal ideas in the postwar era, while Stevenson received the Democratic nomination for president in 1952 and 1956.[9]

Although he initially desired to run for the U.S. Senate and denied any interest in becoming governor, Stevenson proved an able and energetic administrator during his one term in the statehouse. A gifted, witty orator who spoke often about ethics in government, he won plaudits for improving the moral climate in the state. The governor introduced a new merit system of hiring and promotion in state employment, reorganized the corrupt state police, and led a successful drive against organized crime in East St. Louis, Peoria, Rock Island, Joliet, Decatur, and Springfield. Blessed with a budgetary surplus left over from the war, he invested heavily in education, public health, welfare, and highway construction. A Republican-controlled general assembly rebuffed his call for a convention to rewrite the state constitution but met the governor halfway in 1950 by acceding to a "gateway amendment" that streamlined the procedure for amending the existing constitution. A few minor scandals, none of which involved the governor directly, failed to dim the overall picture of an honest and efficient Stevenson administration.

William G. Stratton, the Republican who served as governor from 1953 to 1961, echoed Stevenson's call for good government. He reformed the state court system and fought successfully for the adoption of a constitutional amendment that altered the state's malapportioned legislative districts for the first time since 1901. (U.S. congressional districts had not been redrawn since 1947, when an attempt to grant Cook County proportional representation in the general assembly was defeated by downstaters' refusal to relinquish their historic legislative majorities.) At his first inauguration, Stratton pledged to devote special attention to building and highway construction projects. In the following eight years, he sponsored bond issues that funded the construction of mental health centers and the expansion of state universities, and he supervised the most extensive road-building program in the state since the Len Small administration—including 7,057 miles of new roadways, 638 bridges, and the widening of U.S. Route 66 from Chicago to St. Louis to four lanes. Utilizing funds made available by the federal interstate highway program, he worked with Cook County officials to complete the expressway system emanating from Chicago's Loop. At his urging, the general assembly created the Toll Highway Commission, which issued $415 million in bonds for the construction of the 187-mile network of toll roads traversing northeastern Illinois.

State and local officials authorized the building of new roads, buildings, and other facilities in response to the pressures generated by a rapidly expanding population, with the impact of the baby boom felt most acutely in the area of education. A high school diploma, which only one or two generations earlier had been considered an anomaly, had by the 1960s become a necessity in the job market, and an increasing number of high school graduates moved on to higher education. Many elementary and secondary schools in Illinois seemed hopelessly inadequate in the postwar world, unable to offer curricula appropriate to rapidly increasing knowledge and new technology. As the movement to urban areas continued within the state, such problems became especially egregious in the rural areas, where more than ten thousand one-room schools still operated in 1942. Illinois supported twelve thousand school districts that year, the most of any state. After the war, many of the better-qualified instructors left rural school districts for urban classrooms that offered better pay and working conditions, and more than one-fourth of rural schools employed teachers with only high school degrees themselves. Calls for the repair and modernization of aged schoolhouses in the countryside went unheeded.

Farmers and small-town residents finally settled on consolidation as the answer to the rural schools problem. Neighboring districts pooled their resources and, with additional financial aid from the state, built modern schools with newer books and better facilities. The state helped also by purchasing the ten thousand buses needed to transport hundreds of thousands of students to the new schools centrally located in sparsely populated rural areas. Some small-town residents regretted the disappearance of neighborhood schools, expressed concern about the lengthy bus rides required of the students, and rued the loss of local control over their children's education, but also agreed that the disparity between rural and urban education could not be allowed. By 1948 the number of school districts in the state had been reduced 50 percent, to six thousand; twenty years later, only six hundred remained.

Higher education boomed after the war as the GI Bill paid tuition charges for veterans, the number of high school graduates increased, and a prosperous economy made a college education affordable for a broader spectrum of people. Contrary to the fears expressed by University of Chicago president Robert Maynard Hutchins, who predicted that the GI Bill would turn colleges into "hobo jungles," veterans proved to be serious and capable students. Higher education enrollment in Illinois increased from 107,000 in 1940 to 164,000 in 1956 and reached 500,000 in the late 1970s. After the war the University of Illinois, which ranked eighth nationally in full-time student enrollment, opened satellite campuses in Galesburg and at Chicago's Navy Pier; the Galesburg campus closed in 1949, and the Chicago branch remained at Navy Pier for twenty years until a permanent campus opened near the Loop. The state upgraded the normal schools at Carbondale, DeKalb, Macomb, Charleston, and Normal, founded originally for teacher training, into state colleges and then universities. Southern Illinois University made especially noteworthy progress under the leadership of Delyte Morris, who successfully exploited the desire to improve the quality of life in the most backward part of the state. In his twenty-two years as president, Morris presided over a twelvefold enrollment increase in Carbondale and helped lay the foundation for a new campus in Edwardsville. The University of Chicago and Northwestern University grew less dramatically than the state institutions but retained their first-rate reputations for teaching and research. In 1945, protesting against racial and religious discrimination at the Central YMCA College, its president along with approximately 80 percent of the faculty and much of the student body withdrew and founded Roosevelt College in Chicago. Housed in the old Auditorium Hotel, the college tripled its enrollment of twelve hundred within a year. Medical education became so prominent in Chicago in the decade following the war that 20 percent of all physicians in the country received at least part of their instruction there.[10]

The postwar boom in the state's four-year colleges and universities likewise resulted in the significant growth of junior colleges. Illinois had been in the forefront of the junior college movement (Joliet Junior College, one of the nation's first two-year colleges, opened its doors in 1901), but few such institutions appeared throughout the state in subsequent decades. With the passage of the Junior College Act in 1965, the general assembly established a state regulatory board and funding guidelines, and enrollments increased rapidly at the growing number of junior colleges scattered around the state. Two-year community colleges expanded educational opportunities for a variety of publics. They minimized costs by

The founding of the University of Illinois at Chicago Circle (later called the University of Illinois at Chicago) was part of the phenomenal post–World War II expansion of higher education in Illinois. *Illinois State Historical Library*

allowing college students to live at home for two years and provided vocational instruction to high school graduates uninterested in pursuing a baccalaureate degree, while also offering (especially at night) continuing education courses to members of their communities.

The post–World War II years in Illinois brought phenomenal change as a rapidly expanding population enjoyed the beginning of a prolonged period of economic growth. Producers and consumers shared in the affluence made possible by the nation's triumphs over depression and foreign enemies. At the same time, demographic shifts signaled the coming of political, economic, and social transformations in the years ahead. Between 1950 and 1960, the population of Chicago decreased by 2 percent, even as the number of people residing in the metropolitan area outside the city increased by 72 percent—a metamorphosis that people living outside the half dozen counties in the northeastern corner of the state watched intently, with a resolve to safeguard their own interests. Illinois remained an industrial and agricultural giant in the middle years of the twentieth century, but significant challenges lay ahead.

Park Forest

Aghast at America's degenerating central cities, a growing number of architects and planners called for metropolitan decentralization in the years following World War II. Unfortunately, random growth in the late nineteenth and early twentieth centuries had resulted in suburban sprawl, snarled commuter traffic, and unsightly community design. Instead of haphazard suburban growth and a total absence of planning, reform-minded developers urged the building of new towns outside of existing metropolises. Each new town would be part of a comprehensive regional plan encompassing transportation, housing, public utilities, and leisure facilities for approximately twenty thousand people from varied social and economic strata. Construction of thousands of housing units simultaneously, rather than piecemeal, would result in economies of scale. Because of the enormous cost involved in creating entire infrastructures for wholly new communities, few new towns appeared in the postwar years. Park Forest, Illinois, was one of the few successful ventures.

Receiving an FHA-approved loan of twenty-eight million dollars, one of the largest in the agency's history, developer Philip Klutznick selected a tract of three thousand acres approximately thirty miles south of Chicago for the site of Park Forest. Commuters to the Windy City could ride on the Illinois Central Railroad, which bordered the community on the west, or drive straight to Chicago on Western Avenue, which bisected the new town from north to south. A forest preserve on the east and south lent protection against future development. The first bulldozers began breaking unoccupied farmland on the site in October 1948, and almost exactly one year after the beginning of construction and several months after the incorporation of the Village of Park Forest, the first residents moved into apartments in October 1949. The first houses became available for purchase in 1951. American Community Builders, Klutznick's development company, offered eight different home designs in two-, three-, four-, and five-bedroom plans, which sold for a variety of prices ranging from ten thousand to thirty-five thousand dollars. In all, Klutznick's company constructed 5,500 single-family homes and 3,010 apartments. The developers and the village's first residents named the streets for Illinois servicemen who had won the congressional Medal of Honor in World War II.

In 1953 William H. Whyte Jr. published in *Fortune* magazine a series of articles on postwar suburbs that prominently featured Park Forest. Three years later, he expanded the articles into a book, *The Organization Man,* which became a best-selling analysis of suburban social structures, folkways, and values. He reported that Park Forest residents enjoyed the lush lawns, sidewalks, quiet streets, and good neighborhood schools they had found lacking in Chicago but complained about the lack of stability in what they perceived to be a rootless and transient environment. Ownership of one out of every five homes changed annually, and new families occupied 30 percent of rental units each year.

Park Forest's population grew rapidly; the U.S. census counted more than eight thousand inhabitants in 1950 and thirty thousand in 1960. Philip Klutznick bought a house in Park Forest and lived there alongside his customers for many years. The idealistic developer had hoped to build a heterogeneous community, but it was mostly professionals, academics, and other white-collar workers who bought the homes in the early years. Despite the absence of racially restrictive covenants or local statutes enforcing segregation, no African American families moved into Park Forest until 1959.

Adlai E. Stevenson

Born on February 5, 1900, in Los Angeles, California, Adlai E. Stevenson was the scion of a wealthy Bloomington family. His paternal grandfather served one term as Grover Cleveland's vice president; his mother, Helen Davis Stevenson, and other members of her family owned the *Bloomington Pantagraph*. After attending Choate prep school and graduating from Princeton University and Northwestern University Law School, Stevenson alternated between the practice of law in Chicago and a career in public

Tennessee Senator Estes Kefauver, the Democratic nominee for vice president, joins hands with Illinois Governor Adlai Stevenson, the presidential nominee, at the party's 1956 national convention in Chicago. At the extreme left in the photo are Chicago Mayor Richard J. Daley and Massachusetts Senator John F. Kennedy. *Chicago Historical Society.*

service. He served on the legal staff of the Agricultural Adjustment Administration and later acted as special assistant to Secretary of the Navy Frank Knox during World War II. He represented President Roosevelt in several overseas diplomatic initiatives and became a member of the American delegation that established the United Nations after the war. A local leader of the Chicago Council of Foreign Relations, he hoped to parlay his extensive diplomatic experience into the Democratic U.S. Senate nomination in 1948. Instead, the Democratic party slated Paul H. Douglas for the U.S. Senate seat and Stevenson for governor. He became a national figure overnight, winning the governorship by 570,000 votes while President Harry S Truman mustered a victory margin of less than 34,000 votes in Illinois.

Governor Stevenson constantly called for nonpartisanship and disinterested public service, expressing a willingness to work closely with Republicans as well as Democrats for the good of the state. Many partisan Democrats grumbled that the patrician governor seemed more at ease with the rich and well-born he entertained at his Libertyville farm north of Chicago than with the humbler members of his own party. Nevertheless, the Republicans controlled both chambers of the general assembly for most of Stevenson's four years in office and managed to derail many of his initiatives. Political experts and newspaper editors judged his attempts at political reform in the state only moderately successful. Despite the governor's repeated disavowals of interest in running for the presidency, he quickly emerged as one of the leading candidates for the Democratic nomination. After Truman announced that he would not seek reelection and named Stevenson as the party's best candidate in 1952, the governor continued to demur. Only after the Democratic National Convention in Chicago nominated him on the fourth ballot did Stevenson agree to become a candidate.

The Democratic party chose Stevenson to run for president in 1952 and again in 1956, both times opposing Republican Dwight D. Eisenhower. Probably no Democrat could have beaten Eisenhower, the beloved military hero of World War II, and Stevenson lost by considerable margins both times. Still, he campaigned with style and grace, discussing complicated issues thoroughly and refusing to launch ad hominem attacks against his opponent. His carefully crafted speeches, infused with wit and reason, elevated the tone of political discourse in two presidential contests. He won the respect and admiration of the American people, if not their votes.

After failing in 1960 to attract a third presidential nomination, Stevenson served as U.S. ambassador to the United Nations during the Kennedy administration and part of the Johnson presidency. He died of a heart attack in London, England, on July 14, 1965. The darling of liberal intellectuals, the urbane Stevenson rightly considered himself a political moderate. No fierce advocate for the downtrodden and slow to warm to the plight of African Americans, he urged carefully modulated change to cure societal ills.

CHAPTER FOURTEEN

Turbulence and Change

Unlike their parents who survived the economic deprivations of the 1930s and made great sacrifices to win a global conflict in the 1940s, Americans born after World War II grew to adulthood in an environment of privilege and plenty. Rather than celebrate the affluence that surrounded them, however, many members of the Baby Boom generation concentrated on society's shortcomings and challenged authority figures to address the inequities still persisting. In protests often originating on college campuses, dissidents demanded an end to the war in Southeast Asia, greater access to political power, and equality for African Americans, women, and other oppressed groups. They questioned many of the middle-class values and behavioral norms underpinning American society as well as the legitimacy of specific laws, which resulted in a widening generation gap between young and old. It is not surprising, with so many vital issues at stake, that the 1960s and 1970s proved a turbulent time. Liberals and conservatives, whites and nonwhites, men and women, all argued and sometimes fought over the future of the nation. While far-reaching demographic changes continued to unfold in Illinois, the state's people avidly debated the divisive issues and fully participated in the tumultuous events that defined the era.

In the decades following World War II, Illinois's population grew at a steady rate, comparable to other Midwestern states but significantly less than in the South and Southwest. The state's population of 10,081,158 in 1960 ranked fourth nationally; its 1970 total of 11,113,975 stood fifth. As in previous decades, population increase occurred unevenly in Illinois; Chicago lost population, its suburbs recorded huge increases, and the remaining areas of the state experienced moderate growth (see table 2). The state's population generally shifted northward from 1950 to 1980, and the metropolitan area surrounding Chicago attracted the most people. Although it remained the nation's second-largest city, Chicago lost hundreds of thousands of people during each of those decades. While large numbers of immigrants from the American South and other nations continued to arrive in the Windy City, greater numbers of people departed for suburban destinations.

TABLE 2—Percent Population Growth by Region, 1950–1980

Region	1950–60	1960–70	1970–80
Chicago	-1.9	-5.1	-10.8
Suburban Cook	+77.9	+34.5	+5.8
Collar Counties	+63.1	+35.7	+24.9
Northern Illinois	+18.1	+11.2	+4.0
Central Illinois	+7.9	+6.3	+5.2
Southern Illinois	+4.3	+4.8	+4.1

Adapted from Cheng H. Chiang and Ann Geraci, "Regional Demographic Trends in Illinois, 1950–85," in Peter F. Nardulli, ed., *Diversity, Conflict, and State Politics: Regionalism in Illinois* (Urbana: University of Illinois Press, 1989), 126.

In the postwar years, as Midwestern populations relocated in the burgeoning Sunbelt, large numbers of whites left Illinois for Southern climes. The white population of the state decreased by an estimated 700,000 to 900,000 during the 1970s, while the number of African Americans and Hispanics increased by approximately 400,000. Chicago remained the primary destination for nonwhite immigrants. During the 1960s, the city's African American population increased by 300,000, and more blacks lived in Cook County than in any other county in the nation. The Mexican population in Chicago—stimulated by the bracero program in World War II that recruited several thousand temporary workers—had risen to 45,000 by 1960. The closing of the stockyards, a major source of employment for Mexicans, did little to stem the rising tide of Chicano immigration, and the number of Mexicans in the city surpassed 100,000 in the 1970s. The first large-scale migration of Puerto Ricans to Chicago came in the 1960s, a generation after the flight of thousands from the island to New York City and other East Coast destinations. From 1960 to 1970 the Puerto Rican population of the Windy City more than doubled, from 32,371 to 78,963. Still, Puerto Ricans remained largely invisible in Chicago until a June 1966 race riot, which resulted in sixteen injuries, the destruction of more than fifty buildings, and millions of dollars' worth in property damage.

Race riots erupted in Chicago and other large Northern cities in the mid-1960s even as the postwar civil rights movement came to fruition. The struggle for racial equality in America unfolded in several stages, having begun earlier in the twentieth century with litigation in the courts that resulted in some landmark decisions. During the 1950s and early 1960s, the nation's attention turned to the South, where a number of civil rights organizations led by Martin Luther King Jr. and other courageous protesters staged nonviolent demonstrations to challenge the Jim Crow system of racial discrimination. Meanwhile, a small number of senators and congressmen in Washington, D.C., including Illinois's tireless champion of liberal causes, Senator Paul H. Douglas, battled to pass federal legislation that would eradicate segregation. These disparate efforts over several decades culminated in a burst of legislation—the Civil Rights Act of 1964, the Voting Rights Act of 1965, and the Twenty-fourth Amendment, in particular—that completely undermined the legal foundations of racial segregation. Senator Everett M. Dirksen of Illinois, a conservative Republican with no history of favoring racial equality, ironically played a leading role in mustering support within his party in 1964–1965 for what he called "an issue whose time has come." Almost immediately after the triumph over de jure segregation, which had prevailed in Southern states for generations, African Americans faced de facto segregation in the Northern cities where sprawling black ghettos had appeared in recent years.[1]

As in the immediate postwar years, whites continued to escape integration by heading for the suburbs. Some African Americans who sought to follow the same path found success (the percentage of blacks living in the suburbs of metropolitan Chicago increased from 9 percent in 1960 to 16 percent in 1980, for instance), but most of them encountered a series of obstacles designed to preserve the homogeneity of the communities surrounding the central city. In a series of decisions in the 1970s, the U.S. Supreme Court rejected discrimination based solely upon race but countenanced exclusion based upon social class—a critical distinction because of the lower economic status of many African Americans. The landmark case involved the refusal of Arlington Heights, Illinois, to rezone land for the construction of an apartment complex intended for occupancy by working- and lower-middle-class black families. The Court held in 1977 that only restrictions "with racially discriminatory intent" violated the Constitution. White suburbs discovered that they could avoid any mention of race and still use class-based zoning to maintain their exclusivity.[2]

Blacks and whites lived in rigid segregation throughout Illinois, with African American ghettos of several thousand people extant in Joliet, Decatur, Rockford, Champaign-Urbana, and Evanston. Indeed, cynics remarked, East St. Louis consisted of little else. Chicago attracted the lion's share of attention, however, with massive ghettos on the South and West sides that dwarfed all other minority settlements in the city. More blacks resided in Chicago than in the entire state of Mississippi; in fact, more blacks occupied some of the city's largest public housing projects than populated Selma, Alabama, the 1965 site of Martin Luther King Jr.'s greatest civil rights victory. In 1966, eager to build upon his celebrated achievements in the South, King designated the Windy City as the first target of his new Northern campaign. Dismissing the objections of other civil rights leaders who feared the Cook County Democratic machine and who warned against doing battle with its powerful boss, Richard J. Daley, King would not be dissuaded. He thought that Chicago would be a good target for civil rights reform, because unlike other Northern metropolises where power was diffused and decentralized, change could be effected there with the consent of just one man. Despite its size, King believed, Chicago would be changed if Mayor Daley's opposition could be overcome.

At first greeted by African Americans as a vast improvement over the hated Martin Kennelly, Daley maintained good relations with black Chicagoans during his early years in office, but the situation deteriorated as his determination to maintain strict separation of the races became clear. In deference to his white ethnic constituency, he opposed open housing ordinances and used federal funds to build mammoth public housing projects within African American ghettos. Between 1955 and 1966, the city approved fifty-one public housing sites, forty-nine of which were situated in the ghetto areas of the South, West, and Near North sides. The Robert Taylor Homes, recognized as the largest public housing project in the world at the time of its completion in 1962, contained 4,415 units in twenty-eight identical sixteen-story buildings and housed 27,000 people—of whom 20,000 were children, all were poor, and almost all were black. The mammoth project, said architecture critic W. Joseph Black, was "one of the worst tragedies that architects have created, and surely among the world's ugliest buildings." Newspaperman M. W. Newman called it a "seventy million dollar ghetto."[3]

Daley denied that his policies favored white residents of the city's bungalow belts, affirmed that no other municipal government in the country was doing more for African Americans, and even steadfastly maintained that no ghettos existed in Chicago. When blacks complained about the substandard education afforded minority children in the city's public schools, the mayor stood behind the segregationist policies of the imperious education superintendent, Benjamin Willis. Black Democratic aldermen representing the South Side wards remained quietly subservient to the mayor. Known as the Silent Six for their refusal to offer an opinion on city council business until receiving a signal from Daley, they contributed their votes to the city council's automatic support of the machine agenda. In 1965 the rising disenchantment with the local perpetuation of segregation boiled over in Chicago's first race riot of the decade. The August uprising in the African American West Side led to 80 injuries, 169 arrests, but no fatalities; it was a minor outburst in comparison with the conflagration that broke out that year in the Los Angeles neighborhood of Watts in which 31 people died, but it was also a worrisome harbinger of violent times ahead in Chicago.[4]

King confronted his greatest challenge yet when he arrived in Chicago in January 1966. A heterogeneous African American community there was fractured into groups of Democratic machine loyalists, impatient civil rights advocates willing to employ violence, and devotees of the nonviolent protest that King and his followers had been using effectively in the South. Daley was every bit as determined to safeguard segregation as King's antagonists had been in places like Selma and Montgomery, but he proceeded less confrontationally and more successfully. Under the mayor's direction, the police took no action to curtail civil disobedience. When King led open-housing marchers into all-white neighborhoods, phalanxes of police provided protection against angry white mobs. To King's dismay, a race riot broke out on the West Side in July that required the National Guard to quell. Hopelessly stalemated and afraid that his initial civil rights foray into the urban North was doomed to defeat, King agreed to a face-saving summit meeting with Daley where the two protagonists crafted an open-housing agreement. King and his followers left Chicago claiming an important victory, but savvy local blacks characterized the agreement as both weak and unenforceable. Housing segregation persisted in Chicago, and King secretly acknowledged he had failed to effect any meaningful change.

Earl Bush, Daley's press secretary, looked at the outcome of the 1966 contretemps and concluded, "What Daley did was smother King. What Daley couldn't smother was the civil rights movement." Black unrest in Chicago ignited again in April 1968, when an assassin fatally shot King in Memphis, Tennessee. The day after the shooting, Chicago's West Side rapidly degenerated into a nightmare of mayhem, vandalism, and arson. Rioters inflicted fourteen million dollars' worth of property damage before the National Guard regained control of the smoldering ghetto. Casualties included forty-six civilians who suffered gunshot wounds, nine of whom died, and ninety policemen who were injured; civil authorities reported making more than three thousand arrests. A distraught and angry Daley lauded the handling of the riot by law enforcement authorities and urged them to take more forceful action by shooting arsonists on sight and maiming looters. From across the nation, clergymen, officeholders, political liberals, and civil libertarians, whites as well as blacks, denounced his ill-advised remarks. Daley and his spokesmen backtracked somewhat from his inflammatory remarks but also reported the overwhelming public support he had received in thousands of letters and telegrams. In the age of white backlash and at a time when "law and order" became code words for racial fear and antipathy, Daley's hard line against the rioters seemingly pleased more people than it disturbed.[5]

A short time later, another dramatic event shattered the uneasy racial calm in Chicago. At 4:45 a.m. on December 4, 1969, a detachment of fourteen Chicago policemen with a warrant authorizing a search for illegal weapons entered a slum apartment on the city's West Side. The resulting eight-minute gun battle left dead two officials of the Black Panther party, Fred Hampton and Mark Clark, who had been at odds with local law enforcement officers. The policemen reported they had properly identified themselves and had returned fire only after they were shot at, but investigations by independent authorities drew very different conclusions about what transpired. What the police portrayed as a heated exchange of gunfire had actually been a one-sided peremptory strike in which police shot the defenseless Black Panthers in their beds. Cynical African Americans saw the episode as yet another example of how white policemen brutalized minorities with the tacit approval of city hall—just more business as usual, they charged, in the repressive, racist Daley regime.

Like so many other mayors of Northern cities caught between defensive, dwindling white populations and swelling African American populations, Daley faltered when attempting to deal with the deepening racial crisis of the 1960s and 1970s. The mayor gave blacks some of what they wanted—jobs, recognition, and welfare—and did so in gradually increasing amounts, but at the same time he reserved for his white constituency what they demanded, which was segregation. For many years, despite the city's failure to meet the black community's housing, education, and employment needs, a quiescent black population remained loyal to Daley and constituted one of the key components of the Democratic machine's electoral coalition. Unlikely to vote Republican, the overwhelmingly Democratic black electorate could do little but vote for the machine—or, as increasingly happened in the 1970s, not vote at all. When Daley died in 1976, during his unprecedented sixth consecutive term as mayor, he received plaudits for his administrative acumen. Chicago became known during his tenure as "the city that works," but it was a city that clearly worked better for whites than for blacks.

Chicago also emerged as the center for one of the most important black separatist movements, the Nation of Islam. The Black Muslims had moved their national headquarters to the South Side from Detroit in the 1930s and, under the charismatic leadership of Elijah Muhammad, were attracting thousands of followers in the Windy City by the 1940s. By the 1960s, more than six hundred thousand African Americans nationwide subscribed to the Nation of Islam's newspaper, *Mr. Muhammad Speaks*. The Black Muslims indicted the white race for its systematic oppression of African Americans and exhorted its membership to work hard, live abstemiously, and worship faithfully. The group's emphasis on self-help and black capitalism helped to revitalize portions of Chicago's sprawling African American ghettos. After Elijah Muhammad's death in 1975, the Black Muslims splintered into two factions—one group basing itself upon Islamic orthodoxy, the other group following the path of the original Nation of Islam under Minister Louis Farrakhan. The existence of twenty African American mosques in the Chicago area at the end of the twentieth century testifies to the group's continued vitality.

The issue of racial inequality, so volatile in Chicago, reverberated throughout Illinois in the 1960s and 1970s. Otto Kerner served as governor from 1961 to 1968 and fashioned a strong record on civil rights. He successfully championed the passage of a bill creating a state commission for fair employment practices, legislation previously backed by Governors William G. Stratton and Adlai E. Stevenson but killed in the state senate. When the general assembly balked at passing an open occupancy law, the governor issued an executive order that prohibited discrimination in the sale and rental of real estate. The state supreme court likewise approved open occupancy laws adopted by local governments. Kerner achieved such acclaim for his efforts against discrimination that President Lyndon B. Johnson selected him in 1967 for the chairmanship of the National Advisory Commission on Civil Disorders, the blue-ribbon panel charged with investigating the causes and consequences of the urban race riots plaguing the nation in the mid-1960s. The report of what came to be known as the Kerner Commission strongly denounced racial discrimination and affirmed the nation's commitment to equality for all citizens.

The goodwill and earnest efforts of Governor Kerner notwithstanding, racial violence occurred repeatedly in Illinois cities during the decade. Following the disturbances in Chicago in 1965 and 1966, rioting African Americans took to the streets in Cairo, East St. Louis, Elgin, Peoria, and Rockford in 1967. The death of Martin Luther King Jr. the following year provoked full-scale riots in Evanston, Maywood, Aurora, Joliet, Chicago Heights, East St. Louis, Alton, and Carbondale as well as Chicago. Violence flared suddenly in these cities, usually precipitated by altercations involving black ghetto residents and the representatives of white institutions; often a confrontation between African Americans and white police officers provided the necessary spark. Outbursts fueled by the frustrations of ghetto life, the riots typically lasted a short time, with the destruction of property more common than violence against persons. Few whites participated, usually only the policemen, National Guardsmen, and firemen dispatched to the ghetto flash points. The vandalism, looting, and arson, hypothesized the Kerner Commission, constituted a vivid protest against the poverty and marginalization experienced by so many African Americans living in urban squalor.

In the 1960s East St. Louis became the perfect setting for racial violence, a "tinderbox," as historian Richard J. Jensen aptly termed it. Beset by a collapsing economy, deserted by those who could afford to leave, and ruled by a corrupt political machine, the crumbling Mississippi River city faced a hopeless future. In a 1964 comparison with other Illinois cities having at least fifty thousand people, East St. Louis ranked first in the percentage of families with annual income less than three thousand dollars, first in the percentage of unsafe housing units, first in the percentage of adults possessing fewer than eight years of education, and second in criminal offenses. Although African Americans comprised two-thirds of the city's population

in 1967, an all-black slate of candidates received only 25 percent of the
vote in municipal elections dominated by Mayor Alvin Fields's political machine. A poorly conceived urban renewal project that demolished forty-
nine acres of decrepit housing and empty storefronts downtown left thousands of poor people without shelter and filled up only 30 percent of the
cleared land with new buildings; the remaining thirty-four acres stood vacant for years. Beginning in the late 1960s, black reformers fought against
the local political machine and applied for massive amounts of federal aid
in an attempt to halt the downward spiral of economic decline.[6]

In Cairo, another stagnant river town suffering from high unemployment, dwindling population, and inadequate housing, periodic guerrilla
warfare raged between the races in the late 1960s and early 1970s. The
nearly equal white and black populations became armed camps in 1967 after the apparent murder of an AWOL African American soldier by local police precipitated three days of rioting. The state's attorney of Alexander
County organized the White Hats, an armed vigilante group numbering
approximately five hundred men who wore white construction helmets
while patrolling the city in cars equipped with citizen-band radios. Pitched
gun battles first broke out between the White Hats and African Americans
around Pyramid Court, the sprawling public housing complex where one-
third of the city's blacks resided, and later spread to other areas of Cairo.
When the White Hats disbanded in 1969, hastily commissioned deputy
sheriffs and coroners replaced them. In the ensuing two years, the state
police counted more than 140 incidents of gunfire between whites and
blacks. The National Guard came and went over a period of years as the violence surged and waned. Demanding greater employment in Cairo businesses and more representation in civil service jobs, local blacks staged a
prolonged boycott of the downtown shopping district, which became an
uneasy stalemate when the mayor and white community leaders resisted
demands. Whereas Chicago, East St. Louis, and the other major racial battlefields of the 1960s settled into a restive equilibrium, the shootings in
Cairo continued well into the 1970s.

Along with the thorny question of race, the people of Illinois also divided over U.S. involvement in Vietnam. As the struggle to contain Communism dragged on in Southeast Asia and American casualties rose
steadily, previously strong supporters of the war began to waver. Journal-
ists contradicted the optimistic reports issued by U.S. military personnel,
whose accounts of American combat successes seemed as disingenuous as
their predictions of a quick victory seemed increasingly unlikely. Tales of
atrocities committed by American soldiers left a dazed public unsure of the
nation's role in Vietnam. Was this a war in which the United States should
be involved? Given the nature of the fighting, was it winnable by America's conventional forces? Was the sacrifice of so many lives justified in a
far-off land where this country claimed no compelling economic interests?

Such questions arose more frequently as the television networks provided instantaneous coverage of events complete with dramatic film footage.

The nation's young people were the first to make Vietnam a national issue of importance, and college campuses became the focal points for antiwar protest. By the mid-1960s, the first swell of the huge Baby Boom generation was graduating from high school, and more of them than ever before matriculated in institutions of higher learning. More than six million men and women were attending colleges and universities by the end of the decade, roughly four times as many as in their parents' generation. Their idealism stirred by the civil rights movement, they questioned authority and demanded accountability from the elected officials who shaped American foreign policy. Their defiance of the establishment set them at odds with military and civilian leaders in Washington, D.C., as well as with university administrators. Most students who engaged in antiwar activities participated in peaceful demonstrations, teach-ins, and vigils, but a militant minority occupied campus buildings, destroyed property, and battled with police and National Guard troops. The most sensational antiwar activity first occurred on a handful of campuses, such as the University of California at Berkeley, Columbia University, the University of Michigan, and the University of Wisconsin, but few colleges escaped the contagion of protest altogether.

With more than thirty thousand students enrolled at the Champaign-Urbana campus, the University of Illinois emerged as the collegiate center for antiwar activity in the state. The local chapter of Students for a Democratic Society, the Committee to End the War in Vietnam, and the Champaign-Urbana Draft Resistance Union led the early antiwar protests that, in comparison with more disruptive activities at several other Midwestern universities, seemed relatively mild. Participation broadened and protests became violent for the first time when two developments in the spring of 1970 triggered a new level of student unrest. First came the news of covert connections between the university and the U.S. Department of Defense in bringing the Illiac IV computer project to campus. Student protesters demanded that the university sever its connections to Illiac and cancel the ROTC program as a first step in repudiation of the military-industrial complex. In the wake of the university's failure to comply, students rioted, broke windows in classroom buildings and campustown businesses, and threw firebombs into air force and navy recruiting stations. Local police reported six incidents of arson during February and March 1970.

The announcement of the U.S. invasion of Cambodia in May 1970 and the subsequent shooting deaths of protesting students at Kent State University and Jackson State University by National Guardsmen ignited a second round of violence in Champaign-Urbana. State police and the National Guard battled with protesters for several days as a strike called by antiwar organizations lured many students away from classrooms. As thousands of students smashed windows and attacked police vehicles in the campustown area, university officials refused to countenance the strike and urged faculty to continue holding classes. University administrators breathed a sigh of relief when no strike materialized in the fall semester of 1970 and the few antiwar demonstrations remained peaceful. In a quiet denouement to the preceding year's raucous events, the Defense Department announced in February 1971 that Illiac would be relocated to a government facility in California.

Antiwar fervor on college campuses in Illinois, as well as throughout the nation, crested in the spring of 1970. In Bloomington-Normal, students battled with local police and community residents when Illinois State University officials prohibited lowering flags to half-mast in honor of the slain students at Kent State. The president at Southern Illinois University canceled all classes and closed the institution after a week of violence and vandalism in which police gassed and arrested hundreds of students. The turmoil in Carbondale, sparked by the Kent State killings, represented the culmination of a months-long controversy involving the opening there of the Center for Vietnamese Studies and Programs the previous September. Student and faculty protesters argued that the government intended to use the center, the recipient of a million-dollar grant from the Agency for International Development, to perpetuate U.S. involvement in Southeast Asia. Denying any CIA presence at the center, university officials called protesters' fears groundless and identified their goal simply as the dissemination of knowledge about Vietnamese culture. Angry and confused about the disorder at the state's colleges, members of the Illinois house of representatives devoted a special session to a discussion of how to deal effectively with campus unrest. The legislators questioned university presidents and student leaders summoned to Springfield and debated the legitimacy and appropriateness of student grievances. The hearing ended inconclusively, and colleges continued to be hothouses of dissent.

The collision between antiwar protesters and establishment forces occurred most dramatically in August 1968, when the Democratic party held its presidential nominating convention in Chicago. The performance of the police during the race riots in April, coupled with the dissidents' threats to disrupt the August proceedings, set the stage for a bloody confrontation. Still smarting from the criticism he had received earlier that year, Mayor Daley vowed repeatedly to control protest activities at the convention; he had no intention of allowing the events in his city to be disrupted or the safety of Democratic leaders to be threatened by unruly mobs. "As long as I am mayor," he asserted, "there will be law and order in Chicago. Nobody is going to take over this city."[7] Arrayed against the antiwar activists, in addition to the twelve-thousand-member Chicago Police Department, the mayor assembled five thousand Illinois National Guardsmen, six thousand riot-trained federal troops, hundreds of state and county police, a private security force deployed at the convention site, and a large contingent of secret service agents. The military claimed that one of every six demonstrators was an undercover federal agent. The mayor having assembled the largest military force in an American city since the Civil War, the forces of law and order outnumbered the ten thousand dissidents who came to Chicago by a ratio of five-to-one.

During the convention, antiwar activists and police fought several battles in Lincoln Park and Grant Park. Warming to the task, Chicago policemen removed their badges so they could not be identified, used tear gas and clubs to disperse crowds, and beat the protesters who resisted. The major clash occurred on the final night of the convention while the delegates were selecting their presidential candidate, Hubert Humphrey. At the intersection of Michigan and Balbo avenues outside the Conrad Hilton Hotel, police ordered approximately seven thousand people who were milling around the streets to disperse. Law enforcement officers clubbed, beat, and kicked demonstrators and onlookers, shoved hapless victims through broken restaurant windows, and chased unfortunate bystanders into the hotel lobby, giving vent to the rage that had accumulated over several long days of intense riot duty. The sudden outburst lasted only about twenty minutes, after which the streets outside the hotel emptied completely, but

Protesters in downtown Chicago clashing with law enforcement officials during the 1968 Democratic National Convention. *Chicago Historical Society*

sporadic violence continued for hours thereafter. Television crews captured the "Battle of Michigan Avenue" in dramatic detail, and the crowd chanted, "The whole world is watching."[8]

The fallout from the 1968 Democratic National Convention proved far-reaching. Hubert Humphrey left Chicago with the presidential nomination of a divided and demoralized party, which arguably never completely recovered from the convention debacle. Humphrey failed to carry Illinois in November, a crucial factor in his razor-thin loss to Republican Richard Nixon. Liberal Democrats and civil libertarians excoriated Daley for the shocking spectacle of August 1968, and a number of Chicago businessmen expressed concern about the damage inflicted upon the city's image. A number of professional and religious organizations, including the United Church of Christ (with two million members) and the American Psychological Association (with twenty-six thousand members) cancelled annual conventions scheduled in the Windy City. *Rights in Conflict,* the report of the National Commission on the Causes and Prevention of Violence compiled by Chicago attorney Daniel Walker and a complement of 212 investigators, meticulously documented "unrestrained and indiscriminate police violence." The Walker report coined the term "police riot" to describe the events viewed on television by spellbound audiences in August 1968.[9]

While Chicago's lakefront liberals lambasted Daley, the denizens of the city's bungalow belts commended his work. City hall reported the receipt of thousands of telephone calls and letters applauding the stringent measures taken by police against youthful protesters. Like millions of other working-class Americans, the blue-collar Chicagoans approved of "law and order" and wanted a mayor who would act forcefully to quell civil unrest. Impatient with a permissiveness that they felt contributed to a moral breakdown of the social order and unsympathetic to the countercultural lifestyles as well as to the cause of the antiwar protesters, the "silent majority" found a champion in Chicago's combative mayor. When Daley stood up to long-haired revolutionaries, many Americans raised on old-fashioned patriotism rallied to his defense. When he referred derisively to left-leaning East Coast television and newspaper elitists, millions of alienated workers found their resentments and fears confirmed. The inarticulate, unassuming mayor became a spokesman for the values that so many Americans felt were under siege in a confusing, threatening time. In a year notable for the assassinations of Robert F. Kennedy and Martin Luther King Jr., student takeovers of college campuses, ghetto riots, and anarchic antiwar protests, Daley stepped forward to restore order.

The fact that a public figure like Daley could be both demonized and lionized at the same time reflects the divisiveness pervading American society in that era. His ascending popularity in some quarters after 1968 further demonstrates the onset of a conservative backlash to the incessant demand for change by aggrieved minorities. Youthful protesters' bold attacks on government institutions unsettled the respect for authority ingrained in those older Americans who reflexively supported wars against those foreign nations that Washington, D.C., identified as the enemy. Although liberals sympathized with black aspirations and found the destructiveness of the 1960s' disturbances in the cities understandable, many middle- and working-class whites recoiled at the arson and looting they witnessed on television. A Joliet housewife commented that the demonstrators she had seen on television made her think of savages. White ethnic residents of working-class neighborhoods fought to retain the homes and jobs they had secured through hard work, saving, and years of self-denial; they saw desegregation as an attack upon their communities and hard-won economic status. The political consequences of white backlash could be seen in 1966, when the furor over open housing contributed to the defeat of Paul H. Douglas, a liberal stalwart and crusader for civil rights in the U.S. Senate since 1949, at the hands of Republican Charles Percy. In 1968 the historically impenetrable Democratic vote fell significantly in areas of Chicago targeted by Martin Luther King Jr.'s crusade two years earlier, and segregationist presidential candidate George Wallace won a surprising 30 percent of the white vote in Cairo.

Illinois liberals and conservatives clashed again over the ratification of the Equal Rights Amendment (ERA) in the 1970s. The struggle for rights in the postwar years raised questions about the status of women in American society, and many veterans of the civil rights and antiwar movements became involved in the drive for women's liberation. Organizations such as the National Organization for Women (NOW) identified reproductive freedom, the repeal of antiabortion statutes, and equality in the workplace as their principal goals. Although many women expressed a willingness to work for piecemeal change of federal and state laws, more militant feminists advocated passage of a constitutional amendment to ensure the permanence of reform. (The National Woman's party had been fighting for various versions of a constitutional amendment since the 1920s.) Old-line women's organizations such as the American Association of University Women and the League of Women Voters, which originally denied the need for a constitutional amendment, had altered their position by 1970, and such liberal groups as the Americans for Democratic Action and the American Civil Liberties Union jumped on the bandwagon. In 1972 Congress passed the ERA, which stated that "equality of rights under the law shall not be denied or abridged by the United States or by any State on account of sex," and set the time limit for ratification by three-fourths of the states at seven years.[10]

Obtaining ratification by the necessary thirty-eight states proved a formidable task for ERA supporters, and Illinois became one of the key battlegrounds in a struggle that raged for years. Nineteen states ratified the amendment within three months, twenty-three by the end of 1972. The total rose to thirty-one in 1973, but the momentum slowed and the Nebraska legislature became the first to rescind its approval. By 1977, with only two years remaining for ratification, supporters still needed the approval of four states (including Illinois) and introduced a joint resolution into the Senate and the House of Representatives for an extension of seven years. Congress responded instead with a three-year extension, pushing the deadline back to 1982.

At the time that the Illinois General Assembly began consideration of the ERA, only three women served in the state house of representatives and one woman in the state senate. Elections in subsequent years sent increasing numbers of women legislators to Springfield, but the amendment failed to pass in 1972, 1973, and 1976. Civil rights organizations, labor unions, churches, and other civil groups joined NOW in a massive lobbying campaign to persuade the state's legislators to pass the measure, but conservatives worked every bit as diligently in opposition. Phyllis Schlafly, the national leader of the movement against ratification, directed the "STOP ERA" effort in Illinois from her home in Alton. Schlafly enlisted thousands of housewives who wore old dresses and handed lawmakers freshly baked apple pies with the accompanying poem:

> My heart and my hand went into this dough
> For the sake of the family, please vote no.

STOP ERA women brought their infant daughters wearing signs that read, "Please don't draft me" to the state capitol. Schlafly and her followers affirmed their belief that women belonged in the home, taking care of their husbands and families, and that professional careers for women merely undermined wholesome family life.[11]

The last major industrial state not to ratify the ERA, Illinois attracted considerable media attention as the deadline for ratification drew nearer. In 1978 feminists anticipated a positive vote in the general assembly, but the last-minute defection of several African American representatives from Chicago left supporters six votes short of the three-fifths majority needed for passage. In 1980 with only three more states needed for ratification, a coalition of women's organizations staged a lakefront rally of fifty thousand men, women, and children in Chicago four days before the vote on the ERA in the general assembly. Controversy arose as Thomas Hanahan—a McHenry County Democrat who once described feminists as "braless, brainless broads"—charged that NOW volunteers had offered legislators bribes in return for positive votes. Sangamon County officials announced that a grand jury would be convened to consider the allegations of impropriety, and the general assembly decided to postpone the vote indefinitely. Feminists never triumphed in Illinois, one of the sixteen states that failed to ratify the ERA.[12]

Women activists played a crucial role in another leading reform episode, the writing of a new state constitution. Post–World War II governors and other leading citizens had been calling for a wholesale revision of the state's century-old governing document, but cautious legislators hesitated to call for a constitutional convention. The League of Women Voters took up the issue, and a former president of the organization and state representative, Marjorie Pebworth, championed the issue in Springfield. In 1967 the general assembly ordered a statewide referendum, and the following year the voters by more than a two-to-one margin authorized the calling of a constitutional convention. Against the backdrop of the turbulent 1960s, the delegates resolved to consider such timely issues as the rights of minorities and women as well as the need to modernize state government.

The constitutional convention met for the first time in Springfield on December 9, 1969, and conducted most of its sessions in the historic Old Capitol, the site of three earlier conventions. The voters selected the 116 delegates, 2 from each of the state's senatorial districts, in nonpartisan elections, and the Democrats and Republicans split the number of seats almost exactly in half. The selection of fifteen women and thirteen African Americans made the convention the most heterogeneous in state history. A plurality of the delegates were attorneys, but the inclusion of teachers, farmers, trade union officers, and businessmen made for broad representation of occupation groups. The delegates occasionally left the Old Capitol and met elsewhere in Springfield and across the state so that the public could participate directly. The convention chose a Republican attorney from the Chicago suburb of Kenilworth, Samuel Witwer, as president and under his persistent prodding completed the task within one year. Governor Richard B. Ogilvie, Mayor Daley, and the state's major newspapers endorsed the final product, and the voters ratified the new constitution on December 15, 1970. With a few exceptions, the constitution's provisions went into effect on July 1, 1971.

The new constitution initiated several changes to improve the efficiency of state government, in many instances redistributing political power in the process. Invested with a new measure of authority, the governor could use the line-item veto to expunge portions of a bill passed by the general assembly, reduce funding appropriated for programs, and reorganize government agencies by executive order instead of having to seek legislative approval. On the other hand, the percentage of the vote necessary to override a gubernatorial veto in the legislature was lowered from 66 percent to 60 percent. To eliminate partisan friction between the governor and lieutenant governor, the party's candidates for the two executive offices would henceforth be elected as a team. (In 1968 the voters had elected a Republican governor, Richard B. Ogilvie, and a Democratic lieutenant governor, Paul Simon.) A home rule article granted cities with at least twenty-five thousand population and counties with at least two hundred thousand population additional authority to levy taxes, borrow money, and make laws without approval from Springfield. Mayor Daley's delegates to the convention lobbied furiously for these changes, and Chicagoans celebrated the new constitution's enhanced home rule provisions as a great breakthrough for metropolitan governance.

The new constitution finally settled the issue of a state income tax, a nettlesome issue that had been hanging over Illinois for years. Most other industrial states had adopted income taxes in the twentieth century, but a 1932 ruling by the Illinois Supreme Court that the 1870 constitution prohibited them served as a deterrent to scores of governors and legislators. The increasing cost of public aid in the 1960s and the strong public opposition to raising the regressive sales tax threatened to produce a revenue shortfall by the time that Richard Ogilvie became governor, however. Ogilvie championed a state income tax and, after the general assembly passed the measure at the close of the 1969 legislative session, the Illinois Supreme Court unanimously upheld its constitutionality. Accordingly, the new constitution included provisions for an income tax, an urgent necessity that allowed Illinois to escape the fiscal crises experienced by other state governments in the 1970s.

The new constitution also addressed contemporary issues pertaining to individual rights and the fair treatment of women and minorities. A new bill of rights guaranteed women equal protection under the laws and proscribed discrimination against the handicapped. With a nod to the recent turmoil in the state, a section prohibited "discrimination on the basis of race, color, creed, national ancestry and sex in the hiring and promotion practice of any employer or in the sale or rental of property." Thus, delegates inserted several provisions into the 1970 constitution as much to reflect problems arising in the preceding decade as to deal with changes accumulating over the previous century.[13]

Despite the splendid bipartisan cooperation that produced a new constitution, however, public confidence in the state's elected leaders plummeted as a spate of political scandals erupted in the late 1960s and 1970s. Set against the backdrop of the Watergate investigation in Washington, D.C., the shenanigans of Illinois politicians contributed to the erosion of faith in public institutions. A special commission's investigation of bank stock transactions forced two Illinois Supreme Court justices to resign in disgrace, and a federal judge sentenced former-Governor Otto Kerner to prison for income tax evasion and mail fraud in connection with racetrack bribes. After the death of Paul Powell, longtime secretary of state from Vienna, shoeboxes stuffed with more than eight hundred thousand dollars and illicit racetrack stock turned up in his Springfield hotel room. Several years after serving one term as governor, reformer Daniel Walker went to prison for bank fraud and perjury. Republican James R. Thompson, the crusading federal district attorney for northern Illinois, sent a plethora of

Three powerful Illinois politicians—Paul Powell, Richard J. Daley, and Otto Kerner—in earnest conversation. The careers of Powell (posthumously) and Kerner ended in disgrace because of financial improprieties. Despite rumors of corruption in the Chicago Democratic machine, Daley was never charged with any crimes. *Illinois State Historical Library*

the state's top-ranking Democrats to jail, including Kerner and a number of Mayor Richard J. Daley's closest associates, for a variety of criminal offenses. The sensational string of convictions catapulted Thompson to the top of the Illinois Republican party—he served as governor for an unprecedented four consecutive terms from 1977 to 1991—and contributed to the pervading sense of upheaval in the state.

Portentous events in Illinois served as a microcosm of the turmoil sweeping America in the 1960s and 1970s. Powerful social movements involving race, gender, and the war in Vietnam produced changes in society, albeit only after considerable conflict. For many Americans, the violent clash of forces at the Democratic National Convention in Chicago in 1968 symbolized the deep cleavages dividing the nation. In Illinois, as elsewhere in the United States, the forces of reaction withstood the assaults on existing conditions with a fierce and unwavering determination. Demographic and economic alterations proceeded inexorably, however, and the people of the state had no choice but to adapt. Illinois remained a wealthy and populous state, but the turbulence of the 1960s and 1970s left Illinoisans wary of the future.

Champaign-Urbana

The twin cities of Champaign and Urbana, which rest side by side approximately 125 miles south of Chicago, function as entirely separate municipalities. The University of Illinois campus straddles the street dividing the two communities and dominates the economic, social, and political lives of Champaign-Urbana residents. Located in the midst of a vast prairie, the two cities have long served as an agricultural marketing center for some of the world's most fertile corn and soybean fields. Yet despite their importance as a trade and transportation nexus for a prosperous farming hinterland and a smattering of local industries, the two cities owe their vitality and collective identity to the estimable university in their midst.

Originally settled in 1822 and named the seat of newly formed Champaign County in 1833, Urbana existed for more than thirty years before Champaign was founded. In 1854, as the Illinois Central Railroad crews laid track southward through east central Illinois, engineers devised two possible routes through Urbana and another path just outside of the town. Amid rumors of bribes and backroom real estate deals, the workers completed the track and a railroad depot two miles west of the settlement. The citizens of Urbana discussed the possibility of tearing down the community's existing structures and rebuilding around the depot but decided to keep them in their original location. Soon a town known as West Urbana grew up along the railroad tracks. When Urbana residents applied to the general assembly for incorporation as a city, they also sought authority to annex the new town to the west. Indignant inhabitants of West Urbana resisted and, desiring to distance themselves from their presumptuous neighbors to the east, won incorporation under the name of Champaign. Boosted by the railroad, Champaign became a thriving trade center and soon surpassed Urbana in population. The fast-growing upstart's attempt to wrest the county seat away from Urbana failed, and the courthouse remained in the older town.

When the U.S. Congress passed the Morrill Act in 1862, providing substantial land grants to offset the cost of establishing industrial colleges in the states, a spirited competition ensued among several Illinois communities. Champaign and Urbana had already cooperated in building a seminary between the two towns, and their leading citizens drew up a plan for the agricultural college with the seminary building as the nucleus of the proposed campus. A delegation from the two towns lobbied tirelessly in Springfield and, to the great surprise of overconfident competitors in Chicago and elsewhere, received the charter from the general assembly in 1867. The Illinois Industrial University, which accepted its first class of 110 male students in 1868, changed its name to the University of Illinois in 1885.

In the twentieth century, Champaign continued to grow at a faster rate than Urbana and maintained a reputation for aggressive recruitment of business and industry unmatched by the adjacent county seat. But even as both communities grew farther out into the prairie, the heart of the twin cities remained the leafy university campus—the stately red brick buildings enclosing the quadrangle, the largest number of fraternities and sororities in the nation, and the rooming houses and apartment buildings radiating out from its core. For nine months a year, Champaign and Urbana pulsate with the added weight of thousands of students. In the summer months, following the annual exodus, the slower pace underscores the importance of the school to the twin cities.

Phyllis Schlafly

Born in St. Louis on August 15, 1924, Phyllis Stewart grew up a devout Roman Catholic and staunch Republican in suburban Normandy, Missouri. Her father lost his job with the Westinghouse Electric Corporation during the Great Depression, and her family moved to an apartment in St. Louis to save money. She briefly attended Maryville College, a young women's academy in South St. Louis, before receiving a bachelor's degree from Washington University and a master's degree from Radcliffe College. (Later she received a law degree from Washington University.) She worked at the American Enterprise Institute in Washington, D.C., for one year before returning to St. Louis and marrying Fred Schlafly, a Republican lawyer and politician who lived across the river in Alton, Illinois. The couple settled in Alton and raised six children there. In addition to her activities as housewife and mother, Phyllis became active in Republican politics and ran unsuccessfully for the U.S. Congress in 1952 and 1970.

In 1964 she published her first book, *A Choice, Not an Echo,* a history of Republican national conventions and a scathing critique of the party's Eastern liberal wing. The book sold more than three million copies and, Schlafly claimed, launched the modern conservative movement. She subsequently published a monthly newsletter, the *Phyllis Schlafly Report,* catering to an expanding conservative constituency that balked at the extension of New Deal–Fair Deal reforms. She gained some notoriety as an impassioned anti-Communist and devoted supporter of Republican politician Barry Goldwater but became a household name in the 1970s as the

Phyllis Schlafly, a prominent conservative who successfully led the fight against the Equal Rights Amendment. *Chicago Historical Society*

leading opponent of the ERA. In 1972 she founded STOP ERA, a national organization with a membership of eighty thousand people that later became known as the Eagle Forum. She assailed the ERA as a fraud and claimed the bill would add nothing to the rights already guaranteed women as U.S. citizens. The law would take away the right of a wife to be supported by her husband, Schlafly charged, and would undermine the family by forcing mothers outside of the home. Furthermore, the measure's refusal to exempt women from military service would be harmful both in forcing the sexes together immorally in fox holes and in weakening the fighting capabilities of the armed forces. Critics pointed out that Schlafly hardly lived the life of the traditional stay-at-home mother that she so extolled in her speeches, for her nationwide campaigning against the ERA regularly took her away from her family, but respondents in public opinion polls routinely chose her as the most admired woman in the country. Allies and foes alike credited her with defeating the ERA in Illinois and the nation.

Having helped to vanquish the ERA, Schlafly returned to the advancement of other conservative principles she had long espoused. On religious grounds, she opposed abortion, permissive education, bloated government bureaucracies, and homosexuality—a position that elicited considerable media attention when her eldest son proclaimed himself gay in 1992. She wrote a column that appeared in more than one hundred newspapers, broadcast weekly radio commentaries that aired on forty stations, and wrote sixteen books; such tomes as *The Power of the Positive Woman* and *Who Will Rock the Cradle?* urged women to remain mothers and homemakers, while *Strike from Space* and *Kissinger on the Couch* critiqued U.S. foreign policy. A great admirer of President Ronald Reagan, she found his successor in the White House, George H. W. Bush, too moderate and became a delegate for the more conservative Pat Buchanan in 1996.

CHAPTER FIFTEEN

An Uncertain Future

In the early 1990s, twenty-eight-year-old Rajesh Dhawan came to the United States from India in search of economic opportunity. After receiving a master's degree from Indiana State University, he accepted a job as a software engineer at a high-tech firm in suburban Lisle, west of Chicago. Dhawan and his wife bought a home in Aurora and became part of a vibrant expatriate community that included Indian restaurants, Hindu temples, and movie theaters that regularly showed the latest Bollywood releases. Their experience might have been uncommon even a generation earlier, but by the end of the twentieth century, sweeping demographic changes were reshaping northern Illinois. A study by the Fund for Immigrants and Refugees published in 2001 found 628,000 foreign-born people, roughly one-fourth of them undocumented, in the Chicago metropolitan area, and 42 percent of them lived in the suburbs (up from 34 percent in 1970). The suburban immigrants came most often from Mexico, which was followed by India, Poland, and the Philippines. Waves of newcomers had reshaped Illinois throughout its history, and the immigrants arriving in the 1980s and 1990s were doing the same.

As Illinois approached the millennium, two significant demographic developments altered the character of the state. First, beginning in the years following World War II and accelerating in the last decades of the century, the vast suburban region surrounding Chicago grew in population, wealth, and political influence. The percentage of the state's people residing in the collar counties increased from 62 percent in 1980 to 63.5 percent in 1990 to 65 percent in 2000 (see table 3). No longer merely a significant but secondary force existing in the shadow of the metropolis, the conglomeration of suburbs surrounding Chicago became instead the dominant geopolitical region in the state. Second, the emigration of whites and the simultaneous influx of people from other countries changed the population composition of the state. Between 1970 and

2000, more than a million whites left Illinois while hundreds of thousands of immigrants from Latin America and Asia replaced them. During the 1990s, the Latino population of the state grew from 904,446 to 1,530,262 (a 69 percent increase), and the Asian population grew from 282,569 to 423,603 (a 50 percent increase).

TABLE 3—Population Growth in Collar Counties, 1980–2000

County	1980	1990	2000
Cook	5,253,655	5,105,067	5,376,741
DuPage	658,835	781,666	904,161
Lake	440,372	516,418	644,356
Will	324,460	357,313	502,266
Kane	278,405	317,471	404,119
McHenry	147,897	183,241	260,077
TOTAL	7,103,624	7,261,176	8,091,720
Illinois	11,426,518	11,430,602	12,419,293

Source: All population data are taken from the 1980, 1990, and 2000 census reports.

The arrival of large numbers of Latinos and Asians at century's end helped to reverse five decades of population loss in Chicago, but increasing numbers of immigrants established homes in smaller communities stretching from the collar counties to the metropolitan region across the Mississippi River from St. Louis. Bypassing Pilsen, Humboldt Park, and other Chicago neighborhoods that had long served as ports of entry for recent arrivals to America, immigrants sought to avoid the same high crime rates and wretched public schools that had driven whites out of the inner city. Census data from 1990 and 2000 indicate that nearly half the immigrants located initially in suburbs or downstate communities and had not relocated there from Chicago. Newcomers with low skills and limited education sought manufacturing jobs in industrial suburbs such as Waukegan, North Chicago, and St. Charles, for example, while immigrants with graduate degrees and higher aspirations flocked to the high-tech industries clustered around Interstate 88 in Chicago's western suburbs.

Arriving directly from Mexico and various Central American countries or relocating from Chicago, the Latino population in the suburbs grew by 83.5 percent in the 1980s alone (from 158,531 in 1980 to 291,053 in 1990). In the Chicago metropolitan region, the greatest increase occurred in the western suburbs of Cook and DuPage counties. By 1990 high birthrates and both legal and illegal immigration elevated the percentage of the Latino population to 58 percent in Stone Park, 37 percent in Cicero, 30 percent in West Chicago, 23 percent in Aurora, and 19 percent in Elgin. In many cases suburban-bound Latinos encountered resistance from home owners associations and individuals who violated national and state open-housing statutes, and the U.S. Department of Justice filed housing discrimination suits against Cicero, Addison, and Waukegan. The arrival in the collar counties of so many Latinos who had been stalwart Democratic voters in Chicago threatened to introduce an element of political competition into traditionally Republican turf—especially if naturalization and voter registration narrowed the disparity between the low incidence of Latino political participation and the rising population rates.

While Latinos moved into the western suburbs, significant numbers of African Americans pushed southward out of Chicago in search of new homes. Because of their relatively low socioeconomic status and the persistence of discrimination, they typically clustered in a relatively small number of suburbs. In 1990 more than 40 percent of black suburbanites lived in just fourteen suburbs, and most African Americans in Cook County suburbs lived on blocks that were less than 10 percent white. The *Chicago Tribune* reported in 1995, "When wealthier African Americans moved to predominantly white suburbs, most picked those close to majority black communities." Although some southern suburbs already contained predominantly black populations, others saw the color line crack for the first time in the 1980s and 1990s. Only 36 blacks resided in Riverdale in 1980, but the number grew to 5,557 (40 percent of the population) within ten years. Dolton's African American population went from 2 percent in 1980 to 38 percent in 1990. Blacks became the majority of home owners in Hazelcrest and Country Club Hills during the same years.[1]

Chicago's southwestern suburbs received substantial numbers of immigrants from yet another corner of the globe, the Middle East. Changes in U.S. immigration law and the Israeli occupation of Jordan's West Bank sparked a sizable movement of Arabs to the Chicago metropolitan area in the late 1960s, and the exodus intensified in the 1980s and 1990s. By the end of the century, approximately one-third of the Chicago region's 150,000 Arabs (the nation's third-largest concentration of Middle Easterners) resided in the southwestern suburbs. In communities such as Oak Lawn, Bridgeview, Burbank, Chicago Ridge, Hometown, and Palos Heights, Palestinian restaurants, Lebanese grocery stores, and Egyptian bakeries appeared alongside Seven-Elevens, White Castles, and IHOPs on busy commercial streets. Ethnic tensions surfaced occasionally, most notably when a Muslim group attempted to purchase a church in Palos Heights for conversion into a mosque and the mayor and the city council scotched the deal. Claiming an infringement on their religious freedom, the Muslims took the city to court and won. Never known for their eagerness to embrace diversity during the civil rights era of the 1950s and 1960s, residents of the southwestern suburbs nevertheless received the influx of Arab immigrants with remarkable equanimity.

Chicago's metropolitan area became increasingly decentralized and its population more diverse, but the central city still served as the cultural center for the surrounding region. Suburbanites continued to visit Chicago to take advantage of the services and entertainment available there. Linkages to the city remained strong, and many people read the suburban editions of Chicago daily newspapers, conducted excursions downtown for special events, and cheered for the city's professional sports franchises. Loyalty to perennially disappointing athletic teams underscored the strength of these attachments. With the exception of their 1985 Super Bowl victory, the Bears enjoyed little success in the last decades of the century, and the White Sox and Black Hawks consistently performed at a mediocre level. Playing in charming Wrigley Field, the Cubs attracted large crowds and maintained a trendy following as baseball's lovable losers. Only the Bulls, led by Michael Jordan, excelled, winning six National Basketball Association championships in the 1990s. Devoted fans throughout the metropolitan area and the state still followed the exploits and wore the licensed merchandise of their beloved "home teams."

Suburban sprawl, never a phenomenon triggered solely by white flight, affected downstate communities as well as municipalities in the collar counties. According to the Illinois House Smart Growth Task Force, the pace of metropolitan growth in certain central and southern Illinois cities equaled the more heralded rates in the northern part of the state. Cookie-cutter residential developments, strip malls, office buildings, parking lots, and chain stores became commonplace in the outlying areas of Springfield, Peoria, Bloomington-Normal, and Champaign, and along the Route 13 corridor stretching from Carbondale to Marion. New suburban developments—with curvilinear streets, cul-de-sacs, and homes with multicar garages—consumed farmland and empty spaces as they crept outward from existing prairie cities. Local businessmen and city fathers invariably endorsed growth as a sign of progress, although some dissenters questioned the replication of the drab sameness existing in so many other suburban communities throughout the United States. In their pursuit of profit and homogenized living, noted the writer and social critic James Howard Kunstler, these cities embraced "the geography of nowhere."[2]

Meanwhile, small towns scattered throughout Illinois were struggling to survive. Between 1980 and 1990, while the state's metropolitan areas grew, population in rural areas and small towns declined by almost 6 percent. During the same years, seventy of the state's seventy-four nonmetropolitan counties lost population. Relieved of their dependence upon local stores by the ubiquity of automobiles and paved roads, rural and small-town folk sought the best selection and prices at the Wal-Marts, K-Marts,

Targets, and other retailing giants arrayed on the outskirts of nearby cities. Population inevitably followed commerce as people took jobs in larger communities. In the 1990s, the plight of small towns improved somewhat as population decreases slowed and in some cases reversed. Between 1990 and 1995, population grew in forty-seven of the state's rural counties. Some small towns, which had historically been trade centers for agricultural hinterlands, rebounded after recasting themselves as tourist sites. Arthur, Arcola, and Tuscola in Douglas County offered themselves as gateways to the Amish country, for example, and several towns became part of a "chocolate trail" across northern Illinois. More commonly, small towns prospered as bedroom communities for larger cities when commuters sought greater distance from their work as well as the slower pace of life and greater sense of community available on Main Street. Yet the arrival of too many new residents could spoil the quality of life and undermine the close-knit sense of community that had made small-town life so appealing in the beginning. Survival came at a price for the state's small towns.

While most cities and towns in Illinois grew in the last decades of the twentieth century, Chicago underwent a very different experience. Once the fourth-largest city in the world, the Windy City in 1990 ranked thirty-seventh, just ahead of Yokohama, Japan. Between 1945 and 1990, while its suburbs gained 3,000,000 residents, Chicago lost more than 800,000 people. Between 1990 and 2000, however, the city's population increased from 2,783,726 to 2,896,016 as a rising tide of immigrants surpassed the number of emigrants. The fastest-growing segment of Chicago's population, Latinos increased from 545,000 in 1990 to 753,000 in 2000. Comprising more than one-fourth of the city's population by the end of the 1990s, the Latino community supported two Spanish-language newspapers—*La Raza* and *Exito!*—and a Spanish-language television station. The number of African Americans in the city grew at a slower rate than in past decades and remained steady at approximately 15 percent of the population. Although increasing numbers of upwardly mobile blacks left for the suburbs, Chicago still contained a large and vital African American middle-class community centered in such South Side neighborhoods as Washington Heights, Roseland, Chatham, and Gresham.

Chicago's white population dwindled, but young professionals and empty nesters found residence attractive in many of the city's upscale neighborhoods. The revivification of the Loop and the growth of North Michigan Avenue led to a construction boom of high-rise condominiums on the Near North Side. Many ethnic enclaves thrived in the 1970s and 1980s at the same time that extensive renovations of old, neglected housing rekindled interest in previously forsaken neighborhoods. Gentrification and urban homesteading breathed new life into several decaying lakefront areas, then moved into the streets adjacent to the University of Illinois at Chicago campus, southwest of the Loop, and the Wicker Park and Bucktown neighborhoods farther north. Chicago remained a sharply divided city racially, but the burgeoning market for upscale housing led increasingly to a segregation based on social class—and an unprecedented measure of racial integration, at least on a limited scale.

A series of Democratic mayors labored to manage the manifold changes confronting Chicago in the last quarter of the twentieth century. Occupying city hall for more than twenty years, Richard J. Daley provided strong leadership and stability during perilous times for big cities; his death in 1976 triggered a political free-for-all that elevated five different politicians to the mayoralty in the next thirteen years. Daley's death jeopardized the rule of the Democratic machine, the political leviathan that had guided the city's fortunes since the Great Depression. Declining support for Daley by black voters during his later years in office, along with the increase of the city's minority population, raised important questions concerning race and politics in the Windy City. Could white politicians maintain control of the Democratic party or would African Americans and Latinos translate the potential of their rising numbers into real political power? And could officeholders, either white or minority, configure effective policies to deal with the city's imposing challenges?

The machine's initial effort to preserve business as usual failed dismally. To replace Daley, party leaders chose as acting mayor eleventh ward alderman Michael Bilandic, a staid party loyalist of Croatian descent who subsequently won a special mayoral election in 1977. A quiet, colorless bureaucrat, Bilandic compiled an undistinguished record as mayor but still might have won reelection had it not been for an unpredicted meteorological disaster—a series of record-breaking snowstorms in January 1979 that paralyzed the city and called into question the Democratic machine's ability to deliver basic services. Stranded cars prevented snowplows and salt trucks from doing their work; the city's side streets, many of which went unplowed for the whole winter, froze into single-lane, two-rutted ice roads; garbage went uncollected and the rat population soared; and grocery store shelves remained bare as delivery trucks waited interminably for streets to become passable. Denying the severity of the problem, Bilandic seemed preoccupied and belatedly announced a costly snow-removal plan that removed very little snow. Chicagoans expressed outrage at the mayor's indifference and incompetence.

Bilandic's blunders redounded to the benefit of Jane Byrne, whose defeat of the incumbent mayor in the 1979 election supposedly constituted a political revolution in Chicago. Byrne turned out to be an odd revolutionary, however. Although she had campaigned as an antimachine reformer and inveighed against the "evil cabal" of men who ran the city behind the scenes, the new mayor was very much a product of the Democratic organization. To the dismay of the reformers and African Americans whose support had been essential in her election, Byrne quickly discarded her antimachine rhetoric and forged alliances with leading machine aldermen. Beset by financial problems throughout her mayoralty, she raised city taxes and fired municipal workers to balance the budget. Arguing that the city could no longer afford the costly benefits packages customarily proffered to city workers, she challenged demands made by transit workers, firefighters, and teachers unions and successfully weathered protracted strikes. Byrne won the battle for fiscal responsibility, but the frequent disruptions caused by work stoppages created the impression of government-by-chaos. Whatever the mayor had managed to achieve disappeared in an atmosphere of contentiousness and upheaval.[3]

Black restiveness, escalating for several years under the iron rule of the Democratic machine, grew exponentially under mayors Bilandic and Byrne, both of whom seemed to play racial politics more blatantly and to affront African American sensibilities more openly than had Richard J. Daley. In the 1983 mayoral campaign, Harold Washington became the beneficiary of the rising discontent. Like Byrne a product of the Daley machine who had broken away to become an independent Democrat, Washington ran as a reformer in a three-cornered primary race against the mayor and state's attorney Richard M. Daley, the former mayor's eldest son. When Byrne and Daley split the white vote, Washington won the primary and defeated the Republican candidate to become Chicago's first black mayor. For most of his first administration, he found himself embroiled in the nefarious "council wars," in which twenty-nine white aldermen brought municipal government to a virtual standstill by blocking the initiatives of the mayor and the remaining twenty-one aldermen. The gridlocked city council approved few of the mayor's appointments, rejected his budgets, and refused to pass a tax increase he termed necessary to avoid a budgetary shortfall. After the outcome of a special aldermanic election in 1986 altered the balance of power, the mayor was finally able to work cooperatively with the city council—but very briefly. Just seven months after winning reelection in April 1987, Washington died of a massive heart attack. Chicago's first African American mayor had scant opportunity to govern.

The abrupt end to Harold Washington's mayoralty extended the turmoil that had surrounded city hall since Richard J. Daley's death eleven years earlier. Resigned to choosing an African American as interim mayor, the city council selected a machine loyalist, Eugene Sawyer. Chicago's second black mayor presided over an ephemeral coalition and, unlike Harold Washington, failed to command the loyalty of a united black electorate. In the 1989 mayoral election, Richard M. Daley achieved a melding of the bungalow and condo votes while attracting a significant number of ballots from Latinos and African Americans, to defeat Sawyer by approximately 150,000 votes. Assailing the race baiting, demagoguery, and acrimony of the preceding years, the younger Daley appealed to Chicagoans as a healer who intended to work for the best interests of all groups. His low-key button-down style had a tonic effect, and many voters undoubtedly associated his name with an earlier age of solidity and competence. Although machine oldtimers spoke of the son's election in terms of a "restoration," the new mayor went to great lengths to convince the people that he was no "Son of Boss." Determined to be more of a chief executive officer than an autocrat, Daley modernized city management, balanced a series of municipal budgets, eliminated patronage jobs, privatized some public works jobs, and convinced onlookers that Chicago was again the city that worked. Appreciative voters returned him to city hall in 1991, 1995, 1999, and 2003 by comfortable and sometimes overwhelming margins.[4]

Even with the solid support of the voters, the absence of viable political opposition, and firm control over the city's varied bureaucracies, Daley faced a number of seemingly insoluble problems that plagued urban America at the end of the twentieth century. Against a backdrop of dwindling human and financial resources, for instance, the mayor fought to stem rising crime rates and to alter the city's image as a hostile and unsafe place. In Chicago's worst ghettos, youngsters grew up in a hellish environment in which murder, incarceration, and shortened life expectancies were commonplace. In 1992 the city reported investigating 936 homicides, with 80 percent of the victims African American. The violent crime rate in Chicago stood at 30.3 violent crimes per thousand people in the early 1990s, more than nine times the rate in the collar counties. According to a *Chicago Tribune* survey, 77 percent of the people who left the city for the suburbs in 1992 listed greater safety as an "extremely" or "very" important reason for deciding to move. In the sweltering summer of 1995, in fact, hundreds of elderly people died because of their fear of the hostile environment. Terrified of being robbed if they opened a door or window, the isolated, fearful shut-ins perished in suffocating apartments without air conditioning. In other public opinion surveys, emigrants from the city cited the fear of gangs as the most important factor driving them away—just ahead of the inadequacy of public education.[5]

The sorry state of Chicago's public schools, a lingering problem for decades, became a national scandal in 1987 when U.S. Secretary of Education William Bennett proclaimed them the "worst in the nation." With 400,000 students in 540 schools, the Chicago public school system was the third-largest in the nation. In 1993 its student body was 56 percent African American, 30 percent Latino, 12 percent white, and 3 percent Asian and other. Almost half the students came from impoverished families, one-fourth from homes without fathers present. Promising students with any means at all fled the schools and enrolled in private academies or magnet schools. Historically, Chicago's huge Roman Catholic population supported one of the nation's largest and most generously funded parochial school systems so that, critics maintained, the Irish-dominated political machine ignored public education. Meanwhile, hailing back to the days of the Kelly-Nash machine, the public schools became a patronage dumping ground with little attention to pedagogical quality. An impoverished student body and decades of negligence produced a dysfunctional educational system. By the 1980s the dropout rate approached 50 percent, and thirty-five of the city's sixty-five high schools ranked in the bottom 1 percent in national test scores. In 1988 the *Chicago Tribune* plaintively labeled the public schools "hardly more than daytime warehouses for inferior students, taught by disillusioned and inadequate teachers, presided over by a bloated bureaucracy, and constantly undercut by a selfish, single-minded teachers union."[6]

Cognizant that deficient schools contributed to population loss and concerned about the fact that Chicago businesses could not find qualified entry-level workers, corporate executives and concerned parents banded together to demand action. The Illinois General Assembly passed the Chicago School Reform Act of 1988, which cut the school system's bureaucracy by 25 percent and established 540 local school councils to decentralize administration. The local councils, composed of principals, teachers, parents, and community members, clashed repeatedly with unions and school bureaucrats; test scores remained disappointingly low, and the board of education continued to report enormous deficits. In 1995, working with the full support of Republican Governor Jim Edgar, the Republican-controlled general assembly passed legislation that prohibited Chicago teachers from striking and turned the operation of the public schools over entirely to Mayor Daley. With complete autonomy, Daley and his top aide, Paul Vallas, implemented a new model of reform that imposed draconian budget cuts and established new accountability standards. The mayor's aggressive actions brought a new degree of fiscal responsibility to the Chicago public school system but only modest improvements in graduation rates and standard test scores. The task remained daunting.

Crumbling, overcrowded schools in Chicago often stood in the shadows of grim fortresses housing the city's poor. Massive public housing projects—built with the best of intentions by optimistic planners and architects—became dumping grounds for society's unfortunates, where crime, drug usage, and vandalism prevailed. The second-largest landlord in the nation in the mid-1970s, the Chicago Housing Authority (CHA) supervised 140,000 tenants in more than 42,000 housing units. Fully 95 percent of tenants were African American, and single parents headed 87 percent of the living units. With gangs ruling the projects, CHA maintenance workers and policemen rarely responded to residents' complaints. Vacancy rates soared even as the number of homeless rose throughout the city. In 1995, citing a long history of mismanagement by the CHA, the

U.S. Department of Housing and Urban Development assumed control of Chicago's public housing program. (Federal housing officials did the same in a number of other cities, including Springfield and East St. Louis.) In 1999 federal bureaucrats returned control of public housing to the CHA but not before outlining a new set of policies for the city.

In the 1990s, Chicago began razing thousands of public housing units in projects scattered primarily throughout the West and South sides. The CHA designated all twenty-eight buildings in the Robert Taylor Homes for demolition, a process that would take years to complete. The federal government ordered the city to privatize its Section 8 program, which offered subsidies to low-income residents for market-rate housing, to ensure that former residents of the public housing projects could obtain shelter. Determined to provide subsidized private housing, the CHA announced plans to replace the razed high-rises with low-rise apartment buildings and townhouses in neighborhoods where low-income housing would intermingle with middle-class dwellings. The strength of government's commitment to house the poor remained uncertain, but Chicagoans appalled at the CHA's track record found hope in the disappearance of the massive projects that had blighted African American neighborhoods for decades.

A series of urban problems similarly plagued long-suffering East St. Louis. Crippled by the flight of industry and the middle class, the poverty-stricken city proved unable to deliver services to residents and failed to pay its bills to a host of government agencies and private creditors. State officials and private auditors found the city's financial records in such disarray that its precise level of indebtedness could not be ascertained; estimates in the mid-1980s ranged from eight million dollars to more than fifty million. Following the lead of the federal government, which had taken over the city's public housing in the mid-1980s, the state of Illinois assumed an unprecedented role in the operation of local government. To bolster the efforts of the tiny and ineffective local police force, Illinois state police troopers began patrolling East St. Louis streets. The Illinois state board of education placed the public school system, the fourth-largest in the state, under its direct supervision. In 1994 Governor Jim Edgar created the East St. Louis Financial Advisory Board to provide guidance to the city's frenetic efforts at budget balancing and debt repayment. At century's end, local politicians expressed guarded optimism because of increased financial aid from Springfield and substantial revenues generated by a riverboat casino docked at the East St. Louis riverfront.

In an attempt to revive the economies of struggling river cities, the general assembly passed a law in 1990 that legalized riverboat gambling. At least in theory, state and local governments would realize huge tax windfalls, and the casinos would attract throngs of tourists, stimulate riverfront development, and create new jobs. Opponents of the proposal questioned the morality of the state promoting gambling, predicted higher crime rates, and, noting the preponderance of poor people patronizing existing casinos elsewhere in the nation, called legalized gambling a regressive tax on the lower classes. Supporters of the plan carried the day in the legislature, however, pointing to the state's urgent need for revenue. (Opponents and proponents of a state lottery had made essentially the same arguments when Illinois adopted that new revenue source in 1973.) In addition to the East St. Louis site, riverboat casinos soon appeared in Alton, Joliet, Peoria, Rock Island, and Aurora and in Jo Daviess County near Galena. Although cynics continued to rail against the pernicious influences of the paddle wheelers, by 1994 the enterprise had generated more than $220 million in state and local taxes. In Joliet, a declining city with the highest unemployment rate in the nation (25 percent) in the 1980s, the mayor and other civic leaders pointed to its two riverboat casinos as the catalyst for a remarkable renaissance on the DesPlaines River. Joliet's population increased from 76,836 to 106,221 during the 1990s, making it the third-fastest-growing community in the Chicago metropolitan area. With such a glittering economic success story at his doorstep, Mayor Daley began lobbying in Springfield for permission to open five riverboats and the state's first land-based casino in Chicago.

The willingness of the state's leaders to accept such revenue-generating schemes as lotteries and riverboat gambling owed to the desultory performance of the Illinois economy in the last decades of the twentieth century. In virtually every economic category, the state's businesses and industries lagged behind several of their counterparts in the ascending Sunbelt. Illinois's gross state product (the sum total of goods and services produced in a year) continuously declined as a percentage of the national total, down from 6.4 percent in 1972 to 5 percent in 1992. Simply put, the state's economy grew slower than the national economy during this time. Unemployment rates rose and fell along with national figures, but the metamorphosis of the United States from an industrial-based to a service-based economy came at a particularly heavy price in Illinois and in other manufacturing states. The conversion proved especially wrenching for blue-collar workers forced into lower-paying service occupations. In the production of machinery and other durable goods, for example, statewide employment declined from more than 900,000 jobs in 1975 to 575,000 jobs in 1992.

Although much attention focused on the impact of deindustrialization in the northeastern corner of Illinois, people living in the rest of the state felt the effects just as keenly if not more so. The huge numbers of inner-city poor in Chicago notwithstanding, southern Illinois communities contained the highest percentage of indigents. In 1990 in Alexander County, 263 of every 1,000 residents received public aid; Pulaski County reported 225 per 1,000 on welfare; Cook County listed 212. Desperate to attract revenue-producing businesses, downstate communities competed to be the sites for industries that decades earlier they would have shunned. Small towns and cities vied to attract new prisons, more of which were built during the 1990s under Governor James R. Thompson than at any other time in history. Towns even sought to have landfills and gigantic garbage incinerators located in the vicinity.

No community in Illinois felt the sting of economic contraction more severely in the 1990s than Decatur, which became known as "Striketown, U.S.A.," when strikes and lockouts kept nearly four thousand workers off the job over a span of four years, at three locations—the American-owned Caterpillar heavy equipment factory, the British-owned Staley and Company plant, and the Japanese-owned Bridgestone/Firestone tire factory. Caterpillar's workforce dropped from more than five thousand to twenty-five hundred in a few years, and the Bridgestone/Firestone works closed completely in 2001. Decatur officials identified the diversification of the local economy as the key to offsetting the loss of so many manufacturing jobs, but they found the competition to attract more white-collar jobs intense.[7]

Economic uncertainty beset Illinois farmers as well. The disappearance of farmland, ongoing in modest fashion for generations, accelerated in the last three decades of the twentieth century. According to the annual surveys of the Cooperative Crop Reporting Service, Illinois farmland disappeared at an average yearly rate of 100,000 acres in the 1970s because of paving, flooding, strip mining, and other forms of development. Between 1981 and 1996, the state lost nearly 600,000 acres—or, as the head of the Illinois Department of Agriculture's farmland protection program calculated it, 4.4 acres every hour for fifteen years. Nearly one-third of that loss occurred in the six collar counties (Cook, Lake, McHenry, DuPage, Will, and Kane) directly in the path of the state's greatest metropolitan expansion. Will County suffered the greatest overall loss of arable land (52,114 acres), while DuPage County registered the greatest percentage loss (63 percent). The American Farmland Trust, a private conservation agency identifying the regions most at risk from urban sprawl, ranked the farmland surrounding Chicago as the nation's third-most-endangered area.

Farmers compensated for the loss of land by growing more crops on the acres left for cultivation. More than a century of scientific experimentation in crop genetics and soil science brought to Illinois agriculture a wealth of knowledge and expertise. By the 1990s farmers drove across their land in air-conditioned John Deere tractors costing $135,000 apiece and in combines listed at $200,000. State-of-the-art agricultural implements contained sophisticated computer systems linked to banks of sensors that provided instantaneous analyses of environmental conditions. Back in the farmhouses, desktop computers constantly displayed oscillating market rates and provided access to the five web sites maintained for farmers by the U.S. Department of Agriculture. With more than eight thousand agricultural web sites at their finger tips, farmers in the 1990s never suffered for lack of information.

More know-how and greater efficiency could not solve all of the economic problems confronting modern agriculture, however. Illinois farmers continued to produce astounding yields of corn, soybeans, and other crops, but the vagaries of international markets threw prices up and down in unpredictable convulsions. From 1997 to 1999, the price of soybeans plummeted from $7.62 a bushel to $4.00 a bushel; from 1996 to 1999, the price of corn fell from $4.70 a bushel to $1.75 a bushel. How could farmers survive such plummeting prices and income? The answer rested largely with government agencies in Washington, D.C. In 2000 the average net farm income in Illinois stood at $32,414, of which $15,816 came from one federal program or another. From 1996 to 2001, the federal government targeted $5.6 billion in subsidies to farmers in Illinois, making Illinois third among all states, following Iowa and Texas, in the amount of federal farm subsidies received. The sturdy yeoman farmers, whose rugged independence Thomas Jefferson lionized two centuries earlier, had become grateful clients of the American limited welfare state.

While the U.S. government made a commitment to preserve agriculture, which provided a safety net for the dwindling cohort of Illinois farmers, the situation for the state's coal miners remained even more precarious. Tensions persisted between the mine owners and the heavily unionized miners over such issues as pay rates, safety, health benefits, and pension eligibility rules. In 1978 the UMW conducted the longest nationwide coal strike in history, idling nearly all of the 15,000 miners in Illinois for 110 days. Strikers voted down two proposed contracts and then approved the final version by a margin of only 57 to 43 percent. Meanwhile, the supply of coal had nearly run out in many communities, which left a concerned public to condemn the intransigence of both strikers and management. Coal miners applauded President Jimmy Carter's announcement of a new national energy plan that called for a doubling of coal production by 1985, especially good news because of Illinois's heavy reliance upon nuclear energy as a source of power. But industry representatives questioned the realism of such a goal—particularly with the tightening of environmental laws against strip-mined coal.

Prospects for coal mining worsened with Congress's passage in 1990 of several amendments to the Clean Air Act of 1977. Among the several pollutants that were singled out for elimination by the amendments was sulfur dioxide, a substance in abundance in most of the coal mined in Illinois. Utilities considered two responses for complying with the new industry standards established by the 1990 legislation—either switch to cleaner coal produced in Western states or install smokestack "scrubbers" to trap sulfur dioxide before emission. They increasingly chose the former. An average of one thousand Illinois coal miners lost their jobs each year from 1987 to 1995, leaving only six thousand employees to labor in twenty-six mines statewide. (As late as 1979, there had been more than fifteen thousand men working in seventy-one mines across the state.) Moreover, Chicago and the ten surrounding counties in northeastern Illinois lost more than seven thousand jobs related to the mining industry in such fields as printing, advertising, financial services, and public relations. In the economically depressed southern counties, hopes for resuscitating the coal-mining industry rested with the development of new, cheaper technology for "scrubbing" coal and the discovery of new markets for high-sulfur coal in other countries.

Hard times in the coal industry reflected the Illinois population's growing concern with environmental issues. Urban residents worried about air pollution caused by automobile and factory emissions, rural and small-town inhabitants about land erosion and contamination. Everyone feared the despoliation of drinking water from industrial waste. State government responded to the rising concerns by creating a series of agencies— the Illinois Environmental Protection Agency, the Pollution Control Board, and the Department of Energy and Natural Resources—to monitor compliance with state and local conservation laws. Although the general assembly passed a forceful solid waste management act in 1986, the state's overall record on environmental legislation remained mediocre. Illinois lagged behind dozens of more progressive states because, as a highly industrial state, questions concerning economic development and employment rates intruded into policy discussions about the environment. Powerful interest groups such as the Illinois State Chamber of Commerce, the Chemical Industries Council, and the Illinois Manufacturers Association proved especially skillful in lobbying against environmental legislation in Springfield. At century's end, the question remained as to how economic development could be reasonably balanced with the protection of Illinois's natural resources. Such concerns seemed certain to engage the state's voters and policy makers in the twenty-first century.

Naperville

DuPage County's oldest community, Naperville was settled in 1831 by Captain Joseph Naper of Ohio. Naper platted the town in 1835 on an area covering eighty acres adjacent to the DuPage River. The east–west road between Chicago and Galena passed through Naperville, which was incorporated as a village in 1857. Linked by rail to Chicago twenty-eight miles to the east in 1864, Naperville became a city in 1890. Throughout the nineteenth century, it was an agricultural trade center within the Windy City's vast hinterland. In the first half of the twentieth century, the city became a small-scale industrial center but remained largely outside the radius of bedroom communities whose residents navigated the daily commute to Chicago.

Naperville began growing significantly during the post–World War II suburban boom. In 1947 the Atomic Energy Commission established the Argonne National Laboratory in nearby Lemont, and many of the scientists employed there commuted from Naperville. The completion of the East-West Tollway (a segment of Interstate 88) in 1958 brought the city more comfortably within distance of Chicago and enhanced its appeal as a bedroom community to the Windy City. Yet Naperville's remarkable growth came as an "edge city," an autonomous business and residential hub located on an interstate highway far removed from the central city. Whereas satellite cities once existed firmly within the economic orbit of the urban core, edge cities thrived in the late twentieth century even as big cities and inner suburbs stagnated. Beginning in the 1960s, a number of corporations built large research and office complexes straddling the tollway, which local boosters designated the "Illinois Research and Development Corridor" or, more colloquially, "Silicon Prairie." With the arrival of such high-tech enterprises as the Amoco Research Center, Bell Laboratories, Naico Chemical Company, and the Northern Illinois Gas Company, Naperville had by the 1970s become one of the leading "technoburbs" in Chicago's western suburbs. Between 1980 and 1985, the amount of office space available to businesses interested in relocating to the Naperville area increased nearly tenfold to approximately twenty million square feet.

Naperville's population grew by nearly 40,000 in the 1980s, the largest increase among the communities in the collar counties of northeastern Illinois, and reached the 100,000 mark in 1994; the 2000 census reported an increase in the total population to more than 128,000. The community remained overwhelmingly homogeneous, with the nonwhite population rising only to 3 percent in 1980 and 7 percent in 1990. A federal agency filed suit against Naperville with the charge of racially discriminatory housing practices but dropped the charges for lack of evidence; in the wake of the negative publicity, a movement to enact a fair housing ordinance failed. In 2000 Asians constituted the largest portion of the minority population (9 percent), while Latinos and African Americans each accounted for approximately 3 percent.

To offset the less salutary effects of such astonishing growth, Naperville launched a highly publicized attempt in the 1980s to retain an atmosphere of small-town intimacy. The community preserved its quaint central business district and built a living history museum, the "Naper Settlement," in the heart of downtown. Thus, residents and visitors could discover the slower pace of nineteenth-century village life a brief automobile ride away from the ribbons of divided-lane highways and high-tech campuses on the edge of the edge city.

Jesse Jackson

Jesse Jackson became the nation's most visible civil rights activist after the death of Martin Luther King Jr. and, in the 1980s, became the most influential African American in the Democratic party. Born to an unwed mother on October 8, 1941, in Greenville, South Carolina, Jackson excelled as a student and an athlete in high school. In inspirational speeches to young people over the years, he often related how his being born out of wedlock had not held him back from success. He accepted a football scholarship from the University of Illinois but left after one year, claiming to be a victim of racism. He attended North Carolina Agricultural and Technical University, where he became the star quarterback and student government president, and graduated in 1964. After enrolling the following year at the Chicago Theological Seminary, he became involved in local civil rights activities. He quickly became director of the Coordinating Council of Community Organizations, a consortium of Chicago civil rights groups, and dropped out of the seminary to participate more fully in voting rights protests in Selma, Alabama. (He was ordained into the Baptist clergy in 1968.) Jackson joined Martin Luther King Jr.'s Southern Christian Leadership Conference (SCLC) and in 1967 became national director of Operation Breadbasket, the northern arm of the SCLC. Headquartered in Chicago, Operation Breadbasket obtained more employment opportunities for African Americans by conducting boycotts of some of the city's leading businesses. Jackson's successes enhanced his political power in Chicago and raised his profile within the SCLC leadership.

After King's assassination in 1968, Jackson's stature rose further within the civil rights movement. Resigning from the SCLC in 1971, he created Operation PUSH (People United to Save Humanity) and named himself president of the organization. Operation PUSH expanded upon Operation Breadbasket's boycotts and economic protests to include more political activism and electioneering, and Jackson toured the country preaching moral responsibility to inner-city minority youths. His Wall Street Project sought to place minorities as executives and board members with Fortune 500 companies. As a self-styled "citizen diplomat," he conducted summit meetings between warring nations and negotiated the release of American prisoners of war in the Middle East, Africa, and Latin America.

Jackson's rise in national politics began in 1972, when he charged that Chicago Mayor Richard J. Daley had excluded women and minorities from the Illinois delegation to the Democratic National Convention and cochaired an alternate delegation, which unseated the Daley group. He sought the Democratic nomination for president in 1984 and 1988, receiving widespread support from minority voters and registering thousands of new voters into the party. Jackson did surprisingly well in the

Jesse Jackson in his youth reached a temporary truce with Richard J. Daley but later clashed with the Chicago mayor over control of the Democratic party in the state.

Chicago Historical Society

presidential preference primaries, especially in 1984, although ultimately he fell far short of receiving the necessary number of votes at the conventions to receive the nomination. He established the Rainbow Coalition as a liberal adjunct to the Democratic party and in 1995 merged his two principal organizations to form the Rainbow/PUSH Coalition. His reputation was besmirched in 2001 by allegations of financial irregularities and an extramarital relationship with a member of his staff, and Jackson's popularity declined as critics questioned his moral authority. His political legacy survived through his oldest son, Jesse Jackson Jr., who won election to the U.S. House of Representatives from Chicago in 1996.

ILLINOIS

Epilogue

At the outset of the twenty-first century, the people of Illinois face a host of challenges. While the state's population is predicted to grow at a comparatively slow rate, the increasing number of minority groups puts an additional burden on cultural, educational, and social welfare institutions. Sweeping economic changes generated by national and international trends will have profound consequences for Illinois capitalists, workers, farmers, and families. A continental crossroads that for centuries has welcomed waves of immigrants, Illinois has been no stranger in the past to broad cultural and social transformations. Certainly, the future holds more of the same.

The results of the 2000 decennial census and forecasts of future demographic change indicate that the state's population will become even more heterogeneous. According to the 2000 data, approximately one-fourth of Illinois's immigrants have most recently come from Europe, one-fourth from Asia, and fully one-half from Latin American nations. Census takers that year counted 1.5 million Latinos in the state, 12 percent of the total population. According to estimates by the U.S. Bureau of Citizenship and Immigration Services, the Latino population included as many as 432,000 undocumented immigrants. Projections for the 2020 census include a decline in the state's white population, very little change in the number of African Americans, and more than a twofold increase in the Latino population. These demographic trends will be most evident in the regions of most substantial growth, the Chicago and East St. Louis metropolitan areas, while population in rural counties in the northwestern, southeastern, and east central portions of the state will continue to decline slowly.

An increasingly diverse population will place greater demands on a public education system already facing significant challenges and hamstrung by the lack of resources. For schools attempting to close the performance gap between white and minority students, the struggle often

Movement of the Geographical Center of Population in Illinois

1830 to 2000

begins with the establishment of bilingual education programs. According to the U.S. Department of Education, the number of Illinois students needing help understanding English rose by 95 percent between 1992 and 2002—and the Illinois State Board of Education reported that 78 percent of students enrolled in "English as a Second Language" classes spoke Spanish as their first language. In 2002 Latinos accounted for approximately 16 percent of the state's public school enrollment, and many schools in Chicago and the Metro East region across the Mississippi River from St. Louis serve communities where half of the residents speak Spanish. Employers join reformers in pointing to the schools as a key institution in the effort to assimilate the great number of newcomers apparently bound for Illinois in the future.

The state's schools face the task of preparing future generations of students, regardless of their primary language, to compete in a changing global economy. The creation of employment in the service sector will likely compensate in part for the continued loss of industrial occupations in future decades, as information technology, biotechnology, and bioinformatics assume increasingly important positions in Illinois's economy. Much remains uncertain about employment prospects in the postindustrial world, however, and many of the new service jobs fail to pay as well as the manufacturing jobs that disappeared in the late twentieth century. At the same time, business and government leaders will be faced with important choices regarding energy sources. Can new technology resuscitate Illinois's declining coal industry and will the state fully embrace atomic power as the primary source of its energy needs? And what will be the fate of farmers in a state that has long been part of the most fertile agricultural area in the nation? At the end of the twentieth century, with metropolitan expansion, the consolidation of arable land into larger and larger holdings, and the triumph of agribusiness over the family-owned homestead, many Illinois farmers wonder how much longer they can make a living on the land.

In the state's expanding cities and suburbs, provision of adequate housing for an expanding population will inevitably be a priority. As soaring real estate prices at the beginning of the twenty-first century threaten to exclude many gainfully employed members of the working class, concerns intensify about the fate of those who could not obtain affordable shelter in the private housing market. In Chicago, where the first stages of a plan to overhaul public housing have begun with the demolition of high-rise projects, Mayor Richard M. Daley has outlined plans for scattered-site, subsidized housing in mixed-income communities. Critics have lambasted the Chicago Housing Authority (CHA) for doing a better job of razing public housing than replacing it, however, and even the CHA has acknowledged that the construction of new units has lagged far behind the destruction of old projects. How can the city ensure that displaced tenants end up in better circumstances instead of in inadequate housing in equally blighted neighborhoods? The campaign to refashion public housing launched by Daley and the CHA will be watched closely by other mayors across the state, for Peoria, Rockford, and other Illinois cities, as microcosms of Chicago, struggle against the same intractable problems of declining revenues, white flight, and rising costs for service provision.

Public officials, business leaders, and planners also point to improved transportation as one of the keys to Illinois's future development. To maintain the state's position at the center of the national trade and transportation network, existing roads, bridges, and other facilities will need to be maintained and renovated. In addition, state transportation officials aver, new projects will need to be completed. At the top of the state's transportation wish list in 2004 was a new bridge over the Mississippi River to connect St. Louis to the expanding Metro East region in Illinois. As he has throughout much of his tenure in city hall, Mayor Richard M. Daley continues to call for the construction of a third Chicago-area airport. Discussions of a site have included the lakefront, the southern suburbs, northwestern Indiana, and even the Rockford area, but Daley and state leaders have agreed only on the inability of O'Hare and Midway airports to accommodate the growing volume of air traffic. The snarl of vehicular traffic in and around Chicago, which will only worsen as the metropolitan area continues to spread across northeastern Illinois, calls for additional roadways. Planners and civil engineers urge the construction of circumferential superhighways beyond Interstates 94 and 294, better roads serving O'Hare Airport and the burgeoning western suburbs, and the extension of commuter trains westward.

Clearly, a number of important policy issues confront future generations of the state's leaders. As daunting as some of the challenges appear, Illinoisans can take heart in the belief that the assets that have served the state well in the past should continue to do the same in years to come. Though they will need to adapt to changing conditions, industry and agriculture will surely continue to be the primary underpinnings of the state's economy. Blessed with considerable natural and human resources, Illinoisans must exhibit the same resilience and creativity as was shown by their forebears. With an enlightened political leadership that strives to safeguard the interests of all the people, the residents of Illinois can look to the future with confidence as well as hope.

NOTES

1—The Indians and the French

1. Cullom Davis, "Illinois: Crossroads and Cross Section," in James H. Madison, ed., *Heartland: Comparative Histories of the Midwestern States* (Bloomington: Indiana University Press, 1988), 132, 133.

2. Raymond E. Hauser, "The Illinois Indian Tribe: From Autonomy and Self-Sufficiency to Dependency and Depopulation," *ISHS Journal* 69 (May 1976): 129.

3. Quoted in Raymond E. Hauser, "Warfare and the Illinois Indian Tribe during the Seventeenth Century: An Exercise in Ethnohistory," *Old Northwest* 10 (Winter 1984–1985): 371.

4. Quoted in Lois A. Carrier, *Illinois: Crossroads of a Continent* (Urbana: University of Illinois Press, 1993), 9.

5. Quoted in Hauser, "Illinois Indian Tribe," 135.

6. Quoted in Carl J. Ekberg, *French Roots in the Illinois Country: The Mississippi Frontier in Colonial Times* (Urbana: University of Illinois Press, 1998), 261.

2—British Colonial Rule and American Independence

1. Theodore Calvin Pease, *The Story of Illinois* (Chicago: University of Chicago Press, 1949), 20.

2. Reginald Horsman, "Great Britain and the Illinois Country in the Era of the American Revolution," *ISHS Journal* 69 (May 1976): 101.

3. Quoted in Robert P. Howard, *Illinois: A History of the Prairie State* (Grand Rapids. MI: William B. Eerdmans, 1972), 50.

4. Lowell H. Harrison, *George Rogers Clark and the War in the West* (Lexington: University Press of Kentucky, 1976), 17.

5. Howard, *History of the Prairie State,* 56.

6. Arthur C. Boggess, *The Settlement of Illinois, 1778–1830* (1908; reprint, Freeport, NY: Books for Libraries Press, 1970), 54.

3—From Territory to Statehood

1. Edwards quoted in Boggess, *Settlement of Illinois,* 107.

2. Richard White, *The Middle Ground: Indians, Empires, and Republics in the Great Lakes Region, 1650–1815* (Cambridge, England: Cambridge University Press, 1991).

3. R. Carlyle Buley, *The Old Northwest: Pioneer Period, 1815–1840* (Indianapolis: Indiana Historical Society, 1950), 1:530.

4. Howard, *History of the Prairie State,* 101.

5. Quoted in Kurt E. Leichtle, "The Rise of Jacksonian Politics in Illinois," *Illinois Historical Journal* 82 (Summer 1989): 102.

4—Settling the Frontier

1. Quoted in Douglas K. Meyer, *Making the Heartland Quilt: A Geographical History of Settlement and Migration in Early-Nineteenth-Century Illinois* (Carbondale: Southern Illinois University Press, 2000), 9.
2. James E. Davis, *Frontier Illinois* (Bloomington: Indiana University Press, 1998), 254.
3. Ibid., 304.
4. Mark Wyman, *Immigrants in the Valley: Irish, Germans, and Americans in the Upper Mississippi Country, 1830–1860* (Chicago: Nelson-Hall, 1984), 2.
5. Howard, *History of the Prairie State,* 159.
6. Paul W. Gates, *The Illinois Central Railroad and Its Colonization Work* (Cambridge, MA: Harvard University Press, 1934).
7. James E. Davis, *Frontier Illinois,* 413.

5—Slave State or Free?

1. Howard, *History of the Prairie State,* 188.
2. Eric Foner, *Free Soil, Free Labor, Free Men: The Ideology of the Republican Party before the Civil War* (New York: Oxford University Press, 1970), 78.
3. Norman A. Graebner, "Abraham Lincoln: Conservative Statesman," in *The Enduring Lincoln,* ed. Norman A. Graebner (Urbana: University of Illinois Press, 1959), 69.
4. Pease, *Story of Illinois,* 156.
5. John M. Rozett, "Racism and Republican Emergence in Illinois, 1848–1860: A Reevaluation of Republican Negrophobia," *Civil War History* 22 (June 1976): 114.
6. Robert W. Johannsen, ed., *The Lincoln-Douglas Debates* (New York: Oxford University Press, 1965), 14.
7. Rozett, "Racism and Republican Emergence in Illinois," 107.

6—Civil War

1. Robert E. Sterling, "Civil War Draft Resistance in Illinois," *ISHS Journal* 64 (Autumn 1971): 250.
2. Ibid., 254.
3. Carrier, *Crossroads of a Continent,* 115.
4. Benton McAdams, *Rebels at Rock Island: The Story of a Civil War Prison* (DeKalb: Northern Illinois University Press, 2000), xi.
5. Robert P. Howard, Peggy Boyer Long, and Mike Lawrence, *Mostly Good and Competent Men: The Illinois Governors,* 2nd ed. (Springfield, IL: Institute for Public Affairs, 1999), 107–8.
6. Richard J. Jensen, *Illinois: A Bicentennial History* (New York: W. W. Norton, 1978), 70.
7. Carrier, *Crossroads of a Continent,* 118.
8. Quoted in Pease, *Story of Illinois,* 172.

7—A Modernizing World

1. Howard, *History of the Prairie State,* 333.
2. Carl Smith, *Urban Disorder and the Shape of Belief: The Great Chicago Fire, the*

Haymarket Bomb, and the Model Town of Pullman (Chicago: University of Chicago Press, 1995), 120.

3. Ely quoted from Robert G. Spinney, *City of Big Shoulders: A History of Chicago* (DeKalb: Northern Illinois University Press, 2000), 96.

4. Paul W. Gates, "Frontier Landlords and Pioneer Tenants," in Clyde C. Walton, ed., *An Illinois Reader* (DeKalb: Northern Illinois University Press, 1970), 197–211.

5. Richard M. Doolen, "'Brick' Pomeroy and the Greenback Clubs," *ISHS Journal* 65 (Winter 1972): 436.

6. Roger D. Bridges, "Equality Deferred: Civil Rights for Illinois Blacks, 1865–1885," *ISHS Journal* 74 (Summer 1981): 96.

7. Sundiata Keita Cha-Jua, "'Join Hands and Hearts with Law and Order': The 1893 Lynching of Samuel J. Bush and the Response of Decatur's African American Community," *Illinois Historical Journal* 83 (Autumn 1990): 195.

8. Roberta Senechal, *The Sociogenesis of a Race Riot: Springfield, Illinois, in 1908* (Urbana: University of Illinois Press, 1990), 2.

8—The Spirit of Reform

1. Jon C. Teaford, *The Twentieth-Century American City: Problem, Promise, and Reality* (Baltimore: Johns Hopkins University Press, 1986), 30.

2. David R. Wrone, "Illinois Pulls Out of the Mud," *ISHS Journal* 58 (Spring 1965): 54–78.

3. Teaford, *Twentieth-Century American City,* 26.

4. Quoted in Spinney, *City of Big Shoulders,* 148–49.

5. Ibid., 149.

6. Quoted in Lloyd Wendt and Herman Kogan, *Bosses in Lusty Chicago* (Bloomington: Indiana University Press, 1974), 192.

7. Harold M. Mayer and Richard C. Wade, *Chicago: Growth of a Metropolis* (Chicago: University of Chicago Press, 1969), 280.

8. Maureen A. Flanagan, *Seeing with Their Hearts: Chicago Women and the Vision of the Good City, 1871–1933* (Princeton, NJ: Princeton University Press, 2002), 5.

9. Joan K. Smith, "Ella Flagg Young and the Chicago Schools, 1905–1915," *ISHS Journal* 73 (Spring 1980): 36.

10. Neil Thorburn, "John P. Altgeld: Promoter of Higher Education in Illinois," in Donald F. Tingley, ed., *Essays in Illinois History: In Honor of Glenn Huron Seymour* (Carbondale: Southern Illinois University Press, 1968), 41.

9—An Artistic Renaissance

1. Howard, *History of the Prairie State,* 394.

2. Donald L. Miller, *City of the Century: The Epic of Chicago and the Making of America* (New York: Simon and Schuster, 1996), 498.

3. Quoted in Mayer and Wade, *Growth of a Metropolis,* 128.

4. Donald F. Tingley, *The Structuring of a State: The History of Illinois, 1899–1928* (Urbana: University of Illinois Press, 1980), 118.

5. Ibid., 124.

6. Quoted in Bernard Duffey, *The Chicago Renaissance in American Letters: A Critical History* (East Lansing: Michigan State College Press, 1954), 256.

7. Quoted in Donald F. Tingley, "The 'Robin's Egg Renaissance': Chicago and the Arts, 1910–1920," *ISHS Journal* 63 (Spring 1970): 47.

8. Ibid.

10—World War I and the Red Scare

1. Quoted in Tingley, *Structuring of a State*, 197.

2. Quoted in Melvin G. Holli, "Teuton versus Slav: The Great War Sinks Chicago's German *Kultur*," *Ethnicity* 8 (December 1981): 425.

3. Quoted in Tingley, *Structuring of a State*, 198.

4. Quoted in William T. Hutchinson, *Lowden of Illinois: The Life of Frank O. Lowden*, 2 vols. (Chicago: University of Chicago Press, 1957), 1:328.

5. Quoted in Arthur C. Cole, "Illinois and the Great War," in Ernest Ludlow Bogart and John Mabry Mathews, *The Modern Commonwealth, 1893–1918* (Springfield: Illinois Centennial Commission, 1920), 464.

6. Quoted in Carrier, *Crossroads of a Continent*, 189.

7. Quoted in Tingley, *Structuring of a State*, 202.

8. Quoted in Jensen, *Bicentennial History*, 110.

9. Quoted in Hutchinson, *Lowden of Illinois*, 1:376.

10. Arthur W. Thurner, "The Mayor, the Governor, and the People's Council: A Chapter in American Wartime Dissent," *ISHS Journal* 66 (Summer 1973): 131.

11. Quoted in William Preston Jr., *Aliens and Dissenters: Federal Suppression of Radicals, 1903–1933* (New York: Harper and Row, 1963), 253.

12. David Dechenne, "Recipe for Violence: War Attitudes, the Black Hundred Riot, and Superpatriotism in an Illinois Coalfield, 1917–1918," *Illinois Historical Journal* 85 (Winter 1992): 236.

13. Tingley, *Structuring of a State*, 218.

11—Prosperity and Depression

1. Michael E. Parrish, *Anxious Decades: America in Prosperity and Depression, 1920–1941* (New York: W. W. Norton, 1992), 107.

2. Ibid., 75–76.

3. Lizabeth Cohen, *Making a New Deal: Industrial Workers in Chicago, 1919–1939* (Cambridge, England: Cambridge University Press, 1990), 103.

4. Quoted in Frederick Lewis Allen, *Only Yesterday: An Informal History of the 1920s* (New York: Harper and Row, 1931), 83.

5. Cohen, *Making a New Deal*, 102.

6. St. Clair Drake and Horace R. Cayton, *Black Metropolis: A Study of Negro Life in a Northern City* (Chicago: University of Chicago Press, 1993), 84.

7. Roger Biles, *A New Deal for the American People* (DeKalb: Northern Illinois University Press, 1991), 24.

8. Samuel I. Rosenman, ed., *The Public Papers and Addresses of Franklin D. Roosevelt*, 2 vols. (New York: Random House, 1938), 1:788.

9. Quoted in John M. Allswang, *The New Deal and American Politics* (New York: Wiley, 1978), 26.

10. Roger Biles, *Big City Boss in Depression and War: Mayor Edward J. Kelly of Chicago* (DeKalb: Northern Illinois University Press, 1984), 83.

11. Ibid., 81.

12—World War II

1. Masako M. Osako, "Japanese-Americans: Melting into the All-American Pot?" in Melvin G. Holli and Peter d'A. Jones, eds., *Ethnic Chicago* (Grand Rapids. MI: William B. Eerdmans, 1981), 327.
2. Mary Watters, *Illinois in the Second World War,* 2 vols. (Springfield: Illinois State Historical Library, 1951), 1:133.
3. Ibid., 281.
4. Quoted in Biles, *Big City Boss,* 117.
5. Lionel Kimble Jr., "I Too Serve America: African American Women War Workers in Chicago, 1940–1945," *ISHS Journal* 93 (Winter 2000–2001): 426.
6. Biles, *Big City Boss,* 126.

13—Postwar Boom and Suburban Growth

1. Watters, *Illinois in the Second World War,* 1:236.
2. Kenneth T. Jackson, *Crabgrass Frontier: The Suburbanization of the United States* (New York: Oxford University Press, 1985), 294.
3. Mayer and Wade, *Growth of a Metropolis,* 430.
4. Arnold R. Hirsch, *Making the Second Ghetto: Race and Housing in Chicago, 1940–1960* (Cambridge, England: Cambridge University Press, 1983), 3.
5. Quoted in Ibid., 41.
6. James R. Ralph Jr., *Northern Protest: Martin Luther King Jr., Chicago, and the Civil Rights Movement* (Cambridge, MA: Harvard University Press, 1993), 139.
7. Quoted in Roger Biles, *Richard J. Daley: Politics, Race, and the Governing of Chicago* (DeKalb: Northern Illinois University Press, 1995), 46–47.
8. Carl W. Condit, *Chicago, 1930–1970: Building, Planning, and Urban Technology* (Chicago: University of Chicago Press, 1974), 141.
9. Roger Biles, "Jacob M. Arvey: Post–World War II Political Reform," in David L. Anderson, ed., *The Human Tradition in America since 1945* (Wilmington, DE: Scholarly Resources, 2003), 212.
10. Watters, *Illinois in the Second World War,* 1:250.

14—Turbulence and Change

1. Quoted in Roger Biles, *Crusading Liberal: Paul H. Douglas of Illinois* (DeKalb: Northern Illinois University Press, 2002), 173.
2. Andrew Wiese, *Places of Their Own: African American Suburbanization in the Twentieth Century* (Chicago: University of Chicago Press, 2004), 228.
3. Quoted in Biles, *Richard J. Daley,* 89.
4. Ibid., 93.
5. Quoted in William J. Grimshaw, *Bitter Fruit: Black Politics and the Chicago Machine, 1931–1991* (Chicago: University of Chicago Press, 1992), 125.
6. Jensen, *Bicentennial History,* 166.
7. Biles, *Richard J. Daley,* 148.
8. Ibid., 159.
9. Daniel Walker, *Rights in Conflict: The Violent Confrontation of Demonstrators and Police in the Parks and Streets of Chicago during the Week of the Democratic National Convention of 1968* (New York: Signet, 1968), ix, xix.

10. Susan M. Hartmann, *From Margin to Mainstream: American Women and Politics since 1960* (New York: Alfred A. Knopf, 1989), 106.

11. Ibid., 137.

12. "ERA Marches On to Another Loss," *Time Magazine* 115 (May 26, 1980): 23.

13. Carrier, *Crossroads of a Continent,* 247.

15—An Uncertain Future

1. Quoted in Wiese, *African American Suburbanization in the Twentieth Century,* 268.

2. Quoted in Bill Steinbacher-Kemp, "It Isn't Just the Suburbs Anymore," *Illinois Issues* 25 (March 1999): 20.

3. Biles, *Richard J. Daley,* 235.

4. Ibid., 240.

5. Samuel K. Gove and James D. Nowlan, *Illinois Politics and Government: The Expanding Metropolitan Frontier* (Lincoln: University of Nebraska Press, 1996), 27–28.

6. Quoted in Ibid., 191.

7. Kevin McDermott, "Decatur, Down and Out," *Illinois Issues* 27 (November 2001): 3.

BIBLIOGRAPHICAL ESSAY

Two bibliographies are comprehensive and recent enough to be useful. See John Hoffmann, ed., *A Guide to the History of Illinois* (Westport, CT: Greenwood Press, 1991), and Janice A. Petterchak, ed., *Illinois History: An Annotated Bibliography* (Westport, CT: Greenwood Press, 1995).

A handful of general histories of Illinois exist. Theodore Calvin Pease, *The Story of Illinois* (Chicago: University of Chicago Press, 1949) remained the standard one-volume account for decades. Recently, the most popular single-volume history of the state has been Robert P. Howard, *Illinois: A History of the Prairie State* (Grand Rapids, MI: William B. Eerdmans, 1972), which concludes in the early 1970s. It can be read profitably along with Robert P. Sutton, ed., *The Prairie State: A Documentary History of Illinois*, 2 vols. (Grand Rapids, MI: William B. Eerdmans, 1976). Richard J. Jensen, *Illinois: A Bicentennial History* (New York: W. W. Norton, 1978) appeared in the American Association for State and Local History's bicentennial series of state histories. Like the other books in that series, Jensen's slender volume is more an extended interpretive essay than a comprehensive history. Lois A. Carrier, *Illinois: Crossroads of a Continent* (Urbana: University of Illinois Press, 1993) is a lively anecdotal account of the state's history and is well suited for students. Also consult Federal Writers' Project for the State of Illinois, *Illinois: A Descriptive and Historical Guide* (Chicago: A. C. McClurg and Company, 1947); Roger D. Bridges and Rodney O. Davis, *Illinois: Its History and Legacy* (St. Louis: River City Publishing, 1984); Donald F. Tingley, ed., *Essays in Illinois History: In Honor of Glenn Huron Seymour* (Carbondale: Southern Illinois University Press, 1968); and Cullom Davis, "Illinois: Crossroads and Cross Section," in James H. Madison, ed., *Heartland: Comparative Histories of the Midwestern States* (Bloomington: Indiana University Press, 1988).

Daniel J. Elazar, *Cities of the Prairie* (New York: Basic Books, 1970); Daniel J. Elazar with Rozann Rothman, *Cities of the Prairie Revisited: The Closing of the Metropolitan Frontier* (Lincoln: University of Nebraska Press, 1986); and Daniel Johnson and Rebecca Veach, *The Middle-size Cities of Illinois* (Springfield, IL: Sangamon State University, 1980), all include valuable information on Illinois cities. Robert P. Howard, *Mostly Good and Competent Men: The Illinois Governors*, 2nd edition revised and updated by Peggy Boyer Long and Mike Lawrence (Springfield, IL: Institute for Public

Affairs, 1999), provides short biographical sketches of all the state's governors. *The Encyclopedia of Chicago*, edited by James R. Grossman, Ann Durkin Keating, and Janice L. Reiff (Chicago: University of Chicago Press, 2004), is an invaluable reference for the history of the Second City.

The history of Native American tribes and early French explorers has attracted considerable scholarly attention, increasingly so in the late twentieth century. Regarding the Paleo-Indian settlements in and around Cahokia, see the following: Thomas E. Emerson, *Cahokia and the Archaeology of Power* (Tuscaloosa: University of Alabama Press, 1997); Timothy R. Pauketat and Thomas E. Emerson, eds., *Cahokia: Domination and Ideology in the Mississippian World* (Lincoln: University of Nebraska Press, 1997); Biloine Whiting Young and Melvin L. Fowler, *Cahokia: The Great Native American Metropolis* (Urbana: University of Illinois Press, 2000); and Sally A. Kitt Chappell, *Cahokia: A Mirror of the Cosmos* (Chicago: University of Chicago Press, 2002). The standard work on the early period when the Indians and the French controlled Illinois was for many years Clarence W. Alvord, *The Illinois Country, 1673–1818* (Springfield: Illinois State Historical Society, 1920), and this remains useful for its detail. Enriched by anthropological insights, Raymond E. Hauser's work on the early Native Americans in Illinois is insightful: see "The Illinois Indian Tribe: From Autonomy and Self-Sufficiency to Dependency and Depopulation," *ISHS Journal* 69 (May 1976): 127–38, and "Warfare and the Illinois Indian Tribe during the Seventeenth Century: An Exercise in Ethnohistory," *Old Northwest* 10 (Winter 1984–1985): 367–87.

The best recent general study of the French presence in Illinois is Carl J. Ekberg, *French Roots in the Illinois Country: The Mississippi Frontier in Colonial Times* (Urbana: University of Illinois Press, 1998). His more specific studies on the topic include "Agriculture, *Mentalites,* and Violence on the Illinois Frontier," *Illinois Historical Journal* 88 (Summer 1995): 101–16; and, with Anton J. Pregaldin, "Marie Rouensa-8cate8a and the Foundations of French Illinois," *Illinois Historical Journal* 84 (Autumn 1991): 146–60. Natalia M. Belting's *Kaskaskia under the French Regime* (Urbana: University of Illinois Press, 1948) is a careful study of French Illinois's most important settlement. Helen W. Mumford, *The French Governors of Illinois, 1718–1765* (Evanston, IL: National Society of the Colonial Dames of America in the State of Illinois, 1963) provides brief biographical sketches of the colonial administrators.

On the struggle for empire among the European powers, begin with Clarence W. Alvord, *The Illinois Country, 1673–1818* (Urbana: University of Illinois Press, 1920), and Arthur C. Boggess, *The Settlement of Illinois, 1778–1830* (1908; reprint, Freeport, NY: Books for Libraries Press, 1970). On the influence of the Spanish, see John Francis Bannon, S.J., "The Spaniards and the Illinois Country, 1762–1800," *ISHS Journal* 69 (May 1976): 110–18. Clarence Edwin Carter, *Great Britain and the Illinois Coun-*

try, 1763–1774 (Washington, D.C.: American Historical Association, 1910), considers the deterioration of colonial ties to the British Empire.

Several studies explicate the role played by Illinois in the American Revolution, including Donald Chaput, "Treason or Loyalty? Frontier French in the American Revolution," *ISHS Journal* 71 (November 1978): 242–51; Reginald Horsman, "Great Britain and the Illinois Country in the Era of the American Revolution," *ISHS Journal* 69 (May 1976): 100–109; and David G. Thompson, "Thomas Bentley and the American Revolution in Illinois," *Illinois Historical Journal* 83 (Spring 1990): 2–12. The best biography of George Rogers Clark remains Lowell H. Harrison, *George Rogers Clark and the War in the West* (Lexington: University Press of Kentucky, 1976).

The politics of statehood and slavery are covered in several key works. On statehood, see Solon Justus Buck, *Illinois in 1818* (Urbana: University of Illinois Press, 1967); and James A. Edstrom, "'With candor and good faith': Nathaniel Pope and the Admission Enabling Act of 1818," *Illinois Historical Journal* 88 (Winter 1995): 241–62. Janet Cornelius, *A History of Constitution Making in Illinois* (Urbana: University of Illinois Press, 1969), is essential for understanding the 1818 constitution, as well as later constitutions. Robert M. Sutton, "Edward Coles and the Constitutional Crisis in Illinois, 1822–1824," *Illinois Historical Journal* 82 (Spring 1989): 36–46, is a thorough discussion of Governor Coles's role in the affair. Kurt E. Leichtle's "The Rise of Jacksonian Politics in Illinois," *Illinois Historical Journal* 82 (Summer 1989): 93–107, puts the events of 1822–1824 into a larger political context. James Simeone, *Democracy and Slavery in Frontier Illinois: The Bottomland Republic* (DeKalb: Northern Illinois University Press, 2000), is a sophisticated look at the clash over slavery in the state's most populous region. The role played by Ninian Edwards, the most important Illinois political figure of the age, is discussed in James Simeone, "Ninian Edwards's Republican Dilemma," *Illinois Historical Journal* 90 (Winter 1997): 245–64; and in Joseph E. Suppiger, "Amity to Enmity: Ninian Edwards and Jesse B. Thomas," *ISHS Journal* 67 (April 1974): 201–11.

The antebellum frontier era in Illinois is discussed in Theodore Calvin Pease, *The Frontier State, 1818–1848* (Springfield: Illinois State Historical Society, 1949), and James E. Davis, *Frontier Illinois* (Bloomington: Indiana University Press, 1998). The standard account of the Black Hawk War remains Cecil Eby's *"That Disgraceful Affair": The Black Hawk War* (New York: W. W. Norton, 1973), which is sympathetic to the Indians' plight. Also see Roger L. Nichols, *Black Hawk and the Warrior's Path* (Arlington Heights, IL: Harlan Davidson, 1992). For an understanding of early nineteenth-century settlement patterns, see Douglas K. Meyer, *Making the Heartland Quilt: A Geographical History of Settlement and Migration in Early-Nineteenth-Century Illinois* (Carbondale: Southern Illinois University Press, 2000). Various aspects of the role played by transportation are discussed in Paul W. Gates, *The Illinois Central Railroad and Its Colonization Work* (Cambridge, MA: Harvard University Press, 1934); John F. Stover, *History of the Illinois Central Railroad* (New York: Macmillan, 1976); David L. Lightner, "Construction Labor on the Illinois Central Railroad," *ISHS Journal* 66 (Autumn 1973): 285–301; John M. Lamb, "Canal Boats on the Illinois and Michigan Canal," *ISHS Journal* 71 (August 1978): 211–24; and Thomas L. Hardin, "The National Road in Illinois," *ISHS Journal* 60 (Spring 1967): 5–22. Mark Wyman's superb *Immigrants in the Valley: Irish, Germans, and Americans in the Upper Mississippi Country, 1830–1860* (Chicago: Nelson-Hall, 1984) puts the early nineteenth-century Illinois immigration story into a Midwestern context; Ernst Wilhelm Olson, ed., in collaboration with Schon Anders and Martin J. Engberg, *History of the Swedes of Illinois*, 2 vols. (Chicago: Engberg-Holmberg Publishing, 1908), is a useful study of one ethnic group. The experiences of antebellum farmers are discussed in Allan G. Bogue, *From Prairie to Corn Belt: Farming on the Illinois and Iowa Prairies in the Nineteenth Century* (Ames: Iowa State University Press, 1994); Robert E. Ankli, "Agricultural Growth in Antebellum Illinois," *ISHS Journal* 63 (Winter 1970): 387–98; and Paul W. Gates, "Frontier Landlords and Pioneer Tenants," in Clyde C. Walton, ed., *An Illinois Reader* (DeKalb: Northern Illinois University Press, 1970), 170–220.

To understand community building on the Illinois frontier, begin with a pair of general studies: Timothy R. Mahoney, *River Towns in the Great West: The Structure of Provincial Urbanization in the American Midwest, 1820–1870* (Cambridge, England: Cambridge University Press, 1990); and Carl Abbott, *Boosters and Businessmen: Popular Economic Thought and Urban Growth in the Antebellum Middle West* (Westport, CT: Greenwood Press, 1981). Don Harrison Doyle, *The Social Order of a Frontier Community: Jacksonville, Illinois, 1825–1870* (Urbana: University of Illinois Press, 1978), is a model study of a frontier community. Kay J. Carr, *Belleville, Ottawa, and Galesburg: Community and Democracy on the Illinois Frontier* (Carbondale: Southern Illinois University Press, 1996), provides a useful comparative perspective. Also see Susan Sessions Rugh, *Our Common Country: Family Farming, Culture, and Community in the Nineteenth-Century Midwest* (Bloomington: Indiana University Press, 2001), a case study of Fountain Green, Illinois; and Richard S. Alcorn, "Leadership and Stability in Mid-Nineteenth-Century America: A Case Study of an Illinois Town," *Journal of American History* 61 (December 1974): 685–702, on Paris, Illinois. On the Mormon communitarian experiment in Illinois, see John E. Hallwas and Roger D. Launius, eds., *Cultures in Conflict: A Documentary History of the Mormon War in Illinois* (Logan: Utah State University Press, 1995); and Annette P. Hampshire, "Thomas Sharp and Anti-Mormon Sentiment in Illinois, 1842–1845," *ISHS Journal* 72 (May 1979): 82–100. The Bishop Hill experiment is discussed in Paul Elman, *Wheat Flower Messiah: Eric Jansson of Bishop Hill* (Carbondale: Southern Illinois University Press, 1976).

Any discussion of frontier Chicago begins with the three volumes of Bessie Louise Pierce's *History of Chicago,* published by the University of Chicago Press in 1937, 1940, and 1957, respectively. Harold M. Mayer and Richard C. Wade, *Chicago: Growth of a Metropolis* (Chicago: University of Chicago Press, 1969), traces the spatial growth of the city across time. Robin L. Einhorn, *Property Rules: Political Economy in Chicago, 1833–1872* (Chicago: University of Chicago Press, 1991), offers a provocative interpretation of Chicago's early economic development. Also see Glen E. Holt, "The Birth of Chicago: An Examination of *Economic* Parentage," *ISHS Journal* 76 (Summer 1983): 82–94; John Denis Haeger, "Eastern Money and the Urban Frontier: Chicago, 1833–1842," *ISHS Journal* 64 (Autumn 1971): 267–84; Patrick E. McLear, "William Butler Ogden: A Chicago Promoter in the Speculative Era and the Panic of 1837," *ISHS Journal* 70 (November 1977): 283–91; and Patrick E. McLear, "John Stephen Wright and Urban and Regional Promotion in the Nineteenth Century," *ISHS Journal* 68 (November 1975): 407–20. The early development of Chicago's suburbs is discussed in Carl Abbott, "'Necessary Adjuncts to Its Growth': The Railroad Suburbs of Chicago, 1854–1875," *ISHS Journal* 73 (Summer 1980): 117–31; Ann Durkin Keating, *Building Chicago: Suburban Developers and the Creation of a Divided Metropolis* (Columbus: Ohio State University Press, 1988); and the early chapters of Michael H. Ebner, *Creating Chicago's North Shore* (Chicago: University of Chicago Press, 1988). The story of African Americans in early Chicago is told in Christopher R. Reed, "African American Life in Antebellum Chicago, 1833–1860," *ISHS Journal* 94 (Winter 2001–2002): 356–82; and Stanley L. Jones, "Joseph Wentworth and Anti-Slavery in Chicago to 1856," *Mid-America* 36 (July 1954): 147–60.

By the 1850s, slavery had become a corrosive issue in Illinois life and politics. Paul Finkelman, "Slavery, the 'More Perfect Union,' and the Prairie State," *Illinois Historical Journal* 80 (Winter 1987): 248–69, is a good overview of the issues. Slavery and the rise of the Republican party in the state are examined in Stephen L. Hansen, *The Making of the Third Party System: Voters and Parties in Illinois, 1850–1876* (Ann Arbor: UMI Research Press, 1980); and John M. Rozett's revisionist "Racism and Republican Emergence in Illinois, 1848–1860: A Reevaluation of Republican Negrophobia," *Civil War History* 22 (June 1976): 101–15. More specialized studies include Larry Gara, "The Underground Railroad in Illinois," *ISHS Journal* 56 (Autumn 1963): 502–28; Carol Pirtle, "*Andrew Borders v. William Hayes:* Indentured Servitude and the Underground Railroad in Illinois," *Illinois Historical Journal* 89 (Autumn 1996): 147–60; and John A. Lupton, "'In View of the Uncertainty of Life': A Coles County Lynching," *Illinois Historical Journal* 89 (Autumn 1996): 134–46. Paul Simon's *Freedom's Champion: Elijah Lovejoy* (Carbondale: Southern Illinois University Press, 1994) is a biography of Illinois's most famous martyr to the antislavery cause.

Victor Hicken's *Illinois in the Civil War* (Urbana: University of Illinois Press, 1991) thoroughly details the military exploits of Illinois troops but offers less about economic, political, and social developments in the state. Opposition to the war is discussed in the following: Bob Sterling, "Discouragement, Weariness, and War Politics: Desertions from Illinois Regiments during the Civil War," *Illinois Historical Journal* 82 (Winter 1989): 239–62; Robert E. Sterling, "Civil War Draft Resistance in Illinois," *ISHS Journal* 64 (Autumn 1971): 244–66; Kellee Green Blake, "Abiding and Abetting: Disloyalty Prosecutions in the Federal Civil Courts of Southern Illinois, 1861–1866," *Illinois Historical Journal* 87 (Summer 1994): 95–108; and Craig D. Tenney, "To Suppress or Not to Suppress: Abraham Lincoln and the *Chicago Times*," *Civil War History* 27 (September 1981): 248–59. Illinois's prisoner of war camps are described in Benton McAdams, *Rebels at Rock Island: The Story of a Civil War Prison* (DeKalb: Northern Illinois University Press, 2000); and George Levy, *To Die in Chicago: Confederate Prisoners at Camp Douglas, 1862–1865* (Chicago: Independent Publishers Group, 1994). See also William S. Peterson, "A History of Camp Butler, 1861–1866," *Illinois Historical Journal* 82 (Summer 1989): 74–92. Other useful studies are David Wallace Adams, "Illinois Soldiers and the Emancipation Proclamation," *ISHS Journal* 67 (September 1974): 406–21; Jack Nortrup, "Yates, the Prorogued Legislature, and the Constitutional Convention," *ISHS Journal* 62 (Spring 1969): 5–34; and Robert D. Sampson, "'Pretty Damned Warm Times': The 1864 Charleston Riot and 'the inalienable right of revolution,'" *Illinois Historical Journal* 89 (Summer 1996): 99–116.

Several Illinois politicians played vitally important roles in the Civil War. The best single volume on Abraham Lincoln is David Herbert Donald, *Lincoln* (New York: Simon and Schuster, 1995). The best treatment of Stephen A. Douglas is Robert W. Johannsen, *Stephen A. Douglas* (New York: Oxford University Press, 1985). On Ulysses S. Grant, see William S. McFeely, *Grant: A Biography* (New York: W. W. Norton, 1981). The career of John A. Logan is discussed in two volumes by James Pickett Jones: *John A. Logan, Stalwart Republican from Illinois* (Tallahassee: University Presses of Florida, 1982); and *"Black Jack": John A. Logan and Southern Illinois in the Civil War Era* (Carbondale: Southern Illinois University Press, 1995). Mark A. Plummer, *Lincoln's Rail Splitter: Governor Richard J. Oglesby* (Urbana: University of Illinois Press, 2001), recounts the administration of Illinois's Reconstruction governor.

A rich literature exists on the rise of Chicago in the late nineteenth century. Begin with William Cronon, *Nature's Metropolis: Chicago and the Great West* (New York: W. W. Norton, 1991); Donald L. Miller, *City of the Century: The Epic of Chicago and the Making of America* (New York: Simon and Schuster, 1996); and the relevant portions of Robert G. Spinney, *City of Big Shoulders: A History of Chicago* (DeKalb: Northern Illinois University

Press, 2000). Karen Sawislak, *Smoldering City: Chicagoans and the Great Fire, 1871–1874* (Chicago: University of Chicago Press, 1995), is the most far-ranging discussion of the Great Fire and its aftermath. Carl Smith, *Urban Disorder and the Shape of Belief: The Great Chicago Fire, the Haymarket Bomb, and the Model Town of Pullman* (Chicago: University of Chicago Press, 1995), is sweeping in its interpretive scope. On Chicago's heterogeneous population, see Melvin G. Holli and Peter d'A. Jones, eds., *Ethnic Chicago* (Grand Rapids, MI: William B. Eerdmans, 1984), and such specialized studies of ethnic groups as Dominic A. Pacyga, *Polish Immigrants and Industrial Chicago: Workers on the South Side, 1880–1922* (Columbus: Ohio State University Press, 1991); Humbert S. Nelli, *The Italians in Chicago, 1880–1930: A Study in Ethnic Mobility* (New York: Oxford University Press, 1970); Lawrence J. McCaffrey et al., *The Irish in Chicago* (Urbana: University of Illinois Press, 1987); Antanas J. Van Reenan, *Lithuanian Diaspora: Konigsberg to Chicago* (Lanham, MD: University Press of America, 1990); and Paul S. Taylor, *Mexican Labor in the United States: Chicago and Calumet Region* (Berkeley and Los Angeles: University of California Press, 1932). On ethnic politics, see John M. Allswang, *A House for All Peoples: Ethnic Politics in Chicago, 1890–1936* (Lexington: University Press of Kentucky, 1971).

The plight of African Americans in late nineteenth-century Illinois is discussed in Roger D. Bridges, "Equality Deferred: Civil Rights for Illinois Blacks, 1865–1885," *ISHS Journal* 74 (Summer 1981): 82–108. On the Springfield race riot of 1908, see Roberta Senechal, *The Sociogenesis of a Race Riot: Springfield, Illinois, in 1908* (Urbana: University of Illinois Press, 1990); James Krohe Jr., *Summer of Rage: The Springfield Race Riot of 1908* (Springfield, IL: Sangamon County Historical Society, 1973); and James Crouthemal, "The Springfield Race Riot of 1908," *Journal of Negro History* 45 (July 1960): 164–81. Also see Joanne Wheeler, "Together in Egypt: A Pattern of Race Relations in Cairo, Illinois, 1865–1915," in Orville Vernon Burton and Robert C. McMath Jr., eds., *Toward a New South? Studies in Post–Civil War Southern Communities* (Westport, CT: Greenwood Press, 1982); Christopher K. Hays, "The African American Struggle for Equality and Justice in Cairo, Illinois, 1865–1900," *Illinois Historical Journal* 90 (Winter 1997): 265–84; Beverly A. Smith, "The Murder of Zura Burns, 1883: A Case Study of a Homicide in Lincoln," *Illinois Historical Journal* 84 (Winter 1991): 218–34; Sundiata Keita Cha-Jua, "'Join Hands and Hearts with Law and Order': The 1893 Lynching of Samuel J. Bush and the Response of Decatur's African American Community," *Illinois Historical Journal* 83 (Autumn 1990): 187–200; and August Meier and Elliott M. Rudwick, "Early Boycotts of Segregated Schools: The Alton, Illinois Case, 1897–1908," *Journal of Negro Education* 36 (Fall 1967): 394–402.

Several excellent studies exist of labor unrest in Illinois. Richard Schneirov, *Labor and Urban Politics: Class Conflict and the Origins of Modern Liberalism in Chicago, 1864–1897* (Urbana: University of Illinois Press,

1998), discusses trade union formation, politics, and labor violence in the Windy City. Specialized studies include Paul Avrich, *The Haymarket Tragedy* (Princeton, NJ: Princeton University Press, 1984); Richard Schneirov, Shelton Stromquist, and Nick Salvatore, eds., *The Pullman Strike and the Crisis of the 1890s: Essays on Labor and Politics* (Urbana: University of Illinois Press, 1999); James R. Barrett, *Work and Community in the Jungle: Chicago's Packinghouse Workers, 1894–1922* (Urbana: University of Illinois Press, 1987); John H. Keiser, "Black Strikebreakers and Racism in Illinois, 1865–1900," *ISHS Journal* 65 (Autumn 1972): 313–26; and Robert D. Sampson, "'Honest Men and Law-Abiding Citizens': The 1894 Railroad Strike in Decatur," *Illinois Historical Journal* 85 (Summer 1992): 74–88. On the situation in the coal mines, see Steve Stout, "Tragedy in November: The Cherry Mine Disaster," *ISHS Journal* 72 (February 1979): 57–69; Victor Hicken, "The Virden and Pana Mine Wars of 1898," *ISHS Journal* 52 (Summer 1959): 263–78; and Amy Zahl Gottlieb, "British Coal Miners: A Demographic Study of Braidwood and Streator, Illinois," *ISHS Journal* 72 (August 1979): 179–92.

For an understanding of farmers in the Gilded Age, see Roy V. Scott, *The Agrarian Movement in Illinois, 1880–1896* (Urbana: University of Illinois Press, 1962); and Paul W. Gates, *Landlords and Tenants on the Prairie Frontier: Studies in American Land Policy* (Ithaca, NY: Cornell University Press, 1973). Also useful for understanding late nineteenth-century agriculture in Illinois are Wayne G. Broehl Jr., *John Deere's Company: A History of Deere & Company and Its Times* (New York: Doubleday, 1984); Deborah Fitzgerald, *The Business of Breeding: Hybrid Corn in Illinois, 1890–1940* (Ithaca, NY: Cornell University Press, 1990); and Richard M. Doolen, "'Brick' Pomeroy and the Greenback Clubs," *ISHS Journal* 65 (Winter 1972): 434–50. James W. Neilson, *Shelby M. Cullom, Prairie State Republican* (Urbana: University of Illinois Press, 1962), deals extensively with agricultural issues.

Study of the Progressive Era in Illinois begins with Ernest Ludlow Bogart and John Mabry Mathews, *The Modern Commonwealth, 1893–1918* (Springfield: Illinois Centennial Commission, 1920). Richard Allen Morton, *Justice and Humanity: Edward F. Dunne, Illinois Progressive* (Carbondale: Southern Illinois University Press, 1997), is a fine study of one of the reform-minded governors of the era. The good roads movement is detailed in David R. Wrone, "Illinois Pulls Out of the Mud," *ISHS Journal* 58 (Spring 1965): 54–78. On the prohibition movement, see Thomas R. Pegram, "The Dry Machine: The Formation of the Anti-Saloon League of Illinois," *Illinois Historical Journal* 83 (Autumn 1990): 173–86. Also see Michael T. Bennett, "The Movement for Compulsory Health Insurance in Illinois, 1912–1920," *Illinois Historical Journal* 89 (Winter 1996): 233–46; and the following articles by John D. Buenker: "The Illinois Legislature and Prohibition, 1907–1919," *ISHS Journal* 62 (Winter 1969): 363–84; "Illinois Socialists and Progressive Reform," *ISHS Journal* 63 (Winter 1970): 368–86; and "Illinois and the Four Progressive-Era Amendments to the United States Constitution," *Illinois Historical Journal* 80 (Winter 1987): 210–27. George Pullman's experiment in community-building is detailed in Stanley Buder, *Pullman: An Experiment in Industrial Order and Community Planning* (New York: Oxford University Press, 1967).

Women played an especially important role in reform during the Progressive Era. See Steven M. Buechler, *The Transformation of the Woman Suffrage Movement: The Case of Illinois, 1850–1920* (New Brunswick, NJ: Rutgers University Press, 1986); Lynne Curry, *Modern Mothers in the Heartland: Gender, Health, and Progress in Illinois, 1900–1930* (Columbus: Ohio State University Press, 1999); Maureen A. Flanagan, *Seeing with Their Hearts: Chicago Women and the Vision of the Good City, 1871–1933* (Princeton, NJ: Princeton University Press, 2002); Elizabeth Anne Payne, *Reform, Labor, and Feminism: Margaret Dreier Robbins and the Women's Trade Union League* (Urbana: University of Illinois Press, 1988); and Anthony R. Travis, "The Origin of Mothers' Pensions in Illinois," *ISHS Journal* 68 (November 1975): 421–28. On African American women, see Wanda A. Hendricks, *Gender, Race, and Politics in the Midwest: Black Club Women in Illinois* (Bloomington: Indiana University Press, 1998); and Anne Meis Knupfer, *Toward a Tenderer Humanity and a Nobler Womanhood: African American Women's Clubs in Turn-of-the-Century Chicago* (New York: New York University Press, 1996).

Chicago was one of the primary centers for reform during the Progressive Era. Such muckraking exposés as Upton Sinclair, *The Jungle* (New York: Signet, 2001), and William T. Stead, *If Christ Came to Chicago* (Chicago: Chicago Historical Bookworks, 1990), can still provide valuable context. The crusade to reform local government and improve the delivery of services is discussed in Maureen A. Flanagan, *Charter Reform in Chicago* (Carbondale: Southern Illinois University Press, 1987); Sidney I. Roberts, "The Municipal Voters' League and Chicago's Boodlers," *ISHS Journal* 53 (Summer 1960): 117–48; Paul Barrett, *The Automobile and Urban Transit: The Formation of Public Policy in Chicago, 1900–1930* (Philadelphia: Temple University Press, 1983); Louis P. Cain, *Sanitation Strategy for a Lakefront Metropolis: The Case of Chicago* (DeKalb: Northern Illinois University Press, 1978); David John Hogan, *Class and Reform: School and Society in Chicago, 1880–1930* (Philadelphia: University of Pennsylvania Press, 1985); Michael P. McCarthy, "The New Metropolis: Chicago, the Annexation Movement, and Progressive Reform," in Michael H. Ebner and Eugene M. Tobin, eds., *The Age of Urban Reform: New Perspectives on the Progressive Era* (Port Washington, NY: Kennikat, 1977); Michael P. McCarthy, "Politics and the Parks: Chicago Businessmen and the Recreation Movement," *ISHS Journal* 65 (Summer 1972): 158–72; and Michael P. McCarthy, "Chicago Businessmen and the Burnham Plan," *ISHS Journal* 63 (Autumn

1970): 228–56. Robin Bachin, *Building the South Side: Urban Space and Civic Culture in Chicago, 1890–1919* (Chicago: University of Chicago Press, 2004), discusses the role of urban planning in forging a civic consciousness. On Chicago's African American community, see Allan H. Spear, *Black Chicago: The Making of a Negro Ghetto, 1890–1920* (Chicago: University of Chicago Press, 1967); and Mary E. Stovall, "The *Chicago Defender* in the Progressive Era," *Illinois Historical Journal* 83 (Autumn 1990): 159–72.

Several excellent studies examine the settlement house movement in Chicago. On Hull House, see Rivka Shpak Lissak, *Pluralism and Progressives: Hull House and the New Immigrants, 1890–1919* (Chicago: University of Chicago Press, 1989); Rivka Lissak, "Myth and Reality: The Pattern of Relationship between the Hull House Circle and the 'New Immigrants,' on Chicago's West Side, 1890–1919," *Journal of American Ethnic History* 2 (Spring 1983): 21–50; Jane Addams, *Twenty Years at Hull House* (New York: Penguin Books, 1981); Sandra D. Harmon, "Florence Kelley in Illinois," *ISHS Journal* 74 (Autumn 1981): 162–78; and Louise C. Wade, *Graham Taylor: Pioneer for Social Justice, 1851–1938* (Chicago: University of Chicago Press, 1964). Also see Robert L. Buroker, "From Voluntary Association to Welfare State: The Illinois Immigrants' Protective League, 1908–1926," *Journal of American History* 58 (Winter 1971–1972): 643–60.

Any examination of Chicago's artistic renaissance should begin with the epochal Columbian Exposition. Consult James Gilbert, *Perfect Cities: Chicago's Utopias of 1893* (Chicago: University of Chicago Press, 1991); David F. Burg, *Chicago's White City of 1893* (Lexington: University Press of Kentucky, 1976); Gayle Gullett, "'Our Great Opportunity': Organized Women Advance Women's Work at the World's Columbian Exposition of 1893," *Illinois Historical Journal* 87 (Winter 1994): 259–76; and Anna R. Paddon and Sally Turner, "African Americans and the World Columbian Exposition," *Illinois Historical Journal* 88 (Spring 1995): 19–36. Lisa Woolley, *American Voices of the Chicago Renaissance* (DeKalb: Northern Illinois University Press, 2000), nicely updates Donald F. Tingley, "The 'Robin's Egg Renaissance': Chicago and the Arts, 1910–1920," *ISHS Journal* 63 (Spring 1970): 35–54. On the influence of Chicago writers, see Dale Kramer, *Chicago Renaissance: The Literary Life in the Midwest, 1900–1930* (New York: Appleton-Century, 1966); and Robert Bray, ed., *A Reader's Guide to Illinois Literature* (Springfield: Illinois State Library, 1985). The best overview of the Chicago School of Architecture remains Carl W. Condit, *The Chicago School of Architecture: A History of Commercial and Public Building in the Chicago Area, 1875–1925* (Chicago: University of Chicago Press, 1965). Also see Condit's *Chicago, 1910–1929: Building, Planning, and Urban Technology* (Chicago: University of Chicago Press, 1973). Timothy J. Garvey's *Public Sculptor: Lorado Taft and the Beautification of Chicago* (Urbana: University of Illinois Press, 1988) is the standard biography of the state's renowned sculptor.

For a general overview of Illinois during World War I, see Arthur C. Cole, "Illinois and the Great War," in Ernest Ludlow Bogart and John Mabry Mathews, *The Modern Commonwealth, 1893–1918* (Springfield: Illinois Centennial Commission, 1920). Governor Frank Lowden's critical role in preparing the state for war is detailed in William T. Hutchinson, *Lowden of Illinois: The Life of Frank O. Lowden,* 2 vols. (Chicago: University of Chicago Press, 1957). The treatment of German Americans is discussed in Leslie V. Tischauser, *The Burden of Ethnicity: The German Question in Chicago, 1914–1941* (New York: Garland, 1990); and Melvin G. Holli, "Teuton versus Slav: The Great War Sinks Chicago's German *Kultur,*" *Ethnicity* 8 (December 1981): 406–51. On wartime dissent, see Arthur W. Thurner, "The Mayor, the Governor, and the People's Council: A Chapter in American Wartime Dissent," *ISHS Journal* 66 (Summer 1973): 125–43; Donald Hickey, "The Prager Affair: A Study in Wartime Hysteria," *ISHS Journal* 62 (Summer 1969): 117–34; E. A. Schwartz, "The Lynching of Robert Praeger, the United Mine Workers, and the Problems of Patriotism in 1918," *ISHS Journal* 96 (Winter 2003): 414–37; Tina Stewart Brakebill, "From 'German Days' to '100 Per Cent Americanism,' McLean County, Illinois, 1913–1918: German Americans, World War One, and One Community's Reaction," *ISHS Journal* 95 (Summer 2002): 148–71; David DeChenne, "Recipe for Violence: War Attitudes, the Black Hundred Riot, and Superpatriotism in an Illinois Coalfield, 1917–1918," *Illinois Historical Journal* 85 (Winter 1992): 221–38; and Bruce Tap, "Suppression of Dissent: Academic Freedom at the University of Illinois during the World War I Era," *Illinois Historical Journal* 85 (Spring 1992): 2–22. The standard treatment of the Great Migration of the World War I era is James R. Grossman, *Land of Hope: Chicago, Black Southerners, and the Great Migration* (Chicago: University of Chicago Press, 1989). On the era's race riots, see Elliott Rudwick, *Race Riot at East St. Louis, July 2, 1917* (Urbana: University of Illinois Press, 1982); William M. Tuttle Jr., *Race Riot: Chicago in the Red Summer of 1919* (New York: Atheneum, 1970); and the Chicago Commission on Race Relations, *The Negro in Chicago: A Study of Race Relations and a Race Riot* (Chicago: University of Chicago Press, 1922).

Donald F. Tingley, *The Structuring of a State: The History of Illinois, 1899–1928* (Urbana: University of Illinois Press, 1980), covers the 1920s. A number of biographies detail the careers of the interwar years' key figures, including Douglas Bukowski, *Big Bill Thompson, Chicago, and the Politics of Image* (Urbana: University of Illinois Press, 1998); Alex Gottfried, *Boss Cermak of Chicago: A Study of Political Leadership* (Seattle: University of Washington Press, 1962); Roger Biles, *Big City Boss in Depression and War: Mayor Edward J. Kelly of Chicago* (DeKalb: Northern Illinois University Press, 1984); Thomas B. Littlewood, *Horner of Illinois* (Evanston, IL: Northwestern University Press, 1969); and Forrest McDonald, *Insull* (Chicago: University of Chicago Press, 1962). Depression conditions are described in two books by Studs Terkel: *Division Street: America* (New York: Random House, 1967); and *Hard Times: An Oral History of the Great Depression* (New York: Random House, 1970). Striking visual images of Illinois in the Great Depression are provided in Robert L. Reid and Larry A. Viskochil, eds., *Chicago and Downstate: Illinois as Seen by the Farm Security Administration Photographers, 1936–1943* (Urbana: University of Illinois Press, 1989). Also see Lyman B. Burbank, "Chicago Public Schools and the Depression Years of 1928–1937," *ISHS Journal* 64 (Winter 1971): 365–81; and Lynnita Aldridge Sommer, "Illinois Farmers in Revolt: The Corn Belt Liberty League," *Illinois Historical Journal* 88 (Winter 1995): 222–40. Arvarh E. Strickland, "The New Deal Comes to Illinois," *ISHS Journal* 63 (Spring 1970): 55–68, provides a brief overview of the topic, while Lizabeth Cohen, *Making a New Deal: Industrial Workers in Chicago, 1919–1939* (Cambridge, England: Cambridge University Press, 1990) is a sophisticated interpretation of the interwar years. Labor's story is told in Barbara Wayne Newell, *Chicago and the Labor Movement: Metropolitan Unionism in the 1930s* (Urbana: University of Illinois Press, 1961); and Donald G. Sofchalk, "The Chicago Memorial Day Incident: An Episode in Mass Action," *Labor History* 6 (Winter 1965): 3–43. George J. Mavigliano and Richard A. Lawson's *The Federal Art Project in Illinois, 1935–1943* (Carbondale: Southern Illinois University Press, 1990) examines the New Deal's cultural legacy in the state. St. Clair Drake and Horace R. Cayton's, *Black Metropolis: A Study of Negro Life in a Northern City* (Chicago: University of Chicago Press, 1993) examines African American life in Chicago during the depression years. Richard Lawrence Beyer, "Hell and High Water: The Flood of 1937 in Southern Illinois," *ISHS Journal* 31 (March 1938): 5–21, tells the story of the decade's greatest natural disaster in the state.

Several studies exist of Illinois as the center of midwestern isolationism in the interwar years. See James Colville Schneider, *Should America Go to War? The Debate over Foreign Policy in Chicago, 1939–1941* (Chapel Hill: University of North Carolina Press, 1989); Jerome E. Edwards, *The Foreign Policy of Colonel McCormick's Tribune, 1929–1941* (Reno: University of Nevada Press, 1971); Wayne C. Cole, "The America First Committee," *ISHS Journal* 44 (Winter 1951): 305–22; and the relevant chapters in Richard Norton Smith, *The Colonel: The Life and Legend of Robert R. McCormick, Indomitable Editor of the* Chicago Tribune (Boston: Houghton Mifflin, 1997). The most complete source on Illinois during the war is Mary Watters's encyclopedic *Illinois in the Second World War*, 2 vols. (Springfield: Illinois State Historical Library, 1951). Gubernatorial leadership is the subject of Robert Casey and W. A. S. Douglas, *The Midwesterner: The Story of Dwight H. Green* (Chicago: Wilcox and Follett, 1948). Robert J. Havighurst and H. Gerthon Morgan's *The Social History of a War-Boom Community* (New York: Greenwood Press, 1951) describes wartime conditions in Seneca; W. Lloyd Warner, *Democracy in Jonesville: A Study in Quality and In-*

equality (New York: Harper, 1949), does the same for Morris. On the Japanese Americans who were relocated to Chicago, see Masako M. Osako, "Japanese-Americans: Melting into the All-American Pot?" in Melvin G. Holli and Peter d'A. Jones, eds., *Ethnic Chicago* (Grand Rapids, MI: William B. Eerdmans, 1981), 313–44. Also see Lionel Kimble Jr., "I Too Serve America: African American Women War Workers in Chicago, 1940–1945," *ISHS Journal* 93 (Winter 2000–2001): 415–34; and Iwan Morgan, "The 1942 Mid-Term Elections in Illinois," *ISHS Journal* 76 (Summer 1983): 115–30.

The years following World War II ushered in considerable changes to the Illinois landscape. Demographic changes and their political effects are detailed in Samuel K. Gove and James D. Nowlan, *Illinois Politics and Government: The Expanding Metropolitan Frontier* (Lincoln: University of Nebraska Press, 1996); and Peter Nardulli, ed., *Diversity, Conflict, and State Politics: Regionalism in Illinois* (Urbana: University of Illinois Press, 1989). The most detailed discussion of Adlai E. Stevenson's governorship is in John Bartlow Martin, *Aldai Stevenson of Illinois* (Garden City, NY: Doubleday, 1976). David Kenney, *A Political Passage: The Career of Stratton of Illinois* (Carbondale: Southern Illinois University, 1990), relates the story of Stevenson's successor. The political rise of Stevenson and Paul H. Douglas is discussed in Roger Biles, "Jacob M. Arvey: Post–World War II Political Reform," in David L. Anderson, ed., *The Human Tradition in America since 1945* (Wilmington, DE: Scholarly Resources, 2003). Milton Derber, *Labor in Illinois: The Affluent Years, 1945–1980* (Urbana: University of Illinois Press, 1989), deals more with the operation of trade unions than with the lives of working men and women. Suburbanization is covered in two studies of Park Forest: William H. Whyte, *The Organization Man* (New York: Simon and Schuster, 1956); and Gregory C. Randall, *America's Original G.I. Town* (Baltimore: Johns Hopkins University Press, 2000). On postwar Chicago, begin with Alan Ehrenhalt's readable if romanticized *The Lost City: Discovering the Forgotten Virtues of Community in the Chicago of the 1950s* (New York: HarperCollins, 1995); Carl W. Condit, *Chicago, 1930–1970: Building, Planning, and Urban Technology* (Chicago: University of Chicago Press, 1974); and Roger Biles, *Richard J. Daley: Politics, Race, and the Governing of Chicago* (DeKalb: Northern Illinois University Press, 1995). On race in Chicago, see Arnold R. Hirsch, *Making the Second Ghetto: Race and Housing in Chicago, 1940–1960* (Cambridge, England: Cambridge University Press, 1983); Nicholas Lemann, *The Promised Land: The Great Black Migration and How It Changed America* (New York: Random House, 1991); Martin Meyerson and Edward C. Banfield, *Politics, Planning, and the Public Interest: The Case of Public Housing in Chicago* (Glencoe, IL: Free Press, 1955); and Felix M. Padilla, *Puerto Rican Chicago* (Notre Dame, IN: University of Notre Dame Press, 1987). For discussions of other groups in post–World War II Chicago, see James B. LaGrand, *Indian*

Metropolis: Native Americans in Chicago, 1945–75 (Urbana: University of Illinois Press, 2002); and Dominic A. Pacyga, "Polish-America in Transition: Social Change and the Chicago Polonia, 1945–1980," *Polish-American Studies* 44 (Spring 1987): 38–55.

The 1960s and 1970s proved tumultuous in Illinois. Racial turmoil in Chicago is the subject of Alan B. Anderson and George W. Pickering, *Confronting the Color Line: The Broken Promise of the Civil Rights Movement in Chicago* (Athens: University of Georgia Press, 1986); James R. Ralph Jr., *Northern Protest: Martin Luther King Jr., Chicago, and the Civil Rights Movement* (Cambridge, MA: Harvard University Press, 1993); and Brian J. L. Berry, *The Open Housing Question: Race and Housing in Chicago, 1966–1976* (Cambridge, MA: Ballinger, 1979). William J. Grimshaw, *Bitter Fruit: Black Politics and the Chicago Machine, 1931–1991* (Chicago: University of Chicago Press, 1992), offers a revisionist interpretation of black politics in the Windy City. Two contrasting views of the rise of Harold Washington are offered in Paul Kleppner, *Chicago Divided: The Making of a Black Mayor* (DeKalb: Northern Illinois University Press, 1985); and Melvin G. Holli and Paul M. Green, eds., *The Making of the Mayor: Chicago, 1983* (Grand Rapids, MI: William B. Eerdmans, 1984). For discussions of race in other Illinois cities, see Dennis R. Judd and Robert E. Mendelson, *The Politics of Urban Planning: The East St. Louis Experience* (Urbana: University of Illinois Press, 1973); and Jan Peterson Roddy, ed., *Let My People Go: Cairo, Illinois, 1967–1973* (Carbondale: Southern Illinois University Press, 1996). The 1968 Democratic National Convention is the subject of David R. Farber, *Chicago '68* (Chicago: University of Chicago Press, 1988); and Daniel Walker, *Rights in Conflict: The Violent Confrontation of Demonstrators and Police in the Parks and Streets of Chicago during the Week of the Democratic National Convention of 1968* (New York: Signet, 1968). On antiwar protest, see Patrick D. Kennedy, "Reactions against the Vietnam War and Military-Related Targets on Campus: The University of Illinois as a Case Study, 1965–1972," *Illinois Historical Journal* 84 (Summer 1991): 101–18.

Biographies of important Illinois figures of the postwar era include Roger Biles, *Crusading Liberal: Paul H. Douglas of Illinois* (DeKalb: Northern Illinois University Press, 2002); Byron C. Hulsey, *Everett Dirksen and His Presidents: How a Senate Giant Shaped American Politics* (Lawrence: University Press of Kansas, 2000); Bill Barnhart and Gene Schlickman, *Kerner: The Conflict of Intangible Rights* (Urbana: University of Illinois Press, 1999); Taylor Pensoneau and Bob Ellis, *Dan Walker: The Glory and the Tragedy* (Evansville, IN: Smith Collins, 1993); Robert E. Hartley, *Paul Powell of Illinois: A Lifelong Democrat* (Carbondale: Southern Illinois University Press, 1999); and Carol Felsenthal, *The Sweetheart of the Silent Majority: The Biography of Phyllis Schlafly* (Garden City, NY: Doubleday, 1981).

The literature on the history of Illinois in the last decades of the twentieth century is incomplete. The best source on the recent politics and economic development of the state is *Illinois Issues,* which is published eleven times annually by the University of Illinois at Springfield. Several works deal with the growth of the Latino population in Chicago. See Gerald William Ropko, *The Evolving Residential Pattern of the Mexican, Puerto Rican, and Cuban Population in the City of Chicago* (New York: Arno, 1980); Felix M. Padilla, *Latino Ethnic Consciousness: The Case of Mexican Americans and Puerto Ricans in Chicago* (Notre Dame, IN: University of Notre Dame Press, 1985); and Louise Ano Nuevo de Kerr, "Chicano Settlements in Chicago: A Brief History," *Journal of Ethnic Studies* 2 (Winter 1975): 22–32. Sonya Salamon, *Newcomers to Old Towns: Suburbanization of the Heartland* (Chicago: University of Chicago Press, 2003), considers the renaissance of small towns.

INDEX